T0339417

# Reappraising
# State-Owned Enterprise

# Routledge International Studies in Business History

SERIES EDITORS: RAY STOKES AND MATTHIAS KIPPING

**1. Management, Education and Competitiveness**
Europe, Japan and the United States
Edited by Rolv Petter Amdam

**2. The Development of Accounting in an International Context**
A Festschrift in Honour of R. H. Parker
T. E. Cooke and C. W. Nobes

**3. The Dynamics of the Modern Brewing Industry**
Edited by R. G. Wilson and T. R. Gourvish

**4. Religion, Business and Wealth in Modern Britain**
Edited by David Jeremy

**5. The Multinational Traders**
Geoffrey Jones

**6 .The Americanisation of European Business**
Edited by Matthias Kipping and Ove Bjarnar

**7. Region and Strategy**
Business in Lancashire and Kansai
1890–1990
Douglas A. Farnie, David J. Jeremy,
John F. Wilson, Nakaoka Tetsuro and
Abe Takeshi

**8. Foreign Multinationals in the United States**
Management and Performance
Edited by Geoffrey Jones and Lina Galvez-Munoz

**9. Co-Operative Structures in Global Business**
A New Approach to Networks,
Technology Transfer Agreements,
Strategic Alliances and Agency
Relationships
Gordon H. Boyce

**10. German and Japanese Business in the Boom Years**
Transforming American Management
and Technology Models
Edited by Akira Kudo, Matthias Kipping
and Harm G. Schröter

**11. Dutch Enterprise in the 20th Century**
Business Strategies in Small Open
Country
Keetie E. Sluyterman

**12. The Formative Period of American Capitalism**
A Materialist Interpretation
Daniel Gaido

**13. International Business and National War Interests**
Unilever Between Reich and Empire,
1939–45
Ben Wubs

**14. Narrating the Rise of Big Business in the USA**
How Economists Explain Standard Oil
and Wal-Mart
Anne Mayhew

**15. Women and Their Money 1700–1950**
Essays on Women and Finance
Edited by Anne Laurence, Josephine Maltby and Janette Rutterford

**16. The Origins of Globalization**
Karl Moore and David Lewis

**17. The Foundations of Female Entrupreneurship**
Enterprise, Home and Household in London, c. 1800–1870
Alison C. Kay

**18. Innovation and Entrepreneurial Networks in Europe**
Edited by Paloma Fernández Pérez and Mary Rose

**19. Trade Marks, Brands and Competitiveness**
Edited by Teresa da Silva Lopes and Paul Duguid

**20. Technological Innovation in Retail Finance**
International Historical Perspectives
Edited by Bernardo Bátiz-Lazo, J. Carles Maixé-Altés and Paul Thomes

**21. Reappraising State-Owned Enterprise**
A Comparison of the UK and Italy
Edited by Franco Amatori, Robert Millward, and Pier Angelo Toninelli

# Reappraising State-Owned Enterprise

A Comparison of the UK and Italy

**Edited by Franco Amatori,
Robert Millward, and
Pier Angelo Toninelli**

Routledge
Taylor & Francis Group

LONDON AND NEW YORK

First published 2011 by Routledge
4 Park Square, Milton Park, Abingdon, Oxon OX14 4RN
605 Third Avenue, New York, NY 10017

*Routledge is an imprint of the Taylor & Francis Group, an informa business*

First issued in paperback 2018

Typeset in Sabon by IBT Global.

*Library of Congress Cataloging-in-Publication Data*

Reappraising state owned enterprise : a comparison of the UK and Italy / edited by
    Franco Amatori, Robert Millward, and Pier Angelo Toninelli.
       p. cm. — (Routledge international studies in business history ; 21)

    Includes bibliographical references and index.
    1. Government business enterprises—Great Britain—History—20th century.
2. Government business enterprises—Italy—History—20th century.   3. Government ownership—Great Britain—History—20th century.   4. Government ownership—Italy—History—20th century.   5. Industries—Great Britain—History—20th century.
6. Industries—Italy—History—20th century.   I. Amatori, Franco.   II. Millward, Robert.   III. Toninelli, Pier Angelo Maria.
    HD4145.R35 2011
    338.6'20941—dc22
    2010042955

ISBN13: 978-0-415-87832-6 (hbk)
ISBN13: 978-1-138-37798-1 (pbk)

# Contents

List of Figures                                                          ix
List of Tables                                                           xi
Preface                                                                  xiii

## PART I
## Policies, Outcomes, and Funding

1   Introduction                                                          3
    FRANCO AMATORI, ROBERT MILLWARD, AND PIER ANGELO TONINELLI

2   The Nature of State Enterprise in Britain                            11
    ROBERT MILLWARD

3   Does a Model of Italian State-Owned Enterprise Really Exist?         31
    FRANCO AMATORI AND PIER ANGELO TONINELLI

4   Attempts to "Modernize": Nationalization and the Nationalized
    Industries in Postwar Britain                                        50
    GLEN O'HARA

5   Size, Boundaries, and Distribution of Italian State-Owned
    Enterprise (1939–1983)                                               68
    PIER ANGELO TONINELLI AND MICHELANGELO VASTA

6   The Financing of a Large Infrastructure Project: The Case of
    the Channel Tunnel                                                   100
    TERRY GOURVISH

7   Finance and Structure of the State-Owned Enterprise in Italy:
    IRI from the Golden Age to the Fall                               119
    LEANDRO CONTE AND GIANDOMENICO PILUSO


PART II
State-Owned Enterprises in Different Sectors

8   Property Rights, Economic Rents, BNOC, and North Sea Oil    145
    MARTIN CHICK

9   Capabilities, Entrepreneurship, and Political Direction in the
    Italian National Oil Company: AGIP/ENI (1926–1971)          164
    DANIELE POZZI

10  Iron and Steel State Industry in the UK and Italy           182
    RUGGERO RANIERI

11  From Craftsmanship to Post-Fordism: Shipbuilding in the
    United Kingdom and Italy after WWII                         201
    GIULIO MELLINATO

12  State Enterprise in British Electricity Supply: An Economic
    Success?                                                    223
    ROBERT MILLWARD

13  Industrial Policy and the Nationalization of the Italian
    Electricity Sector in the Post-World War II Period          242
    RENATO GIANNETTI

*List of Acronyms*                                              263
*List of Contributors*                                         269
*Index*                                                        273

# Figures

2.1    Rate of return on capital in the UK, 1965–1976 (%).    22

5.1    Example of the structure of the IRI group.    70

5.2    Example of pyramidal control within the IRI group.    72

5.3    Weight of share capital and assets of firms held by IRI, ENI, and EFIM on Imita.db and on Italian joint stock companies.    83

5.4    Control of IRI, ENI, and EFIM under the effective criterion in comparison to the accounting one.    86

5.5    Control of IRI, ENI, and EFIM under the pyramidal criterion in comparison to the accounting one.    87

7.1    Equity and debt of the top 200 Italian manufacturing enterprises (% shares).    123

7.2    IRI capital and debt, 1936–2001 (1970 lire).    128

7.3    IRI bonds and other debts, 1936–2001 (1970 lire).    129

7.4    Net worth and debts of the IRI group (consolidated), 1975–1999 (in 1970 lire).    130

7.5    Debt to equity ratio of Finsider, Finmeccanica, and Stet, 1933–2001.    134

12.1    Price indexes for electricity and other goods in the UK, 1882–1948.    225

12.2    Price indexes for electricity and other goods in the UK, 1948–1998.    230

# Tables

2.1      Annual Profits of the UK Nationalized Industries,
1968–1978 (£ million)      23

2.2      Annual Average Growth Rate of Total Factor Productivity
UK and U.S., 1950–1995 (%)      25

5.1      Number of Firms Included in the Imita.db Census for the
Three Italian State-Owned Groups      73

5.2      IRI, ENI, and EFIM by Typologies of Shareholder
(Number of Firms)      75

5.3      IRI, ENI, and EFIM Firms and Their Weight in Imita.db
(Number of Firms and Percentage)      78

5.4      Weight of Share Capital of Firms Held by IRI, ENI, and
EFIM (Percentage of Imita.db, Total)      79

5.5      Weight of Share Capital of Firms Held by IRI, ENI,
and EFIM in Manufacturing (Percentage of Imita.db,
Manufacturing)      81

5.6      Strength of Shareholding of IRI, ENI, and EFIM
(% Number of Firms)      85

5.7      Regional Distribution of SOEs in Italy (Number,
Number %, and Assets %)      89

5.8      Regional Distribution: Public Firms as Percentage of
Imita.db (Number and Assets)      92

6.1      Channel Tunnel Outturn, 6 May 1994, Compared with
the November 1987 Forecast (£m, Sept. 1985 Prices)      104

6.2      Channel Tunnel Traffic, 1994–2009 ('000s)      107

6.3      Eurotunnel Operating Results and Profit and Loss,
1994–2008 (£m)      110

7.1    Equity and Debt of the Top 200 Italian Manufacturing
       Enterprises, 1951–1991 (% Shares)                                    124

7.2    Ratio of Debt to Net Worth for the Top 200 Manufacturing
       Firms, 1936–1991                                                     126

7.3    Correlation Coefficients between IRI Total Liabilities
       and the Liabilities of Sector Shareholdings (Company and
       Group), 1949–1992                                                    136

7.4    Correlation Indexes between IRI Total Liabilities and the
       Liabilities of Sector Shareholdings (Company and Group),
       1949–1992                                                            136

8.1    British National Oil Corporation Contribution to
       Estimated Expenditure under Fifth Round Licenses
       (Net Exchequer Cash Flows under Alternative Routes
       of Contribution)                                                    154

11.1   UK, Italy, and World Shipbuilding Deliveries, 1947–2004
       (x 1,000 gross registered tons.) (All self-propelled commercial
       vessels over 100 gross tons)                                        209

12.1   Electricity Generation and Sales in Britain, 1920–1998              231

12.2   Electricity Profits and Rates of Return under
       Nationalization: Electricity Boards in England and Wales,
       1948–1987                                                           234

12.3   Productivity Growth in Nationalized Electricity Supply in the
       UK, 1948–1985 (Annual Average Percentage Growth Rate)              235

12.4   Productivity Growth in Electricity Supply in the UK,
       France, Germany, and U.S., 1950–1997 (Average Annual
       % Change in Total Factor Productivity)                              237

13.1   Electricity Plants in Italy, 1951–1973 (Megawatts
       and Shares)                                                        246

13.2   Composition of the ENEL Grid (by Voltage): Length of
       Long-Distance Transmission Lines (in Kilometers) and Losses
       of Transmission and Distribution at 380 Kilovolts (kV)              248

13.3   Flows of Funds in ENEL, 1963–1973 (Percentage)                     250

13.4   Costs and Revenues in ENEL, 1963–1973 (1963 = 100)                 254

13.5   Labor, Capital, and Total Factor Productivity (TFP) in
       ENEL, 1963–1973 (1963 = 100)                                       255

13.6   Sectoral Wages in Italy, 1963–1973 (1963 = 100)                    257

# Preface

This book originated partly from a renewed interest in state enterprise, as the ideas associated with the Washington consensus came under strong criticism. In addition, and quite independently, the Italian Association of Economic Historians was planning a number of bilateral Anglo-Italian meetings on topics relevant to the recent economic history of the two countries. A conference was held in Rome in May 2008 with papers on the history of state enterprise in Italy and the UK. The detail and quality of the papers convinced us and Routledge that publication of the proceedings would be worthwhile, and we believe the outcome is a book that adds significantly to the economic history of both countries and to the general topic of state enterprise.

We are very grateful to Fondazione Istituto per la Ricostruzione Industriale (IRI) for providing financial support for the conference. We would like also to thank the Foundation's president, Antonio Pedone, as well as its secretary general, Franco Russolillo, for all that they did to make the event a success.

During the conference we also benefited from the comments of Luciano Segreto, Daniela Felisini, and Massimo Mucchetti, whom we also wish to thank.

F.A.
R.M.
P.A.T.

# Part I

# Policies, Outcomes, and Funding

# 1 Introduction

*Franco Amatori, Robert Millward,
and Pier Angelo Toninelli*

## AN ECONOMIC ACTOR DISCARDED TOO
## EARLY INTO THE WASTEBIN OF HISTORY

A reappraisal of state-owned enterprises (SOEs) is warranted in the light of the recent renewed interest in state intervention, the limited current literature, and the significant role played by SOEs in the 20th century. After a quarter century of almost general condemnation and rebuttal of the entire nationalization experience, second thoughts about governmental direct intervention in the economy are surfacing. Such a change was induced by the increasingly critical reflection about the globalization paradigm, which has strongly influenced Western culture and society since the 1980s. This in turn grew out of different converging factors: the vanishing of what had previously appeared to be the only socioeconomic model alternative to the capitalistic one, that is, the planned economy; the political overthrow of the states following that model, after the collapse of the Berlin wall; and the new industrial revolution stimulated by the new information and communication technologies. The drive to privatization was actually one of the pillars of the economic and ideological approach dominating the final decades of the last century, an approach soon identified with the prescriptions of the International Monetary Fund and the World Trade Organization or, in other words, with the "Washington Consensus."

Today, the consensus is no longer so clear, a consequence of disillusionment with some of the outcomes of privatization of infrastructure and related industrial sectors and, mostly, of the recent frequent market failures followed by several state rescue acts during the 2008–2010 recession. These include, for instance, the nationalization of the Northern Rock bank in the United Kingdom as well as state support to the Royal Bank of Scotland. Moreover, a recent report of the Commission on Growth and Development (2008) shows that after WWII, the countries which attained sustained economic growth for more than 25 years were precisely the ones that, among the recommendations suggested by the "Washington Consensus," neglected privatization.

Therefore, although the free-market economy no longer exists as a universal panacea, the Western model seems once more to face new ideological, institutional, and cultural challenges. Hence questions come up which increasingly challenge the direction so far followed. Does public enterprise still have a future? Is any specific sector still in need of the visible hand of government? Or, whatever the economic destiny of Western civilization will be, have SOEs been put to rest forever? If so, where will the pendulum of state intervention next swing? This book attempts to provide an unprejudiced assessment of the historical record of state-owned enterprises in two nations: Italy and the United Kingdom. It seems the right time now that some 20 years have elapsed since the sharp decline in the role of SOEs and given also the limited amount of current literature on this topic. The older rich literature on SOEs offered only a scattered collection of comparative case studies that were often narrowly analyzed and that provided only an outline of their basic tendencies. To our knowledge, no specific two-nation comparison is available, offering analysis into detailed, distinguishing aspects: size, performance, and strategies.

It has to be stressed that the two countries examined are very different in history and geography, and, in particular, in their economic evolution: the timing, pace, and pattern of industrialization, the institutional settings, the position on the international market. A few fundamental points should at least be mentioned. From the 17th century, Britain was a well-defined nation; it was the first industrial nation, and it opened the way to the launching of the Western world toward growth and modernization. Only in 1861 was Italy politically unified. It was predominantly agricultural and succeeded in joining the industrialized world only in the 20th century. These differences had an impact, of course, on mentality, values, judicial systems, patterns of innovation, entrepreneurship, and economic policies. The political degeneration of Italy in the interwar period is also relevant even though nationalism, isolation, and power politics were not an Italian peculiarity.

But was the first great insurgence of SOEs in Italy during the interwar period to be entirely ascribed to the specific policy of the fascist regime, or did it have more ancient roots? It should not be forgotten that Italy enjoyed a long tradition of rescue by the state. In 1887, it bailed out a company, Terni (steel), which was, at the time, the major industrial company in the country. In 1911, the same happened to the entire steel sector. A little more than a decade later (1922), the industrial activities linked to the two major banks, Banca Italiana di Sconto and Banco di Roma, were rescued. The procedure was always the same: the national bank printed bank notes in order to accomplish the goal.

As different as the two countries were, a comparison between the ways in which the state enterprises originated and evolved in Italy and the UK can nevertheless offer important insights. In the 20th century, the position (both qualitatively and quantitatively) of SOEs in each country was significant. In the UK, the nationalized industries never accounted for more than 10% of gross domestic product (GDP), but they were located in very capital-intensive sectors, so much so that their annual investment programs accounted for some 20% of the UK total in the 1950s. They provided key intermediate inputs for industry and some basic items of household budgets (e.g., transport, energy, telecoms), and, along with the National Health Service, were leading lights in the public sector of the economy, accounting for one half of total capital formation. In Italy, a government presence in these sectors originated in state activity in railways and telecoms in the late 19th century as well as in oil and electricity in the 20th century. Perhaps even more significant was the emergence from the 1930s of state holding companies like Istituto per la Ricostruzione Industriale (IRI). Such holding companies came to account for 30% or more of the assets of the Italian joint stock companies by the 1980s (see Chapters 2, 3, and 5).

## BEFORE AND AFTER THE WAR

The contributions in this book are organized into two parts. Part I (Chapters 1–7) focuses on the general nature, aims, and quantitative dimensions of SOEs. In Part II, Chapters 8 through 13 contain case studies of specific sectors: steel, oil, shipbuilding, and electricity in both countries. It is possible to identify certain phases in the role and characteristics of SOEs which were common to the two countries.

Before World War II, strategic factors played a strong role in both nations with the postal service, telegraph, telephone, and airlines taken into state ownership, as well as railways in Italy, international cables in Britain, and some shared participation in oil companies. Ideology was not, up until the 1940s at least, a prominent rationale for nationalization in Italy and UK, if for no other reason than because at the time there was some political confusion about what nationalization really meant and implied (for instance, as shown by O'Hara in Chapter 4).

When politics came into play, it was in its most specific field, that of protecting national interests. It was strategic policy aimed at controlling activities that were crucial for security or economic independence. In the UK, there was state control over telephone and telegraph services to safeguard communication channels with the peripheral regions of the empire as well as the financial channels of the city; in Italy, instead, politics showed its presence in postal services, railroads, and supply of crude and distribution of oil products. Yet, in both countries, control of oil resources was felt to be a basic need to be secured through a large government share in the Anglo-Iranian Oil Company (AIOC) in the UK or the founding of Azienda Generale Italiana Petroli (AGIP) in Italy during the fascist period, when the issue of energy dependence on imports was unsuccessfully fought by a country launched toward autarky. In neither case, however, was the political side capable of following a straight strategy. In 1937 the fascist government in Italy set the regime's own interests above those of economic logic, ridding itself (for political reasons) of the rich oil fields of the Mossul region,[1] while in the late 1950s Mattei had to struggle against government hostility toward the investments of Ente Nazionale Idrocarburi (ENI) abroad, which threatened to crowd out domestic investment, particularly in Italy's southern regions (as shown by Pozzi in Chapter 9). Conversely, for AIOC the end of the war implied stricter bureaucratic burdens and the attempt of the government to interfere in the strategies of the company. In the 1930s, another major political intervention in Italy was of course the rescue of large firms in the financial and production sectors. A banking crisis and problems of industrial investment led to state intervention via the establishment of IRI which, after the war, became the precursor for the other state holding companies, ENI and Ente Finanuziamento Industria Marifatturiera (EFIM).

After World War II, government policies for promoting economic development and social justice became more prominent generally in Europe and the late 1940s saw wholesale nationalization of railways, gas, electricity, and coal in the UK. In part, this was a product of regulatory failure as well as of the more general crisis of the private sector following the depression of the 1930s and a socialist influence in some sectors like coal. The late 1940s was a period of national reconstruction after the war, and the Attlee government was able to heavily intervene in the UK economy. In Italy (given its earlier fascist past), the state had to keep a lower profile, albeit without any diminution of the role of SOEs.

In the 1950–1980 period, there is little doubt that SOEs in both countries were perceived as a vehicle for modernization and innovation. The term "modernize" even appears in the title of O'Hara's chapter (Chapter 4), as modernization stands at the center of the Labour Party's political platform, even with the necessary caveats concerning the ambiguous interpretation it was sometimes later given. However, the clear aspiration of public enterprises to innovate and modernize runs through practically all of the chapters in this book. In the British case, this can be seen easily not only from O'Hara's Chapter 4 but also in the transport sector (cf. Gourvish, Chapter 6), starting from the Railway Modernization Plan of 1955 (even though, in the end, it turned out to be a partial failure) to the major motorway building program of the late 1950s; in the iron and steel industry with the 1967 creation of the British Steel Corporation characterized by a managerial team with "a strong focus on restructuring and modernization" (Ranieri, Chapter 10); and, finally, in the energy sector. If the short-lived British National Oil Corporation (BNOC) tried to optimize search and production of North Sea oil, it was in the electricity sector where the best yields were obtained. As early as the 1920s, the state established the Central Electricity Board, which created the first European integrated network of power transmission; in the 1940s, this was merged with all generating and distribution in the form of the nationalized British Electricity Authority and Area Boards (Millward, Chapter 12). Such a dynamic approach curiously contrasts with the conservative one of private shipbuilding (highlighted by Mellinato, Chapter 11), which seems to have also conditioned state behavior in this sector.

Similarly, modernization and innovation emerge as characterizing traits of the Italian experience, particularly in the quarter century following WWII, that is, in the heyday of the entire history of public enterprise when the size of Italian SOEs, measured in terms of capital and assets, reached its maximum extension (see Toninelli and Vasta, Chapter 5). This was especially true in the cases of oil and steel, where the development of a modern technocracy marked a fundamental step toward managerial capitalism. In Chapter 13, Giannetti also shows that in the electricity sector, the nationalization of most of the production and distribution system greatly increased the technical efficiency of the grid and accelerated the transition toward thermal power generation. Finally, and in contrast to the UK, direct state intervention in shipbuilding in Italy meant rapid technical transformation in at least two phases: in the construction of big liners in the 1930s (though this penalized the rest of the fleet), which brought international recognition and prestige to the nation, and, in more recent years, when a managerial and technical revolution based on automation and flexibility relaunched Italian engineering in passenger/cruise shipbuilding (Mellinato, Chapter 11). In the period 1945–1973, the so-called golden age, the economies of both France and Italy grew robustly while the UK started to experiment with new economic policies, in part imitating the former two. In the 1960s, it was economic planning on the French model. In the 1970s, it was Italy that was copied as the Industrial Reorganization Corporation was established to promote mergers and act somewhat like a state merchant bank (as shown by O'Hara in Chapter 4) along the lines of IRI.

The 1970s provided the second major economic turning point of the 20th century, as the oil crisis of 1973/1974, rising inflation and unemployment, and the abandonment of fixed exchange rates in the Bretton Woods system led to a questioning of the state intervention that had characterized the postwar years. The ideological lead in the shift to more use of markets, deregulation, fiscal restraint, and a smaller state sector was taken by Thatcher's Britain but, in the context of privatization, there were also underlying technological and structural currents affecting telecoms and airlines in particular (Gourvish, Chapter 6; Conte and Piluso, Chapter 7; Chick, Chapter 8; Mellinato, Chapter 11). Over the course of the 1980s, the two countries moved in opposite directions. Whereas in the UK, privatizations multiplied under the lead of Margaret Thatcher and her mentor, Keith Joseph, starting with the first big privatization in November 1984 (British Telecom), in Italy the existence of state-owned enterprise continued to be stubbornly defended. Not infrequently, IRI and ENI were compelled to take over private activities in difficulties as in the case of Teksid, the steel sector of Fiat which was taken over by IRI and some chemical activities of Montedison that ENI acquired.

## FINANCE, ENTREPRENEURSHIP, AND GOVERNANCE

One of the strong themes that emerges from the contributions to this book is the interrelated problems of finance, entrepreneurship, and governance and the clear differences between the two countries.

As for the first, the difficulties faced by the banking system and industrial investment in the 1930s prompted strong intervention by the Italian state, leading to the emergence of the nation's state holding companies. The UK never experienced the same problems. There, finance was readily available for SOEs by bond issues or by direct loans from the central government. After 1945, nationalized industries struggled to make profits and self-financed a smaller share of their investment programs than the private sector but, given the strength of the London Stock Exchange, access to finance as such was not a problem. In Italy, on the contrary, in the early 1930s the perverse relationship between bank and industry broke down. The universal banks had, in practice, become financial holdings of the leading Italian firms. To give relief to Italy's tied up capital market, and to put an end to the intricate liaison, a special body was created for the purpose: IRI, a state-owned corporation which took over all the banks' industrial securities, while the banks themselves came under its control. Then after the war, and especially from the 1960s, increasing financial needs induced by "improper burdens" assigned to the SOEs (such as to reduce unemployment and foster growth) were met by "endowment funds" granted by the government (Conte and Piluso, Chapter 7).

With regard to entrepreneurship and governance, because of the way the state holding companies were set up in Italy, considerable discretion was left to enterprising managers and directors (Amatori and Toninelli, Chapter 3). The boundaries of their economic activity were not severely circumscribed; this allowed entrepreneurs like Mattei and others to flourish. On the other hand, since the beginning of the 20th century, the bureaucratic structure of the state was flanked by concerns where functionaries could act entrepreneurially without being bound. This tendency has been defined as "escape from the State" (Melis 2010, 180). It represented a big difference with the UK where, for much of the 20th century, there was a strong line dividing the private from the public sector with the latter treated largely as a setting for public administration rather than entrepreneurship (Millward, Chapter 2). Attempts to break out of that mold in the 1960–1980 period are discussed in Chapter 4 (O'Hara). The contrast between the two countries' involvement in the exploitation and delivery of oil and natural gas are revealed by Chick in Chapter 8, where he examines the British National Oil

Corporation, and in Chapter 9, where Pozzi discusses AGIP. Similar contrasts emerge in Ranieri's analysis (Chapter 10) of the steel industry in both countries. Mellinato's description in Chapter 11 of the fortunes of both shipbuilding industries suggest that the greater flexibility in Italy allowed that industry to cope with the declining role for all European shipbuilders more robustly than the UK industry. Most SOEs in the UK were in the governance framework first used in local government and taking the form, post 1945, of public corporations with their own legal identity, an influential managing board and chief executives acting not too differently from civil servants. This was the case not only for the classic network utilities like railways, telecoms, post, gas, and electricity but also airlines, coal, oil, and the small manufacturing firms like British Aerospace. In broad terms, this was also true of the classic utilities in Italy—railways and trunk telephones (both placed initially in government departments) and electricity, with the establishment of Ente Nazionale per l'Energia Elettrica (ENEL) in 1962. The big difference was in manufacturing, construction, oil and natural gas, non-trunk telephones, airlines, and commerce where state involvement was exercised through the Italian state holding companies.

It is hoped that the detail and range of this book will provide material for further research and reflection on the role of SOEs in the Western world. Each of the contributions includes some attempt to provide a qualitative assessment of the performance of managers and their relationship to the state. It is clear that the latter's inability to act from a distance, with unambiguous guidelines for managers, was a problem in both countries. Quantitative assessments of performance have proved difficult. In Chapter 13, Giannetti presents important findings on productivity in the electricity supply industry, but this is restricted mainly to the period 1960–1973. More generally the sheer spread of SOEs in the Italian economy and the complexity of shareholdings have rendered quantitative isolation of the SOE sector difficult to achieve. The evidence for the UK on profitability and productivity (cf. Chapters 2 and 12 by Millward) suggest that although the profit record of SOEs was poor (except for electricity supply), the productivity performance compared favorably with their privatized successors and with comparable (and more privately owned) industries in the U.S. However, the aims of state enterprise were not simply to raise profitability or productivity but also to modernize, innovate, and create well-founded personnel programs and good relations with trade unions. More sophisticated quantitative measures of performance are clearly needed, and it is hoped this book will stimulate more work along these lines.

## NOTES

1. In fact, early development of AGIP was hindered by the will not to collide with the majors, as shown first by the 1932 removal of the president, Alfredo Giarratana, who during his 3 years in office had given quite a dynamic spur

to the company both at home and abroad. In 1936, AGIP sold to the Iraq Petroleum Co. its 40% share of the Mossul Oil Field Co., which controlled very rich oil concessions in Iraq. According to comments at the time, the move was gracefully solicited by Britain in order to alleviate the economic embargo imposed on Italy after her African adventure (see, e.g., Jacobini 2006).

## BIBLIOGRAPHY

Commission on Growth and Development 2008, *The Growth Report. Strategies for Sustained Growth and Inclusive Development*, Washington, DC: World Bank.

Jacobini O. 2006, *La questione petrolifera italiana. Studi di Oreste Jacobini fra primo e secondo dopoguerra*, Roma: Quaderni dell'Archivio Storico ENI.

Melis, G. 2010, "Amministrazione e dirigismo economico: Una storia lunga," in *Inseparabili: Lo stato, il mercato e l'ombra di Colbert*, ed. D. Felisini, Soneria Mannelli, Italia: Rubbettino.

# 2 The Nature of State Enterprise in Britain

*Robert Millward*

## INTRODUCTION

By 1950, state-owned enterprises in energy, telecom, and transport were common in all European countries, but in manufacturing, banking, and commerce there were considerable differences—much higher in Italy, Spain, Germany, and, to some extent, France than in Britain and Scandinavia. Various factors explain this greater intensity: the autarkic policies of Germany in the interwar period (and Spain after the Civil War), the problems of finance and entrepreneurship in Italy, and the French state's determination after 1945 to plan and/or own those industries important for national security. Even in the infrastructure industries, the origins of state enterprises differed quite strongly. State ownership of trunk railway lines, for example, started in the 19th century for Germany and Scandinavia, whereas public ownership of Britain's railways dates from 1948. So a major aim of this chapter is to explain how and why the origin of state enterprise was different in Britain compared with in Continental Europe.

In the early part of the 20th century, the state's involvement sometimes took the form of shares in companies like British Petroleum and Cable and Wireless (for overseas telecommunications), but this practice was not common and here there is another difference with Continental Europe which needs explaining. It was the public corporation under neither company nor civil law but given its own distinctive legal identity by an Act of Parliament which came to typify the state enterprise—the Central Electricity Board, British Rail, the National Coal Board, and so forth. They were often huge enterprises, among the biggest in Britain in the 1950s, raising many problems of organization and finance, which form a second topic for this chapter.

In the 1960s and 1970s, the British government actively intervened in the manufacturing and oil sectors, leading to the establishment of several new state enterprises like British Leyland (the Rover car group), British Aerospace, and the British National Oil Corporation. In some cases they were rescue acts, as for Rolls Royce and the shipbuilding companies which were in danger of complete financial collapse. But there were also strategic and business innovation issues involved. This period and those sectors are covered in detail by Glen O'Hara (Chapter 4) and Martin Chick (Chapter 8) and so the main emphasis in this chapter is on the classic infrastructure industries—energy, telecoms, and transport over the long term. All state enterprises, whatever the sector, came under fire in the 1970s, and their performance was a major debating point in the lead up to privatization from 1980. A third concern of this chapter is therefore to evaluate the economic performance of the nationalized industries, relative to comparable industries in other countries and to the privatized regime which followed in Britain.

## STRATEGIC DIMENSIONS OF STATE ENTERPRISE

The sectors populated by state enterprise, and in particular the differences between countries, reflect the role of the state in each economy and the form of the business–state interface. Problems of regulating natural monopolies like railways and electricity transmission grids have often been at the forefront of explanations of state intervention, and certainly this was an important element in the nationalizations of the late 1940s in Britain. Even here it needs emphasizing that this was a period of national reconstruction after World War II, so security issues were present. More generally, such strategic dimensions are important in understanding both Britain's early ventures into state enterprise and its differences with Continental Europe throughout the 20th century. It is useful in this context to think of the establishment of state enterprises in Britain as falling into three periods:

### 1868–1945

H.M. Telegraph and H.M. Telephone (as part of the Post Office); British Petroleum (shares in); Cable and Wireless (shares in); Central Electricity Board; British Overseas Airways Corporation; Radio Chemical Centre

### 1946–1951

Bank of England, National Coal Board; British Electricity Authority and Area Boards; British Transport Commission (comprising five executives for Railways, Road Transport, London Transport, Hotels, Docks, Inland Waterways); British Waterways; Gas Council and Area Boards; Iron and Steel Corporation

### 1967–1977

British Steel; Rolls Royce; National Water Council; the Rover Group (British Leyland); British Aerospace; British Shipbuilders; British National Oil Corporation

This list uses the names with which these enterprises were 'christened' at the time they were brought into the public sector, and many changed their names later—to British Telecom, British Gas, British Rail, the British Transport Docks Board, and so on.[1]

In the 19th century and early 20th century, the British experience was very different from the countries of Continental Europe, most of whom had hostile neighbors on their borders (think of France, Prussia, Holland) or were keen to promote unification in a new nation-state (Belgium, Italy, Germany) or across scantily populated regions (Sweden, Norway). Resources and services where security might be at stake, or for which strategic issues were involved, were closely regulated, subsidized, or owned by the state (e.g., telegraph, railways, telephone). In the energy field, it was the range of options open to each country and the inability to make short-term substitutions that was central. Hence there were strong moves in the early 20th century by countries poorly endowed with coal (such as Italy and even France) to exploit the technological advances in electricity generation, and especially transmission, and to develop hydro-electric power, typified by the Vattenfall in Sweden established in 1909 and the Nordvestsjællands Elektriciteist-Værk established in Norway in 1920. In times of war, command over such resources was often a decisive factor in alliances; compare, for example, Italy's links with the U.S. and Britain in World War I, Portugal in World War II (see Millward 2008 for more on this topic).

Britain, as an island economy, had few of these worries. It was well endowed with coal, had a massive shipping fleet, left railways and coal to the private sector and gas, electricity, and water to local determination. There were areas where the British government did intervene, and they reflected Britain's key strategic concerns: (1) the empire and the need to forge good links with the colonies; (2) financial channels for the city, a big British asset; and (3) the emergence of oil as a potentially important energy resource.

What we find therefore is, first, close control over telegraph and telephone. As in all European countries, the government felt the telegraph was a security risk and it was absorbed into the Post Office in 1868, followed by the telephone in 1907. Of particular interest is the Cable and Wireless Co., established in the 1930s as a main supplier of overseas telegraph and telephone. Telegraph was technically very suited to transmitting financial transactions, and the importance of Britain's financial sector and the link with colonies generally prompted close government interest in the development of overseas telecommunications. The government subsidized Cable and Wireless and helped in network development. In 1938, under the Imperial Telegraph Act, the Treasury acquired 2.6 million shares in the company. In 1944, there was an agreement among all Commonwealth Ministers that all companies dealing with international communications should be publicly owned. Under the 1946 Cable and Wireless Act, the government acquired the rest of the 27.4 million shares (Tivey 1973, 182–183; Chester 1975, 258–260; Lipartito 2000). Second, the government took shares, in the early 20th century, in the Anglo-Persian Oil Company, which itself held shares in the Turkish Petroleum Company. The British Petroleum Company, which eventually emerged with part government ownership, reflected Britain's major strategic concern about oil. The third and final dimension of Britain's strategic concerns was airspace and airlines, which were, from the beginning, of strategic concern for all governments, especially one like Britain, which was in the 1930s still a major power and concerned with forging strong links with its colonies. It was one of the signatories of the 1919 Paris Air Convention, which granted sovereign rights to airspace (analogous to oil underground). The embryonic domestic airline industry was unstable and there were several bankruptcies, so the government subsidized the largest private airline serving domestic and Continental routes, British Airways, and the Imperial Airways Company on its colonial links. In 1940, the two were absorbed and merged into a new state enterprise, the British Overseas Aircraft Corporation (Dienel and Lyth 1998).

Finally, there was a particular region of the British Isles which had some special strategic concerns. When the south of Ireland broke from the UK in the 1920s, the new Irish Free State (later Republic) started to create a number of state enterprises (well before anything analogous in Britain) in electricity, industrial and agricultural credit, insurance, shipping and steel, dairies, airlines (surface transport later), and the development of turf extraction (a key energy resource). Most historians have argued this had nothing to do with socialism but rather reflected a desire of the new nation-state to show its firm control of key sectors and to demonstrate that it could run a more efficient economy than the ailing British one it had left. Lemass, the Minister of Industry, for example, declared that, as part of its struggle for a "self-sufficient and self-supporting state," the government was to take over the ailing sugar processing industry and to favor local sugar beet producers. Many of the infrastructure industries were still state owned in 2006 (O'Grada 1997, 178–190; Barrett 2006, 2007).

## STATE ENTERPRISE AND THE DEVELOPMENT OF NATIONAL NETWORKS

The analysis so far cannot account for the emergence of state enterprise in coal, railways, electricity, and gas or for the form which public ownership took in Britain in the 1940s. The energy and transport industries had long been regulated by central or local government, but by 1920 they faced three kinds of problems.

1. Structural: how to develop national networks (electricity, telephone) sometimes in the face of stubborn resistance from small-scale municipal and private enterprises and, in the case of railways, in the face of the emergence of a formidable competitor, road transport.

2. Public interest: many of the services of the infrastructure industries came to be demanded by politicians, business, and residential users as public services.
3. The coal industry: this was the one sector where the rise of socialism was having tangible effects through the demand for nationalization from the mining unions and Members of Parliament representing mining constituencies.

In electricity, technological advances promised large economic gains from the development of a national grid, but this was hampered by the strong role of local government. There was a need to establish links between systems previously privately or municipally owned, to close down some operations and to build the grid. The government intervened to promote coordination and the state-owned Central Electricity Board emerged in 1926, with a national grid more or less complete 10 years later. There were still, however, over 500 small private and municipal enterprises involved in retailing electricity or operating small generating plants (see Chapter 12). In the case of gas, there was no technological or economic case for a national grid, but marketing and research and development were weak, as there were still over 900 separate undertakings existing in the late 1930s (Foreman-Peck and Millward 1994). In the case of the railways, rationalization of a set of private companies seemed to be possible as a result of the 1921 Railways Act establishing four regional privately owned monopolies. The chances of this rationalization proving successful were hardly tested before road transport came on the scene so that the railways were in deep financial trouble by the late 1930s.

As to the second problem, by the inter-war period there was a clear expectation that the gas, water, railways, and even electricity enterprises should be supplying something more than simply a market service (Crompton 1985, 1995; Chick 1995). In all of these services, price discrimination was possible and where, as was often the case, perceived marginal costs were small, standardized 'universal' prices emerged—the same rate per mile, per kilowatt hour, per therm, independent of geographical location, for similar classes of consumers (including freight and passenger classes). Insofar as that approach supported a degree of national unification and of 'fairness' in the price of 'necessities' it was supported by politicians. Such trends were often accompanied by pressures from business users and others to keep at low levels the prices of these key ingredients for industry. However, such price structures did not always make proper allowances for variations in costs so that, especially for railways, they led to financial difficulties.

These two problems were classic regulatory issues and, in principle, could have been solved by the establishment of national or regional monopolies, privately owned but regulated by government, as emerged under the Thatcher privatizations of 1979–1996. In the end, capitalist enterprise did not emerge well from the 1930s and the employers, especially in coal and electricity, often proved reluctant participants in schemes for reorganization and rationalization (Hannah 1979; Supple 1986, 1987). The coal industry is not a 'network' industry but the British coalfields in the interwar period were facing growing competition from other countries like Poland and, by World War II, were showing all the signs of an aging industry—less accessible seams, problems in raising output. In the end, public ownership emerged in the late 1940s.

Many of these structural problems were common to all European countries, but several Continental countries had a prior history of state enterprise, as noted earlier. In the late 1940s, a burst of nationalization in France and Britain effectively meant they 'caught up' with the rest of Europe in the infrastructure industries. The net result was that by 1950, railways, airlines, coal, electricity, gas, and telecommunications were fully or partly state owned everywhere in Western Europe, even though public ownership had emerged in a variety of ideological settings (e.g., socialist, fascist, pro-market). In much of Western Europe, state ownership had originated in geopolitical issues. Britain and France saw dramatic nationalizations in the 1940s where the rhetoric was certainly socialist, but we should note the following:

1. There was little nationalization of manufacturing (outside steel and Renault) and hence neither government could be said to own the 'means of production' (Einaudi 1948; Moch 1953; Millward 1997).
2. The nationalizations were concentrated on what the Labour government called the 'basic' industries—energy and transport plus coal and steel. 'Basic' was never defined, but these industries were central to national reconstruction in the desperate conditions of the late 1940s. So also was cotton and motor cars for exports, but as long as the cotton and motor car firms met their national targets, they were able to escape nationalization (Singleton 1995). Thus, nationalization occurred where there were regulatory problems or strategic issues involved.
3. In France, the impetus to planning and the key role of state enterprise in those plans stemmed directly from a determination not to suffer a fourth German invasion; the plan gave priority to six 'basic' sectors: coal, steel, electricity, transport, cement, and farm machinery. It demanded control over Germany's coal industry, and the Commissariat du Plan was located in the Prime Minister's office (Hackett and Hackett 1963; Kuisel 1981).
4. Coal was the only industry in the UK about which it could be said that the pressure, from mining unions and Labour Members of Parliament, to nationalize was clearly an expression of socialism and was influential.

## ORGANIZATION AND MANAGEMENT

The division of the British economy between private and public enterprise had three distinctive features. First, the sectoral incidence of public ownership in the UK was rather different from that in Continental Europe. In Italy, Germany, and Spain, there was much more state activity in manufacturing, banking, and commerce. In the privatizations of the 1980s and the 1990s, the average size of undertaking was distinctly smaller, and the number larger, in Continental Europe than Britain, where it was focused more on the large infrastructure enterprises. Second, for a long time in Britain, there had been a strict dividing line between the public and private sectors. Before the establishment of the Industrial Reorganisation Corporation in the late 1960s (cf. Chapter 4 by Glen O'Hara), the only companies in which the central government had a significant share holding were British Petroleum and Cable and Wireless, in which a strategic motive was present, as noted earlier. There was nothing equivalent to IRI and ENI in Italy, VIAG and VEBA in Germany, INI in Spain, or the state companies in Sweden in road haulage, provincial railways, or tobacco (brought together in the 1970s under an umbrella state commission Statsforetag). At the local level, the sharing of profits between private companies and local governments—which can be seen in the activities of the Paris Gas Company, the Berliner Elekctrzitäts-Werke and the Danish Gas Company (in dealings with the Copenhagen City Council)—had no counterpart in Britain. Indeed, the common practice in the 19th century of British municipal enterprises transferring some of their profits to the coffers of local government was frowned on by Parliament in the early 20th century (Joint Select Committee1902–1903). Even in the 1960s and 1970s, when the state came to be involved much more in share participation in manufacturing firms, the typical pattern was 100% state ownership—Rolls Royce, British Shipbuilders, British Leyland.

Third, the main form of public ownership in Britain was an institution which was legally and functionally quite separate from the private sector. This 'public corporation' dominated transport and energy, the largest early runners in the 1950s being the British Transport Commission, the National Coal Board plus the British Electricity Authority and Gas Council (together with the lower layers of regional distribution boards and the Central Electricity Generating Board). The employees were not civil servants but neither were the corporations operated under company law. They had their own legal identity, established by Act of Parliament and very similar to ENEL in Italy and EDF and GDF in France (Ostergaard 1954; Hirschfield 1973). The key characteristics of this institution relevant here included the fact that the state enterprises were not enjoined in their Acts of Parliament to make a profit. If any profits were made, they had to be reinvested in the industry. They were given a 'public purpose' to distinguish them from profit maximizers. For example, the British Transport Commission was to provide "an efficient, adequate, economic and properly integrated system of public inland transport and port facilities" (Transport Act 1947, C.49) while the National Coal Board was to be geared to "securing the efficient development of the coal mining industry . . . making coal supply available . . . as may seem to them best calculated to serve the public interest" (Coal Industry Act 1946, C.59).

The industries were run not by representatives of interest groups like trade unions but by boards of professional specialists, including engineers, financiers, administrators, personnel advisers, scientists, and former civil servants. The chairmen of the boards were sometimes of military origin—army officers who had worked in the colonies. The corporation was not seen as a setting where entrepreneurship was especially valued and fostered (in contrast to the situation in Italy). The corporations were to be regulated and administered, reflecting the need to regulate what were often natural monopolies and the need to administer businesses which were perceived to be of strategic importance nationally. In this sense they continued a tradition of local government supervision and management of electricity, gas, water, and tramways in the 19th century and the new local or regional public corporations of the early 20th century: the Port of London Authority, the Merseyside Docks and Harbour Boards, the London Passenger Transport Board. It is significant that the major academic literature in the 1945–1964 period was 'Public Administration'. This was not a management literature. The scholars were in university politics departments not business schools. Some even had a legal background, reflecting the fact that the public corporation was a new legal entity. A voluminous literature emerged on the problems of managing these enterprises which, in the 1950s, were regarded as unprecedentedly large (Robson 1952, 1962; Tivey 1973). Several Select Committees of Parliament devoted considerable time to auditing their management and organization. In retrospect, these enterprises were no different in size to the large multinationals which then existed and which proliferated in the second half of the 20th century. The key questions are whether we can quantitatively appraise their performance (see later) and whether Britain wanted its public enterprises to be as entrepreneurial and innovative as the Italian firms (cf. Chapter 4).

Some of these organizational issues stemmed from the influence of the Labour Party and the 1945–1951 Labour government. It was not a narrow socialist or Marxist party, rather more a social democratic one with close links to the trade union movement. The high minded 'public purpose' has been characterized by some historians (Barnett 1986) as a vain attempt to create a 'new Jerusalem'. The public corporation format was very much favored by the influential Herbert Morrison, who was instrumental in the establishment of the London Passenger Transport Board as a public corporation. He envisaged board members as being above sectional interests. They "must regard themselves as the high custodians of the public interest.

In selecting the Board, these considerations must be in the mind of the Minister" (Morrison 1933).

Each corporation was to be an enterprise which had a public purpose but with a clear commercial orientation (selling services and goods), breaking even financially and operating honestly and efficiently. The Acts of Parliament which established them also reflected the Labour government's deep involvement with national reconstruction after the war. On the one hand, there was a consensus that the two large industries, railways and coal, were in structural decline and needed a national rescue act. More generally, reconstruction after the war called for clear upgrading of the capital stock of the nationalized industries and training of the labor force. Overarching central councils like the British Electricity Authority and the British Transport Commission were set up with responsibility for research, training, and drawing up investment programs, as also was the Gas Council. This broad approach was carried through for all the nationalized industries even to the airlines (Civil Aviation Board), British Steel, and the National Coal Board. The latter were not natural monopolies, and the government's basic interest in securing air links with the colonies and enough investment in coal and steel to facilitate the reconstruction of Britain might have been better achieved by the leverage which would have been afforded by simple share ownership. However, the airlines were in great financial difficulties and the nationalization of coal was demanded by the miners and their Members of Parliament. Steel had been on the agenda for a long time though, as Ranieri (1995) has written, the new arrangements proved difficult to implement because civil servants and the Labour Party had little experience dealing with oligopolistic industries like steel.

## FINANCE, INVESTMENT, AND PROFITABILITY

Even though the nationalized industries had duties related to the public interest, their finances were important because of the amount of compensation which was paid to the former owners, the demands made on the UK capital market by the industries' investment programs, and because the level of profits gave some indication of the extent to which they met the one objective which could be readily quantified: breaking even.

In one limited sense, securing finance for investment was not a problem (unlike Italy) insofar as London was the world's premier stock market and the issue of bonds or the acquisition of short-term credit was not difficult, especially if backed up by a government guarantee. Moreover, government oversight of the banking system—which emerged after World War II and into which the nationalized industries' finances were immersed—had been strengthened. In its 1945 election manifesto, the Labour Party declared that the "Bank of England and its financial powers must be brought under public ownership, and the operation of the other banks harmonized with industrial needs." Some thought the transfer unnecessary. For centuries there had been close links between the Bank of England and the Treasury. The Bank had a Charter and Acts of Parliament dating from as early as 1694 such that the private bank owners had little freedom of action. Nor was compensation difficult to calculate since "the rate of return on Bank Stock had not changed [from 12%] during the past twenty three years [and] ... the capital stock ... had stood at £14,533,000 since 1816" (Chester 1975, 237, 240). At the least, however, with such firm control from the center, there was no need to take over the commercial banks, and here Britain differed significantly from Continental Europe. In proposing the bill which formed the basis of the 1946 Bank of England Nationalisation Act, the Chancellor of the Exchequer in 1945 thought that "the Bill made the law fit the facts ... and ensured an integrated and coherent system of financial institutions" (quoted in Robson 1962, 28).

Although compensation was straightforward for the Bank of England, matters were more complicated for the main industries nationalized. Here there is a vivid contrast with what happened in the 1980s when privatization was dogged by much debate about the appropriate share prices for the industries on sale and whether the taxpayer got a good deal. The shares were often undervalued and, on issue, were therefore strongly oversubscribed—for example, 3 times for British Telecom in 1984 and British Gas in 1986, and 11 times for British Airways in 1987 (Parker 2009, 197, 393, 418; Millward 2010). The reverse process in the 1940s involved calculating how much the private owners of coal companies, electricity enterprises, and railway companies should receive in the forced sale of their assets to the government. Compensation was estimated as amounts approximating the market value of the companies. A variety of methods were used to measure this, including an annual average of recent stock market quotations, the assessment of sustained earnings and purchase years in terms of risk, and the valuation of the real capital stock. The general principle, according to Chester's official history, was that the compensation would be "the amount which the operating company's undertakings might be expected to realize if sold in the open market on the appointed day as a going concern by a willing seller to a willing buyer on the basis of—a) the net maintainable revenue; and b) the number of years' purchase to be applied thereto" (Chester 1975, 324).

The capital sum thereby assessed (£927 million for the railways, e.g.) was then paid to existing shareholders often in the form of government-guaranteed, fixed-interest corporation stock, such as British Transport Stock. This whole process was time consuming, often involving tribunals, but the taxpayer paid the best approximation to market value. Hence compensation proved not to be a major hurdle, except for the coal industry. The miners did not like the idea of the private owners being compensated by 'Coal Industry Stock' because that sounded as though nothing had changed from the 1930s, and the miners objected to any whiff of capitalism around their new National

Coal Board. So the private coal owners received gilt-edged government bonds in compensation, and the National Coal Board obtained government loans for its investment programs. For the other industries, fixed-interest corporation stock was to be used both for compensation and for all new long-term capital needs. This method had already been used with the Central Electricity Board, established in 1926 for constructing the national grid, but it elected not to use the Treasury guarantee on the stock market because, at the time, the government was keen to cover up any appearance of public ownership, even though the reality was that there was no equity capital in the enterprise (see Chapter 12). In the late 1940s, the nationalized industries stock did not sell so well, the early financial results were not promising, and, by the late 1940s, the early popular enthusiasm for nationalization was waning. So, resort was made to loans from the central government (essentially financed by the issue of more government gilt-edged bonds) with interest and repayment made to the government rather than bond holders—the method already adopted for the National Coal Board.

All of the industries were subject to the requirement that, taking one year with another, their revenues should cover all outgoings, including depreciation, interest charges, and capital redemptions. A central feature of the history of the nationalized industries is that this financial target often conflicted with the public interest obligations and the pressures imposed by supervising Ministries. Nonfinancial activities, such as not closing a steel works because of local unemployment problems, were in the early days rarely accompanied by explicit subsidies so that profitability was initially quite low. The losses of the National Coal Board were considerable, and British Rail never covered its interest charges. A particular concern which emerged by the early 1960s was the extent to which the nationalized industries had become less able to finance their ambitious investment programs from their own resources. The broad idea was that the trading surpluses of the enterprises were expected to cover all interest payments and redemption of stock and generate ploughed back profits which would finance an (unspecified) share of expenditure on capital formation, including that for replacement of depreciated assets. The industries' aggregate annual surplus of revenues over outgoings on operating account (wages, fuel, raw materials, etc.) in the early 1950s was equivalent to about 66% of annual fixed capital formation. This had fallen to 50% by the early 1960s, and the capital expenditure was not just new investment but included all replacement of depreciating assets (Central Statistical Office 1960–1979). Comparisons were often made with private manufacturing industry, which tended to finance a major part of its new investment, let alone depreciation, from internal sources—though whether that is commendable is a moot point because external financing usually carries stronger scrutiny. Two government White papers of the 1960s (H.M. Treasury 1961, 1967) stressed the importance of self-finance, and by the end of the 1960s the figure had risen to 75%.

In addition to the degree of self-financing, some observers have compared rates of return on capital in public and private enterprise. To do this, we should perhaps measure profit in both sectors before deducting interest charges, as these are large for public corporations which have no equity. The estimates in Figure 2.1 relate to net trading surpluses, after capital consumption but before deducting interest charges, as a percentage of the capital stock. By the late 1960s, the nationalized sector was earning 3%, less than the private sector but more than previously and nearly enough to cover all interest charges. Another way to look at this is given in Table 2.1 which shows, for example for 1968, that the net trading surplus, including subsidies and after making provision for depreciation of assets and inventory appreciation, was $475 million. Rent and other income added £79 million, but interest charges were £680 million so that the overall net profit (which was required to be zero over good and bad years) was a loss of £126 million. Moreover, that figure masked great differences between sectors in that the Electricity Boards accounted for more than 80% of the aggregate net trading surplus. Even worse was to follow as losses rose to over £1 billion by the mid-1970s, the rate of return fell to -0.2% by 1974 and, net of subsidies, to -3.4%. To a large extent, this was a product of the nationalized industries' prices being held down as part of the anti-inflation policies of the Heath and Wilson governments of the 1970s (Hannah 2004). Explicit subsidies were provided, as shown, but they were not enough to offset the

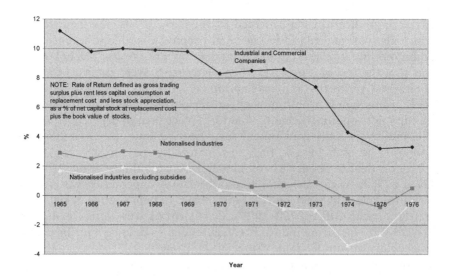

*Figure 2.1*   Rate of return on capital in the UK, 1965–1976 (%).
*Source: Chancellor of the Exchequer 1978.*

decline, and the picture of gloom surrounding the industries' finances was an important element in the push to privatization.

## EFFICIENCY, PRODUCTIVITY PERFORMANCE, AND BUSINESS MODELS

The poor profit record of the nationalized industries has led many to conclude that this reflected bad management. The problem with profits as an index of efficiency is that prices and therefore profit margins may on the one hand be reflecting a monopoly position and on the other hand be reflecting ministerial pressure to hold down prices, rather than indicating bad management. For this reason, attention has been directed more to productivity and, in particular, total factor (labor plus capital) productivity. There are good reasons for looking at efficiency and productivity growth because, as noted earlier, there was a clear injunction in the Acts of Parliament for the nationalized industries to be efficient. Moreover, there is no doubt that by 1980, as the Official History of Privatisation puts it: "the notion that nationalisation was inefficient and private ownership efficient and therefore privatisation was crucial for

*Table 2.1*    Annual Profits of the UK Nationalized Industries, 1968–1978 (£ million)

|  | A<br>Trading<br>Surplus after<br>Depreciation[a] | B<br>Other<br>Income[b] | C<br>Interest and<br>Dividends | Total=<br>Net Profits<br>A+B-C |
|---|---|---|---|---|
| 1968 | 475 | 79 | 680 | (-)126 |
| 1969 | 450 | 95 | 726 | (-)181 |
| 1970 | 227 | 104 | 794 | (-)463 |
| 1971 | 150 | 102 | 896 | (-)644 |
| 1972 | 209 | 107 | 973 | (-)657 |
| 1973 | 286 | 222 | 1212 | (-)704 |
| 1974 | 117 | 298 | 1642 | (-)1227 |
| 1975 | (-)26 | 324 | 1971 | (-)1673 |
| 1976 | 820 | 515 | 2363 | (-)1128 |
| 1977 | 917 | 502 | 2618 | (-)1199 |
| 1978 | 709 | 474 | 2640 | (-)1457 |

[a] Sales revenue plus subsidies, less wages and other costs on operating account and less depreciation and stock appreciation.
[b] Rent and other income which rose in the 1970s mainly in line with the contemporary high level of inflation (often 20% per annum).
*Source:* Central Statistical Office 1979.

achieving productivity gains and cost reductions, became a prominent theme of Ministerial speeches" (Parker 2009, 441).

Although some of the earliest work on productivity (cf. Pryke 1971) concluded that the nationalized industries' performance in the 1950s and 1960s was good, later observers, writing in the period from the early 1980s, as the industries' finances deteriorated and the threat of privatization became a real one, cast the record in a much more pessimistic light (Pryke 1981; Molyneux and Thompson 1986, 1987; Dunkerley and Hare 1991; Hannah 2004). The evidence is however far from clear. In an earlier piece of work (Millward 1990), I found that the growth of total factor productivity in the UK nationalized industries 1950–1985 was better than manufacturing and compared favorably with similar sectors in U.S., where public ownership was much less common. A very large study by Iordanoglou (2001) compared the performance of several UK manufacturing industries with that of public enterprises. His sample included those British industries which were ranked above median by output growth, plant size, and capital intensity in the period 1950–1975. This generated 30 industries, including 5 in the public sector (gas, electricity, water supply, telecoms, airlines) and 25 private sector industries, such as oil refining, organic chemicals, radio and electronic computers, and motor vehicles. Labor productivity growth rates of the public sector were consistently higher than those of the private sector and of comparable U.S. infrastructure industries, while the U.S.–UK productivity gap was narrowed much more successfully in the infrastructure sectors than in manufacturing.

It is important, however, to place these findings in the context of the literature on long-term productivity changes and on total factor productivity for which Iordanoglou provided no new information. Recent research by O'Mahony, Broadberry, and others has generated better data, especially on the use of the capital stock. These writers have been more circumspect in identifying the influence of nationalization, but I still cannot see any evidence for the inference made by some that the 'anti-competitive regimes' in mid-20th-century Britain hampered productivity growth and that privatization improved it (Broadberry 1997, 258; 2000, 8; Broadberry and Ghosal 2001, 21). The productivity patterns are clearly affected by a number of factors, in some cases unconnected with the institutional setting: catch-up effects from World War II, technology growth and imitation, resource endowments. At the overall economy level, productivity had been much higher in the U.S. than in the UK from the early 1900s, but it grew slightly faster in the UK in the period 1950–1973.

On the new evidence, the British total factor productivity growth record in most of the nationalized industries was significantly better than that of their US counterparts and better than that in the whole of the British economy. To be more specific, the average annual rate of total factor productivity growth from 1950 to 1973 was higher in Britain than in the U.S. for airlines, electricity, gas, and coal, as may be seen in Table 2.2. The proposition that privatization in Britain led to an improvement is contradicted by a comparison of these figures with those for 1973–1995 (Table 2.2), when the growth rates for airlines, gas, and electricity were lower. Nor was there any clear improvement relative to the U.S.; among the above industries, the only one that Britain gained under private ownership relative to the U.S. was gas, with the advantage of the new North Sea deposits of oil and natural gas. The coal figure certainly rose, but coal was not privatized until 1994 and its rapid contraction from 1973 to 1995 was accompanied by a productivity growth of 7.89% per annum, largely under public ownership.

Productivity growth in British Rail was only 1.34% and 1.17% for the two periods, well below the U.S. figures. However, the very high figures for the U.S. of 4.5% and 5.9% were reflecting the huge contraction of U.S. railways in the face of severe competition from airlines. The British system was not privatized until 1996, so the comparison of the two countries is more a matter of expansion versus decline, rather than ownership. In telecommunications, British state enterprise showed a productivity growth of 2.13 % in the period 1950–1973 (U.S. 1.73%), but in the second period it grew even faster and much better that the U.S. industry— the major exception to most of the above. In summary, as Parker (2006, 381–382) states about the infrastructure industries, "the labour and total factor productivity gap between the UK and other countries has narrowed but in most cases this narrowing dates back to the late 1970s or before." Any benefits from the post-1979 regime in Britain have come, he suggests, from deregulation and enhanced competition rather than from the change in ownership. Interestingly, other evidence from O'Mahony (1999) and O'Mahony and Vecchi (2001) suggests that in coal mining, electricity, and telecommunications, the publicly owned French industries performed better than either the UK or the U.S. throughout all the second half of the 20th century.

*Table 2.2*　Annual Average Growth Rate of Total Factor Productivity UK and U.S., 1950–1995 (%)

|  | 1950–1973 | | 1973–1995 | |
|---|---|---|---|---|
|  | *UK* | *U.S.* | *UK* | *U.S.* |
| A) Airlines | 11.53 | 9.55 | 4.48 | 2.81 |
|     Electricity | 5.51 | 3.93 | 1.53[a] | 2.57[a] |
| B) Coal | 1.34 | 0.82 | 7.89 | 3.09 |
| C) Gas | 4.71 | 3.02 | 4.16 | -4.09 |
| D) Railways | 1.60 | 4.45 | 1.17 | 5.9 |
| E) Telecoms | 2.13 | 1.73 | 4.08 | 2.84 |
| F) Manufacturing | 3.28 | 1.95 | 1.85 | 1.21 |

[a] 1979–1997.
Source: Derived from O'Mahony 1999; O'Mahony and Vecchi 2001.

There were in fact significant differences between public corporations and their privately owned successors, but one suspects this was not so much about business efficiency, as captured in productivity figures, but rather more about the scope for entrepreneurship. It is possible to conceive of a British state enterprise business model with the following features. The successful public corporations had public interest obligations (relating to security of supply, developing rural areas, integrating transport, etc.), were achieving a healthy grow of sales, had well-developed personnel programs, and had modest managerial salary levels. Last but probably most important, they were profitable—profit being important not for itself but because the enterprise had an objective to break even (including subsidies), and meeting that objective was consistent with being an enterprise with a clear set of objectives which were quantified, monitored, and generally realized. Near to that model were probably the Electricity Boards, Cable and Wireless, British Aerospace, Amersham International, British Gas, the British National Oil Corporation, and the British Transport Docks Board (arguably the most efficient section of the dock industry). This business model was respected and was supported by management. Some of the latter opposed the breakup of their business as privatization loomed (cf. BTDB), and some, like Sir Denis Rooke at British Gas and Lord Keaton at BNOC, fought against privatization itself (Parker 2009, 89, 117, 132, 136, 148).

The corporations' weaknesses were lack of investment, modest salaries, and the often severely circumscribed activities (contrast Italy, Germany, Spain). Thus, the BTDB and National Freight Company could not develop property and land as its successors could. As a public corporation, British Telecom could not expand overseas. The business model for the newly privatized firms was for some public interest obligations, good sales growth, profits constrained by a regulator, more scope for entrepreneurship in the scale and width of its activities (such as oil and natural gas exploration for British Gas), and better access to the financial institutions as a key to expanded investment opportunities. Clearly some of these prospective features of privatization were enticing for state enterprise managers, whose eventual commitment to privatization was also sweetened by employee bonus share schemes and the possibility of better salaries.

## CONCLUSIONS

In the period before 1945, the state enterprise sector in Britain looked very different from that in Continental Europe. It was much smaller and largely reflected the fact that as an island economy with a large empire, large navy, and merchant fleet, strategic concerns were focused mainly on overseas telecommunications, oil, and airlines; hence Cable and Wireless, British Petroleum, British Overseas Airways Corporation. The state-owned enterprises which emerged in the late 1940s reflected three forces. One was the set of regulatory problems arising from the financial problems of the railways, the development of national networks in the infrastructure sectors, and the political pressures on pricing policies. Second, the depression years of the 1930s yielded a legacy of distrust of arm's length regulation of private sector monopolies. Third, there was socialist pressure for nationalization whose main effect seems to have been in the coal industry. By 1950 then, energy, telecommunications, and transport were all run by state enterprises (as largely elsewhere in Europe). Their organization reflected, in part, a continuing theme of British institutional history: that of keeping the private and public sectors quite separate. The 'public corporation' was a distinct legal form, and the industries were given a 'public purpose', and initially 'administered' rather than managed in an entrepreneurial way. Raising capital, given the strength of the British stock market, was a political rather than a technical problem.

Problems arose, not so much from underlying managerial or efficiency issues as from the inability to reconcile the public purposes and their attendant waves of government intervention, with financial targets. It is clear that these central problems of nationalized industries explain, to a great extent, the financial weaknesses. As a whole, the sector did not break even over the 1948–1978 period, and this was true for most of the individual years and for some of the major industries—coal and railways especially. However, these are different issues from the question of whether each industry was efficient in its use of resources. To the question did each industry produce its range of services with excess labor and capital, the answer is no. The state enterprise in Britain compared favorably in productivity growth with comparable sectors in (the more privately owned) U.S. industries and with the privatized regimes which followed in Britain. It is instructive, as argued in the last section, to think in this context of two British business models, one for public corporations and one for regulated private utilities, with the latter given more scope for entrepreneurship and hence expansion. Both have a potential role.

The arguments concerning the origins of state enterprise in Britain suggest some nonideological reasons why state enterprise gave way to privatization. Telecommunications and airlines were the first major industries to be privatized in the 1980s. This largely reflected, on the one hand, the technological developments in jet airlines, telephones, e-mail, and computing, which made the old centralized monopolies look inappropriate and allowed a wider range of market solutions. In addition, the need to have telephones and airlines under close government control for strategic purpose was no longer obvious: there was no need to have telecoms in a government department, no need for strategic links with colonies, and no need for Britain to have only one airline. Moreover, by the 1980s, the mistrust of arm's length regulation of private monopolies inherited from the depression years of the 1930s had diminished, paving the way for privatization of the energy industries and the railways and for the introduction of new regulatory schemes. What is intriguing for the future, given the behavior and growth of enterprises like Gazpom, cross-national enterprises like Électicité de France (EDF) and E.ON (German power and gas company), is what will replace railways, telecoms, and coal as productive sectors vital for national unification and defense and what mechanisms will be put in place by government.

## NOTES

1. The list excludes airports, Royal Ordnance Factories, the Royal Dock-yards, and all public enterprises owned by local authorities. Telecommunications were separated from the Post Office as British Telecom in 1981. British European Airways Corporation was separated from British Overseas Air in 1946, but the two were merged as British Airways in 1975. The Radiochemical Centre started in 1940, later becoming part of the Atomic Energy Authority and lastly Amersham International, its name prior to privatization. The British Electricity Authority later became the Electricity Council, overseeing the Central Electricity Generating Board and the Area Boards for distribution. British Waterways was a research and supervisory body with the water supply undertakings still owned by municipal and private companies up to 1973, when the industry was nationalized in the form of 11 Regional Water Authorities under the National Water Council. The Gas Council and Area Boards later became British Gas. The Iron and Steel Corporation was denationalized in 1953, but the industry was later nationalized as British Steel. The British National Oil Corporation was renamed Britoil shortly before privatization.

## BIBLIOGRAPHY

Barnett, C. 1986, *The Audit of War: The Illusions and Realities of Britain as a Great Nation*, London: Macmillan.

Barrett, S.D. 2007, "Transforming Air Transport in Ireland," in *Transforming Public Enterprise in Europe and North America*, ed. J. Clifton, F. Comin, and D. D. Fuentes, Basingstoke, UK: Palgrave.

Barrett, S.D. 2006, "Privatisation in Ireland," in *Privatisation Experiences in the European Union*, eds. M. Köthenbürger, H.-W. Sinn, and J. Whalley, Cambridge, Mass.: MIT Press.

Broadberry, S.N. 1997, "Anglo-German Productivity Differences 1870–1990: A Sectoral Analysis," *European Review of Economic History* 1(2): 247–268.

Broadberry, S.N. and S. Ghosal 2002, "From the Counting House to the Modern Office: Explaining Comparative Productivity Performance in Services since 1870," *Journal of Economic History* 62(4): 967–998.

Central Statistical Office 1960–1979, *National Income and Expenditure*, London: HMSO.

Chancellor of the Exchequer 1978, *The Nationalised Industries*, Command 7131, London: HMSO.

Chester, Sir N. 1975, *The Nationalisation of British Industry 1945–51*, London: HMSO.

Chick, M. 1995, "The Political Economy of Nationalization: The Electricity Industry," in *The Political Economy of Nationalisation in Britain 1920–50*, eds. R. Millward and J. Singleton, Cambridge: Cambridge University Press.

Coal Industry Nationalisation Act 1946, *Public and General Acts and the Church Assembly Measures of 1946*, 9 and 10 Geo. VI, C.59. London: HMSO.

Crompton, G.W. 1985, "'Efficient and economical working'? The Performance of the Railway Companies 1923–33," *Business History* 27(2): 222–237.

Crompton, G.W. 1995, "The Railway Companies and the Nationalisation Issue," in *The Political Economy of Nationalisation in Britain 1920–50*, eds. R. Millward and J. Singleton, Cambridge: Cambridge University Press.

Dienel, H.-L. and P.J. Lyth, eds. 1998, *Flying the Flag: European Commercial Air Transport since 1945*, Basingstoke, UK: Macmillan.

Dunkerley, J. and P.G. Hare 1991, "The Nationalised Industries," in *The British Economy since 1945*, Oxford: Oxford University Press.

Einaudi, M. 1948, "Nationalisation in France and Italy," *Social Research* 15(1): 22–43.

Foreman-Peck, J. and R. Millward 1994, *Public and Private Ownership of British Industry 1820–1990*, Oxford: Oxford University Press.

Hackett, J. and A. Hackett 1963, *Economic Planning in France*, Cambridge, Mass.: Harvard University Press.

Hannah, L. 1977, "A Pioneer of Public Enterprise: The Central Electricity Generating Board and the National Grid," in *Essays in British Business History*, ed. B. Supple, Oxford: Clarendon Press.

Hannah, L. 1979, *Electricity before Nationalisation*, London: Macmillan.

Hannah, L. 2004, "A Failed Experiment: The State Ownership of Industry," in *The Cambridge Economic History of Modern Britain: Structural Change and Growth 1939–2000*, eds. R. Floud and P. Johnson, Cambridge: Cambridge University Press.

Hirschfield, A. 1973, "The Role of Public Enterprise in the French Economy," *Annals of Public and Collective Economy* 44: 225–269.

Iordanoglou, C.F. 2001, *Public Enterprise Revisited: A Closer Look at the 1954–79 U.K. Labour Productivity Record*, Cheltenham: Edward Elgar.

Joint Select Committee of the House of Lords and the House of Commons 1902–1903, *Report on Municipal Trading*, Parliamentary Papers 1900 VII and 1903 VII, London: HMSO.

Kuisel, R.F. 1973, "Technocrats and Public Economic Policy: From the 3rd to the 4th Republic," *Journal of European Economic History* 2: 53–99.

Kuisel, R.F. 1981, *Capitalism and the State in Modern France*, Cambridge: Cambridge University Press.

Labour Party 1945, *Let Us Face the Future: A Declaration of Labour Policy for the Consideration of the Nation*, London: Labour Party.

Lipartito, K. 2000, "Failure to Communicate: British Telecommunications and the American Model," in *Americanisation and Its Limits: Reworking US Technology and Management in Post-War Europe and Japan*, eds. J. Zeitlin and G. Herrigel, Oxford: Oxford University Press.

Millward, R. 1990, "Productivity in the UK Services Sector: Historical Trends 1856–1985 and Comparison with USA 1950–85," *Oxford Bulletin of Economics and Statistics*, 52(4): 423–436.

Millward, R. 1997, "The 1940s Nationalisations in Britain: Means of Production or Means to an End?" *Economic History Review* 50(2): 209–234.

Millward, R. 2008, "Business and the State," in *Oxford Handbook of Business History*, eds. G. Jones and J. Zeitlin, New York: Oxford University Press.

Millward, R. 2010, "The Family Silver, Business Efficiency and the City," *Business History* 52(1): 169–185.

Moch, J. 1953, "Nationalisation in France," *Annals of Collective Economy* 24: 97–111.

Molyneux, R. and D. Thompson 1986, "The Efficiency of the Nationalised Industries since 1978," *Institute of Fiscal Studies Working Paper* 100.

Molyneux, R. and D. Thompson 1987, "Nationalised Industry Performance: Still Third Rate?" *Fiscal Studies* 8(1): 48–82.

Morrison, H. 1933, *Socialisation and Transport*, London: Constable.

O'Grada, C. 1997, *A Rocky Road: The Irish Economy since the 1920s*, Manchester: Manchester University Press.

O'Mahony, M. 1999, *Britain's Productivity Performance: An International Perspective*, London: National Institute of Economic and Social Research.

O'Mahony, M. and M. Vecchi 2001, "The Electricity Supply Industry: A Study of an Industry in Transition," *National Institute Economic Review* 177: 85–99.

Ostergaard, G.N. 1954, "Labour and the Development of the Public Corporation." *Manchester School* 22: 192–226.

Parker, D. 2006, "The United Kingdom's Privatisation Experiment: The Passage of Time Permits a Sober Assessment," in *Privatisation Experiences in the European Union*, eds. M. Köthenbürger, H-W Sinn, and J. Whalley, Cambridge, Mass.: MIT Press.

Parker, D., 2009, *The Official History of Privatisation, Vol. 1, The Formative Years 1970–87*, London: Routledge.

Pryke, R. 1971, *Public Enterprise in Practice*, London: MacGibbon and Kee.

Pryke, R. 1981, *The Nationalised Industries: Policies and Performance since 1968*, Oxford: Martin Robertson.

Ranieri, R. 1995, "Partners and Enemies: The Government's Decision to Nationalise Steel 1944–8," in *The Political Economy of Nationalisation in Britain 1920–50*, eds. R. Millward and J. Singleton, Cambridge: Cambridge University Press.

Robson, W.A., ed. 1952, *Problems of Nationalised Industry*, London: Allen and Unwin.

Robson, W.A. 1962, *Nationalised Industry and Public Ownership*, London: Allen and Unwin.

Singleton, J. 1995, "Debating the Nationalisation of the Cotton Industry, 1918–50," in *The Political Economy of Nationalisation in Britain 1920–50*, eds. R. Millward and J. Singleton, Cambridge: Cambridge University Press.

Supple, B. 1986, "Ideology or Pragmatism? The Nationalisation of Coal 1916–46," in *Business Life and Public Policy: Essays in Honour of D.C. Coleman*, eds. N. McKendrick and R.B. Outhwaite, Cambridge: Cambridge University Press.

Supple, B. 1987, *The History of the Coal Industry, Vol. 4, 1913–46: The Political Economy of Decline*, Oxford: Clarendon Press.

Tivey, L. 1973, *The Nationalised Industries since 1960: A Book of Readings*, London: Allen and Unwin.

Transport Act 1947, *Public General Acts and the Church Assembly*, 10 and 11 Geo. VI, C.49, London: HMSO.

Treasury, H.M. 1961, *The Financial and Economic Obligations of the Nationalised Industries*, Command 1337, London: HMSO.

Treasury, H.M. 1967, *Nationalised Industries: A Review of Financial and Economic Objectives*, Command 3437, London: HMSO.

# 3 Does a Model of Italian State-Owned Enterprise Really Exist?

## Franco Amatori and Pier Angelo Toninelli

## INTRODUCTION

This chapter aims to show that an Italian model of public enterprise actually did exist and, subsequently, to delineate its main characteristics.

Here we anticipate that Italy's most original contributions to the international constellation of state-owned companies in the field were the public holdings created in the 1930s and 1950s, namely IRI (Institute for Industrial Reconstruction) and ENI (National Agency for Hydrocarbons). The peculiar nature of these institutions was the matching of state property with the style of private entrepreneurship and management. Therefore, even if IRI and ENI coincided with a significant portion of the Italian economy, we're looking at a form of nationalization more apparent than real, which gave birth to a system capable of blending state and market. For sure, such a discourse is valid for IRI and ENI in their golden age—the 1950s and the 1960s.

A quick glance shows that Italy was not the only country that adopted this formula. For instance, think of Anglo-Iranian Oil in the United Kingdom or Renault in France. Even though the origins of their nationalization were entirely different, both were state-owned enterprises (SOEs) and perfectly suited to compete in the market. Similar cases can also be found in Germany, Austria, and the Netherlands. However, as we will see further ahead, in those countries the overall experience of public enterprises was not as extensive as in Italy (Toninelli 2000a). Moreover, in Italy there was a real SOE system: a system with a precise chain of command and a system that implied a controversial relationship between political powers and the entrepreneurial forces that were supposed to be alive and well in the companies. In other words, we think that the general formula (state property and market conduct), the extent of the experience, the interface between politics and economics, and the real impact on the country's history offer sufficient justifications to confirm our thesis that an Italian model of SOE does indeed exist.

However, IRI and ENI are not the sole examples of Italian public enterprise, nor is their formula for the extent of corporate governance and finance that characterized the different forms of direct public

activity in the country. In fact, the complexity of forms and organizations assumed by the state's direct intervention in the economy (just to
limit our analysis to the central level) reached heights of imagination
and ingeniousness that were probably unknown abroad. A plethora of
state companies, state monopolies, state shareholding companies, state
concerns, and so on coexisted throughout the 20th century.[1] Therefore,
an overall evaluation of the dimension, the governance, the finance, and
the viability of Italian public enterprise is extremely difficult. Still, the
chapters contained in this book will try to at least supply some partial
answers to these questions.

This chapter is organized in the following manner: the first two sections
offer a rapid outline of the history of state intervention and nationalization
since Italy's unification. The next two sections focus on the debate about
the origins and the motives, as well as the peculiar aspects, of the Italian
case. The following section dwells on the organizational characteristics of
SOEs during their golden age, and in the final section we'll try to analyze
the causes of their progressive degeneration starting in the 1970s before we
arrive at our concluding remarks.

## STATE INTERVENTION IN THE ECONOMY
## BETWEEN UNIFICATION AND WORLD WAR II

This period can be divided into three phases: in the first two (1861–1912
and 1912–1932) the foundation was laid for the subsequent outburst
(1932–1940), as suggested by the creation of the first state monopolies
and special agencies together with the establishment of a climate and
an environment favorable to stronger government intervention in the
economy, given that the latter was racked by major political and financial difficulties.

### Phase 1: 1861–1912

The unification process was led by a ruling class which greatly desired that
the nation once again become one of Europe's great powers. But Italy in
the mid-19th century was a backward area, with fundamental differences
between the various regions and a lack of spontaneous forces capable of
realizing the economic transformation that the political goals of its leaders demanded. Thus, the state was obliged to become the major economic
actor of the country. It issued public debt bonds and imposed taxes, which
had never been done in the pre-unification states. It conducted a monetary
policy that went beyond the limits of the gold standard system. Moreover,
in the first five decades following unification (1861–1912), direct interference by the state in the economy was remarkable; at times, it should be
added, against its own intentions.[2]

The railways business was emblematic. In 1865, budget constraints tempted the government to sell off most of the network which had already been completed to a few private companies who were allowed to finish construction with some financial support from the state. Yet, the threat of bankruptcy on the part of rail companies forced the government to abandon this plan in 1885. Property belonging to the network was taken back while management, still subsidized by the government, remained in private hands. Poor maintenance and inadequate service to the public finally prompted the state to also nationalize the rail service in 1905. As a result, a special state company (Azienda Autonoma delle Ferrovie dello Stato [FFSS]) was entrusted with the entire organization, but it had no autonomous legal status and was incorporated in the public administration.

The new state had inherited from previous Italian governments mining activities as well as a huge amount of public land, later sold into private hands by auctions that were not always transparent. For a while in fact, the government was transformed into the country's major real-estate company. Furthermore, following the example of other European countries, tobacco and salt monopolies were set up to guarantee considerable fiscal revenue to the exhausted Treasury (Vetritto 2005). The state also took charge of the mail and telegraph services and created a full-scale department. More uncertain would have been the policy toward the telephone service: it was soon declared a state monopoly, but it had to face huge investment (and yet high yields). Even though in the long run the state monopoly option was to prevail, up to the 1950s different public–private mix combinations would occur: only the trunk lines were tightly kept for strategic reasons in state hands and financed through special funding (Bottiglieri 1987). In 1912, still in a monopolist spirit, INA (Istituto Nazionale Assicurazioni, National Institute of Insurance) was created, a public corporation endowed with a margin of autonomy with respect to public administration in general. This could be considered a major step in constructing the Italian welfare state.

From these few examples one can already grasp what the main features of Italian state intervention had been and what they later would become. On the one side, in the public utilities sector, which was most easily affected by natural monopolies and which historically needed state intervention, either via regulation or through direct ownership and management (Toninelli 2000b), the second option was preferred—either at the local or at the national level. On the other side—the direct undertaking of economic activities—from early on, the state was reluctantly forced to intervene in order to make up for private capitalism's inadequacies, which were too feeble on both financial and entrepreneurial fronts.[3]

## Phase 2: 1912–1932

The 20 years (1912–1932) following the creation of INA can be seen as a sort of dress rehearsal for the next performance by the entrepreneurial state. The dramatic events of the period—war, inflation, Depression—brought with them a new attitude toward the state's role in the economy and society.[4]

Certainly one sector in dire need of the government's special attention was that of banking, as it suffered from chronic instability and a shortage of intermediaries. Although the founding of a few German-type universal banks in the 1890s had provided a partial remedy for the latter, it conversely increased potential instability. Therefore, apart from a number of measures directly connected with the war, the government's main concern after 1913 was to strengthen the financial market, primarily through investment in the military and defense industries and, after the war, in social overhead capital. In 1914, CSVI (Consorzio Sovvenzioni Valori Industriali) was created by Banca d'Italia (the Bank of Italy, the corporate bank which since 1894 acted as the central bank, albeit still subject to private law), Banco di Napoli, and Banco di Sicilia (the only other institutions able to issue currency), together with several savings banks to support national industry at the eve of the huge conflict. It was followed by a number of new public finance institutions: CREDIOP (Consorzio di credito per opere pubbliche, 1919), ICIPU (Istituto di credito per le imprese di pubblica utilità, 1924), and IMI (Istituto Mobiliare Italiano, 1931).

These institutions, as well as IRI which was soon to come on the scene, were conceived primarily by Alberto Beneduce,[5] and they shared some common features. Their capital was publicly owned and shared among a few public groups such as INA, Banca d'Italia, Cassa Nazionale per le Assicurazioni Sociali (the agency for social security created in 1919, and later transformed into INPS), and so on, while the source of finance was mostly from the issue of debenture bonds guaranteed by the state[6] (Posner and Woolf 1967; Cassese 1985).

Finally, a major intervention in the productive system that was destined to have extremely important consequences was the creation of AGIP (Agenzia Generale Italiana Petroli) in 1926. An SOE heartily supported by Mussolini, AGIP was assigned the task of exploring and supplying hydrocarbons and distributing oil products in Italy. The fascist regime's expectations were that the new state company would reduce the country's dependence on foreign energy. However, up to the start of World War II, results were negligible as the company was virtually paralyzed by contrasting economic and political interests (Sapelli et al. 1993).

## Phase 3: 1932–1940

In the early 1930s, the perverse relationship between bank and industry came closer and closer to a breaking point. The universal banks had almost lost the character of mixed banks and had become financial holdings, intertwined with most of the leading Italian firms, which in turn depended on them for finance (Rodano 1983). IMI's creation had been an attempt to give relief to Italy's tied up capital market, without actually putting an end to the intricate liaison. The time had come to make a clean break and, at the same time, to restructure the entire financial and industrial system. The proposed solution was ingenious indeed—"so surprisingly innovative as to deserve extra special attention" (Zamagni 1989, 377)—because it implied replacing the mixed bank with the state at the core of the country's economic system (Toniolo 1980, 268).

The body created for the purpose was IRI, a state-owned corporation which took over all the banks' industrial securities, while the banks themselves came under its control. As a consequence, in 1933—through IRI—the state came to control a substantial part of the Italian economy: about 21.5% of total capital of Italian joint-stock companies, a percentage which actually increased to about 42% when indirect chain-shareholding was taken into account (Cianci 1977, 275ff.; Toniolo 1980, 249ff.)[7]

IRI was conceived as a temporary institution, with the aim of restoring and reorganizing the suffering companies before placing them back on the market. A number of outstanding firms (Edison, Italgas, etc.) were soon given back to private hands, but the bulk of them remained under IRI's control. Later, the absence of private buyers and changes in the international climate (autarchy, rearmament) paved the way for its transformation into a permanent institution (1937). It was organized as a super-holding on top of a few sectorial financial holdings which coordinated the activity of the controlled companies.[8] IRI itself was a public-law corporation, wholly owned by the state, albeit autonomous at the legal and financial levels: the firms it controlled remained joint-stock companies under private law. Therefore, it can be said that, by the eve of World War II, the Italian State-entrepreneur had come into its own: Italy at the time "was second only to the Soviet Union in the extent of its state property ownership" (Romeo 1998:135).

## PUBLIC ENTERPRISE AFTER WORLD WAR II

In the postwar period, Italy, unlike the other defeated powers, not only resisted pressure to progressively divest public properties and encourage a free market ideology, but also gradually enlarged its control over the economy and production through what in short was to become an organized shareholding system.

IRI stood out as the main character in the story as well as the pillar of the system. Two new sectorial holdings were added soon after the war: Finmeccanica, where machinery and engineering companies converged (including Alfa Romeo, the renowned sportscar company) and Finelettrica (for electrical companies). An additional subholding, Fincantieri, where shipyards converged, was later created in 1959.

The oil sector would soon become the second pillar of the state-holding system. In 1945, Enrico Mattei was appointed AGIP's special administrator, entrusted with overseeing the approaching process of privatization (see Chapter 9). A large section of the political and economic world, urged on by the big oil companies, was behind the move to privatize. But once he was in charge, Mattei, highly impressed by management's technical expertise as well as the great expectations of oil prospecting in the Po Valley (which would later prove to be disappointing), changed his mind. Within the space of a few years, AGIP was transformed into an aggressively dynamic oil company eager to compete on the international market with the major players. It also created highly innovative policies, both on the internal market, where prices and tariffs were substantially reduced, and toward the less-developed crude-producing countries, which were brought in as joint partners in the economic exploitation of oil. In 1953, Mattei was the driving force behind the creation of ENI (Ente Nazionale Idrocarburi), the state super-holding that operated in energy. ENI was organized on the model of IRI, with a couple of private legal operating entities such as AGIP, ANIC (Azienda Nazionale Idrogenazione Carburanti), and SNAM (Società NAzionale Metanodotti, in the natural gas sector). Mattei directed the group until his untimely death in an airplane crash in 1963. Thanks to his managerial abilities as well as his political skills, ENI revealed itself to be a closely integrated and centralized group on the inside, while maintaining a high degree of autonomy toward the external world (i.e., political parties and economic lobbies) (Orsenigo, Sapelli, and Toninelli 1992; Sapelli et al. 1993).

ENI and IRI became two of the main agents of Italy's economic policy and growth, as the statutes of both state holdings contemplated social as well as economic goals. As a result, both groups undertook initiatives to relieve unemployment and stimulate growth, particularly in the South. It meant that maximizing profit was at times second to other goals, giving rise to "improper financial burdens" in the balance sheet, burdens that were supposed to be offset by a special state endowment fund (Saraceno 1975). As can be imagined, this was bound to become one of the causes of the ensuing explosion of public debt, particularly when electoral and political goals replaced the socioeconomic ones (Balconi, Orsenigo, and Toninelli 1995). For some analysts, the beginning of the decline occurred in 1956, when a new state department—the Ministry of State Shareholdings—was instituted. The Ministry was established to take control and reorganize all state holdings (enti di gestione)—IRI, ENI, and later EGAM (Ente Gestione Attività Minerarie, mining companies, 1958)—as well as other patrimony then organized in two further smaller state holdings—EAGC (Ente Autonomo Gestione Cinema, cinema) and EAGAT (Ente Autonomo Gestione Aziende Termali, thermal baths).

For the State-entrepreneur, the 1960s was the period of greatest expansion. A new state holding (EFIM, Ente Finanziamento Industria Manifatturiera) was created to take care of the machinery, glass, and aluminum industries. But undoubtedly the most important move was the nationalization of the electrical industry (ENEL, Ente Nazionale per l'Energia

Elettrica). This was the first and only industry nationalized since the railways had been taken over in 1905. To a certain extent, the decision was also different from all the others concerning SOEs, as this was neither a case of market failure leading to a rescue by the state nor of compensating for insufficient private entrepreneurship. It was more of a "political" decision, supported by the classic arguments that the profits of this most typical public service should not remain in private hands and that it was technically necessary to wield full control in order to increase the country's supply as well as to provide the public with the best service (Posner and Woolf 1967, 40ff.).

The 1960s and early 1970s were years of continuous growth for the entire SOE system, due to an increasing emphasis on its anticyclical role and the effort to maintain a high level of employment, particularly in the South. New steel plants and automobile factories were set up there, even if this move did not correspond to purely economic criteria (Amatori 2000). Moreover, ENI began to expand outside its core business into the textile sector as well as into chemicals, opening the door to the battle for control of Montedison, the ailing private giant of the Italian chemical industry.

While reaching its peak, however, the Italian SOE system began to show its inherent fragility. In the 1950s, the relationship between state holdings and the political system had been cooperative rather than hierarchical. In short, they were an active part of the political system, capable of influencing and transforming it. In the 1960s, however, the requisites needed to keep the system viable gradually weakened, as the confluence of interests and visions between the SOEs and the political system began to vanish. This was primarily the consequence of a major change in the political environment: a Center-Left government coalition was formed. This coalition introduced new parties, and thus new interests, into the administration of state-owned companies. In general, however, the very growth of the system had raised the issue of the relationship between the state and its companies.[9] In the following period (from the mid-1970s onward), the economic condition of SOEs became highly critical. The economic depression that followed the two oil shocks, together with serious social conflicts that afflicted the country for more than a decade, significantly affected Italian big business and the SOEs in particular. Moreover, the economic and financial conditions of state holdings worsened as a result of overleveraging and a decline in self-financing (Amatori 2000). Therefore, the company was subjected to the constraining power of the political system. Political institutions gained the latitude to make decisions regarding the provisions of direct financing (in its position as sole shareholder) through the mechanism of "endowment funds" (fondi di dotazione). As a result, the system was increasingly exposed to political pressures: parties, rather than the body of citizens, became the principal of SOEs, operating as agent, while increasing corruption and illegal practices penetrated its internal mechanisms (Balconi, Orsenigo, and Toninelli 1995). Several attempts to reform the system and restore the entrepreneurial spirit of the 1950s failed to have the desired effect. Instead, a policy of removing deadwood began: in 1978, EGAM, a financial disaster, was dismantled. Shortly afterward, ENI gave up its textile company and IRI sold Alfa Romeo to FIAT. In 1988, Finsider was de facto bankrupt. Thus, a creeping process of privatization can be said to have already begun in the 1980s, though it would be nowhere as forceful as the process undertaken by Margaret Thatcher's government in the UK.

## WAS IT NECESSARY?

Was it really necessary to create IRI in the 1930s?[10] Ernesto Cianci, a scholar and manager, examines this question in his fascinating book on the birth of the State-entrepreneur in Italy (Cianci 1977). The book was published when the difficulties of the system were already apparent.

We will now briefly elaborate on some of Cianci's argumentation. Italy was the only nation in southern Europe to have achieved a stable level of industrialization before World War II in spite of a serious obstacle: from the very beginning of its economic development, the financial needs of industrial investors far exceeded the supply of private savings, as seen in the issuance of securities. Nevertheless, the general improvement in the economic outlook after 1935 could have allowed an alternative to direct state intervention to materialize. The alternative was a governmental policy able to completely mobilize the resources of private business. The first goal would have been to create better channels for the financing of industry, promoting a more courageous initiative by IMI, strengthening the traditionally weak Italian stock exchange, and fostering the creation of institutional investors. Also very important would have been a massive investment in both visible and invisible infrastructures: education, transportation, and communications. Equally decisive could have been a liberal policy that at least mitigated the country's heavy protectionism and, above all, dismantled the industrial cartels made compulsory by a 1933 law. Finally, to make up for the weaknesses of Italian entrepreneurship, it would have been necessary to create a favorable environment for foreign investments. Certainly this mixture of measures would have been effective, but it must be recognized, as Cianci does, that, combined with the difficulties of attracting foreign capital to Italy in a period of fragmented markets, all this would have been heresy to the fascist government. Mussolini much preferred to have at his disposal a centralized instrument for his aim of power (as was provided by IRI) rather than beginning a pervasive, long-term program of general improvements to the Italian economic system. Moreover, in addition to the contingent economic and political environments, there was the pressure of the long-lasting tradition of direct state intervention that, as we have seen, goes back to the birth of Italy as a politically unified nation in 1861. Not by chance, the first Italian big business grew side-by-side with the state, as was the case, for example, of the railway company Società Italiana per le Strade Ferrate Meridionali and of Società Veneta, a firm involved in major public construction works financed by the state. The system seems to confirm fully the affirmation of Franco Bonelli, a scholar of modern Italian economic history, who defined the Italian model as "precocious state capitalism" (Bonelli 1978, 1204; see also Romeo 1965).

All of the major phases of Italian economic development have been marked by industrial rescues. In 1887, at the end of the first wave of industrialization, only state intervention helped prevent the closure of the first large Italian corporation, the Terni steel plant, founded 3 years earlier (thanks to the same generous state support) to produce battleship armor for the navy (Bonelli 1975, 26). Again in 1911, at the end of the so-called Italian industrial revolution, it was the turn of almost the entire steel sector, whose companies had expanded unwisely while accumulating impressive debts (Bigazzi 1981a, 96–98). In 1922, following the growth caused by World War I, which definitively positioned Italy among the industrialized nations, the state set about rescuing the industrial activities of two major banks, Banca Italiana di Sconto and Banco di Roma (Cianci 1977, 43–54).[11] In each of these three episodes, the Bank of Italy[12] played a crucial role. Particularly revealing was what happened in 1922. We have already mentioned CSVI, the consortium of banks promoted by the Bank of Italy to reinforce the financing of national industry. To rescue Banca Italiana di Sconto and Banco di Roma, an Autonomous Section of the consortium was created, which was nothing more than the Bank of Italy. Every time one of the companies that had previously worked with Banca Italiana di Sconto or Banco di Roma needed money to pay its debts, it issued a promissory note on the order of Autonomous Section of the consortium, which signed it over the same day to the Bank of Italy, which in turn issued new banknotes to pay the debts (Cianci 1977, 44).

If we consider the three main actors in Gerschenkron's (1962) typology— the entrepreneur, the universal bank, and the state—it would be unrealistic to think that only the state was active in the process of Italian industrial development. The universal banks were formed in Italy in the last decade of the 19th century on the basis of German capital and technical know-how. At the beginning of the 20th century, with their financial resources and management expertise, they backed the most important industrial initiatives in the start-up phase (Confalonieri 1974–1976). But their stability was always rather precarious because, given the scarcity of Italian private savings available, they were compelled to collect money in highly unstable international markets (De Cecco and Pedone 1995, 259). There was a serious contradiction between this uncertain source of financing and the longterm commitment required by the companies, a contradiction that could be resolved only by state intervention in the form of rescues, a sort of ex-post financing by the state (Bonelli 1978, 1231).

In the early 20th century, Italy had capable entrepreneurs who understood the critical needs of their companies in production, distribution, and management. These forward thinkers included Giovanni Agnelli in the automobile industry and Giovan Battista Pirelli in rubber; they were entrepreneurs who vigorously competed in both national and international markets. But when IRI eventually tried to sell its assets to private business, it did not find a crowd of potential buyers, especially in sectors such as steel, heavy machinery, telecommunications, and shipping, where deep pockets were necessary not only to purchase but also to keep the business going. After its transformation into a permanent institution, IRI became so embedded in the evolution of the Italian economy that, following the war, when the political and ideological climate was free-market-oriented as never before, even a strong advocate of private business such as Angelo Costa (then the president of Confindustria, the Italian confederation of industrialists) was forced to admit before the Economic Committee of the Constitutional Assembly that IRI was an economic necessity (Maraffi 1990, 146–147).

Therefore, in spite of the clear continuity between what happened in the 1930s and previous Italian economic-political history, the birth of IRI represented a decisive turning point in the economic and business history of Italy. From that point on, the state became the direct owner of companies operating in the market. This had never happened before, not even in the years of fascism, as Mussolini wanted to shape the Italian economy but he did not intend to nationalize it.[13]

## SERENDIPITY OR STRATEGY?

An important challenge for historians is to understand whether this major change, that is, direct state ownership, grew out of a conscious design or simply happened under the pressure of the bank crash.

In his comparative work on different national industries systems, Andrew Shonfield inclines toward the second alternative. In general, he believes that in Italy the "proliferation of nationalized and semi-public enterprise is more the result of historical accident than of deliberate political decision"; in particular, IRI's transformation into a permanent public agency in 1937 appears to be "perhaps the most absent-minded act of nationalization in history" (Shonfield 1965, 178–179). Pasquale Saraceno, an economist who worked for IRI for his entire professional career[14] had a more moderate opinion. Yet he, too, emphasized the pragmatism of the early years and the special attention given to not scaring private business with a nationalization policy. According to Saraceno (1975, 8–9), this is the reason IRI's companies maintained the legal status of private enterprises.

The weight of private business in the origins of IRI is stressed by Marco Maraffi, who sees IRI basically as a rationalization of Italian big business and considers the entire operation, as shaped by the country's principal capitalists, as influencing the government. He offers as proof of his argument the quick privatization of the two giants Edison (the electric company that was the biggest Italian corporation at the time) and Bastogi (Italy's major financial holding company) (Maraffi 1990, Chap. 3).

With the catastrophe of the early 1930s, totally unexpected in its dimensions, IRI needed a good dose of pragmatism. Until the eve of IRI's foundation, for example, documents circulated about the creation of a state holding company for long-term industrial financing, IFI (Cianci 1977, 244–245). Fascism was unable to ignore the interests of the elite of the industrial bourgeoisie.

Nevertheless, Shonfield, Saraceno and Maraffi seriously underestimated the intellectual consistency and managerial capacities of the group that conceived and carried out the reform of the 1930s, especially those of its leader, Alberto Beneduce. Although he was a socialist, Beneduce never displayed any sympathy for a nationalized economy in which companies would be a bureaucratic appendage of the state. Given these premises, Beneduce, to whom Mussolini gave full powers in the IRI operation, certainly had in mind precise guidelines, if not a detailed action plan, at the beginning. These guidelines are demonstrated above all by the general framework of the reform. Drastically separating banks from industry, the state fully assumed its responsibilities as industry owner, directing industrial development (not managing it) and leaving the companies to compete in the market. With regard to private interests, it appears that Beneduce recognized the importance of sociopolitical balances and understood perfectly that IRI had to have boundaries; after all, he also knew the scarcity of managerial resources in his headquarters. Nonetheless, he fiercely opposed the idea of underselling "his" companies to private ones, as in the case of Alfa Romeo with Fiat, or the synthetic fibers manufacturer Chatillon with SNIA, or the electric company SIP with Edison (see Castronovo 1995, 294–301). Finally, Beneduce's IRI developed a distinctive element of rationalization based on the industrial sector in a period previously characterized by confusing multisectorial groups. Furthermore, IRI favored fostering the development of the best managers and technicians at both sectorial holding and corporate levels.

## PROBLEMS OF A GIANT CONGLOMERATE

At the peak of its expansion in the mid-1970s the state shareholding system appeared to be a giant conglomerate, in other words, a mix of companies belonging to different, unrelated sectors, whether considered as a whole or as the various super-holding companies such as IRI, ENI, EFIM, and EGAM.

Giant groups of unrelated companies are a reality of our time, existing both in advanced nations and in those trying to catch up with them.[15] They arise for various reasons: (1) to avoid being trapped in a saturated sector; (2) to avoid the risk of antitrust sanctions; (3) to respond to the necessity of diversifying, given the impossibility of exploiting scale economies in a weak domestic market; or (4) for reasons having to do with the nation's particular historical evolution (as in the cases of IRI in Italy and the Japanese zaibatsu, family-owned horizontal groups of companies in nonrelated sectors).

However, in a highly diversified group to avoid a serious fracture between companies and headquarters, the latter must be not only lean but also act as guarantor of the companies. Beneduce took pride in having limited the size of IRI's headquarters to a simple office in downtown Rome no larger than a typical family apartment and in having operated with a small staff. "IRI's presence was little noticed," writes Gian Lupo Osti (Sinigaglia's assistant and, since the 1960s, one of the most important managers of the state-owned steel sector) in his magnificent autobiography.

We should not forget, however, that IRI came subsequently also to manage directly a few, by no means secondary, owned companies such as the telecommunications and the broadcasting monopolies, the nation's leading airline, and highway companies, as well as to act as a general contractor for the construction of turnpikes and other infrastructures.

In any case, the 1950s are considered the golden era of state shareholding companies: the fact is that there was no strong, external political reference point. The realization of Sinigaglia's plan in the steel sector seems to be similar to any other great entrepreneurial action in a Western market economy. He opened up a big new plant of the right scale in the right place, he specialized the production of existing plant, and he shut down those that were obsolete (see Chapter 10). Particularly surprisingly in a state entrepreneur, the last action involved the dismissal of thousands of workers. To such a change, Sinigaglia (who was very attentive to social problems) used to answer that by producing better steel at lower prices, he would powerfully foster the development of the machinery manufacturing industry and consequently the expansion of employment in both the machinery and steel sectors, which would more than compensate for the previous loss of jobs. This did indeed happen, but such a line of reasoning became unthinkable a few years later inside the state shareholding system.

Mattei's contributions, too, appear to be those of a great industrial leader. Even if he started from the privileged position provided by the legislation on ENI and hydrocarbons, his model was rational and vertically integrated from oil and natural gas research and extraction to distribution, refining, and the sale of gasoline products. It was able to reduce costs per unit and to increase market share in both the oil and chemical field. Particularly relevant was the success attained with the construction of the Ravenna petrochemical plant, thanks to which ENI succeeded in destroying Montecatini's monopoly of nitrogen fertilizers, to the advantage of Italian farmers. In the end, big state enterprises able to compete in the market better than private ones and acting in the best interests of the country became the winning formula of the golden age of state shareholding companies in the 1950s.

## POLITICS TAKES OVER

The turning point, or what we might also call the trap, came with the creation of the Ministry of State Shareholdings and a precise chain of command. At the top of this chain, not visible in the organizational charts, was a silent partner made up of the political parties forming the government coalition. Political parties have always played an important role in Italy, given the necessity for mediation and adaptation in the relationship between the state (considered as a universalist, bureaucratic body) and society because of the latter's weakness and fragmentation (see Sapelli 1990). The lifeline of political parties is consensus, but state shareholding companies were started in a period that was dictatorial and offered no political competition, a fact that kept them relatively free of political strife. Things naturally changed after the war, when competition heated up and the parties realized that an extended system of state firms was a formidable weapon.

But something made the Italian case more complicated. The major opposition party was that of the Communists. In Italy it is a competitive party, but its international connection made it unthinkable as a possible governing party, an alternative to the Christian Democrats and their allies (among which, from the early 1960s, was the Socialist Party). So a one-way spoils system arose in which a set of parties had enormous economic power and would not be punished in the next elections even if they used power badly. Competition was concentrated among the members of the government alliance in occupying, thanks to their coalition power, the largest possible number of positions that permitted them to distribute favors and resources so as to increase their consensus and hence their power (Balconi, Orsenigo, and Toninelli 1995). From this perspective, the state shareholding system above all needed to grow larger without concern for profits and losses.

Some may object that this infernal mechanism did not begin with the birth of the Ministry of State Shareholdings. In the first years, often the minister was little more than a yes-man to the heads of the super-holding companies. This may be true, but it is also true that property rights and legal channels to exercise them are important in the Western world. Once such a precise formal arrangement was formed, it carried a specific weight that was fully understood from the mid-1970s, when SOEs found themselves in trouble and needed financial support from the government and the Parliament, which were, in turn, controlled by the parties (Castronovo 1995, 495–500). The mix of politics and economics that characterized SOEs after 1960 has not always been judged in a critical manner by scholars and practitioners. On the contrary, for a while it was deemed the appropriate cure to increase the economic and social welfare of a nation. A good example of this point of view is found in Pasquale Saraceno's essay, with his explanation that the only appropriate choice for the SOE is *economicità*, which can be translated as "economic health or fitness."[16] For Saraceno, the structure of state shareholdings must not be seen as a hierarchy but, rather, as a continuous exchange and confrontation between political goals and management needs. This intellectual position is appealing, but it does not hold up to reality. In the second half of the 1950s, top management at Finsider (made up of Oscar Sinigaglia's followers) was confirmation of Saraceno's reasoning. Finsider's managers went to the southeastern port city of Taranto to construct a big steel plant. Taranto had been reduced to a pitiful state when orders for its shipyards from the navy dried up. At the end of the 1950s, the country needed greater productive capacity in steel, but for Finsider it would have been more convenient to simply increase the size of existing plants. Nevertheless, the economic and social condition of Taranto demanded a response, and management accepted the new industrial location. They wanted to build a factory with a precise market goal: large pipelines for natural gas and armored plates for ships. Finsider's management understood clearly that simple quantitative expansion was not as important as targeting highly specialized production, which would be less subject to attacks by the new emerging countries. But quantitative expansion meant more employment and hence more political consensus. On this basis, Finsider started an alliance between political powers and a part of management that had never accepted Sinigaglia's ideas. The Taranto plant, which finally opened in 1965, was expanded enormously in the 1970s to produce cheap steel, but it had no market strategy. For Finsider, it would be the beginning of the end (Osti 1993, Chap. 3).

A similar tale can be told of Alfa Romeo, which was compelled to open a new factory near Naples. The company's president, Giuseppe Luraghi, who had brought it to its peak in the postwar period, accepted the challenge, preparing for the new production of a small car that would seriously compete with those of Fiat. When he was forced to hire workers on the basis of political and territorial criteria rather than their skills and attitudes (and was subjected to other nonsensical requests), Luraghi found himself with no choice but to resign (Luraghi 1979).

Detailed research on single companies demonstrates that in some cases, thanks to a strong esprit de corps and a favorable market situation, management's resistance was stronger and the firms were not overwhelmed. This seems to be the case for AGIP, a sectorial holding of ENI (Sapelli et al. 1993). But it does not change the overall picture of management held hostage by politicians and subject to progressive degeneration. Even ENI is an excellent illustration of how the nature of enterprise can change. After Mattei's death in 1962, ENI, in addition to its core business of oil, was also engaged in industrial rescues of companies operating in mining, in chemicals, and in totally unrelated sectors such as textiles. It became increasingly a state holding company for economic development. Even more striking is the fact that ENI had to take over first the mining and machinery manufacturing activities of EGAM (1977) and then, in 1980, SIR's and Liquichimica's plants (the so-called Italian smoking chemical ruins) under a set of laws passed by Parliament. The Soviet-style expropriation of top management's prerogatives was impressive.

## CONCLUSIONS

The first privatization initiatives of the 1980s de facto brought to an end a century-old experience. Certainly Italy's nationalization process has been characterized by shadows and light. Dark moments especially characterized the final phase: in the early 1990s the entire structure of Italian SOEs, already subjected to serious shocks by the crisis of the previous decade, began to collapse, the result of several converging factors.

As already mentioned, the first factor was the degeneration of corporate governance induced by unbearable levels of political interference. Second, while state enterprises during the golden age and up to the end of the 1960s followed the behavior of private ones (at times performing better) (Toninelli and Vasta 2007), later their economic and financial conditions, particularly in the cases of IRI and EFIM, continued to worsen. In 1992, IRI alone registered losses amounting to more than 4,000 billion liras (about 2.2 billion Euros). A year later these losses had grown to more than 10,000 billion liras (Barca and Trento 1997, Table 1). The Treasury bore enormous financial burden for implementing both the endowment funds and the payment of matured interest on the borrowed funds. Third, SOEs had become increasingly identified, by public opinion, with inefficiency and waste. They were held largely responsible for the state's financial crisis—a destiny shared with practically all the other countries characterized by a large public sector after World War II, "Felix Austria" included (Toninelli 2000a).

The final outcome, however, should not make us forget the reasons that led to the building of the shareholding system or the role historically played by SOEs in the Italian economy. Therefore, the final assessment cannot be altogether negative: in Italy, unlike other countries such as France or England (where the nationalization process gained momentum under left-wing governments), ideological and political reasons seem to have been less important. Instead, in the most crucial phase of the country process of growth convergence toward the level already reached by the first comers, the state was called upon to remedy structural deficiencies such as capital scarcity, lack of infrastructures, and feeble entrepreneurial spirit: this was quite evident in the cases of canals, railways, oil producing and refining, iron and steel, banking and finance. Besides, state intervention was even more decisive when private business showed itself unable to compete on the free market: in fact the largest part of the SOE system came from rescue operations performed by the state. Finally the growth of the entrepreneurial state in Italy was also the consequence of the post-WWII decision to implicitly renounce a regulatory policy like the one followed, for instance, by the U.S. Not by chance, the establishment of special American-type regulatory agencies and authorities has been the necessary prerequisite for the privatization of wide sectors of public activities which occurred in the late 1990s.

One can wonder if it wouldn't have been better to leave private business to its fate. The answer is not easy and would imply a very sophisticated counterfactual analysis, starting with a reliable measure of the long-time performance of the entire SOE system. But this would imply finding a way to also quantify the spillover effects on the diffusion of technology, of innovative managerial practices on capital formation (e.g., see Giannetti and Pastorelli 2007), and, in addition, the extensive program of investments carried out during the difficult 1970s. All of these were not negligible assets of the growth of public enterprise as they manifest themselves both in the golden age as well as in critical times like the 1970s.

## NOTES

1. According to Cassese (1985, 18–19), by the early 1980s there were about 500 public economic bodies active in the country in addition to the three state super-holdings (IRI, ENI, and EFIM). The first ones were ruled by private law and characterized by an entrepreneurial stance: that is, they were expected to break even with the sale of products and services. The super-holdings, instead, had a double nature, as they were organized according to public law and audited by a comptroller or auditor-general, but ruled by private law. Moreover, there were hundreds of companies characterized by variable state-shareholdings equally governed by private law: in a few special cases, the companies providing public services under license were ruled directly by the state. Still a different kind of state direct activity needs to be considered: the autonomous state agencies (such as railways, telephones, highways and agricultural markets) and the state administrations (state-controlled monopolies as well as postal and telegraph services). These were under the authority of specific ministries and wholly reliant on the same for their financing; only the railways were governed slightly differently as they were able to issue bonds.

2. This situation can be seen, for instance, in the initial economic enterprise of taking over the ownership and management of thermal spas in the towns of Montecatini, Salsomaggiore, and Recoaro, which were part of the Demanio Industriale (State Industrial Properties). Notwithstanding numerous attempts to sell them, they remained in government hands for decades. The same occurred with Società del Canale Cavour, a canal system in the Piedmont region that was constructed shortly after unification. It became part of the state domain in 1874, when the private (mostly British) corporation (that had acquired ownership and a 50-year license to manage the canal) went bankrupt. (For further information and examples, see Toninelli 2004, 55ff., from which the present section draws.)

3. This can also be demonstrated with regard to the founding of the country's modern iron and steel industry, discussed later in this chapter.

4. During the war, even eminent Italians sharing sound liberal beliefs, such as Luigi Einaudi, Maffeo Pantaleoni and Pasquale Jannaccone, began to talk about how it would be desirable that the State take over shares of

companies operating in crucial industries such as foodstuffs and the military (Cianci 1977). Although that vision might have been distant from the ideas of those who wanted to either overthrow or deeply reform the capitalist system, it helped to create the climate that gave rise to a certain number of public corporations.

5. Hence the frequent reference to them as "Beneduce institutions."
6. Such a guarantee could be either direct (i.e., state) or implicit (i.e., issued in the name of IMI, IRI, etc.). The debt was acquired primarily by institutions and public bodies obliged to invest their assets in government or state guaranteed bonds. For more details on the evolution of the financing of SOEs, see Conte and Piluso, Chapter 7.
7. IRI controlled 40% of the military iron and steel industry and 100% of the military industry as a whole, 90% of shipyards, 80% of the telephone industry, the shipping lines and railways production, about 40% of the banking and finance system and the metallurgic industry, as well as about 30% of the electrical industry, plus minor shares in the textile, engineering, cinema, and construction industries.
8. STET (Società Torinese per l'Esercizo Telefonico, telephones), Finmare (shipping), Finsider (iron and steel).
9. This generated a complex and sophisticated discussion regarding the extent and mechanisms of political control over the management of the companies (Shonfield 1965; Amato 1972; Colitti 1972; Cavazza-Graubard 1974; Scalfari and Turani 1974; Saraceno 1975).
10. The present section draws upon Amatori 2000, 133ff.
11. Ansaldo (heavy machinery, shipbuilding, automobiles, and the like) was at the time the largest Italian corporation to be among the companies rescued.
12. The country's most important issuer of currency and, after 1926, the only institution able to issue currency
13. Thus, in 1926 the Autonomous Section of CSVI became the Istituto di Liquidazioni (Institute of Liquidations), a clear sign that all the activities that the state had taken over from Banca Italiana di Sconto and Banco di Roma were to be sold to private business (Cianci 1977, 57).
14. In the early 1930s, Saraceno served as assistant to Alberto Beneduce, making a substantial contribution in 1936 when the bank bill was drawn up.
15. The literature about business groups is the widest. See, among others, Leff 1978; Encaoua and Jacquemin 1982; Goto 1982; Koike 1993; Barca et al. 1994; Granovetter 1995; Shiba and Shimotani 1997; Amatori and Brioschi 1997; Zeitlin and Ratcliffe 1998; Barbero 1997; Bargigli and Vasta 2003.
16. As we have already noticed, this meant that the aim was not to maximize profits but to focus on economic goals established within the framework of social and political constraints. On the other hand, the law stated that these kinds of constraints were considered "improper financial burdens," for which the Parliament had to compensate with an endowment fund (Saraceno 1975, Chap. 2).

## BIBLIOGRAPHY

Amato, G., ed. 1972, *Il governo dell'industria in Italia*, Bologna: Il Mulino.

Amatori, F. 2000, "Beyond State and Market: Italy's Futile Search for a Third Way," in *The Rise and Fall of State-Owned Enterprises on the Western World*, ed. P.A. Toninelli, Cambridge: Cambridge University Press.

Amatori F. and F. Brioschi 1997, "Le grandi imprese private: Famiglie e coalizioni," in *Storia del capitalismo italiano dal dopoguerra a oggi*, ed. F. Barca, Rome: Donzelli.

Balconi, M., L. Orsenigo, and P.A. Toninelli 1995, "Tra gerarchie politiche e mercati: Il caso delle imprese pubbliche in Italia (acciaio e petrolio)," in *Potere, mercati, gerarchie*, ed. M. Magatti, Bologna: Il Mulino.

Barbero, M.I. 1997, "Argentina: Industrial Growth and Enterprise Organization," in *Big Business and the Wealth of Nations*, eds. A.D. Chandler, F. Amatori, and T. Hikino, Cambridge: Cambridge University Press.

Barca, F., et al. 1994, *Assetti proprietari e mercato delle imprese, Vol. 2, Gruppo, proprietà e controllo nelle imprese italiane medio-grandi*, Bologna: Il Mulino.

Barca F. and S. Trento 1997, "La parabola delle partecipazioni statali in Italia," in *Storia del capitalismo italiano dal dopoguerra a oggi*, ed. F. Barca, Rome: Donzelli.

Bargigli, L. and M. Vasta 2003, "Proprietà e controllo nel capitalismo italiano (1911–1972)," in *L'impresa italiana nel Novecento*, eds. R. Giannetti and M. Vasta, Bologna: Il Mulino.

Bonelli, F. 1975, *Lo sviluppo di una grande impresa in Italia*, Turin: Einaudi.

Bonelli, F. 1978, "Il capitalismo italiano. Linee generali di interpretazione," in *Storia d'Italia, Annali 1, Dal feudalesimo al capitalismo*, Turin: Einaudi.

Bottiglieri, B. 1987, *STET. Strategie e struttura delle telecomunicazioni*, Milano: Angeli.

Cassese, S., ed. 1985, *L'amministrazione centrale*, Turin: UTET.

Castronovo, V. 1995, *Storia economica d'Italia*, Turin: Einaudi.

Cavazza, F. and S.R. Graubard 1974, *Il caso italiano*, Milan: Garzanti.

Cianci, E. 1977, *La nascita dello stato imprenditore in Italia*, Milan: Mursia.

Colitti, M. 1972, *Le grandi imprese e lo stato*, Turin: Einaudi.

Confalonieri, A. 1974–1976, *Banca e industria in Italia 1894–1906*, 3 vols., Milan: Banca Commerciale Italiana.

De Cecco, M. and A. Pedone 1995, "Lo stato investitore," in *Storia dello stato italiano dall'Unità a oggi*, ed. R. Romanelli, Rome: Donzelli.

Encaoua, D. and A. Jacquemin 1982, "Organization Efficiency and Monopoly Power. The Case of French Industrial Groups," *European Economic Review* 19: 25–51.

Gerschenkron, A. 1962, *Economic Backwardness in Historical Perspective*, Cambridge: Harvard University Press.

Giannetti, R. and S. Pastorelli 2007, "Il sistema nazionale di innovazione negli anni Cinquanta e Sessanta," in *Innovazione tecnologica e sviluppo industriale nel secondo dopoguerra*, ed. C. Antonelli et al., Rome-Bari: Laterza.

Goto, A. 1982, "Business Groups in a Market Economy," *European Economic Review*, 19: 53–70.

Granovetter, M. 1995, "Coase Revisited: Business Groups in the Modern Economy," *Industrial and Corporate Change* 4(1): 93–130.

Koike, K. 1993, "Business Groups in Developing Economies," *Developing Economies* 31(4): 363–377.

Leff, N. 1978, "Industrial Organization and Entrepreneurship in the Developing Countries: The Economic Groups," *Economic Development and Cultural Change*, 26: 661–675.

Luraghi, G., 1979, "La verità sull'Alfa Romeo," *Epoca* 11 August: 5–10.

Maraffi, M. 1990, *Politica ed economia in Italia*, Bologna: Il Mulino.

Orsenigo, L., G. Sapelli, and P.A. Toninelli 1992, "The Evolution of the Strategy and Structure of a State-Owned Company: The Case of Agip Petroli s.p.a., 1960–1990," *Business and Economic History* Second series, 21.

Osti, G. 1993, *L'industria di stato dall'ascesa al degrado*, Bologna: Il Mulino.

Posner, M.V. and S.J. Woolf 1967, *Italian Public Enterprise*, London: G. Duckworth & Co.

Rodano, G. 1983, *Il credito all'economia. Raffaele Mattioli alla Banca Commerciale Italiana*, Milan-Naples: Ricciardi.

Romeo, R. 1965, "Lo stato e l'impresa pubblica nello sviluppo economico italiano," *Elsinore* March–June: 14–55.

Romeo, R. 1988, *Breve storia della grande industria in Italia*, Milan: Cappelli.

Sapelli, G. 1990, "Lo stato italiano come imprenditore politico," *Storia contemporanea* 2: 243–296.

Sapelli, G., et al. 1993, *Nascita e trasformazione d'impresa. Storia dell'AGIP Petroli*, Bologna: Il Mulino.

Saraceno, P. 1975, *Il sistema della imprese a partecipazione statale nell'esperienza italiana*, Milan: Angeli.

Scalfari, E. and G. Turani 1974, *Razza padrona*, Milan: Feltrinelli.

Shiba, T. and M. Shimotani 1997, *Beyond the Firm*, New York: Oxford University Press.

Shonfield, A., 1965, *Modern Capitalism*, London: Oxford University Press.

Toninelli P.A., 2000a, *The Rise and Fall of State-Owned Enterprises in the Western World*, Cambridge: Cambridge University Press.

Toninelli, P.A., 2000b, "The Rise and Fall of Public Enterprise: The Framework" in *The Rise and Fall of State-Owned Enterprises in the Western World*, ed. P.A. Toninelli, Cambridge: Cambridge University Press.

Toninelli, P.A. 2004, "Between State and Market: The Parabola of Italian Public Enterprise in the 20th Century, *Entreprise et histoire* 37: 53–74.

Toninelli, P.A. and M. Vasta 2007, "Public Enterprise and Public Networks in Italy 1952–2001: A Quantitative Profile," in *Transforming Public Enterprise in Europe and North America. Networks, Integration and Internationalization*, eds. J. Clifton, F. Comin, and D. Diaz Fuentes, London: Palgrave-Macmillan.

Toniolo, G. 1980, *L'economia dell'Italia fascista*, Bari: Laterza.

Vetritto, G. 2005, *La parabola di un'industria di stato. Il monopolio dei Tabacchi 1861–1997*, Venice: Marsilio.

Zamagni, V. 1989, *Dalla periferia al centro*, Bologna: Il Mulino.

Zeitlin, M. and R. Ratcliffe 1988, *Landlords and Capitalists: The Dominant Class of Chile*, Princeton: Princeton University Press.

# 4 Attempts to 'Modernize'

## Nationalization and the Nationalized Industries in Postwar Britain

*Glen O'Hara*

## INTRODUCTION

"These measures of ours are not theoretical trimmings. They are the essential part of a planned economy that we are introducing into this country": Prime Minister Clement Attlee's justification of the nationalization of 20% of British industry (Attlee 1947, 42). His rhetorical confidence in physical planning was matched by Hugh Dalton, Labour's first postwar Chancellor, but it was to conflict with other Labour politicians' visions for 'socializing' industry. Some of Attlee's ministers held quite different views, faithful to a potent amalgam of liberal Keynesian that originated primarily with the economist James Meade and his colleagues in the Cabinet Office's Economic Section. Douglas Jay and Hugh Gaitskell, who both served in the Treasury under Attlee, are good examples of this concept's devotees (Toye 2003, 196, 225). "We are seeking a combination of public ownership, public accountability and business management for business ends," Attlee's deputy, Herbert Morrison, had written in his 1933 *Socialisation and Transport*: hardly the same ends as his immediate superior envisaged in 1946 (Hennessy 1992, 197–198, 185–186; Marquand 1996, 7, 12).

This confusion was to lie at the heart of dilemmas over how to govern and manage nationalized industries throughout the postwar golden age, as the Attlee government launched nationalization as an economic imperative that would permit greater interventionist dirigisme. The scale of the project was enormous. Public sector employment rose from 2 million before the war to 7 million after it; and from 10% to 30% of the workforce. The nationalized industries' output was £980m in 1950, and the sector accounted for 20% of gross domestic capital formation (Hogwood 1992, 129–130). Civil aviation, inland transport in the form of railways, long distance road haulage and canals, electricity, gas, iron and steel, and the coal industry became, respectively, the British Overseas Airways Corporation (BOAC), and then British Airways in 1974; the Transport Commission, incorporating rail and road haulage (though the latter was re-privatized from 1953); British Waterways; the Central Electricity Generating Boards and the regional suppliers; the 12 Area Gas Boards; the Iron and Steel Board, privatized in 1953 but re-nationalized as British Steel in 1967; and the National Coal Board. The Bank of England was also nationalized in 1946. Some areas in which Labour's party conference called for nationalization remained immune: large-scale builders and retail banks, to name but two. But, in general, Labour's rank-and-file and leaders believed that they had indeed seized the 'commanding heights' of the industrial economy (Saville 1993, 37, 43).

But what really lay behind most of the decisions over what to nationalize, what to leave in the private sector, and how to govern each nationalized industry, was Britain's desperate economic situation in the 1940s. The crisis of supply, which was the legacy of war, the country's shortage of dollars, and the political strength of the metals industry, dictated both which areas were subject to controls and which owners were mollified with concessions. Ministers seized on the most technocratic option before them: a single board of appointed expert managers, who would be accountable to Parliament for breaking even over an undefined period of time (Chester 1975, 560–563). Alternative Labour suggestions—for instance, radical decentralization, democratization, or scrutiny by Parliamentary Select Committee or Whitehall 'efficiency unit'—were all rejected (Cairncross 1985, 275–284, 489–493). The situation was rather different in the iron and steel industry, though in ways that once again demonstrate the role of immediate economic contingencies. Because the need for those exports was so great, and the Conservative Party in Parliament was so vociferous in defense of the private industry, government's 1948 nationalization bill gave the steel owners much of what they wanted. Although a new Iron and Steel Corporation now controlled most of the industry, including many engineering plants, most of the individual companies and their managements survived (Dunkerley and Hare 1991, 389).

There had been, in other words, much less of a break with the past than Labour wished to imagine. The public sector's relatively 'hands-off' corporate governance, its centralization, and its insulation from Parliamentary scrutiny brought to mind another series of public-sector 'rationalizations' in the 1930s: namely, the Conservatives' subsidies for the run-down of inefficient coal mines and companies, the creation of the British Broadcasting Corporation, and the British Overseas Airways Corporation (Ramsden 1987, 53–55). The cartelization and reorganization of the interwar years was to some extent simply being continued (Millward and Singleton 1995, 316–318). Indeed, it may be speculated that at a time of relative political consensus about the ends of policy, the means by which to achieve those ends became even more controversial. Debates over ownership stood in for clearer, and perhaps politically dangerous, new ideas about even more divisive subjects: redistribution, equality, or even nationality (Gamble and Walkland 1984, 104–107; Kavanagh and Morris 1989, 27–29; Cronin 1991, 221).

This chapter will show how these uncertainties affected attempts to modernize Britain's state-owned enterprises between the 1950s and 1970s and how this uncertain rationale for state control opened up a very large ideological space for dissension as to their governance. Neither Labour nor the Conservatives had a clear and straightforward agenda: this formed a constant backdrop to attempts to reform the sector, a fact that was eventually to undermine its very existence. The Conservatives in power would try to subject the sector to more rigorous economic tests; Labour would attempt to cut through these dilemmas by creating a whole new concept of 'state entrepreneurship'. Drawing on the Italian experience, and that country's policies that had circumvented the dilemmas of public benefit and state control, Labour's idea of 'selective intervention' involved a long search for a more flexible public sector. But this chapter will also show just how confused British politicians' ideas about 'foreign' concepts really were; another reason why this search proved fruitless.

## POLITICAL CONFUSION OVER NATIONALIZATION

Most Conservatives thought that a more dynamic economy should make questions of ownership obsolete. "Managements have as their main function the detailed planning of the concerns for which they are responsible," their Automation Group's report declared. "[T]hey are far better qualified than innumerable extra Civil Servants to judge how to apply [change] to their particular operations" (Conservative Political Centre 1956, 19). But though these views expose Conservatives' hostility toward state-owned enterprises, they also demonstrate why little was done to disassemble the sector while the party held power between 1951 and 1964. Their continued existence was thought of as a necessary part of the new welfare state, and as the economy grew, their significance and power might gradually wither in any case. Rab Butler, the party chairman who drew up the Conservative Industrial Charter of 1947, deliberately aimed to make a statement of the Conservatives' adherence to the 'middle way' in politics (Ramsden 1980, 109–115). There would be no widespread privatization. Nationalization and denationalization also appeared at the time irrelevant to Britain's economic problems, which the Conservatives during the 1950s came increasingly to see as rising prices, stagnant industrial relations, and an uncompetitive— and mainly private—export sector (Ramsden 1996, 29–36).

Spending on the nationalized industries, reckoned the chairman of the Conservative expert committee on economic growth, was 'unnecessary and wasteful' (Conservative Party Archive 1961). The party's Committee on the Nationalized Industries, which deliberated in the run-up to the 1959 general election, was privately very critical of this sector's performance and floated the idea of a 'British Petroleum solution' or halfway house between privatization and the status quo (Green 2002, 224–225). But even then, little was done to change the balance between public and private. It is true that the iron and steel industry was denationalized—although, as we have seen, its structure made this an easier task than privatizing other state-owned enterprises. Even here, the Ministry of Supply and the Bank of England were deeply skeptical about going over this ground yet again, and an Iron and Steel Board retained the right to cap prices and veto developments in the industry (Burk 1988, 6–7, 81–88).

There was, even so, another, quite different impulse to the Conservatives' hostility. This was simply that nationalization was very unpopular with the public. To some extent, this issued from the general weariness with controls and austerity that formed part of the folk memory of the 1940s (Zweininger-Bargielowka 2000, 60–98). In 1957, a Gallup Poll for the *News Chronicle* showed that only 18% of the electorate wanted more nationalization (Harvester Archives of the British Conservative Party [HABCP] 1957). Public hostility was not just a matter of unfocused resentment: it also had much more specific connotations. It was, for instance, associated with high taxation, especially as state subsidies for these industries rose from the late 1950s onward, and consumer subsidies rose for 'affluent' workers who hardly needed them (HABCP 1961). Conservative politicians and officials also knew that the biggest trade unions within this sector of the economy were perceived as left-wing, obstructive, and inefficient (National Archives of the United Kingdom [NAUK] 1961).

In lieu of more radical changes, the Conservatives attempted to make the nationalized industries behave in a more 'businesslike' manner. The management of the railways was liberalized, for instance, and a government stipulation that they had to charge uniform prices was removed (Harris 1972, 190–195). The electricity industry was regionalized, with only a coordinating and weak advisory role reserved for the Electricity Council at the center (Hannah 1982, 161–167, 183–184). The Conservative White Paper of 1961 tried to bring more precision to the vague nationalization statutes. The statutory obligation to break even 'over a period' was clarified by reference to a specific planning cycle of 5 years. The Treasury also stipulated that the difference between the historic and the replacement cost of assets should be spelled out and that future capital needs had to be more clearly taken into account (Tomlinson 1994, 204). Nationalized industries' need for capital would be discussed on a 5-year planning horizon, and upper limits would be set two years out from any negotiations with the government. *The Financial and Economic Obligations of the Nationalized Industries* argued that nationalized industries had enjoyed lower rates of return than the private sector. This was "sooner or later damaging to the economy as a whole," and it was a situation the government declared itself determined to reverse (Cmnd. 1357, 1961, 5–6). More specific reforms of the same period included the breakup of the state's inland transport interests, with the constituent parts of the British Transport Commission given their own autonomy and targets (Cmnd. 1248, 1960, appendix).

## THE ROLE OF THE INDUSTRIAL
## REORGANISATION CORPORATION

Labour Party politicians, and especially Harold Wilson as leader from 1963, were acutely aware of the nationalized sector's unpopularity among the electorate. Wilson therefore attempted to reshape Labour's commitment to further nationalization on the 'old' model of 1945–1951, beyond a totemic intent to renationalize the steel industry (NAUK 1964; Cmnd. 2651, 1965). Wilson's answer was to stress the need for seedcorn money in order to gain the government a presence in the 'new' and more technologically advanced industries and new types of corporate governance which would be more responsive and less bureaucratic than the huge corporations Labour had created under Attlee. The party's 1964 election manifesto called for a greater role for the National Research and Development Corporation and declared that Labour in power would "go beyond research and development and establish new industries, either by public enterprise or in partnership with private industry" (Labour Party 1964, 9–10).

One major instrument of Labour's ambitions for such new industrial conglomerations was to be the Industrial Reorganisation Corporation (IRC), which would encourage, fund, and organize mergers and then provide capital for new plants and machinery within the new merged organizations (Tomlinson 2004, 700). Reorganization and a greater sense of strategic priorities might then stand in for expensive industrial and regional policies in the form of grants and loans, which would have to take their place alongside Labour's promise of higher expenditure on the welfare state (Labour Party Archive 1962). The IRC was supposed to act as a 'state merchant bank'. Wilson used his personal friendship with the banker Siegmund Warburg and chose one of Warburg's associates, Ronnie Grierson, to be IRC's first head. Despite thinking the idea 'absurd', Grierson agreed to take the job in order to stop the new body 'doing harm' (Ferguson 2010, 391).

This was, however, hardly the limit of the group's interests. Given the intellectual miasma that hung over these questions in the UK, it was little wonder that British planners turned to an ambitious ready-made foreign example while designing the IRC. In this case the exemplar they chose was Italy, and in particular that country's state holding company IRI: the Istituto per la Ricostruzione Industriale (NAUK 1965b). IRI had been founded in 1933 to rescue three of Italy's failing banks, though IRI soon expanded its remit to help industrial firms as well. Italian banks were prevented from taking holdings in the wider economy at the same time, to prevent another industrial crisis threatening the financial system. The entire banking system had been at risk of collapse, because of both the monetary contraction managed by the authorities attempting to defend the lira's value against gold and the widespread panic as other countries' banking systems broke down (Mattesini and Quintieri 1997, 284–285).

## ITALY: THE INAPPROPRIATE EXEMPLAR

Policymakers' interest in Italy should come as little surprise in terms of the overall culture of economic thought, for the economic league tables published at the time by the United Nations and the Organisation for European Co-Operation and Development showed the UK to have a relatively slow, and Italy a relatively rapid, rate of growth (Tomlinson 1996b). In 1950, Italian GDP per capita amounted to $3,502 in 1990 U.S. dollars; by 1965, that figure was $7,580, an increase of 116%. The UK, on the other hand, could muster economic growth per head of only 41% over the same period (Maddison 2001, Table C1-c, 276–277). Nor was the particular example of state-led growth particularly novel: left-leaning economic authors from the Marxist far left to the reformist soft left—from Thomas Balogh, to Stuart Holland and then (on Labour's right wing) to Michael Posner—were extolling its virtues throughout this period (NAUK 1965a; Cairncross 1997, 30).

Holland believed that IRI provided a means by which to attack 'structural' imbalances in the economy which would not be susceptible to Keynesian demand management (Holland 1972, 6–7; 1975, 182–194). Posner, though much less enthusiastic than Holland, believed that "the determined attack on basic infra-structure deficiencies in the Italian economy made by the public sector . . . provided the indispensable stimulus to the Italian miracle" (Posner and Woolf 1967, 70; see also Posner and Pryke 1966). Both men were in a position to spread their ideas in the mid- to late 1960s. Holland assisted Balogh as an Economic Assistant to the Prime Minister in 1966 and 1967, and was later influential in *Labour's Programme 1973* (Adlam 1980, 16–21). Posner was also a Special Adviser, and served as the Ministry of Power's first Director of Economics (*The Independent* 9 March 2006; *The Guardian* 17 March 2006).

Only the disastrous experience of IRI's politicization in the recessions of the 1970s and 1980s could expose its real flaws (Hine 1992, 38–39). This phenomenon was a constant theme throughout the sector and the period under discussion here, and involved prolonged wrangling among political factions—notoriously in the state oil and chemicals holding giant ENI (Ente Nazionale Idrocarburi) (Grant, Martinelli, and Paterson 1989, 78–79). It had not simply begun with the relative political polarization of the 1970s (Fratianni and Spinelli 1982, 239–240). But, at the time, even economists who looked at which elements IRI could spin off into the private sector believed IRI to have stabilized Italy's banking system and provided a valuable channel through with private savings and foreign investment could flow (Einaudi, Byé, and Rossi 1955, 235–236). When Grierson visited Italy in 1963 to drum up business for Warburg's, IRI executives indeed told him that they were "literally flooded with offers of 15 year money from US sources on very attractive terms" (Warburg Archives [SGW] 1963). Warburg executives were constantly amazed at the enormous amounts that IRI could raise, especially in the U.S. (SGW 1970).

Labour's enthusiasm for the Italian model seems, in retrospect, to have been entirely overdone—especially because many of the conditions allowing IRI to succeed in Italy were not present in the UK. It was indeed the case, as economist Andrew Shonfield argued, that IRI companies refused to use their privileged financial position to spend money on the prevention of unemployment (Shonfield 1965, 181). But this was partly because it was easy to take on new staff when there was so much surplus labor to draw into the factories from the shrinking farm sector, a source of manpower long since exhausted in Britain (Denison 1967, 46–48). More generally, Italian GDP was far behind Britain's in the late 1940s, as the 'long boom' got under way. Italian industries were also much smaller than British industries, with the number of employees in each business far below her competitor's: all metals and engineering industries accounted for only 8% of Italy's GDP on the eve of World War II, while labor productivity had actually fallen progressively behind Britain's in the interwar period (Federico 1996, 772). That left an enormous space for economies of scale and scope to be grasped, much less painfully than in Britain (Cohen and Federico 2001, 99–101).

Italy's economy was managed by what the British writer Tobias Jones has recently termed 'parallel paths', just as familiar among the Italian public as they became to businessmen: "the official one written on paper, and the hidden one going on in verbal agreements between 'gentlemen'" (Jones 2003, 140). A network of financial links, cross-shareholdings, shared board memberships and joint ventures tied Italian business together at the top, and provided the capital for the rise of heavy industry (Rinaldi and Vasta 2005, 193–198). Enrico Cuccia's dominance of the monopoly investment bank Mediobanca is one of the best-known examples of such networks in action in the private sector (Amyot 2004, 33–38, 56–57; Segreto 1997, 654–657). It was these links, rather than the corporatist state, that controlled and drove IRI and the other holding companies, especially in the 1950s and early 1960s (Maraffi 1980, 510–512). It may even be the case, as Amatori has argued, that IRI paradoxically worked well when it was 'headless', that is, when the silent partners at the top, namely, the political partners and the heads of the individual businesses themselves, could exert little or no direction over these networks (Amatori 2000, 149–150). With the creation of a Ministry of State Holdings in 1956–1957, greater government direction confined IRI's constituent parts; this was an important reason for Labour's enthusiasm in the first place but was a development which tended to undermine the whole system's rationale.

There was little sign here of Wilson's more centralized, directed, and 'purposive' governance. Increased government control seems rather to have deepened the client relationships between individuals, political parties, and managers within this semi-public and semi-private sector (Martinelli 1979, 77–83). More and more capital was directed toward high-profile and expensive 'prestige' projects to garner popularity in Italy's regions, particularly in the South, although this seems to have done little to make that region more economically competitive or more widely to have updated its social infrastructure (Padoa Schioppa 1993, 80, 83). It is difficult to escape the impression that Italy's postwar miracle was, at least in terms of heavy industry, caused by a virtuous circle of strong demand, cheap labor, rapid European integration, and easy credit. Once these conditions had changed, the 'model' fell apart: the state holding companies' investment and economic returns plunged during the 1970s, even as they attempted to mop up the unemployment attendant upon stagflation (Locke 1995, 54–55).

Enormous spaces were also left in the British official imagination with regard to the Italian economy more widely. Despite IRI and ENI's success in mobilizing foreign direct investment and encouraging exports, their continued expansion also appealed to the Italian political parties and business elites because they ensured that actual ownership remained in Italian hands (Posner 1977, 821–823). This was an idea less likely to recommend itself to an economic elite more open to foreign ownership, such as Britain's. Nor were the two countries' private sector firms of similar size, with the Italian economy dominated, on the one hand, by very large and well-connected family groups and, at the local level, very small businesses (Barca and Trento 1997, 536–541). A banking system in which independent financial markets were weak, and in which funds were channeled to large industrial concerns by powerful state holding companies and Mediobanca, allowed family firms such as Fiat, Pirelli, and Pesenti to become even more powerful (Aganin and Volpin 2003, 16–18). Even in Emilia-Romagna, the heartland of Italy's motorbike and mechanical industries, clusters of small family firms dominated the textiles and clothing industries throughout the period (Cooke and Morgan 1998, 123). But such a system also encouraged such small businesses to fund themselves: an ideal situation, perhaps, if one wanted to reinforce a 'dual economy' such as Italy's, but hardly appropriate in the UK (Bianchi 1995, 106–107).

## THE TRAVAILS OF 'DIRECT INTERVENTION': THE 1960S

Even though the IRC spent only £103m in capital (during a period when manufacturing investment as a whole was nearly £7bn), it was extremely influential in a number of industrial concentrations, especially in electronics, mechanical engineering, and the car industry. The IRC stood behind, or approved, mergers of English Electric and Elliott Automation, Plessy's takeover of English Electric's data processing arm, and then English Electric's merger with International Computers and Tabulators to form International Computers Limited (ICL), conceived by Labour's Minister of Technology, Tony Benn, as a 'national champion' and worldwide competitor with IBM (Benn 1989, 83). The 'restructuring' of the mechanical engineering industry absorbed much of IRC's time, partly because it was such a complicated and fragmented sector. Most controversially, the IRC encouraged hostile takeovers in both the ball-bearing and scientific instruments industries: even Warburg thought that the corporation had 'damaged its image' in appearing to 'take sides' in the latter bid (SGW 1968). In the former case the IRC even took control of one company, Hoffman, in order to buy up another (Pollard's) and thus frustrate the latter's attempt to merge with a Swedish company. Another large and apparently 'competitive' British corporation was thus created (Graham 1972, 190–191).

Perhaps inevitably, the IRC soon also became increasingly involved in the new techniques and strategies that the new national champions might adopt. It provided £25m in retooling loans to help encourage and support the merger of British Motor Holdings (BMH) and the Leyland Motor Corporation, which came with advice and conditions on how the money might be spent (Church 1994, 86). The English Electric–ICT deal, too, came with conditions for government help: in this case, that ICL develop leasing rather than selling techniques, so as to speed up adoption of computers in industry (Hendry 1989, 155–157). The IRC showed some tendency as it became more established to intervene outside the range of mergers *per se*: a loan of £1.5m was made to the Reed Paper Group in 1968 to finance plants that would reconstitute printed paper for reuse. In the IRC's last year of operation, 10 out of 17 such projects were launched, mostly spent under a Conservative government dedicated to its abolition. This was duly achieved in May 1971 (Mottershead 1974, Table 10.1, 436).

The creation of British Leyland (BL) was the most famous case of IRC intervention, and it was an absolutely critical deal if the new corporation's integrity and relevance was to be asserted. Donald Stokes, the dynamic head of Leyland, had been in discussion with BMH since 1964, and the government was keen to encourage a merger rather than a takeover of BMH by the younger and commercially more vigorous group (NAUK 1966; SGW 1967). Several meetings were held in private with the Prime Minister to encourage Stokes and his opposite number, Sir George Harriman, to approve a deal (Benn 1988, 483, 511; 1989, 16, 20, 31). The IRC's ambition was clear: to re-equip BMH using the skills and capital available to Leyland and to subsidize this process if necessary with a cheap loan during a period of high interest rates (Young and Lowe 1974, 65–66). This would create a British motor group that could compete across a whole range of vehicle types and to achieve that end without a damaging public battle. It achieved these ends through its intermediary role, backed up by the capital it could offer (Hague and Wilkinson 1983, 120–128).

But there were limits to what the IRC could do to boost 'efficiency', without exerting actual control, and the problem BL now faced was that its constituent parts were themselves hardly amalgamated. BL contained the remnants of Austin, Morris, Daimler, Standard Triumph, Leyland, Rover, and Jaguar, virtually unintegrated and with very few links to one another at lower levels. Replication of parts, suppliers, and research was commonplace. Donald Stokes, Leyland's new head as well as deputy chairman of the IRC, remembered that "[there were] 50 or 60 different companies all trying to retain their independence even though they had been taken over" (Church 1994, 87). The group went bankrupt in 1974 and had to be rescued through nationalization. Strategic thought, at least in regard to initiating new nationalizations, appeared to have failed by this stage. Even so, BL had half the British market as late as 1978, although that had shrunk to 35% by 1989, as Vauxhall, Ford, and new Japanese competitors came to dominate the market. Its workforce had shrunk by two thirds since 1978 (Dankbaar 1994, 175).

Similar phenomena were evident in other mergers: the Coventry Gauge–Tube Investments union of 1969 showed no gain in efficiency by the mid-1970s, while Alfred Herbert's expansionist takeover of other machine tool manufacturers saw the group on the verge of bankruptcy at the same time. The Herbert Group was split up again in 1979, although not before it had absorbed several tranches of government money (Broadberry 1997, 344). The entire intellectual rationale for the contemporary wave of monopolies and mergers is, to some extent, questionable. Evidence from the U.S. and UK alike seems to show that that the profitability of those companies proposing the merger or mounting the takeover was not consistently higher than those firms being absorbed. These deal initiators were almost certainly bigger, and thus were able to draw on the capital the deal required, but this was unlikely to mean that the merged group did any better than the two companies had done separately (Morris 1998, 216–217). One analysis of UK mergers between 1964 and 1972 has demonstrated that the majority of companies experienced a mild decrease in profitability thereafter (Meeks 1977, 24–25).

The IRC has never attracted the sustained academic criticism to which other elements of Labour's program have been subjected. As late as 1986, some academics were noting that "there was fairly broad agreement that it was a success" (Utton 1986, 6). But not only were Italian-style holding companies and state finance entirely inappropriate to British conditions, but the large-scale creation of national champions on the U.S. model was hardly likely to work either. The enormously cheap raw materials and land that U.S. capitalism absorbed very early during the 'second industrial revolution' of the late 19th century entrenched vast economies of scale and scope that kept labor productivity in manufacturing at about double the UK level throughout the 20th century. Attempting to ape corporate structures more appropriate to that economic environment—without the factor endowments that so assisted U.S. firms—was doomed to failure (Broadberry 1997, 395–396).

## THE TRAVAILS OF 'DIRECT INTERVENTION': THE 1970S

Some of this emphasis on 'flexibility', and on agreements in specific sectors and with individual companies, was very prescient given the developing nature of government intervention. Little was done in the first two years of the Heath government, as the Conservative leadership tried to ignore or circumvent pressure from junior radicals such as Nicholas Ridley. Ridley's policy group on the industries had reported in 1968, recommending some privatizations and above all that "the managers . . . must be left alone to manage." It was a familiar refrain, and early in the Heath government the free-marketeers made some gains. But when the Heath government began systematically to engage with these issues, it was in precisely the opposite manner to that which Ridley intended. Ridley was moved from the Department of Trade and Industry in 1972, where he had presided over a short-lived laissez-faire experiment (Taylor 1996, 148–152).

Glasgow's shipyards, reorganized into the Upper Clyde Shipbuilders (UCS) consortium by Labour in 1967–1968, were rescued from bankruptcy at this point: three out of the four dockyards were to remain open. During shop stewards' protests, Heath had told the Scottish Trades Union Congress that "it is not a basis in which the country can be run to pour money into debt-making companies. There is no future except in companies which can build ships and sell them at a profit. UCS has not been a success and there is no point in endeavouring to keep it alive" (NAUK 1971b). The Cabinet believed that UCS had "now become a symbol of ailing enterprise, bedevilled by bad labour relations and poor management, in whose future prospects there could be little confidence" (NAUK 1971a). Their decision to keep the docks open, despite their own doubts and apparently to lessen their political embarrassment, helped to bring the entire idea of state intervention into question.

Meanwhile, Labour had been steadily moving to the left as to both the shape and purpose of nationalization. A wave of left-wing radicalism, strikes, and protests against the Heath government's 1972 Industrial Relations Act helped to encourage Labour further in this direction. Alternatives to the Morrisonian public corporation came increasingly into focus, including the idea of workers' control as promoted by Ken Coates and the Institute for Workers' Control. The economic sections of *Labour's Programme 1973* were mostly written by Holland, and called for a National Enterprise Board (NEB) with many more powers than the IRC had possessed. A new NEB, Holland imagined, would be granted the equity in 25 of Britain's 100 largest companies (Wickham-Jones 1996, 64–66). It would then be able to intervene directly in each sector of industry, promote industrial democracy and job security, and allow the government to control multinational corporations (Foote 1997, 298–312).

The outcome was much less coherent, ordered, and purposeful. The commitment to industrial democracy was quietly dropped once Labour came back to power in 1974; a rate of return of 15% to 20% was to be expected from investments; and the NEB was to be subject to the same monopolies and mergers legislation as private industry (Coates 1980, 115). The two White Papers issued on the NEB were vague; the second was published in 1975 after the NEB's main advocate, Tony Benn, had been demoted to the energy brief, and it was particularly unforthcoming as to the new body's powers and responsibilities. At a time when the Cabinet was becoming increasingly fearful of the effects of an international loss of confidence in both Labour and sterling, there seemed little room to buy up new industries (Kramer 1988, 4–14, 18–28).

NEB spending peaked at £368m in 1977–1978, before falling back to £70m in the following financial year (Tomlinson 1996a, Table 7.1, 169, 183). The NEB had spent £1bn of Labour's approximately £8bn total support to private industry. But over half of this, £569m in all, had gone to BL. Some 95% of the NEB's total spending went to support for companies that would otherwise have collapsed. Only one planning agreement was reached with a private company, the Chrysler car corporation, which would also have been bankrupt had it not been funded by the NEB. Although the company's performance improved marginally, it then broke the agreement by selling out to Peugeot Citröen in 1978, only a year after the deal with the government (Wickham-Jones 1996, 141–142). Together with the nationalization or retention of companies facing collapse—BL, for one, but UCS too—the record of selective intervention seemed to have done little to confirm Wilson's faith in 'scientific' socialism.

## CONCLUSIONS

Some of the key elements in this survey are all too easily ignored, particularly the politicization inherent in making choices between the private and public sectors, and the transnational nature of economic policymaking in the post–World War II era. As Terry Gourvish has remarked, it can be very difficult for economic and business historians to integrate these aspects into their research (Gourvish 1987, 18). It has long been clear among historians of Britain's state-owned enterprises that political impulses were crucial in terms of which industries to take into the public sector, and the form of their governance. John Singleton and John Wilson, in their approaches to the Attlee government's nationalization and the gas industry respectively, have shown how other variables do little to explain the scale and scope of nationalization (Singleton 1995, 29; Wilson 1995, 161). Martin Chick, for instance, has demonstrated how the interests of the French bureaucracy, and French politics, explain the rapid adoption of marginalist pricing principles in that country's electricity industry in comparison with Britain (Chick 2006, 163–166; see Chick 2007). But it can be very difficult to operationalize these insights in the archives, and less work has been done on the 1960s and 1970s than on the Attlee period. A number of widely informed and book-length histories of competitiveness, entrepreneurship and Britain's public sector have been emerging, and it is hoped that such studies will continue mixing together political, economic, and international insights (e.g., Gourvish 2008).

The contrast between Italy and the United Kingdom, the first experiencing a period of very fast and apparently 'concerted' economic growth and the second perceived as stagnating, was felt very acutely in this period. But the causal links behind these different political economies—the transnational element to policymaking—have remained rather hidden. There are only a limited number of studies, especially in English and apart from textbooks, of the different political dynamics of British and Italian economic strategies in the state sector (Tolliday 2000, 244). Francesca Carnevali's study of the oil and gas giant, the ENI (Ente Nazionale Idrocarburi), and Ilaria Favretto's comparative work on British and Italian and British on the political left, are relatively rare examples (Carnevali 2000; Favretto 2003). There are still fewer examples of historiographically informed work explicitly comparing the governance of Italian politicians state-owned enterprises using new archival material: Ruggero Ranieri's work on the steel industry in both countries is an example of might be achieved in this respect (Ranieri 1995, 2004). There is clearly a great deal of scope for more international histories comparing differential performance, and probably still more in the discovery and delineation of the networks of experts and politicians who carried those concepts across national borders.

The general picture revealed in this chapter—of ambiguity, ideological disputation, and slow reform, usually inspired by foreign models that remained opaque to most of the policymakers involved—helps to explain the relative loss of confidence in these bodies during the 1970s. Even prior enthusiasts, such as Richard Pryke, lost confidence in their ability to generate and sustain economic growth (Pryke 1971, e.g., 453–467; 1981, e.g., 262–263). It was a period when earlier gains seemed to die away: only British Airways, British Gas, and British Telecom were able to claim above-average gains in productivity in that decade. They were all in high-demand industries that allowed the process of reequipment and technological advance to continue (Brech 1985, Table 25.2, 789). This was, however, a period of general crisis for British industry; nationalized industry could hardly have remained immune. Total factor productivity also rose more quickly than in the private sector throughout the postwar era (Foreman-Peck and Millward 1994, Table 9.2, 310). Most of Britain's state-owned enterprises also did better than the same sectors in other industrialized countries (Millward 2006, 2, 12). They hardly deserved identification as the lumbering and outdated 'lame ducks' of neoliberal lore (Gamble 1989, 74). But the political impression made by their new losses, especially when the rationale for their creation and consolidation had been so uncertain, would be fatal to their survival in the Thatcherite era.

## BIBLIOGRAPHY

### Archival Sources

Conservative Party Archive, Bodleian Library, Oxford
CRD 2/9/47, Preliminary Notes by Paul Chambers, Policy Committee on Economic Growth, 21 June 1961.

Harvester Archives of the British Conservative Party series one (Brighton 1977), 1957/29, "Socialism Creeps in: Plans for Taking over Britain by the Back Door," 1957.

HABCP 1961/15, D. Howell, "Expanding Prosperity," in CPC, Principles in Practice (February 1961).

National Archives of the United Kingdom, Kew, London T 298/213, Minutes of meeting in the Chancellor's room, "The Pay Pause," 22 November 1961.

CAB 128/39, Cabinet minutes, 26 November 1964.

PREM 13/254, Balogh to Wilson, "The Domestic Outlook," 7 July 1965.

EW 27/171, Preparatory group report on ICFC, 19 November 1965.

CAB 128/41 pt. 3, Cabinet minutes, 20 December 1966.

PREM 15/679, Prime Minister's meeting with the STUC, 21 June 1971.

CAB 128/49, Cabinet conclusions, 14 June 1971.

Labour Party Archive and Study Centre, John Rylands Library, Manchester

LPA NEC subcommittee files, Labour Party Research Department memorandum to home policy subcommittee, "Planning and the Common Market," May 1962.

S.G. Warburg Archives, Hatton Gardens, London

Box 9, Grierson note, "Visit to Rome and Milan by SGW and RHG," 22 March 1963.

Box 20, Warburg to Grunfeld, "Leylands," 25 October 1967.

Box 22, Warburg to Grunfeld, "Plessey," 3 September 1968.

Box 25, Eric Roll note for the file, "Italian Financing," 11 March 1970.

## Secondary Sources

Adlam, D. 1980, *Problems in Labour Politics*, London: Routledge.

Aganin, A. and P.F. Volpin 2003, "The History of Corporate Ownership in Italy," European Corporate Governance Institute Finance Research Paper Series 17/2003.

Amatori, F. 2000, "Beyond State and Market: Italy's Futile Search for a Third Way," in *The Rise and Fall of State-Owned Enterprise in the Western World* ed. P.A. Toninelli, Cambridge: Cambridge University Press.

Amyot, G. 2004, *Business, the State and Economic Policy: The Case of Italy*, London: Routledge.

Attlee, C.R. 1947, *Purpose and Policy: Selected Speeches*, London: Hutchinson.

Barca, F. and S. Trento 1997, "State Ownership and the Evolution of Italian Corporate Governance," *Industrial and Corporate Change* 6: 533–559.

Benn, T. 1988, *Out of the Wilderness: Diaries 1963–67*, London: Hutchinson.

Benn, T. 1989, *Office without Power: Diaries, 1968–72*, London: Hutchinson.

Bianchi, P. 1995, "Italy: The Crisis of an Introvert State," in *Industrial Enterprise and European Integration: From National to International Champions in Western Europe*, ed. J. Hayward, Oxford: Oxford University Press.

Brech, M.J. 1985, "Nationalized Industries," in *The Economic System in the United Kingdom*, Third Edition, ed. D. Morris, Oxford: Blackwell.

Broadberry, S.N. 1997, *The Productivity Race: British Manufacturing in International Perspective, 1850–1990*, Cambridge: Cambridge University Press.

Burk, K. 1988, *The First Privatisation: The Politicians, the City and the Denationalisation of Steel*, London: Historians' Press.

Cairncross, A. 1985, *Years of Recovery: British Economic Policy 1945–51*, London: Methuen.

Cairncross, A. 1997, *The Wilson Years: A Treasury Diary, 1964–1969*, London: Historians' Press.

Carnevali, F. 2000, "State Enterprise and Italy's 'Economic Miracle': The Ente Nazionale Idrocarburi, 1945–1962," *Enterprise and Society* 1: 249–278.

Chick, M. 2006, "The Marginalist Approach to Fuel Policy in Britain and France," *Economic History Review* 59: 143–167.

Chick, M. 2007, Electricity and Energy Policy in Britain, France and the United States since 1945, Cheltenham: Edward Elgar.

Church, R. 1994, *The Rise and Decline of the British Motor Industry*, Basingstoke: Macmillan.

Cmnd. 1248, 1960, *Reorganisation of the Nationalised Transport Undertakings*, London: HSMO.

Cmnd. 1357, 1961, *The Financial and Economic Obligations of the Nationalised Industries*, London: HSMO.

Coates, D. 1980, *Labour in Power? A Study of the Labour Government of 1974– 79*, London: Longman.

Cohen, J.S. and G. Federico 2001, *The Growth of the Italian Economy, 1820– 1960*, Cambridge: Cambridge University Press. Conservative Political Centre 1956, *Automation and the Consumer*, London: Conservative Political Centre.

Cooke, P. and K. Morgan 1998, *The Associational Economy: Firms, Regions, and Innovation*, Oxford: Oxford University Press.

Cronin, J. 1991, *The Politics of State Expansion: War, State and Society in Twentieth-Century Britain*, London: Routledge.

Dankbaar, B. 1994, "Sectoral Governance in the Automobile Industries of Germany, Great Britain and France," in *Governing Capitalist Economies: Performance and Control of Economic Sectors*, eds. J.R. Hollingsworth, P.C. Schmitter, and W. Streeck, Oxford: Oxford University Press.

Denison, E.F. 1967, *Why Growth Rates Differ*, Washington DC: Brookings Institution.

Dunkerley, J. and P.G. Hare 1991, "Nationalized Industries," in *The British Economy since 1945*, eds. N.F.R. Crafts and N. Woodward, Oxford: Clarendon Press.

Einaudi, M., M. Byé, and E. Rossi 1955, *Nationalization in France and Italy*, Ithaca, NY: Cornell University Press.

Favretto, I. 2003, *The Long Search for a Third Way: The British Labour Party and the Italian Left since 1945*, Basingstoke: Palgrave Macmillan.

Federico, G. 1996, "Italy, 1860–1940: A Little-Known Success Story," Economic History Review 49: 764–786.

Ferguson, N. 2010, *High Financier: The Lives and Time of Siegmund Warburg*, London: Penguin.

Foote, G. 1997, *The Labour Party's Political Thought: A History*, Third Edition, Basingstoke: Palgrave Macmillan.

Foreman-Peck, J. and R. Millward 1994, *Public and Private Ownership of British Industry 1820–1990*, Oxford: Clarendon Press.

Fratianni, M. and F. Spinelli 1982, "The Growth of Government in Italy: Evidence from 1861 to 1979," *Public Choice* 39: 221–243.

Gamble, A. 1989, *The Free Economy and the Strong State: The Politics of Thatcherism*, Basingstoke: Macmillan.

Gamble, A. and S. Walkland 1984, *The British Party System and Economic Policy 1945–83*, Oxford: Clarendon Press.

Gourvish, T.R. 1987, "British Business and the Transition to a Corporate Economy: Entrepreneurship and Management Structures," *Business History* 29: 18–45.

Gourvish, T.R. 2008, *Britain's Railways 1997–2005: Labour's Strategic Experiment*, Oxford: Oxford University Press.

Graham, A. 1972, "Industrial Policy," in *The Labour Government's Economic Record, 1964–1970*, ed. W. Beckerman, London: Duckworth.

Grant, W., A. Martinelli, and W. Paterson 1989, "Large Firms as Political Actors: A Comparative Analysis of the Chemical Industry in Britain, Italy and West Germany," *West European Politics* 12: 74–95.

Green, E.H.H. 2002, *Ideologies of Conservatism*, Oxford: Oxford University Press.

*The Guardian*, 17 March 2006, "Obituary: Michael Posner."

Hague, D. and G. Wilkinson 1983, *The IRC, An Experiment in Industrial Intervention: A History of the IRC*, London: Allen and Unwin.

Hannah, L. 1982, *Engineers, Managers and Politicians: The First Fifteen Years of Nationalised Electricity Supply in Britain*, London: Macmillan.

Harris, N. 1972, *Competition and the Corporate Society: British Conservatives, the State and Industry 1945–1964*, London: Methuen.

Hendry, J. 1989, Innovating for Failure: Government Policy and the Early British Computer Industry, Cambridge, Mass.: MIT Press.

Hennessy, P. 1992, *Never Again: Britain 1945–1951*, London: Jonathan Cape.

Hine, D. 1992, *Governing Italy: The Politics of Bargained Pluralism*, Oxford: Clarendon Press.

Hogwood, B.W. 1992, *Trends in British Public Policy*, Buckingham: Open University Press.

Holland, S. 1972, "State Entrepreneurship and State Intervention," in *The State as Entrepreneur: New Dimensions for Public Enterprise*, ed. S. Holland, London: Weidenfeld and Nicolson.

Holland, S. 1975, *The Socialist Challenge*, London: Quartet.

*The Independent*, 9 March 2006, "Obituary: Michel Posner."

Jones, T. 2003, *The Dark Heart of Italy*, London: Faber.

Kavanagh, D. and P. Morris 1989, *Consensus Politics from Attlee to Thatcher*, Oxford: Blackwell.

Kramer, D.C. 1988, *State Capital and Private Enterprise: The Case of the UK National Enterprise Board*, London: Routledge.

Labour Party 1964, *Let's Go with Labour for the New Britain*, London: Labour Party.

Locke, R.M. 1995, *Remaking the Italian Economy*, Ithaca, NY: Cornell University Press.

Maddison, A. 2001, *The World Economy: A Millennial Perspective*, Paris: OECD.

Maraffi, M. 1980, "State/Economy Relationships: The Case of Italian Public Enterprise," British Journal of Sociology 31: 507–524.

Marquand, D. 1996, "Moralists and Hedonists," in *The Ideas That Shaped Post-War Britain*, eds. D. Marquand and A. Seldon, London: Fontana.

Martinelli, A. 1979, "Organised Business and Italian Politics: Confindustria and the Christian Democrats in the Postwar Period," *West European Politics* 2: 67–87.

Mattesini, F. and B. Quintieri 1997, "Italy and the Great Depression: An Analysis of the Italian Economy, 1929–1936," Explorations in Economic History 34: 265–294.

Meeks, G. 1977, *Disappointing Marriage: A Study of the Gains from Merger*, Cambridge: Cambridge University Press.

Millward, R. 2006, "The British Privatisation Programme: A Long Term Perspective," *University of Milan Department of Economics Working Papers* 2006–07.

Millward, R. and J. Singleton 1995, "The Ownership of British Industry in the Post-War Era," in *The Political Economy of Nationalisation in Britain*, eds. Millward and Singleton, Cambridge: Cambridge University Press.

Morris, D. 1998, "The Stock Market and Problems of Corporate Control in the United Kingdom," in *Britain's Economic Performance*, Second Edition, eds. T. Buxton, P. Chapman, and P. Temple, London: Routledge.

Mottershead, P. 1974, "Industrial Policy," in *British Economic Policy 1960–1974*, ed. F. Blackaby, Cambridge: Cambridge University Press.

Padoa Schioppa, F. 1993, *Italy, the Sheltered Economy: Structural Problems in the Italian Economy*, Oxford: Clarendon Press.

Posner, A.R. 1977, "Italy: Dependence and Political Fragmentation," International Organization 31: 809–838.

Posner, M.V. and R. Pryke 1966, *New Public Enterprise*, London: Fabian Society.

Posner, M.V. and S.J. Woolf 1967, *Italian Public Enterprise*, London: Duckworth.

Pryke, R. 1971, *Public Enterprise in Practice: The British Experience of Nationalization over Two Decades*, London: MacGibbon and Kee.

Pryke, R. 1981, *The Nationalised Industries: Policy and Performance since 1968*, Oxford: Robertson.

Ramsden, J. 1980, *The Making of Conservative Party Policy: The Conservative Research Department since 1929*, London: Longman.

Ramsden, J. 1987, "'A Party for Owners or a Party for Earners?' How Far Did the British Conservative Party Really Change after 1945?" Transactions of the Royal Historical Society 37: 49–63.

Ramsden, J. 1996, *The Winds of Change: Macmillan to Heath, 1957–1975*, London: Longman.

Ranieri, R. 1995, "Partners and Enemies: The Government's Decision to Nationalise Steel, 1944–48," in *The Political Economy of Nationalisation in Britain*, eds. R. Millward and J. Singleton, Cambridge: Cambridge University Press.

Ranieri, R. 2004, "Remodelling the Italian Steel Industry: Americanization, Modernization, and Mass Production," in *Americanization and Its Limits*, eds. J. Zeitlin and G. Herrigel, Oxford: Oxford University Press.

Rinaldi, A. and M. Vasta 2005, "The Structure of Italian Capitalism, 1952–1972: New Evidence Using the Interlocking Directorates Technique," *Financial History Review* 12: 173–198.

Saville, R. 1993, "Commanding Heights: The Nationalisation Programme," in *Labour's High Noon: The Government and the Economy*, ed. J. Fyrth, London: Lawrence and Wishart.

Segreto, L. 1997, "Models of Control in Italian Capitalism from the Mixed Bank to Mediobanca, 1894–1993," *Business and Economic History* 26: 649–661.

Shonfield, A. 1965, *Modern Capitalism*, Oxford: Oxford University Press.

Singleton, J. 1995, "Labour, the Conservatives and Nationalisation," in *The Political Economy of Nationalisation in Britain*, eds. R. Millward and J. Singleton, Cambridge: Cambridge University Press.

Taylor, R. 1996, "The Heath Government, Industrial Policy and the 'New Capitalism,'" in *The Heath Government 1970–74*, eds. S. Ball and A. Seldon, London: Longman.

Tolliday, S. 2000, "Enterprise and State in the Italian 'Economic Miracle,'" Enterprise and Society 1: 241–248.

Tomlinson, J. 1994, *Government and the Enterprise since 1900: The Changing Problem of Efficiency*, Oxford: Clarendon Press.

Tomlinson, J. 1996a, "British Industrial Policy," in *Britain in the 1970s: The Troubled Economy*, eds. R. Coopey and N. Woodward, London: UCL Press.

Tomlinson, J. 1996b, "'Inventing Decline': The Falling Behind of the British Economy in the Post-War Years," *Economic History Review* 49: 441–459.

Tomlinson, J. 2004, "The Labour Party and the Capitalist Firm, c.1950-c.1970," *Historical Journal* 47: 685–708.

Toye, R. 2003, *The Labour Party and the Planned Economy 1931–51*, Woodbridge: Boydell and Brewer.

Utton, M. 1986, "Developments in British Industrial and Competition Policies," in *European Industrial Policy*, ed. G. Hall, Basingstoke: Palgrave Macmillan.

Wickham-Jones, M. 1996, *Economic Strategy and the Labour Party: Politics and Policy-Making 1970–83*, Basingstoke: Palgrave Macmillan.

Wilson, J.F. 1995, "The Motives for Gas Nationalisation," in *The Political Economy of Nationalisation in Britain*, eds. R. Millward and J. Singleton, Cambridge: Cambridge University Press.

Young, S. and A.V. Lowe 1974, *Intervention in the Mixed Economy: The Evolution of British Industrial Policy 1964–72*, London: Croom Helm.

Zweininger-Bargielowka, I. 2000, *Austerity in Britain*, Oxford: Oxford University Press.

# 5 Size, Boundaries, and Distribution of Italian State-Owned Enterprise (1939–1983)

*Pier Angelo Toninelli and Michelangelo Vasta*

## INTRODUCTION

For the most part of the last century, the role of state-owned enterprises (SOEs) was probably more pronounced, continuous, and prolonged in Italy than elsewhere in the West: in 1990, the economic weight of the public sector was still around 20% of gross national product (GNP) (Malgarini 2000). This was the response to the fact that Italian economic growth had long been penalized by structural frailties such as a narrow internal market, a shortage of capital, financial weakness, and a decline of entrepreneurial initiative and the state. Yet, as shown in a previous chapter (see Amatori and Toninelli, Chapter 3), the complexity of forms and organizations assumed by the state direct intervention in the economy (just to limit our analysis to the central level) reached heights of imagination and ingenuity in Italy that were probably unknown abroad: State companies, State shareholding companies, State concerns, and so on, coexisted throughout the 20th century. This helps in explaining why we do not yet have a precise and thorough measure of the weight of public enterprise on the entire economy, not to say of more specific data concerning their sectoral and/or regional distribution. In fact, only a limited number of empirical studies is so far available (Rapporto Saraceno 1956; Sartori 1957; Posner and Woolf 1967; Arrighetti, Stansfield, and Virno 1982; Rapporto Marsan c. 1992; Bognetti and Spagnolo 1992), and thus it is difficult to identify precisely, at a micro level, the real dimension of Italian public enterprise and hence assess a phenomenon whose actual magnitude remains unknown to us.

The aim of our research is to fill this gap by showing the basic features of the dimension, boundaries, structure, governance, and location of Italian SOEs. The first results have been offered in a previous, recent contribution (Toninelli and Vasta 2010). The present one offers further information concerning the internal organization of the state holdings and a first approximation of SOEs' regional distribution. It is organized in the following way: in the first section, a synthetic account of the results of the previous research will be offered, and in the second section, new evidence on regional distribution will be presented and discussed.

## SIZE AND BOUNDARIES OF ITALIAN SOES

### Sources and Methods

As stated in a previous chapter (see Amatori and Toninelli, Chapter 3), direct state intervention in the economy goes back to 19th century, even though major moves were made in the interwar period when public corporations to administer forests, roads, and the postal and telegraph services joined the already existing state railroad agency and state insurances against illness, industrial injuries, and old age pensions. But it was the direct intervention in the production and industry spheres with the creation of AGIP and IRI which marked a discontinuity in the country's history of public intervention. Over the years, IRI, ENI (created in 1954 on top of AGIP), and finally EFIM (later created to operate in the mechanical industry) came to control larger and larger sectors of the economy to the extent that in Italy, public enterprise had almost become a synonym of them. This is the reason why we have reconstructed the boundaries of these three state holdings, which is therefore only a rounding down of the SOE's real size. The originality of our approach is essentially due to three elements: (1) the time span, which covers about half a century: five benchmark years are likely to give a satisfactory picture of the entire period; (2) the use of a dataset, the Imita.db, which allows us to compare the effective weight of the public enterprise versus the overall Italian enterprise system; (3) the attempt to reconstruct, through the identification of the structure of shareholding, the models of governance adopted.

In order to provide a quantitative mapping of Italian public enterprise, we used a representative sample of Italian firms, the Imita.db dataset (Vasta 2006c; http://imitadb.unisi.it).[1] In the recorded firms, we singled out the state-owned or state-controlled enterprises.[2] The information related to SOEs was gathered directly from the IRI and ENI archives: it is made of documents used to produce consolidated balance sheets, of the various yearbooks published by the two state holdings, and of other sources of various kinds such as balance sheet accounts, board of directors' reports, and so forth. Other classic records of Italian firms were also consulted, such as the *Taccuino dell'azionista*, the *Annuario delle aziende di credito e finanziarie*, the *Calepino dell'azionista*, and the *Annuario R&S*.

The analysis focuses on five benchmark years (1936, 1952, 1960, 1972, and 1983) of the Imita.db.[3] It identifies the shareholders of each individual firm in those years, reconstructing, in particular, those relating to state holdings (in other words, the three groups: IRI, ENI, and EFIM), those held by the sub-holdings of each group (financial and/or operating),[4] and those of all the other firms of the group.[5] A list of the holdings is offered in Appendix 5.1.

Figure 5.1 shows an example, without any reference to time, of the general structure of the IRI group's shareholding. This model is also valid for the two other state holdings, even though they, especially EFIM, had a much simpler group structure. As we have stated, IRI directly entered in a few holding companies (financial or not) with a variable holding share, which was always

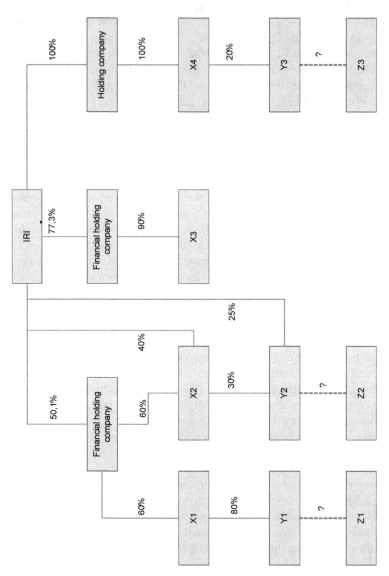

*Figure 5.1*  Example of the structure of the IRI group.

above 50%; moreover, IRI held shares directly in other firms (X2, Y2). In addition, the holding companies held shares in many firms (X1, X2, X3, X4) with variable percentages: these (X1, X2, X4), in turn, could hold shares (Y1, Y2, Y3) in a chain structure which scaled down to a lower level (Z1, Z2, Z3). In some firms, the direct share of IRI was to be added to that of the holding company (X2), whereas, in some cases, the share structure was more complex and could involve up to 10 other subjects.

The sources analyzed have enabled us to reconstruct most of the shares of the three state holdings, of their sub-holdings (financial or not), as well as of the most important firms at the lower levels (X1, X2, X3, X4). Even though the mapping takes a good part of our sample into account, it was not possible to reconstruct further levels of the control chain (Z1, Z2, Z3). Thus, the resulting map underestimates the boundaries of Italian SOEs. The analysis was developed following the recent literature on corporate finance and corporate ownership (La Porta, Lopez-de-Silanes, and Shleifer 1999; for a survey, see Morck, Wolfenzon, and Yeung 2005). It makes it possible to assess the different estimates of the degree and the size of control of the various groups according to two measurements: share capital and assets. In particular, it was decided to adopt four different criteria: (1) accounting, (2) effective control, (3) majority control, and (4) pyramidal control. We will now go into more detail and describe the logic which inspired these criteria.

The accounting criterion attributes to the groups the size of control that emerges from an algebraic calculation of the capital shares. For example, in Figure 5.1, the group is granted control of 100% of X4 share capital, while, for the X2 firm, we have summed the percentage controlled directly by IRI (40%) to IRI's control share of the financial company (50.1%) times the financial holding company's controlling share (60%) of the X2 firm. The percentage of control attributed to the group, therefore, reaches a total of 70.06% (40% + 60% × 50.1%).

This is the main criterion employed in this first section and represents the benchmark to which the other estimates will be compared. Such a criterion offers a quantitative reconstruction of the share of each holder, which is the level of ownership of the diverse public groups, although it does not guarantee a realistic analysis of the level of state control of the Italian enterprise system. For this reason, we have searched for other criteria, diverging from a strictly accountable evaluation and thus broadening the quantitative approach.

The second criterion deals with the effective control: it attributes to the group the entire capital of a firm that is controlled at a level above 20%, while the capital of a firm that is controlled by a percentage of less than 20% is not considered. In other words, as recently suggested in the literature, one assumes that the control by the group of a percentage equal to 20% or more corresponds to the full control of the relative firm (La Porta et al. 1999; Bertrand and Mullainathan 2003).[6]

In order to offer a more realistic, and, at the same time, more prudent assessment of state control, we have experimented with two other criteria.

The third criterion, majority control, attributes to the control of the group the total capital of a firm that is controlled by a percentage of more than 50%,[7] while it excludes the capital of a firm that is controlled with a percentage of equal or less than 50%. The logic of this criterion is similar to the previous one, but it avoids potential overestimation. Moreover, it is appropriate to the particular features of the Italian ownership system.

Finally, the fourth criterion is aimed to ascertain how relevant to the public sector is a very widespread model of governance of Italian private groups: the pyramidal control. In order to obtain this, each group was attributed the capital of the firms controlled through a chain of shareholdings that was greater than 50%. It is appropriate to recall that this case differs from the previous ones because it does not proceed with a simple algebraic calculation, as it looks upon situations of repeated control. The logic behind the pyramidal control enables us to evaluate the weight of the public groups on all Italian firms with regard to the widespread practice of creating chains of firms able to guarantee the total control of the underlying firms, thus limiting the capital directly invested by the parent company. Figure 5.2 clarifies the logic behind the pyramidal control: it shows how

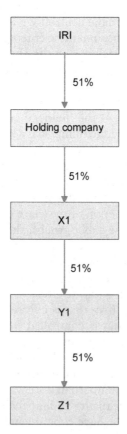

*Figure 5.2*   Example of pyramidal control within the IRI group.

*Table 5.1*　Number of Firms Included in the Imita.db Census for the Three Italian State-Owned Groups

| Years | Italian firms cor- responding with Imita. db (a) | Italian firms not cor- responding with Imita. db (b) | Total firms | Italian firms corresponding with Imita. db on total Italian firms (a)/(a+b) |
|---|---|---|---|---|
| IRI | | | | |
| 1936 | 148 | 32 | 180 | 82.2 |
| 1952 | 120 | 35 | 155 | 77.4 |
| 1960 | 147 | 54 | 201 | 73.1 |
| 1972 | 201 | 53 | 254 | 79.1 |
| 1983 | 230 | 362 | 592 | 38.9 |
| Total | 846 | 536 | 1,382 | 61.2 |
| ENI | | | | |
| 1936 | | | | |
| 1954 | 28 | 7 | 35 | 80.0 |
| 1960 | 40 | 11 | 51 | 78.4 |
| 1972 | 63 | 32 | 95 | 66.3 |
| 1983 | 78 | 95 | 173 | 45.1 |
| Total | 209 | 145 | 354 | 59.0 |
| EFIM | | | | |
| 1936 | | | | |
| 1952 | | | | |
| 1960 | | | | |
| 1972 | 62 | 21 | 83 | 74.7 |
| 1983 | 59 | 47 | 106 | 55.7 |
| Total | 121 | 68 | 189 | 64.0 |
| IRI+ENI+EFIM | | | | |
| 1936 | 148 | 32 | 180 | 82.2 |
| 1952–54 | 148 | 42 | 190 | 77.9 |
| 1960 | 187 | 65 | 252 | 74.2 |
| 1972 | 326 | 106 | 432 | 75.5 |
| 1983 | 367 | 504 | 871 | 42.1 |
| Total | 1,176 | 749 | 1925 | 61.1 |

one unit, in this case IRI, with just one stake (in the holding company) can act as the ultimate owner of all the firms in the chain, including those in which it has not invested directly.[8]

The methodology described above is applied to the firms which belong to the three state holdings registered in the Imita.db archive. However, beyond these firms, our sources enabled us also to identify the firms belonging to the three groups, but which are not included in the Imita.db. This dataset in fact includes the joint stock companies with a share capital greater than a specified threshold (which could change from year to year).[9] Table 5.1 offers some details on the number of Italian SOEs included in the database.

On the whole, about 1,900 firms have been identified, even if those used in the following analysis are about 1,200, which are the ones contained in the Imita.db. In the first four benchmark years, as shown in Table 5.1, the percentages of the total number of recorded firms accounted for by Imita.db are remarkable for IRI, ENI, and, in 1971, also for EFIM. The representativeness decreases in 1983, when only half of the detected firms are registered by the Imita.db. This could be the consequence either of the changes in the capital threshold criteria employed to include firms in the database, as it went from 100 million lire in 1973 to 1 billion in 1984, or of the increase in the number of controlled firms with other legal forms, or both.

## The Governance of the Groups

The different holding share typologies described above have been analyzed in order to determine the various combinations of control for each benchmark year, differentiating among manufacturing firms and firms in other sectors. These data provide, at a first approximation, interesting information concerning the governance adopted by the three public groups.

Table 5.2 shows that within IRI, the form of control changes remarkably over time.

The growth of the group reflected mainly the development of the holding companies (financial or not). In 1936, the main link was direct IRI participation in 137 firms (50 manufacturing firms and 87 firms in other sectors), which were subsequently to be ascribed to the group.

In 1952, the situation was already more fluent, even though direct holding share was still the most common link (44 cases). Shareholding through financial companies was also widespread (19), as well as the joint shareholding by IRI and the financial holding companies (34). In the following years, the shareholding scheme becomes more complex: on the one hand, the number of firms in which IRI directly held shares decreased while the number of those whose share capital was controlled through financial holding companies and other firms of the group increased; on the other hand, the multifaceted shareholding—direct, through financial holding companies and through firms at the second level—became quite frequent. In the period considered, the group structure seemed to move toward a pyramidal

*Table 5.2* IRI, ENI, and EFIM by Typologies of Shareholder (Number of Firms)

| IRI Group[1] | 1936 | 1952 | 1960 | 1972 | 1983 |
|---|---|---|---|---|---|
| IRI direct (1) | 137 | 44 | 28 | 16 | 16 |
| Holding companies (2) | | | 1 | 4 | 4 |
| Financial holding companies (3) | 6 | 19 | 42 | 80 | 94 |
| Other (non holding) group firms (4) | | 18 | 32 | 64 | 61 |
| (1) + (3) | 4 | 34 | 26 | 12 | 12 |
| (3) + (4) | | | 10 | 11 | 27 |
| Other combinations | | 4 | 7 | 13 | 15 |
| Total | 147 | 119 | 146 | 200 | 229 |
| ENI Group[2] | | | | | |
| ENI direct (1) | | 2 | 3 | 3 | 4 |
| Holding companies (2) | | 12 | 22 | 32 | 12 |
| Financial holding companies (3) | | | | | 2 |
| Other (non holding) group firms (4) | | 9 | 6 | 16 | 19 |
| (2) + (3) | | | | | 12 |
| (2) + (4) | | 1 | 7 | 8 | 7 |
| Other combinations | | 3 | 1 | 3 | 21 |
| Total | | 27 | 39 | 62 | 77 |
| EFIM Group[3] | | | | | |
| EFIM direct (1) | | | | 6 | 8 |
| Financial holding companies (2) | | | | 33 | 50 |
| Other group firms (3) | | | | 22 | |
| Total | | | | 61 | 58 |

[1] Excluded state holding IRI.
[2] Excluded state holding ENI.
[3] Excluded state holding EFIM

system. In particular, from a holding with direct control over the manufacturing activities, IRI was transformed into an owner of the last resort controlling the financial holdings: these, in turn, guaranteed the control over the forward firms, both through indirect shareholding—with a chain that allowed the control of a firm with small investment—and through cross shareholding.

In the case of ENI, the forms of control are quite different, but here, too, as in IRI, they become more and more articulated over time. ENI's direct presence remains scarce as firms are mainly controlled by the holding companies and/or by the other firms of the group. From its foundation in 1953, ENI sectors of activity were clearly separated into productive and commercial divisions, and each one was controlled at the top by a holding company. For instance, for most of the 1950s and 1960s, there were four divisions: upstream activities headed by AGIP Mineraria, downstream by AGIP, natural gas by Saipem, chemicals by Anic. Then, the first two were merged into AGIP but, in a short time, the number of holding companies began to increase (Sapelli et al. 1993). Furthermore, after 1983, the number of companies which held shares within the group, as well as cross shares between the holding company and the other firms, grew.

In contrast, EFIM's structure of control was much simpler: the state holding controlled mainly financial firms which, in turn, directly controlled other (mainly) manufacturing firms. EFIM kept direct control of almost all the financial firms and of the shares of the capital of the service firms; in 1982, the control of the capital of the manufacturing firms was almost entirely in the hands of the financial firms of the group.

## The Boundaries

It is well known that the size of the Italian SOEs was by no means insignificant; however, its internal structure was too complex to allow, in the past, a systematic quantitative estimation of its dimensions. Some studies (Mortara 1976; Arrighetti et al. 1982; Bognetti and Spagnolo 1992) have attempted to produce a mapping of SOEs, but only for short periods,[10] and studies on the long-term nature of governance fail to provide a systematic analysis of Italian SOEs (Aganin and Volpin 2005). Furthermore, the lack of quantitative information on the constellation of the Italian firms has precluded any estimate of the real weight of the SOEs in the economic activities of the country. The results presented here provide a first step in the direction of both the study of the evolution of Italian capitalism and, in a broader perspective, the comprehension of the nature of the governance of the Italian firms. This, in turn, would allow the relationship between governance and performance, the evolution of the financial structure and the economic growth in general to be brought to light.

Table 5.3 shows the number of companies whose shares were partly or totally controlled by the three groups and their weight vis-à-vis the total of Italian firms. The percentage of the total of the share capital and assets controlled by the three groups, using the accounting criterion, is presented in Table 5.4. In Table 5.5, the same values are calculated for the different segments of the manufacturing sector.

With regard to IRI, the overall percentages become even more significant as early as 1936. Three years after its foundation, when IRI was still a temporary agency, its weight on the total capital of the Italian joint stock companies was 12.5% (Table 5.4).[11]

In the first two postwar benchmark years (1952 and 1960)—in other words, during the golden age—the weight of IRI rose considerably, reaching values higher than 15%. In the period that followed, the percentage grew further: 21.2% in 1972 and 29.9% in 1983. The weight of ENI also tended to increase: it was about 3% of the total in the two benchmark years after its foundation, but it approached values of around 8% in the last two years. The weight of EFIM, albeit lower, was not negligible, amounting to about 2.5% of the overall share capital of Italian firms. Since the 1960s, these trends have been affected by the state's additions to their endowment funds, the mechanism envisaged by the government to offset the "improper financial burdens" in their balance sheet (Saraceno 1975), which, however, increasingly exposed SOEs to political pressures.

Therefore, when adding up the percentages of control of the three main state holdings in accordance with the structure indicated above (Figure 5.3), we can observe that the values continue to grow considerably during the period analyzed. Their value during the golden age amounts to about 20% of the share capital of Italian firms. In the early 1970s, this percentage rose to almost a third (32.1%), despite the caveat mentioned above, and reached 40% in the early 1980s.[12]

The disaggregated analysis at sector level shows that control by IRI is remarkable in the banking and financial sector, with percentages that oscillate from 22.5% in 1936 to about 50% of the total capital in the period following World War II. It is worthy of note that the transport sector also grew in size such that in 1983, IRI's weight exceeds 60% of the total capital of the firms (Toninelli and Vasta 2007). ENI controls a very high percentage of mining: in 1983 it accounted for almost the entire share capital of the sector. With regard to the utilities sector, the values are somehow misleading: in fact, the 1972 peak (49.6% for ENI; see Table 5.4) was caused by the effects of the 1962 nationalization of electricity. A great part of the electrical activities was given to a new public body, Ente Nazionale per l'Energia Elettrica (ENEL), which was included in the Imita.db sample in 1972. However, in that year, ENEL had not yet been endowed with proper funds by the government. As a consequence, the overall capital values of the electrical companies were strongly undervalued.[13]

The wide impact of SOEs on the economy emerges from the aggregated data of the three groups: in a considerable number of sectors of primary importance—mining, financial, transport, utilities—the weight of SOEs is clear and their presence broadly diffused, and is, no matter how it is viewed, significantly bigger than indicated by the fragmentary estimates previously available.

Focus will now be directed to the manufacturing sector, in order to analyze, with the help of Table 5.5, the weight of the three public groups. All three groups show a strong and growing specialization in manufacturing. Their total weight grew from 7.9% in 1936 to 12.3% in 1972. Clearly, in 1936, this weight depended entirely on IRI, which was joined

*Table 5.3*   IRI, ENI, and EFIM Firms and Their Weight in Imita.db (Number of Firms and Percentage)

| Macro-sector | Imita.db | | | | | IRI Group + ENI Group + EFIM Group | | | | | | | | | | |
|---|---|---|---|---|---|---|---|---|---|---|---|---|---|---|---|---|
| | 1936 | 1952 | 1960 | 1972 | 1983 | 1936 | % | 1952–1954 | % | 1960 | % | 1972 | % | 1983 | % |
| Agriculture and fishing | 188 | 241 | 158 | 256 | 166 | 10 | 5.3 | 2 | 0.8 | 1 | 0.6 | 7 | 2.7 | 6 | 3.6 |
| Mining | 93 | 127 | 144 | 161 | 34 | 6 | 6.5 | 13 | 10.1 | 16 | 11.1 | 10 | 6.2 | 4 | 11.8 |
| Manufacturing | 1,764 | 3,017 | 3,163 | 6,140 | 2,911 | 51 | 2.9 | 58 | 1.9 | 74 | 2.3 | 168 | 2.7 | 157 | 5.4 |
| Utilities | 224 | 169 | 167 | 77 | 26 | 9 | 4.0 | 22 | 13.0 | 27 | 16.2 | 5 | 6.5 | 11 | 42.3 |
| Construction | 139 | 196 | 181 | 427 | 244 | 4 | 2.9 | 2 | 1.0 | 8 | 4.4 | 18 | 4.2 | 11 | 4.5 |
| Services | 1,553 | 2,009 | 2,066 | 3,947 | 1,105 | 42 | 2.7 | 32 | 1.6 | 39 | 1.9 | 81 | 2.1 | 78 | 7.1 |
| Financial intermediation | 285 | 422 | 492 | 795 | 1,100 | 26 | 9.1 | 19 | 4.5 | 22 | 4.5 | 37 | 4.7 | 100 | 9.1 |
| Total | 4,246 | 6,181 | 6,371 | 11,803 | 5,586 | 148 | 3.5 | 148 | 2.4 | 187 | 2.9 | 326 | 2.8 | 367 | 6.6 |

*Table 5.4* Weight of Share Capital of Firms held by IRI, ENI, and EFIM (Percentage of Imita.db, Total)

| Macro-sector | IRI Group | | | | | ENI Group | | | | |
|---|---|---|---|---|---|---|---|---|---|---|
| | 1936 | 1952 | 1960 | 1972 | 1983 | 1936 | 1954 | 1960 | 1972 | 1983 |
| Agriculture and fishing | 27.3 | 16.9 | 0.6 | 4.0 | 0.4 | | - | - | - | 0.4 |
| Mining | 2.7 | 5.0 | 0.8 | 0.5 | - | | 65.4 | 42.1 | 86.7 | 94.8 |
| Manufacturing | 7.9 | 7.4 | 8.5 | 7.1 | 18.9 | | 1.6 | 2.6 | 4.4 | 6.8 |
| Utilities | 6.7 | 8.6 | 7.5 | 1.0 | 0.0 | | 2.9 | 1.3 | 49.6 | 2.9 |
| Construction | 5.8 | 5.5 | 1.7 | 5.0 | 7.3 | | - | 0.8 | 0.5 | 0.4 |
| Services | 19.9 | 17.9 | 18.2 | 13.6 | 29.6 | | 0.0 | 0.7 | 0.1 | 7.9 |
| *of which transport* | 40.9 | 30.5 | 33.3 | 27.4 | 61.4 | | - | 1.4 | 0.1 | 0.4 |
| Financial intermediation | 22.5 | 56.0 | 44.3 | 50.5 | 55.2 | | - | 0.3 | 0.4 | 0.7 |
| Total | 12.5 | 19.4 | 16.0 | 21.2 | 29.9 | | 3.3 | 2.5 | 8.6 | 7.7 |

*(continued)*

*Table 5.4*  (continued)

| Macro-sector | EFIM Group | | | | | Total | | | | |
|---|---|---|---|---|---|---|---|---|---|---|
| | 1936 | 1952 | 1960 | 1972 | 1983 | 1936 | 1952–1954 | 1960 | 1972 | 1983 |
| Agriculture and fishing | | | | - | 0.3 | 27.3 | 16.9 | 0.6 | 4.0 | 1.2 |
| Mining | | | | 0.0 | 0.0 | 2.7 | 70.3 | 43.0 | 87.3 | 94.9 |
| Manufacturing | | | | 0.8 | 1.3 | 7.9 | 9.0 | 11.1 | 12.3 | 27.1 |
| Utilities | | | | - | - | 6.7 | 11.6 | 8.8 | 50.5 | 2.9 |
| Construction | | | | 0.1 | 0.0 | 5.8 | 5.5 | 2.5 | 5.7 | 7.7 |
| Services | | | | 0.2 | 0.2 | 19.9 | 17.9 | 19.0 | 13.9 | 37.8 |
| of which transport | | | | - | 0.4 | 40.9 | 30.5 | 34.7 | 27.5 | 62.2 |
| Financial intermediation | | | | 6.2 | 5.6 | 22.5 | 56.0 | 44.6 | 57.1 | 61.5 |
| Total | | | | 2.3 | 2.6 | 12.5 | 22.7 | 18.5 | 32.1 | 40.2 |

Table 5.5  Weight of Share Capital of Firms Held by IRI, ENI, and EFIM in Manufacturing (Percentage of Imita.db, Manufacturing)

| Sector | IRI Group | | | | | ENI Group | | | | |
|---|---|---|---|---|---|---|---|---|---|---|
| | 1936 | 1952 | 1960 | 1972 | 1983 | 1936 | 1954 | 1960 | 1972 | 1983 |
| Food products and tobacco | 0.2 | 0.1 | 0.0 | 1.2 | 8.2 | | - | - | - | - |
| Textiles and textile products | 3.9 | - | 3.2 | - | - | | - | - | 4.2 | 8.8 |
| Leather and leather products | - | - | - | - | - | | - | - | - | - |
| Wood and wood products | - | - | - | - | - | | - | - | - | - |
| Paper products, publishing and printing | 0.9 | 3.8 | 3.7 | 1.7 | 9.5 | | - | 0.2 | 0.2 | - |
| Coke and petroleum products | 0.4 | 0.1 | 0.1 | - | - | | 13.6 | 10.5 | 16.6 | 44.9 |
| Chemicals and chemical products | 6.6 | 3.6 | 2.0 | 1.1 | 0.0 | | 0.4 | 6.5 | 10.0 | 23.5 |
| Rubber and plastic products | - | - | - | - | - | | - | - | 0.0 | - |
| Other non-metallic products | 2.0 | 2.4 | 2.5 | 1.7 | 2.4 | | - | - | 2.7 | 0.2 |
| Basic metals and metal products | 26.8 | 25.9 | 26.2 | 18.0 | 55.8 | | - | - | - | 0.4 |
| Machinery and equipment | 38.1 | 20.3 | 5.5 | 4.5 | 6.4 | | - | 3.5 | 1.7 | 4.4 |
| Electrical and optical equipment | 1.7 | 11.3 | 9.9 | 9.4 | 13.6 | | - | - | - | 0.3 |
| Transport equipment | 12.2 | 13.0 | 17.9 | 37.4 | 28.3 | | - | - | - | - |
| Manufacturing n.e.c. | 0.0 | - | - | - | - | | - | - | - | - |
| Total manufacturing | 7.9 | 7.4 | 8.5 | 7.1 | 18.9 | | 1.6 | 2.6 | 4.4 | 6.8 |

(continued)

Table 5.5  (continued)

| Sector | EFIM Group | | | | | Total | | | | |
|---|---|---|---|---|---|---|---|---|---|---|
| | 1936 | 1952 | 1960 | 1972 | 1983 | 1936 | 1952–1954 | 1960 | 1972 | 1983 |
| Food products and tobacco | | | | 1.0 | 1.4 | 0.2 | 0.1 | 0.0 | 2.2 | 9.7 |
| Textiles and textile products | | | | 0.1 | - | 3.9 | - | 3.2 | 4.2 | 8.8 |
| Leather and leather products | | | | - | - | - | - | - | - | - |
| Wood and wood products | | | | - | - | - | - | - | - | - |
| Paper products, publishing and printing | | | | 0.2 | - | 0.9 | 3.8 | 3.9 | 2.0 | 9.5 |
| Coke and petroleum products | | | | - | - | 0.4 | 13.8 | 10.6 | 16.6 | 44.9 |
| Chemicals and chemical products | | | | 0.3 | 0.1 | 6.6 | 4.0 | 8.5 | 11.4 | 23.6 |
| Rubber and plastic products | | | | 1.3 | 0.7 | - | - | - | 1.4 | 0.7 |
| Other non-metallic products | | | | 0.5 | 1.7 | 2.0 | 2.4 | 2.5 | 5.0 | 4.3 |
| Basic metals and metal products | | | | 1.4 | 1.0 | 26.8 | 25.9 | 26.2 | 19.4 | 57.2 |
| Machinery and equipment | | | | 1.2 | 2.1 | 38.1 | 20.3 | 9.0 | 7.4 | 12.9 |
| Electrical and optical equipment | | | | 0.9 | 0.8 | 1.7 | 11.3 | 9.9 | 10.3 | 14.7 |
| Transport equipment | | | | 2.6 | 4.9 | 12.2 | 13.0 | 17.9 | 40.0 | 33.3 |
| Manufacturing n.e.c. | | | | - | - | 0.0 | - | - | - | - |
| Total manufacturing | | | | 0.8 | 1.3 | 7.9 | 9.0 | 11.1 | 12.3 | 27.1 |

in the 1950s by ENI and then, in the last two benchmark years, also by EFIM. Here, too, the year 1983 registers a notable expansion: the combined weight of the three groups rises above a quarter of the total. The data disaggregated by sector highlight how the control of the three groups over the whole period was concentrated in the heavy sectors, albeit with an alternate trend.

IRI is strong in the steel (basic metals) industry and in the transport equipment sector. In steel, in the first three benchmark years, the IRI share oscillates around 25%, reaching 55.8% in 1983; in transport equipment, the share increases from 12.2% in 1936 to 37.4% in 1972, attaining 28.3% in 1983. A significant presence can also be found in the machinery and equipment industry, especially in the first years, and also in the electrical equipment industry.

ENI is concentrated in the energy sector, with a significant weight in the oil sector and, especially in 1972 and 1983, in chemicals. In the last two years analyzed, ENI underwent a process of unexpected diversification, as can be seen by looking at the not unsubstantial percentage in the textile industry, where ENI accounted for 8.8% of the total of capital of Italian firms in 1983.

The smallest of the three state holdings, EFIM, was less specialized. Its presence, in general rather low, was, however, well distributed over almost all the heavy sectors and especially in the machinery equipment and transport equipment.[14]

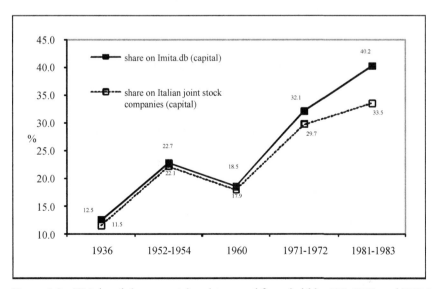

*Figure 5.3*   Weight of share captial and assets of firms held by IRI, ENI, and EFIM on Imita.db and on Italian joint stock companies.

## Forms of Control and Boundaries

In order to assess the "real" weight of public enterprise, in Table 5.6 we present the three different models of the groups previously discussed, that is, effective control, majority control, and pyramidal control.

As for IRI, the majority control is prevalent for all the benchmark years. Moreover, it shows fairly clearly that manifold minority shareholdings are numerous, especially in 1936. In the following years, shareholdings constituting effective control (between 20% and 50%) became more numerous, except for the last benchmark year. The ENI group presents a limited number of small shareholdings throughout the period, but it has a considerable number of shareholdings that allow effective control, especially in 1952 and 1972; this, as in the case of IRI, was considerably reduced in the last benchmark year. The same trend is recorded for EFIM, which, in 1972, owned many shareholdings (48.4% of the total), which allowed effective control. As in the other state holdings, such a percentage diminished considerably in 1983, thus favoring majority shareholdings. Therefore, in the central phase of the period (corresponding to the benchmark years, 1952–1954, 1960, and 1972), the three state holdings took charge of a significant percentage of the shareholdings that allowed them to control the firms without owning the majority of their share capital. The data show that, in the early 1980s, this phenomenon was clearly reduced.

We proceeded then to calculate their control capacity according to the previously identified criteria: this provides an estimate of the real weight of the public groups on the Italian joint stock companies. In light of this, by adopting the accounting criterion, these estimates were referred to the control of share capital. We have assumed that, for all the firms with effective control, the whole capital could, in fact, be entirely attributed to state control. In Figure 5.4, the percentages have been calculated considering 20% to be the inferior threshold for effective control: this considerably broadens the boundaries of Italian SOEs in a way that extensively widens their dimensions. With regard to IRI, for example, it becomes evident how the boundaries of the IRI group appear significantly wider than previously imagined. In particular, for the period between 1952 and 1972, the boundaries reconstructed on the basis of effective control are much larger in comparison to the estimates made upon the basis of the accounting criterion. In the central years, at the very least, the relative weight of the share capital controlled by a value of between 20% and 50% might be large enough to compensate for the value of the share capital of the minority shareholdings that were not considered by using the effective control criterion. In contrast, in the case of the other two groups (ENI and EFIM), the increase of the effective control compared to the accounting control is minor, although, in terms of proportions, it, nevertheless, remains significant, as seen in Figure 5.4.

*Table 5.6* Strength of Shareholding of IRI, ENI, and EFIM (% Number of Firms)

| State holding | 1936 | | | 1952–1954 | | | 1960 | | | 1972 | | | 1983 | | |
|---|---|---|---|---|---|---|---|---|---|---|---|---|---|---|---|
| | <20 | 20≤p≤50 | >50 | <20 | 20≤p≤50 | >50 | <20 | 20≤p≤50 | >50 | <20 | 20≤p≤50 | >50 | <20 | 20≤p≤50 | >50 |
| IRI | 39.9 | 9.5 | 50.7 | 11.7 | 30.0 | 58.3 | 12.9 | 29.9 | 57.1 | 12.9 | 29.9 | 57.2 | 20.4 | 12.2 | 67.4 |
| ENI | | | | 3.6 | 46.4 | 50.0 | 7.5 | 22.5 | 70.0 | 12.7 | 36.5 | 50.8 | 6.4 | 9.0 | 84.6 |
| EFIM | | | | | | | | | | 4.8 | 48.4 | 46.8 | 5.1 | 27.1 | 67.8 |
| IRI+ENI+EFIM | 39.9 | 9.5 | 50.7 | 10.1 | 33.1 | 56.8 | 11.8 | 28.3 | 59.9 | 11.3 | 34.7 | 54.0 | 15.0 | 13.9 | 71.1 |

In addition, we have also calculated the degree of control following the majority criterion, obtaining only marginal differences in comparison to the accounting values.

Finally, the growth of the weight of the three groups when a pyramidal control criterion is adopted, if compared to the weight calculated following the accounting criterion, is presented in Figure 5.5. On this basis, we proceeded to sum up the entire capital of the firms controlled through a chain of shareholdings above 50%. This means that, in situations of repeated control, either direct or indirect, we did not consider the accounting capital value but the entire capital of that firm. The increase of the control of the firm, in this case, highlights different trends for the three groups. With regard to the IRI group, its boundaries again emerge significantly wider than those defined by the accounting criterion, although they are inferior to those obtained using the effective criterion. For the other two groups, the pyramidal criterion shows the opposite trend: we can notice narrower boundaries than those resulting from the accounting criterion for the whole period, with the exception of ENI in the year 1960. These results highlight the different strategies adopted by the three state holdings. On the one hand, IRI is characterized by a strongly pyramidal structure, with permanent indirect and cross shareholdings (cf. Table 5.2), which allowed it to control a vast number of firms. On the other, the other two state holdings show a weaker structure and a more limited (ENI), or even almost completely absent (EFIM), chain of control.

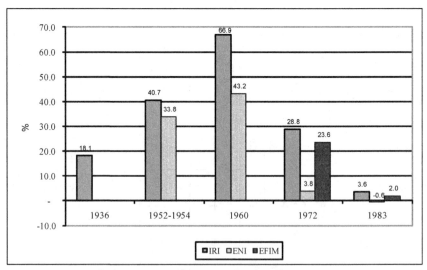

*Figure 5.4*   Control of IRI, ENI, and EFIM under the effective criterion in comparison to the accounting one.

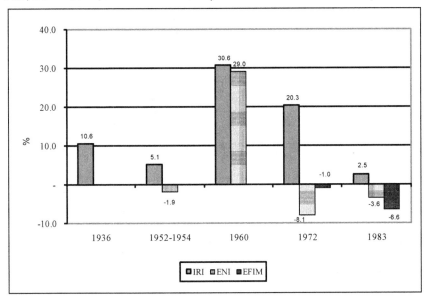

*Figure 5.5* Control of IRI, ENI, and EFIM under the pyramidal criterion in comparison to the accounting one.

## THE REGIONAL DISTRIBUTION

### Number and Size Distribution

A further step toward the comprehension of Italian SOEs dynamics and contribution to the country's economy has been done by breaking down the national series into disaggregate categories, representing four regional macro-areas (North-West, North-East, Central, South and Islands). Each of them has been in turn further subdivided according to the country's administrative regional structure (that is, 19 regions). Such analysis has been performed with regard, first, to number of firms and assets and, second, to their respective shares as compared to the Imita.db universe. For this exercise, we have preferred the data be reconstructed through the effective control criteria, which is likely to give a better idea of the real dimension of the phenomenon.

Before getting more deeply into the analysis, a caveat has to be introduced. SOEs regional distribution data often involve some unavoidable bias, that is, an abnormal concentration in the Lazio region, where the capital is located: in fact, in Rome not only IRI's, ENI's and EFIM's headquarters were located, but also a fair number of holding and operating companies. Such disproportion does not concern so much the absolute numbers as the size of assets. In fact with respect to the first, only in the 1952–1954 benchmark does Lazio show an abnormal value: 35.3% of the country's total. In the other four benchmark years (1936, 1960, 1972, 1983), the results (with values between 21.8% and 27%) are not much different from Lombardy's (20.0% to 25.8%; see Table 5.7). But if we turn to the assets data, the share of the Rome region jumps to much higher values, with a record in 1972 (45.1% of the total assets of Italian SOEs) towering over a set of values around 40%. Such region alone attracted Central Italy's almost entire investment in public firms. Lombardy was still the second more concentrated region, even though at much lower level (between 22.8% and 27.3% of total assets).

In contrast to Lazio, Lombardy's position in the ranking is to be explained by the area's high level of industrialization. Such a position in the public sector contradicts the conventional wisdom tending to contrast Milan, and the core of the private capitalism, with very few public undertakings, with the political capital Rome, the core of state capitalism in Italy.

The disaggregating SOEs series for macro-areas yields clear results. The North-West turns out as the region with the largest share with regard both to number and assets. Here is where the "industrial triangle" (Piedmont, Liguria, and Lombardy) is located and where a good part of the heavy industry was rescued by the state during the Depression years. Emblematic is the case of Liguria, which ranks third among the regions most affected by state intervention (with a 23% share in 1936) and where the shipbuilding industry was deeply involved in the crisis of the sector which persisted throughout the war and its aftermath: not by accident within the North-East area, where all in all state intervention was feeble, only Friuli-Venezia Giulia stands out with a 4.5% share of public assets in 1952–1954 (see Mellinato, Chapter 11).

Looking then at the internal dynamics of the data, we can note that three of the four macro-areas do not show a clear trend: as for number, the North-West is characterized by a stationary tendency until the 1960s, followed by a decline which in reality seems to mask a capitalization of assets, as portrayed by its U-shape behavior; the North-East shows very irregular trends both in number and assets; the same can be said of Central Italy, even though with a more fluctuating behavior as far as numbers are concerned. Only the South shows a neat tendency to grow both in number and assets: here, between 1936 and 1972, the number of public undertakings increases from 9 to 77, followed by a small decline in the next decade: this corresponds to an increase of 13 percentage points (from 10.1% to 23.1%). As for assets, this meant a growth from an almost nonexistent 0.9% in 1936 to 5.0% in 1981, thus marking clearly the change of economic policy toward the South since the postwar period. As said in a previous chapter, ENI and IRI were among the main instruments through which the government tried to pursue the convergence of the southern regions, especially Campania and Sicily (which received the greatest help), toward the North.

Table 5.7  Regional Distribution of SOEs in Italy (Number, Number %, and Assets %)

| Regions | NUMBER | | | | | NUMBER % | | | | | ASSETS % | | | | |
|---|---|---|---|---|---|---|---|---|---|---|---|---|---|---|---|
| | 1936 | 1952–1954 | 1960 | 1972 | 1983 | 1936 | 1952–1954 | 1960 | 1972 | 1983 | 1936 | 1952–1954 | 1960 | 1971 | 1981 |
| VDA | | | | 1 | 1 | - | - | - | 0.3 | 0.3 | - | - | - | 0.0 | 0.0 |
| PIE | 7 | 8 | 10 | 12 | 19 | 7.9 | 6.0 | 6.1 | 4.1 | 6.1 | 5.8 | 5.6 | 5.0 | 3.9 | 7.7 |
| LIG | 8 | 14 | 21 | 29 | 23 | 9.0 | 10.5 | 12.7 | 10.0 | 7.4 | 23.0 | 20.0 | 18.0 | 17.9 | 20.9 |
| LOM | 23 | 34 | 39 | 58 | 70 | 25.8 | 25.6 | 23.6 | 20.0 | 22.4 | 27.3 | 22.8 | 25.6 | 25.3 | 24.7 |
| North-West | 38 | 56 | 70 | 100 | 113 | 42.7 | 42.1 | 42.4 | 34.5 | 36.2 | 56.1 | 48.4 | 48.6 | 47.2 | 53.2 |
| TAA | | | | 1 | 1 | - | - | - | 0.3 | 0.3 | - | - | - | - | 0.0 |
| VEN | 5 | 2 | 4 | 8 | 14 | 5.6 | 1.5 | 2.4 | 2.8 | 4.5 | 0.5 | 1.3 | 1.5 | 0.3 | 0.7 |
| FVG | 7 | 5 | 5 | 10 | 11 | 7.9 | 3.8 | 3.0 | 3.4 | 3.5 | 0.1 | 4.5 | 2.6 | 1.6 | 1.3 |
| EMR | 4 | 1 | 4 | 3 | 8 | 4.5 | 0.8 | 2.4 | 1.0 | 2.6 | 0.6 | 0.6 | 0.8 | 0.0 | 0.2 |
| North-East | 16 | 8 | 13 | 22 | 34 | 18.0 | 6.0 | 7.9 | 7.6 | 10.9 | 1.2 | 6.4 | 4.8 | 2.0 | 2.2 |
| MAR | | | | 2 | 2 | - | - | - | 0.7 | 0.6 | - | - | - | 0.0 | 0.0 |
| TOS | 2 | 3 | 6 | 9 | 18 | 2.2 | 2.3 | 3.6 | 3.1 | 5.8 | 0.2 | 0.2 | 1.8 | 0.7 | 1.7 |
| UMB | | | | 2 | 5 | - | - | - | 0.7 | 1.6 | - | - | - | 0.1 | 0.1 |
| LAZ | 24 | 47 | 42 | 78 | 68 | 27.0 | 35.3 | 25.5 | 26.9 | 21.8 | 41.6 | 41.0 | 40.5 | 45.1 | 37.8 |

(continued)

Table 5.7  (continued)

| Regions | NUMBER | | | | | NUMBER % | | | | | ASSETS % | | | | |
|---|---|---|---|---|---|---|---|---|---|---|---|---|---|---|---|
| | 1936 | 1952–1954 | 1960 | 1972 | 1983 | 1936 | 1952–1954 | 1960 | 1972 | 1983 | 1936 | 1952–1954 | 1960 | 1971 | 1981 |
| Central | 26 | 50 | 48 | 91 | 93 | 29.2 | 37.6 | 29.1 | 31.4 | 29.8 | 41.8 | 41.2 | 42.2 | 45.9 | 39.6 |
| CAM | 7 | 13 | 25 | 34 | 33 | 7.9 | 9.8 | 15.2 | 11.7 | 10.6 | 0.7 | 3.9 | 4.2 | 2.2 | 3.1 |
| ABR-MOL | | | | 1 | 3 | - | - | - | 0.3 | 1.0 | - | - | - | 0.1 | 0.1 |
| PUG | | | | 16 | 10 | - | - | - | 5.5 | 3.2 | - | - | - | 0.3 | 0.2 |
| BAS | | | | 6 | 3 | - | - | - | 2.1 | 1.0 | - | - | - | 0.0 | 0.0 |
| CAL | | | | 3 | 2 | - | - | - | 1.0 | 0.6 | - | - | - | 0.0 | 0.0 |
| SAR | | 1 | 1 | 7 | 8 | - | 0.8 | 0.6 | 2.4 | 2.6 | - | 0.0 | 0.0 | 0.3 | 0.3 |
| SIC | 2 | 5 | 8 | 10 | 13 | 2.2 | 3.8 | 4.8 | 3.4 | 4.2 | 0.2 | 0.0 | 0.1 | 1.9 | 1.3 |
| South | 9 | 19 | 34 | 77 | 72 | 10.1 | 14.3 | 20.6 | 26.6 | 23.1 | 0.9 | 4.0 | 4.3 | 4.9 | 5.0 |
| Total | 89 | 133 | 165 | 290 | 312 | 100.0 | 100.0 | 100.0 | 100.0 | 100.0 | 100.0 | 100.0 | 100.0 | 100.0 | 100.0 |

*Legenda:* VDA: Valle d'Aosta; PIE: Piemonte; LIG: Liguria; LOM: Lombardia; TAA: Trentino Alto Adige; VEN: Veneto; FVG: Friuli Venezia Giulia; EMR: Emilia Romagna; MRA: Marche; TOS: Toscana; UMB: Umbria; LAZ: Lazio; CAM: Campania; ABR-MOL: Abruzzo Molise; PUG: Puglia; BAS: Basilicata; CAL: Calabria; SAR: Sardegna; SIC: Sicilia

## Public and Private Firms

The trend just illustrated is reinforced by Table 5.8, which measures the weight of public firms over the Imita.db universe in each region. As a matter of fact these two tables show clearly that both number and assets of SOEs not only kept growing in the South but also grew at a faster rate than private undertakings.

The share of public firms in the total number of firms registered by Imita.db in the South increased significantly over the entire period, rising from 3.5% in 1936 to 12.2% in 1983, while the relative assets share grew even more (from 2.3% to 18.4%).

Here, too, the two previously mentioned regions (Campania and Sicily) most benefited from state help: up to 1960 they were, in practice, the only southern regions characterized by some presence of SOEs (although with values not comparable to the North-East and Lazio); then in the following two benchmark years, public undertakings gained an important role also in the other regions. For instance, in 1971 the six SOEs registered in Basilicata represented almost one third of the number of the companies recorded in Imita.db and to 9.1% of the region total assets: in the same year SOEs' assets reached, in Puglia, 16.1% of the total and in Abruzzo-Molise 29.3%.

However, something else comes out strongly from these two tables: it is the overwhelming direct presence of the state in the economic activities of Liguria and Friuli-Venezia Giulia, which confirms what was already suggested about the increasing weight of SOEs in heavy industry, particularly in shipbuilding, which is a capital-intensive sector par excellence. In Liguria, the share of SOEs assets fluctuated between 43.2% and 51% up to the 1970s, to break then the 70% level in 1981; in Friuli, it peaked at 51.5% in 1952, to decrease slowly thereafter.

In the end, a further confirmation concerns Lombardy: in three of the five benchmark years, the share of public assets was more than one fifth of total assets, with a peak of 27% in 1981. This value, which was likely to be more the result of private disinvestment than of real expansion of the public sector, concurred with the Liguria abnormal value to push in 1981 the North-West percentage up to one third of the total.

## CONCLUSIONS

The initial hypothesis of our research was that scale of state ownership has been characterized over time by an accentuated variability, which was determined by a continuous stream of acquisitions, mergers, and dismissals. Such variability, together with the scarce availability of quantitative information on the structure of the systems of Italian firms, prevented scholars in the past from identifying the boundaries of Italian

*Table 5.8*  Regional distribution: Public Firms as % of Imita.db (Number and Assets)

| Regions | SOEs as % of Imita.db (number) | | | | | SOEs as % of Imita.db (assets) | | | | |
|---|---|---|---|---|---|---|---|---|---|---|
| | 1936 | 1952–1954 | 1960 | 1972 | 1983 | 1936 | 1952–1954 | 1960 | 1971 | 1981 |
| VDA | - | - | - | 3.0 | 5.0 | - | - | - | 10.0 | 11.5 |
| PIE | 1.5 | 1.2 | 1.5 | 1.0 | 3.1 | 12.1 | 10.8 | 9.0 | 8.8 | 18.1 |
| LIG | 2.2 | 3.4 | 5.8 | 6.4 | 14.3 | 45.2 | 43.5 | 43.2 | 51.0 | 73.1 |
| LOM | 1.2 | 1.2 | 1.4 | 1.3 | 3.6 | 20.7 | 15.1 | 15.8 | 20.3 | 27.0 |
| North-West | 1.4 | 1.4 | 1.8 | 1.6 | 4.1 | 24.3 | 19.6 | 18.8 | 23.0 | 32.7 |
| TAA | - | - | - | 0.4 | 1.0 | - | - | - | - | 0.9 |
| VEN | 2.5 | 0.7 | 1.4 | 1.1 | 2.8 | 3.0 | 8.0 | 9.5 | 4.2 | 7.9 |
| FVG | 6.8 | 3.5 | 3.5 | 3.1 | 7.3 | 0.8 | 51.5 | 42.5 | 28.8 | 32.0 |
| EMR | 2.8 | 0.5 | 1.6 | 0.4 | 1.4 | 8.5 | 8.4 | 10.1 | 0.4 | 2.1 |
| North-East | 3.4 | 1.1 | 1.7 | 1.1 | 2.6 | 2.9 | 19.1 | 15.6 | 8.2 | 8.8 |
| MAR | - | - | - | 2.7 | 3.4 | - | - | - | 2.9 | 1.3 |
| TOS | 1.1 | 1.0 | 2.7 | 2.2 | 6.6 | 0.8 | 1.1 | 10.7 | 5.9 | 11.8 |
| UMB | - | - | - | 4.8 | 6.2 | - | - | - | 22.8 | 10.9 |
| LAZ | 4.0 | 5.9 | 5.5 | 6.4 | 13.1 | 23.9 | 20.0 | 22.7 | 21.0 | 22.7 |
| Central | 3.3 | 4.5 | 4.7 | 5.2 | 10.0 | 21.3 | 18.5 | 21.6 | 20.2 | 21.7 |

| CAM | 4.9 | 7.5 | 11.1 | 8.2 | 19.0 | 2.9 | 13.7 | 17.2 | 14.4 | 23.2 |
|---|---|---|---|---|---|---|---|---|---|---|
| ABR-MOL | - | - | - | 1.4 | 5.9 | - | - | - | 29.3 | 10.7 |
| PUG | - | - | - | 10.1 | 14.9 | - | - | - | 16.1 | 13.5 |
| BAS | - | - | - | 30.0 | 17.6 | - | - | - | 9.1 | 9.1 |
| CAL | - | - | - | 5.7 | 10.0 | - | - | - | 4.5 | 3.7 |
| SIC | 3.7 | 2.7 | 2.2 | 1.6 | 7.3 | 1.3 | 0.2 | 0.5 | 11.1 | 14.0 |
| SAR | | 3.6 | 1.7 | 1.9 | 11.8 | - | 1.5 | 2.0 | 7.1 | 18.2 |
| South | 3.5 | 4.0 | 4.6 | 4.5 | 12.2 | 2.3 | 8.5 | 9.2 | 12.2 | 18.4 |
| Total | 2.1 | 2.2 | 2.6 | 2.5 | 5.6 | 19.7 | 18.2 | 18.8 | 20.1 | 25.2 |

*Legenda:* See table 5.7

SOEs with respect both to the aggregate data and to their regional distribution. The results presented in this chapter offer some innovative answers to these issues.

First, we have shown that the weight of the three public groups, measured by two standard proxies, such as share capital and assets of all the Italian firms, is very significant, especially with regard to manufacturing, especially to the heavy sectors. It kept growing and, in some areas, (mining, transport, finance and utilities) this growth reached remarkable percentages of the total. All in all, the large size of direct state intervention in the economy reconstructed here has not been even approximated by previous studies.

Second, we have seen how complex is the group structure of each of the three state holdings because of the large number of firms distributed all over the sectors of the economy and because of the high level of complexity of the forms of control.

In the third section, we have discussed how the regional distribution changed over time. Two conclusions deserve special attention here, as they only partly confirm the traditional picture offered by historiography. They confirm the growing weight of the state in the South, which seems to compensate for the insufficient investment of private groups and thereby balance, at least partially, the original concentration of the state's efforts in the northern and central regions. On the other end, the research shows more innovative results with regard to the enduring presence of the state in the northern areas, particularly in Lombardy, where the bulk of private initiatives was concentrated.

## APPENDIX 5.1 HOLDING COMPANIES AND FINANCIAL HOLDING COMPANIES OF THE THREE GROUPS

### IRI

1935–1937
STET Società torinese esercizi telefonici
FINMARE Società finanziaria marittima (only for 1936 and 1937)
FINSIDER Società finanziaria siderurgica (only for 1937)

1951–1953
STET Società torinese esercizi telefonici
FINMARE Società finanziaria marittima
FINSIDER Società finanziaria siderurgica
FINMECCANICA Società finanziaria meccanica
FINELETTRICA Finanziaria elettrica nazionale (only for 1952 and 1953)

1959–1961
STET Società torinese esercizi telefonici
FINMARE Società finanziaria marittima
FINSIDER Società finanziaria siderurgica
FINMECCANICA Società finanziaria meccanica

FINELETTRICA Finanziaria elettrica nazionale
FINCANTIERI Finanziaria cantieri navali (only for 1960 and 1961)
AUTOSTRADE Concessioni e Costruzioni Autostrade (only for 1960 and 1961)

1970–1972
STET Società finanziaria telefonica
FINMARE Società finanziaria marittima
FINSIDER Società finanziaria siderurgica
FINMECCANICA Società finanziaria meccanica
FINCANTIERI Finanziaria cantieri navali
ITALSTAT Società italiana per le infrastrutture e l'assetto del territorio
SPA Società finanziaria di partecipazioni azionarie
Società finanziaria per il traforo del Monte Bianco (only for 1970)
RAI Radiotelevisione italiana
ALITALIA Linee aeree italiane
AUTOSTRADE Concessioni e Costruzioni Autostrade (only for 1972)

1981–1983
STET Società finanziaria telefonica
FINMARE Società finanziaria marittima
FINSIDER Società finanziaria siderurgica
FINMECCANICA Società finanziaria meccanica
FINCANTIERI Finanziaria cantieri navali
ITALSTAT Società italiana per le infrastrutture e l'assetto del territorio
SOFIN Società finanziaria di partecipazioni azionarie (già SPA Società finanziaria
    di partecipazioni azionarie)
CREDITO ITALIANO
BANCO DI ROMA
BANCA COMMERCIALE ITALIANA
BANCO DI SANTO SPIRITO
SME Società meridionale finanziaria
FINSIEL Finanziaria per i sistemi informativi elettronici
ALITALIA Linee aeree italiane
SISMA Società industrie siderurgiche meccaniche e affini (only for 1981)
SIFA Società immobiliare e finanziaria per azioni (only for 1983)

# ENI

1954–1955
AGIP Azienda generale italiana petroli
ANIC Azienda nazionale idrogenazione combustibili
SNAM Società nazionale metanodotti
AGIP MINERARIA
ROMSA Raffineria di oli minerali

1959–1961
AGIP Azienda generale italiana petroli
ANIC Azienda nazionale idrogenazione combustibili
SNAM Società nazionale metanodotti
AGIP MINERARIA

1970–1972
AGIP Azienda generale italiana petroli

ANIC Azienda nazionale idrogenazione combustibili
SNAM Società nazionale metanodotti
AGIP NUCLEARE (only for 1972)

1981–1983
AGIP Azienda generale italiana petroli
ANIC Azienda nazionale idrogenazione combustibili (only for 1981 and 1982)
SNAM Società nazionale metanodotti
AGIP CARBONE (only for 1981 and 1982)
SNAM PROGETTI
LANEROSSI
NUOVO PIGNONE Industrie meccaniche e fonderia
OFFICINE SAVIO
SAIPEM
INDENI Società per la promozione di nuove iniziative industriali
SOFID Società finanziamenti idrocarburi
HYDROCARBONS INTERNATIONAL HOLDING S.A.
AGIP NUCLEARE (only for 1982)
ENICHIMICA (only for 1982 and 1983)
SAMIM Azionaria minero-metallurgica (only for 1982 and 1983)

## EFIM

1970–1971
FINANZIARIA ERNESTO BREDA
BREDA FERROVIARIA Partecipazioni e finanziamento costruzioni ferroviarie
MCS
INSUD

1981–1982
FINANZIARIA ERNESTO BREDA
AVIOFER BREDA
MCS
SOPAL Società partecipazioni alimentari

## NOTES

1. This source has already been extensively used for examining the general characteristics of Italian industry in the 20th century (Giannetti and Vasta 2006).
2. A first quantitative analysis that uses Imita.db by comparing the dynamics of SOE to private firms in service sectors can be found in Toninelli and Vasta (2007).
3. It was not always possible to employ data concerning the same year. Data from the Imita.db and those regarding IRI refer to 1952, whereas for ENI, whose first balance sheet was presented on 30 April 1954, we used the 1952 data for controlled firms as well as the 1954 ones for shareholdings, adding the ENI holding data both to the universe and to the firms of the group. Regarding the last two benchmark years, our data refer to two biennials (1971–1972 and 1982–1983): data on share capital refer to the years 1972 and 1983, whereas those on assets refer to 1971 and 1982.

4. In order to identify the shareholding structure of the various groups, we have defined holding companies in a more rigorous way than that adopted in the three state holdings documents, as these reflect their internal routines. In particular, a holding company has been identified as a firm (1) in which one of the three state holdings has a shareholding that is higher than 50%, and (2) which controls at least one other company by a percentage greater than 50%. The sector of activity of a firm allows us, moreover, to follow the terminology adopted, for example, at the IRI Archive and to distinguish between *financial* holding companies (which own and manage, or administer, other companies) and *operative* holding companies (not financial). The first ones pertain to Section J of the 2002 Ateco-Istat classification, based on Eurostat NACE Rev. 1.1 classification of economic activities. Such a definition, which may appear restrictive, guarantees that the firms that are to be referred to as holding companies are only those firms where state holdings were able to maintain the control of forward firms without direct shareholding.

5. Therefore, we consider group firms not only those companies that are defined as such in various state holdings' documents, but all those firms with stakes controlled by the state holding, by a holding company (financial or not), by another firm of the group, or by any combination of them.

6. In a context in which ownership is widely dispersed (e.g., public companies), the control of 20% of the capital of a firm would guarantee that the appointment of a number of directors would be sufficient to secure effective control of an entire firm. However, it is well known that ownership in Italy is far from being dispersed (Rinaldi and Vasta 2005; Bargigli and Vasta 2006).

7. This kind of control has already been described in the Berle and Means' (1932) pioneering work and is today often used in studies on corporate ownership.

8. In other terms, Figure 5.2 shows how IRI, through a limited investment, can control the activities of the group through the majority of share capital and of voting rights of all the firms in the chain. For example, if the Z1 firm had a share capital equal to 100, in the case of a pyramidal structure (like that presented in Figure 3.2), financial commitment of IRI to control Z1 would be equal to 6.8%. In fact, IRI's direct commitment is limited to 51% of the capital of the sub-holding which, back to back, scales down to 26% of X1 (51% × 51%), to 13.3% of Y1 (51% × 26%); and, finally, to 6.8% of Z1 (51% × 13.3%). In the absence of a pyramidal structure, in order to gain control of Z1, IRI would have had to take a shareholding equal to 51% of Z1 share capital, maintaining therefore a financial outlay equal to 51 (51% of 100, share capital of Z1), much greater than the amount maintained under the hypothesis of pyramidal control (6.8%).

9. Small joint stock companies and other firms with different legal forms are therefore not included. Moreover, Italian firms with their headquarters abroad are also excluded. For further information, see Vasta (2006).

10. Mortara (1976) refers to the period 1970–1974, Arrighetti et al. (1982) refer to 1976–1978, and Bognetti and Spagnolo (1992) analyze the 1983–1988 period.

11. For a detailed disaggregation of the share capital of the manufacturing sector controlled by IRI, ENI, and EFIM, see Toninelli and Vasta (2010, Table 3.5)

12. It must be underlined that the representativeness of the Imita.db in the universe of Italian joint stock companies declines in the final benchmark year, 1983. The weight of the three public groups on the Imita.db and on the Italian joint stock companies almost coincides with the first four benchmark years, when the Imita.db always represented more than 90% of the total. Compared to the values presented in Table 5.4, in fact, the weight of the three public groups in the Italian joint stock companies is 11.5% in 1936, 22.1% in 1952–1954, 17.9% in

1960, and 29.7% in 1972. In 1983, instead, there is a large gap: the weight of all three groups on the Imita.db climbs to 40.2%, while the weight on the joint stock company universe is equal to 33.5%.

13. In our analysis, the endowment funds given by governments are considered equivalent to the share capital.

14. Following the hypothesis, advanced earlier, that the control of the capital share of the firm corresponds to the control share of the assets, the analysis of three state holdings' assets weight in the Italian system of firms is offered in Toninelli and Vasta (2010, Tables 3.6 and 3.7).

## BIBLIOGRAPHY

Aganin, A. and P. Volpin 2005, "The History of Corporate Ownership in Italy," in *A History of Corporate Governance around the World*, ed. R. Morck, Chicago: University of Chicago Press.

Arrighetti, A., G. Stansfield, and C. Virno 1982, *Le partecipazioni azionarie pubbliche. Un'analisi strutturale*, Milan: Franco Angeli-Ciriec.

Bargigli, L. and M. Vasta 2006, "Ownership and control in Italian capitalism(1911–1972)," in *Evolution of Italian Enterprises in the 20th Century*, eds. R. Giannetti and M. Vasta, Heidelberg-New York: Physica-Verlag.

Berle, A.A. and G.C. Means 1932, *The Modern Corporation and Private Property*, New York: Macmillan.

Bertrand, M. and S. Mullainathan 2003, "Pyramids," *Journal of the European Economic Association* 1(2–3): 478–483.

Bognetti, G. and C. Spagnolo 1992, *Le riforme mancate. L'intervento pubblico tra vincoli ed efficienza (1983–1988)*, Milan: Franco Angeli-Ciriec.

Giannetti, R. and M. Vasta, eds. 2006, *Evolution of Italian Enterprises in the 20th Century*, Heidelberg-New York: Physica-Verlag.

La Porta, R., F. Lopez-de-Silanes, and A. Shleifer 1999, "Corporate Ownership around the World," *Journal of Finance* 54(2): 471–517.

Malgarini, M. 2000, "Le privatizzazioni in Italia tra il 1992 e il 1999: Iter normativo e risultati quantitativi," in *Le privatizzazioni italiane*, ed. S. de Nardis, Bologna: Il Mulino.

Morck R., D. Wolfenzon, and B. Yeung 2005, "Corporate Governance, Economic Entrenchment, and Growth," *Journal of Economic Literature* 43(3): 655–720.

Mortara, A., ed. 1976, *Il settore pubblico dell'economia. Dati e notizie 1970–1974*, Milan: Franco Angeli-Ciriec.

Posner, M. and S. Woolf 1967, *Italian Public Enterprise*, Cambridge, Mass.: Cambridge University Press.

Rapporto Marsan c.1992, *L'Istituto per la Ricostruzione Industriale—I.R.I. Elementi per la sua storia dalle origini al 1982*, Rome, mimeo.

Rapporto Saraceno (Ministero dell'Industria e del Commercio) 1956, *L'Istituto per la Ricostruzione Industriale—IRI. Origini, ordinamenti e attività svolta*, Turin.

Rinaldi, A. and M. Vasta 2005, "The structure of Italian capitalism, 1952–1972: new evidence using the interlocking directorates technique," *Financial History Review* 12(2): 173–198.

Sapelli, G., et al. 1993, *Nascita e trasformazione d'impresa. Storia dell'AGIP Petroli*, Bologna: Il Mulino.

Saraceno P. 1975, *Il sistema della imprese a partecipazione statale nell'esperienza italiana*, Milano: Angeli.

Sartori, R. 1957, *Le partecipazioni economiche dello Stato*, Rome: Studium.

Toninelli, P.A. and M. Vasta 2007, "Public Enterprise and the Rise of Services: Networks and Performance of Italian Big Business," in *Transforming Public Enterprise in Europe and North America. Networks, Integration and Internationalization*, eds. J. Clifton, F. Comin, and D. Diaz Fuentes, London: Palgrave Macmillan.

Toninelli, P.A. and M. Vasta 2010, "State-Owned Enterprises (1936–83)," in *Forms of Enterprise in 20th Century Italy*, eds. A. Colli and M. Vasta, Cheltenham: Edward Elgar.

Vasta, M. 2006, "Appendix: The Source and the Imita.db Dataset," in *Evolution of Italian Enterprises in the 20th Century*, eds. R. Giannetti and M. Vasta, Heidelberg, Germany: Physica-Verlag.

# 6 The Financing of a Large Infrastructure Project

## The Case of the Channel Tunnel

*Terry Gourvish*

## INTRODUCTION: STATE-OWNED TRANSPORT IN BRITAIN: PROBLEMS AND PERSPECTIVES

Debates about the effectiveness, or otherwise, of the British public sector have not disappeared with the drive to privatize most of the nationalized industries from the mid-1980s. After World War II, much of inland transport was taken into public ownership under the aegis of the British Transport Commission. The move, which was largely dictated by the poor state of the assets and their unattractiveness to private capital, offered the promise of scale economies and operational integration for the railways, bus services, and road transport, activities which were in any case either heavily regulated or already in the public sector (Anson and Crompton 2009). The operational history of nationalized transport, and especially the railways, has been analyzed in some depth (Gourvish 1986, 2002). From the beginning, one of the first things to be controlled was investment, when resources were scarce in the troubled late 1940s. There was a glimmer of light in the mid-1950s. The Railway Modernization Plan of 1955, a rare example of planned investment on a large scale, received substantial support from the Treasury, but many of the investments proved to be a disaster, damaging the reputation of public sector managers for some considerable time. The Treasury quickly moved to scale down the investment program at the end of the decade. British Rail's investment shortages then became more acute again, as the business moved into deficit. The situation was particularly difficult in the bleaker economic conditions of the 1970s, preventing the corporation from making a more competitive response to the dominance of private motoring and road haulage. By 1976, the investments made during the period of the Modernization Plan were reaching the end of their useful lives, and Peter Parker, British Rail's incoming chairman, was moved to warn the government of the risks associated with the "crumbling edge of quality" (Gourvish 2002, 85). The period of financial constraint under the Labour administration of 1976–1979 was followed by equally harsh treatment by Margaret Thatcher's first Conservative government of 1979–1983, though in the latter case parsimony was accompanied by political dogma, notably the promise to "roll back the public sector." There followed a general assault on the public sector, grounded on the neoliberal assumption that the market and private sector institutions would optimize the provision of public services (Martin 1993; Florio 2004, 27ff.; Clifton, Comín, and Díaz Fuentes 2006, 738). However, many public sector managers were excited about the prospects of privatization in all its forms, particularly where it offered the prospect of freeing an enterprise from the straightjacket of investment constraint and ministerial intervention.

Larger schemes, particularly those for rail infrastructure, were more difficult to initiate and manage. All projects above a fairly low threshold required ministerial approval before they could proceed. In transport some important investments were made in the second half of the 20th century. There were the important river crossings by road, in particular, the two Severn Bridges, opened in 1966 and 1996, respectively; the Humber Bridge, opened in 1981; and the three Dartford Crossings—two tunnels, opened in 1963 and 1980, and a bridge, opened in 1991. A major motorway building program began in the late 1950s with the M1, and by the time the London orbital motorway (M25) had been completed in 1986, there was an extensive network in place of some 1,800 miles (Transport Statistics Great Britain [TSGB] 2009, 131). Most of this work was funded directly from the Exchequer and could be justified on a number of counts, not least by the income received from motor taxation. However, the private sector was a partner in the Dartford Bridge and the two Severn Bridge projects. In both cases, a Private Finance Initiative operated, with construction the responsibility of a private consortium. The facilities were run via a Public–Private Partnership in which the private sector was rewarded by taking over collection of the tolls on the entire crossing. In the Dartford case, the tolls were sufficient to repay the accumulated debt and build up a substantial maintenance fund, and the concession was ended in 2003.

On the other hand, not all of these road transport projects would have passed conventional tests of profitability. The Humber Bridge has proved a disappointing project in terms of traffic and revenue generated. The product of a strong political commitment, it would surely have struggled to show either a positive return or a positive cost–benefit calculation at the appraisal stage. Costing £97 million to build, it failed to cover the interest on its debt, which rose to £209 million by 1984 and £435 million by 1995. Government support was required, first to stabilize the debt level in 1995, and then to provide a £6 million maintenance grant in 2009 (Wentworth and Beresford 1998, 53–56; Department for Transport [DfT] 2009). Nevertheless, the bulk of road investments would have comfortably passed conventional tests of profitability and have produced substantially higher economic returns than most railway projects (cf. Affuso, Masson, and Newbery 2003).

Unsurprisingly, then, in loss-making industries such as the railways, large-scale projects were harder to promote. In the period 1960–1980, in addition to the replacement of steam locomotion by diesel traction under the Modernization Plan, there was the electrification of the West Coast Main Line from London to Glasgow (1960–1974) at a cost of approximately £215 million (Gourvish 1986, 512–513), or £8.3 billion in 2009 prices, and an initial attempt to build a channel tunnel in association with the French in 1967–1975.[1] Both schemes highlighted the difficulty of proceeding with a major project which consumed a large part of the government's investible funds when a business (the railways) was unable to generate sufficient resources from its operating profits in a sector where government priorities were lower than, for example, health or education. In the case of the first Channel Tunnel scheme, the decision by the British government to abandon the scheme was greatly influenced by the escalating cost of the Channel Tunnel Rail Link, a new line to connect the tunnel with London which was a project managed by British Rail. The scheme, badly administered by British Rail, had seen costs escalate from £123 million to £373 million (in May 1974 prices) in only 14 months, June 1973–August 1974; inflation was responsible for £50 million, but most of the increase came from omissions and underestimation (Gourvish 2006, 159). The spiraling cost of this part of the Tunnel project, which was the responsibility of the British government, was a material element in its decision to withdraw in January 1975. But there were wider issues at work here. The long period required to carry out the venture, the specificity of the assets, and the high commercial risk acted as deterrents to private investment. The British project manager, Rio Tinto, worked hard to constrain its financial exposure, but its actions had the effect of transferring risk to the public sector. Inevitably, the relationship with the British and French governments deteriorated when Rio Tinto and the other private companies demanded guarantees against cancellation, limits on equity financing, and state guarantees of the loan book. But to accommodate such demands would have prevented the project from avoiding the constraints of public sector funding. This impasse was a material element in the British government's decision to abandon the project (Gourvish 2008, 50–74).

In much of the abundant literature on the British privatization process from the 1980s, the focus has been firmly upon "process" and "performance," the latter generally measured in terms of productivity (both labor and total), profit rates, and value added (cf. Jackson and Price 1994; Martin and Parker 1997; Florio 2004; Parker 2009). Relatively little has been done to assess the differences between the public and private sectors in their approach to investment and project management, and it is comparatively rare to find answers to the question: does the private sector invest more effectively than the public sector? It is not at all clear that the investment appraisal techniques are superior in one type of enterprise than in the other, and if private sector disciplines may establish a more productive use of management time and resources, these gains may be offset by the cheaper cost of capital upon which the public sector is able to draw. On the other hand, the impetus to involve the private sector in transport (and other) infrastructure projects reflected a dissatisfaction with the historical record of conventional, public sector projects. What research has been done suggests that cost overruns and delays in completing construction were common (cf. Grimsey and Lewis 2004, 71–78). When the Channel Tunnel was revived after a favorable banking report in May 1984 (Gourvish 2006, 246–248), there was a determination on the British government's part that the taxpayer's contribution to the scheme should be limited. However, this proved to be a pipedream, and the scheme became an early lesson in some of the pitfalls in public–private partnerships (Hall 1998; Grimsey and Lewis, 2002, 2004; Gourvish 2006). The second Channel Tunnel project, one of the largest investments of the late 20th century, was advanced by the Thatcher and Mitterrand governments during the period of privatization. It is a key example of a large infrastructure project which was intended to be a private sector responsibility but which increasingly drew in government funds and commitment.

The Channel Tunnel eventually cost about £5 billion to construct and double that to finance (Gourvish 2006). How successful was this venture? Robert Millward, in reviewing my official history of Britain and the Tunnel (Gourvish 2006), thought the answer should be no. The Tunnel was commercially marginal, he suggested, and the social benefits far from obvious. "Whether it was ever economically beneficial, even in the widest sense is . . . a moot point." Taxpayers and equity holders probably lost out, and some of the funding banks also (Millward 2007). Ricard Anguera, in a recent article for the journal *Transportation Research*, went much further. His cost–benefit appraisal of the project concluded that "the British economy would have been better off had the Tunnel never been constructed, as the total resource costs outweighs the benefits generated. Users have gained significantly at the expense of owners (producers) . . . The long-term evaluation of the project confirms the poor viability of the investment both in financial and cost benefit terms" (Anguera 2006, 291). Finally, Robert Wearing and David Myddelton included the project in two volumes of case studies. Wearing (2005, 108–124) saw the Tunnel as a failure of corporate governance and an example of principal-agent weaknesses. Myddelton, in a recent Institute of Economic Affairs publication entitled *They Meant Well*, included the Tunnel and its rail link in a list of six projects that "went wrong" disastrously. Taking the view that the Channel Tunnel Rail Link was an essential part of the project, he concluded that "building and running the Channel Tunnel has been ruinous for Eurotunnel" and that the substantial sums eventually provided for the rail link meant that the Tunnel "must rank as a government disaster" (Myddelton 2007, 152–153). These findings merit closer examination, because if the project was not worthwhile, then we should ask: Why was it promoted? What was the role of the public sector in the process? The question of success or failure is a complicated one, and there are many elements in the equation, embracing economic benefits, political considerations, and social costs and benefits, including wider aspects of transport requirements in Europe.

## THE TUNNEL AS A MEGAPROJECT:
## "OVER TIME AND OVER BUDGET"

First of all, the success or failure of the project should be assessed in relation to its performance in terms of project management. Here, the challenges posed by Europe's largest piece of transport infrastructure were clearly considerable. The logistics of tunneling under the sea over such a length certainly stretched the capabilities of the engineers. There were many uncertainties, and project managers could scarcely be criticized for the unexpected hazards encountered, particularly in relation to difficult ground. And while the technology of tunneling may not have been novel, the technologies associated with the fitting out of the Tunnel were unquestionably at the cutting edge, and the differential increases in cost over estimate reflected this (Table 6.1). Second, the cost overruns and time delays, though clearly threatening Eurotunnel's commercial viability, were by no means large in relation to other "megaprojects." The press fastened on to this observation at regular intervals. Eurotunnel's Rights Issue documentation in May 1994 revealed that the Tunnel had opened a year late, with construction costs some 57% to 64% over the estimate in 1987, though total project costs, including financing, had risen more steeply, by 122% (Table 6.1).

*Table 6.1*  Channel Tunnel Outturn, 6 May 1994, Compared with the November 1987 Forecast (£m, Sept. 1985 Prices)

|  | November 1987 Forecast | Actual at 6 May 1994 | Increase (%) |
|---|---|---|---|
| Construction costs: |  |  |  |
| Tunneling | 1,329 | 2,110 | 59 |
| Terminals | 448 | 553 | 23 |
| Fixed equipment | 688 | 1,200 | 74 |
| Rolling stock | 245 | 705 | 188 |
| Bonuses | – | 46 | – |
| Direct works | – | 36 | – |
| Contingency | 132 | – | – |
| Total | 2,842 | 4,650[a] | 64 |
| Project costs: | November 1987 Forecast | Cash requirement to end 1998 est. May 1994 | Increase (%) |
|  | 4,550[b] | 10,116 | 122 |

[a]Includes £194m not spent. The overspend on £4,456m = 57%.
[b]Given as £4,874m in July 1987 prices: deflated by GDP market prices 2Q:87/3Q:85.
*Source*: Eurotunnel, Pathfinder prospectus, November 1987, Rights Issue document, May 1994.

Myddelton (1987, 144) elected to compare the September 1985 estimate with the 1994 outturn, producing a construction cost overrun of 87%. But both overruns were small beer compared with famous megaprojects in the past. As the *Financial Times* (1994, 2004) noted, the Suez and Panama canals cost more than 50 times over budget, and the Concorde airliner cost 7 times more than expected, with profoundly disappointing revenues. And we might also mention the Seikan Tunnel in Japan (14 years late), the Scottish Assembly building (costing 10 times more than the initial estimate), Gaudí's Sagrada Familia, and the ceiling in the Sistine chapel (1508–1512). Academic research supports the contention that the Tunnel was progressed fairly well given the circumstances, which included its "quadripartite" character (two countries [Britain and France] and two sectors [private and public]). A quantitative assessment of the capital cost of 52 large civil infrastructure projects, conducted by the Rand Corporation in 1988, compared outturn costs (*excluding* commissioning and start-up costs) with cost estimates at the "detailed engineering stage." On this basis, the authors found that the average cost overrun was 88%, and the average delay was 17%, which, with a 6-year project like the Tunnel, is equivalent to 12 months (Morrow, McDonnell, and Arguden 1988, v, 7, 18, 30–32, 45–46; see also Winch 1996, 24). Similar results were derived from a study of UK projects undertaken by Mott MacDonald for the Treasury in 2002 (Grimsey and Lewis 2004, 72–74). Flyvbjerg, Bruzelius, and Rothengatter (2003, 14, 19) have placed the Channel Tunnel, which they suggest had a cost overrun of 80%, in the middle of a table of cost overruns for large transport projects, which range from 26% to 196%. Judged in this context, the performance of the contractors, Transmanche-Link (TML) and the concession holders and operators, Eurotunnel, if leaving much to be desired on the public relations front, was satisfactory. And unlike some earlier projects, it was clearly a misfortune for Eurotunnel to embark on a long construction process during a time of relatively high inflation, and then commence operating when the rate of inflation fell and prices became more stable. In such a situation, the weight of the debt burden remained stubbornly in place, creating difficulties for the owners of capital as it became clear that revenues were likely to be insufficient to service the debt.

## THE CHANNEL TUNNEL'S CONTRIBUTION TO TRANSPORT PROVISION, 1994–2009

Although that most valuable of historical tools—hindsight—is in short supply, there has now been a decade and a half of Tunnel operating, and it is possible to provide a tentative evaluation of its contribution to the European transport network. A number of studies have emerged, including a detailed evaluation of the impact on the county of Kent by Hay, Meredith, and Vickerman (2004), more recent work on Ashford by Preston and Wall (2008), and a literature review by Kamel and Matthewman (2008). This research presents a rather gloomy evaluation of the economic impact of the Tunnel and of the high-speed rail lines linking it with London, Paris, and Brussels. Wider economic benefits have been "difficult to detect," as they appear to have been swamped by external factors and are only likely to be found where supportive planning mechanisms are in place. However, there is no doubting the fact that the Tunnel has provided a significant addition to transport services between Britain and the Continent. Table 6.2 summarizes the Tunnel's record in terms of traffic carried from 1994. Despite a slow start, and notwithstanding the setback of a serious fire on a freight shuttle on 18 November 1996, the railways' Eurostar business increased steadily on the London–Paris/Brussels routes, reaching 6 million passengers in 1997 and over 7 million in 2000. Direct services to Disneyland Paris were introduced in June 1996 and a winter ski service to Bourg–St. Maurice began in 1997; a direct summer service to Avignon was introduced in July 2002. However, trial connecting services north of London to and from the British regions proved a failure in the period May 1995–January 1997, as did the night sleeper trains, and when the leasing arrangement for the sleeper trains was terminated in 1998, Britain's Department for Transport had to put up £109.5 million in termination costs. The lack of regional services proved to be a particular disappointment, provoking the criticism of the House of Commons Transport Committee (1999). Total Eurostar traffic slipped back in 2001–2003, but there were further gains once the British high-speed rail link to London St. Pancras was opened in stages, in September 2003 and November 2007. By 2008, passenger numbers exceeded 9 million. The average for 1998–2009 was 7.4 million a year.

These results were, of course, well down on the forecasts of 1987–1994, and losses were experienced. On the other hand, Eurotunnel's "Le Shuttle" traffic built up well, although the ferries' retention of duty-free sales until 1999 and periodic outbursts of price cutting prevented the Tunnel from gaining a higher market share. The number of shuttle passengers reached a peak of over 12 million in 1998, but has fallen steadily since then. The average for 1998–2009 was 8.7 million a year. Taken overall, passenger numbers in 2003 were only about 40% of expectations in 1994 (Table 6.2). Freight was a mixed bag. The railways' trainload operations were clearly disappointing. Planned by British Rail on the British side, then developed by the private sector after the sale of the Railfreight Distribution business to a consortium led by Wisconsin Central in 1997, the traffic remained well below Eurotunnel's expectations. The amount carried rose to 3.1 million metric tons in 1998, but then began to decline with the economic downturn in Europe, and the traffic in 2002 was only half that of the peak, by which time the business was being adversely affected by the moves made to combat the activities of "clandestines" or unauthorized entrants, who are popularly known as "asylum seekers" (cf. Rail Freight Group 2002). The actual rail freight tonnage for 2003, 1.7 million, was well down on the 1987 and 1994

*Table 6.2* Channel Tunnel Traffic, 1994–2009 ('000s)

| Year | Passenger: Eurostar | Shuttle | Total Passengers | Freight: Railway | Shuttle | | Total Freight | |
|------|------|------|------|------|------|------|------|------|
| | (pass no:s) | (pass no:s) | (no:s) | (metric tons) | (metric tons) Gy | Ay | (metric tons) Gy | Ay |
| 1994[a] | n.a. | n.a. | 315 | 452 | 585 | 845 | 1,037 | 1,297 |
| 1995 | 2,920 | 4,161 | 7,081[d] | 1,350 | 3,519 | 5,083 | 4,869 | 6,433 |
| 1996[b] | 4,867 | 7,942 | 12,809[d] | 2,361 | 4,671 | 6,747 | 7,032 | 9,108 |
| 1997 | 6,004 | 8,649 | 14,653 | 2,923 | 2,304 | 3,328 | 5,227 | 6,251 |
| 1998 | 6,038 | 12,367 | 18,405 | 3,141 | 6,345 | 9,165 | 9,486 | 12,306 |
| 1999 | 7,130 | 9,888 | 17,550 | 2,865 | 7,551 | 10,907 | 10,416 | 13,772 |
| 2000 | 7,130 | 9,888 | 17,018 | 2,947 | 10,197 | 14,729 | 13,144 | 17,676 |
| 2001 | 6,947 | 9,366 | 16,313 | 2,447 | 10,782 | 15,574 | 13,230 | 18,021 |
| 2002[c] | 6,603 | 8,649 | 15,252 | 1,487 | 11,079 | 16,003 | 12,566 | 17,490 |
| 2003 | 6,315 | 8,384 | 14,699 | 1,744 | 11,565 | 16,705 | 13,309 | 18,449 |
| 2004 | 7,277 | 7,787 | 15,064 | 1,899 | 11,529 | 16,653 | 13,418 | 18,542 |
| 2005 | 7,454 | 8,073 | 15,527 | 1,588 | 11,781 | 17,017 | 13,369 | 18,605 |
| 2006 | 7,858 | 7,708 | 15,556 | 1,569 | 11,664 | 16,848 | 13,233 | 18,417 |
| 2007 | 8,261 | 7,771 | 16,032 | 1,210 | 12,735 | 18,395 | 13,945 | 19,605 |
| 2008 | 9,113 | 6,831 | 15,994 | 1,240 | 11,286 | 16,302 | 12,526 | 17,542 |
| 2009 | 9,220 | 6,810 | 16,030 | 1,181 | 6,923 | 10,000 | 8,104 | 44,181 |
| 1987 forecast: 2003 | 21,400 | 21,100 | 39,500 | 10,600 | 10,500 | | 21,100 | |
| 1994 forecast: 2003 | 17,120 | 18,650 | 35,770 | 10,450 | 14,850 | | 25,300 | |

[a] Partial opening.
[b] Tunnel fire, 16 Nov. 1996: passenger shuttles resumed 10 Dec. 1996, full freight service 15 June 1997.
[c] Disruption caused by 'clandestines' (asylum seekers).
[d] 7,789 and 13,673 in MMC, 1997, para. 4.17 × implied multipliers = approx. 2.5 passengers per car, 37 passengers per coach.
Gy, Gourvish's estimate based on 9 payload metric tons per vehicle carried.
Ay, Anguera's estimate based on 13 payload metric tons per vehicle carried (note that Anguera's reported figures are 1994 0.8m; 2002 17.1m).
*Source*: TSGB 2003-2009; Eurotunnel, R&A 1994-2008, Press release, 20 January 2010 (restated figures used where given); Pathfinder Prospectus, November 1987, Rights Issue document, May 1994; News Release, 25 January 2005.

forecasts (approx. 10.5 million), and the tonnage carried in 2007–2009 was lower than in 1995 (see Table 6.2). On the other hand, Eurotunnel's HGV shuttles were more successful, in spite of the fire in 1996. The traffic grew steadily from just under 400,000 vehicles in 1995 to 1,300,000 in

2003–2006, and reached a peak of 1,400,000 vehicles in 2007, before the recession, which had a pronounced effect on business in 2009. Although the tonnage carried is impossible to calculate with accuracy, if we assume that the average payload per vehicle was 9 metric tons, then 11.6 million metric tons were carried by shuttle in 2003, 78% of the level forecast by Eurotunnel in 1994 (14.85 million metric tons). The economist Stefan Szymanski (2000) preferred a loading of 12.5 metric tons, while Anguera (2006) favors the recent Eurotunnel estimate of 13 metric tons, both of which produce higher traffic figures, of course. If we accept the Eurotunnel estimate of 13 metric tons per vehicle, then the actual shuttle traffic in 2003, at 16.7 million metric tons, exceeded the 1994 forecast for 2003 by 12% (see Table 6.2). It is difficult to find estimates of Eurotunnel's share of the roll-on/roll-off traffic through the Channel ports. Anguera (2006, 298) provided data only for the port of Dover, but Hay et al. (2004, 28) provided an estimate for all ports of 26% for 1999. This was a not inconsiderable, but by no means overwhelming, share of the market.

Interested parties, and especially aggrieved shareholders, have suggested that the traffic forecasts were consciously fictitious, used to justify support for a private sector project with no subsidy. French sources, notably Guillaume Pepy, chairman of Eurostar from 2002, have leveled the accusation at British officials (*Sunday Times* 2003). This is unfair and, in fact, all forecasts, whether advanced by consultants, companies, civil servants, or academics, have proved to be wide of the mark (Kay, Manning, and Szymanski 1989; Freud 2006) have leveled the accusation at British officials. Szymanski, one of the academics involved in the process of estimation, has conceded that errors were made. There were deficiencies in estimating broad variables such as the rate of growth of the cross-channel market, and the assumptions made about the decline of the ferries after the Tunnel opened were premature. Eurotunnel was overoptimistic about its likely revenues, the product of assuming a market share and prices which did not materialize. On the other hand, there were few precedents if any for modeling the outcome of competition between a privately owned fixed link and private sector ferries (Szymanski 2000, 413–414, 420–423). Clearly forecasting was and is a tricky business, and, indeed, it has been asserted that many transport megaprojects have suffered from overoptimistic forecasts, especially where railway transport is involved (Flyvbjerg et al. 2003, 22–25, 31–34).

Although a detailed analysis of the cross-channel market lies outside the scope of this book, we should observe that forecasting for the Tunnel was affected by the changing nature of the business over the quarter-century from 1980. In the passenger market, the leisure segment was greatly influenced by the fact that this was ceasing to be a simple geographical market, as 1970s forecasters had assumed, but was becoming more of a "what you do with your spare time" market. In this context, the competition offered by a deregulated airline industry might have been—and indeed was—anticipated, but few analysts predicted the success of the low-cost airlines such as Ryanair and Easyjet from the mid-1990s. These companies not only challenged the established airlines but also had an impact on the cross-channel market as a whole. Although their overall market share has been small, they affected all operators by transforming consumers' expectations about price. In addition, they helped to narrow the market for international rail travel, although it should be pointed out that this narrowing was also encouraged by the more conservative business strategies of Eurostar after the privatization of British Rail's company, European Passenger Services (Hay et al. 2004, 23–24, 32–33; Heslop 2004). The leisure market itself was subject to change. British holidaymakers continued to take their cars with them on visits to France, Belgium, and Germany, and there were more short trips in the 1990s, encouraged by the ferries, which were able to increase the number of passenger vehicles carried by over 60% in the 5 years before the Tunnel opened (Monopolies and Mergers Commission [MMC] 1997, para. 2.21). However, the International Passenger Survey revealed that by 2002, France, the mainstay of UK residents' foreign visits in the past, had lost its place as the number one destination to Spain, and Spain has maintained its position in subsequent years. The Tunnel's popularity as a mode of transport for UK residents making foreign visits fell back after peaking in 1998. In that year 12% of visits abroad were made via the Tunnel; by 2002 this had fallen to 9%, and in 2008 the Tunnel's share slipped below 7%, though the losses were offset to some extent by an increased use of the Tunnel by visitors *to* the UK (Department of the Environment, Transport and the Regions [DETR] 1997; Office for National Statistics [ONS] 2002, 2005, 2008). Travel to France remains the core of Tunnel business, and longer-distance train travel has remained unattractive for both leisure and business passengers. Of course, this situation may change if measures to protect the environment and limit carbon emissions are intensified, and/or if the airlines are confronted with higher costs. Nevertheless, the Tunnel has captured a sizeable share of "near-European" passenger markets, and notably 71% of the London–Paris and 64% of the London–Brussels markets (Gourvish 2006, 371; Preston and Wall 2008, 405).

Eurotunnel's financial results have of course proved extremely disappointing (see Table 6.3), way below the documented expectations of 1987–1994 (Cf. Li and Wearing 2000; Wearing 2005). However, it is important to distinguish between (a) the operating results before financial operations; (b) the underlying profit and loss; and (3) the profit/loss after exceptional items, and notably the one-off gains produced by financial restructuring, notably in 1997 and 2007. Once the trials of late opening and the November 1996 fire had been overcome, Eurotunnel achieved a turnover of around £600 million a year over the period 1998–2008, and an operating margin of around 55%. But turnover was way below the prospectus forecasts (cf. Wearing 2005, 116), and after depreciation and financial charges, losses were severe, averaging £137 million a year, 1998–2004, before exceptional items. The company made much of the fact that "cash breakeven" had been

Table 6.3   Eurotunnel Operating Results and Profit and Loss, 1994-2008 (£m)

| | Operating revenue: | | Turnover (Revenue) | Operating margin | Operating profit/loss after depreciation | Profit/loss after financial charges, tax (underlying loss[a]) | exceptional profit[b] | impairment charge | Profit/loss after exceptional items (exceptional profit, impairment charge etc.) |
|---|---|---|---|---|---|---|---|---|---|
| | Shuttles | Railways | | | | | | | |
| 1994[a] | 11 | 12 | 31 | -320 | -465 | -1,103 | 716[c] | | -387 |
| 1995 | 120 | 133 | 304 | -64 | -200 | -925 | | | -925 |
| 1996 | 150 | 207 | 504 | 134 | -29 | -716 | | | -716 |
| 1997 | 113 | 212 | 531 | 209 | 57 | -611 | | | -611 |
| 1998 | 210 | 213 | 666 | 334 | 184 | -215 | 279 | | 64 |
| 1999 | 265 | 210 | 654 | 351 | 210 | -94 | 296 | | 202 |
| 2000 | 315 | 208 | 600 | 345 | 208 | -124 | 1 | | -124 |
| 2001 | 315 | 214 | 574 | 327 | 188 | -147 | 6 | | -132 |
| 2002 | 349 | 227 | 609 | 348 | 207 | -105 | 428 | | 302 |
| 2003 | 306 | 230 | 578 | 313 | 167 | -148 | 115 | 1,300 | -1,334 |
| 2004 | 285 | 234 | 555 | 294 | 128 | -127 | -48 | 336 | -587 |
| 2005 | 295 | 235 | 541 | 299 | 153 | / | / | 1,750 | -1,971 |
| 2006 | 318 | 240 | 568 | 335 | 220 | / | / | - | -143 |
| 2007 | 382 | 199 | 590 | 330 | 196 | / | 2,733 | | 2,733 |
| 2008 | 372 | 214 | 645 | 346 | 215 | / | | | 33 |

[a] Limited operating
[a] Profits from financial restructuring, etc.
[b] Capitalization of own work.
Note: Major changes in the presentation of the accounts from 2005 and with the financial reorganization of June 2007.
Source: Eurotunnel, R&A 1994–2008; News Release, 25 January 2005. Restated figures used where given.

achieved in 2002; that is, operating revenues were sufficient to cover both costs and interest charges. However, exceptional profits from financial operations were a key element in this statistic, and in any case, in the following year a considerable sum—£1.3 billion—was deducted as an impairment charge to reflect the fact that the discounted future value (at 7%) of cash flows was much lower than the net book value of the assets. A further £336 million was deducted in 2004.

Unsurprisingly, the debt burden continued to dominate, and the disgruntled, mainly French, shareholders, disturbed by the unfulfilled promises of Eurotunnel's prospectuses, continued to challenge the company's directors in the courts. In April 2004, French shareholders, led by Nicolas Miguet, ousted the board and installed a French-dominated management team, with Jacques Maillot as chairman and Jean-Louis Raymond as chief executive. However, this radical step failed to produce immediate and effective solutions. Trading continued to be challenging in 2004, and with debt repayment and full interest payments set to resume at the end of 2005, and the minimum usage charge—toll levels guaranteed by the British and French railway operators—expiring in 2006, the search for a stable debt management regime became even more urgent. Maillot gave way to Jacques Gounon in February 2005, and when talks about a further debt restructuring began in April, it was Gounon who demanded that the creditors write off two thirds of Eurotunnel's £6.3 billion debt. He declared himself entirely opposed to a debt-for-equity swap (*Financial Times* 2005a). A challenge to his uncompromising approach was mounted by Miguet and Raymond, who resigned as chief executive, but the threat evaporated at shareholders' meetings in Calais in June. The meetings left nothing resolved, however, heralding a period of intense negotiation about Eurotunnel's future. The situation was complicated by the selling-on of much of the company's debt (*Financial Times* 2005b). In 2005 the method of accounting was changed, and a large impairment charge of £1.75 billion was incurred, producing an overall loss of almost £2 billion. Steps were then taken to write down the debt to more manageable proportions. In June 2007 a second large debt-for-equity swap was arranged, and the company's debt was reduced to €3.8 billion, then approximately £2.8 billion; a £720 million rights issue was also launched, in April 2008 (*Daily Telegraph* 2008). The company was reconstituted as Groupe Eurotunnel (GET), led by Gounon, and shareholders' interests were diluted considerably (Groupe Eurotunnel 2008). When financial information for 2007 was published, in April 2008, it revealed a £2.7 billion gain from the promised financial restructuring, an adjustment which helped to establish a modest "profit" in 2008 (Table 6.3). The draconian steps taken in 2007 may have put Eurotunnel on a more even keel, but it would be brave to predict the future of the company given the financial pressures it clearly continues to face, and in the light of recent operating problems, including a second fire, in September 2008, and interruptions to Eurostar services produced by bad weather and technical failures in December 2009–February 2010 (*Times* 2009, 2010; *Daily Telegraph* 2010).

## THE POLITICAL ECONOMY OF THE "MEGAPROJECT"

The Channel Tunnel was completed successfully without the direct involvement of public money. But construction costs and deadlines were exceeded, the Concession was revised twice, and the financial structure renegotiated. It was twenty years before Eurotunnel was able to pay its first dividend, a modest €0.04 a share in 2008, and despite the draconian reduction in shareholders' interests, the burden of debt is still heavy. Although the post-2007 position appears more stable, uncertainty about the company's long-term prospects remains a constant element. Usage charge payments and the start of the requirement to repay debts provide enormous challenges. Anguera's calculations of the cost–benefit deriving from the Tunnel produce a negative net present value (NPV) of £10 billion (in 2004 prices), and the conclusion is that the benefits to users were substantially outweighed by the costs to producers (i.e., owners) (Anguera 2006, 312). On the other hand, Anguera conceded that his cost–benefit analysis was only a partial one. It covers a much shorter period (10 years, 1994–2003) than the period of the Tunnel Concession (99 years), and excludes environmental, energy, and employment effects. There are also grounds for believing that Anguera has been too gloomy about the plight of producers: Eurotunnel, the cross-channel ferry companies, the banks, and equity investors (see below). In fact, it is all too easy to dismiss the Tunnel as a failure. The other side of the argument is that the project represents an enormous achievement in terms of construction, financial, and political engineering. And in terms of transport provision, it has captured a large share of the cross-channel and London–Paris/Brussels markets, even if the overall results have been much lower than initial expectations in the late 1980s, and the carriage of rail freight in particular has proved disappointing. However, the patent fact was that as an investment project the Tunnel cost too much, and revenues were much lower than forecast. Of course, had costs been closer to the original estimate of £2 billion for the tunneling and £4 billion in total project costs, then Eurotunnel's profit and loss account would have been more satisfactory. But whatever the trading picture, the Tunnel remains a monument to the imagination, a potent symbol of what can be achieved in the face of skepticism and financial difficulty. No doubt more surprises are in prospect, but few would currently challenge the view that the Tunnel is an essential piece of European transport infrastructure, with economic gains in France, even if the initial impact in Kent has been relatively modest (Hay et al. 2004, 46–65; Preston and Wall 2008, 410–415).

When Eurotunnel's preliminary prospectus was released in 1986, Malcolm Binks, an American banker with Merrill Lynch Capital Markets of

New York, noted that the investment "could hardly be less attractive." He referred, somewhat cynically, to the five stages of a major project: "Euphoria; Disenchantment; Search for the Guilty; Persecution of the Innocent; and Rewards for the Uninvolved" (Binks 1986). More seriously, the Channel Tunnel has several lessons to offer to those interested in the development and management of large projects (cf. Mackie and Preston 1998, 2–4; Winch 2002, 13–15, 68, 402–403; Flyvbjerg et al. 2003, 96–97; Wearing 2005). As the European Conference of Transport Ministers has recognized, it is important to work with a concessionaire that is distinct from the promoters (banks and construction companies) and which can act as project "champion"; responsibility for risk-taking should be established and clearly defined among the several parties; it is difficult to finance large infrastructure schemes with evident social benefits but speculative private gains without public guarantees; and there is a real challenge in balancing project flexibility against the need to establish a strong framework of safety and service quality (European Conference of Ministers of Transport [ECMT] 1999).

The way in which Eurotunnel was established, and, in particular, the nature of its contractual relations with TML and the railways, contributed to its difficulties. The tortuous relationship with TML owed much to the fact that the contractors were initially the promoters, and it took some time to appreciate that Eurotunnel's role was to establish a sophisticated piece of transport infrastructure and not just an engineered tunnel. At a critical stage, Eurotunnel was a fledgling company, short of expertise, and there were clear information asymmetries between it and TML, and between the banks and TML. TML began as a loose confederation of five British and five French construction companies, and it took time before the individual members of the consortium were able to function effectively as a team. In this environment, the construction contract invited difficulties, especially given the rudimentary nature of the design work before it was signed. Only the tunneling was contracted for at a fixed price, with an incentive to restrain costs: the rolling stock was procured on a cost-plus basis, the equipment as a lump sum. It was no surprise to find that the latter elements gave rise to disagreements and disputes or that construction costs rose. Graham Corbett, Eurotunnel's finance director from 1989 to 1996, offered a number of "simple lessons" to follow in large infrastructure projects, such as the need to keep credit arrangements flexible, including the introduction of public sector mezzanine finance at an early stage, the ability to protect against inflation and interest rate movements, and use of a performance-related element in rewarding debt; the need to avoid design and build contracts where the contractor is not going to be the operator; avoidance of unwieldy construction consortia; and above all, the need to embark on the design work before construction starts (Corbett 1996a, 69–71; 1996b). The overoptimism of successive traffic and revenue forecasts also came to haunt the company and certainly produced a legacy in the Railway Usage Contract, with its minimum usage charge that few felt would become operational. In all this, the responsibility lay firmly with the private sector players, although the two governments presided over the arrangements and did not seek to challenge them.

## THE CHANNEL TUNNEL AND THE
## ROLE OF THE PUBLIC SECTOR

The Tunnel also provides important and salutary lessons for government–industry relations, especially with international megaprojects, in areas such as the tension between economic and political evaluations of major investment schemes; and the tension between the Treasury and sponsoring departments in evaluating, distributing, and managing risk in public–private ventures. Above all, it provided valuable experience for those embarking enthusiastically upon the British government's Private Finance Initiatives. As we have seen, at several points in this long story, the project foundered or was put on ice. One cannot emphasize enough how difficult it was for the "tunnelistas" to wage their campaigns through the serried ranks of skeptics and opponents. Undoubtedly, much of the problem from the 1950s lay in uncertainty over ownership and governance issues. Should the Tunnel be built and operated by the public sector? Should it be constructed with private capital and operated publicly? Should it be constructed and operated by the private sector? These questions were not straightforward and were influenced by the fact that skepticism about the prospect of financial returns was an enduring feature from the early 1960s. There were to be two decades of fluctuating debate before a solution was found, and the one chosen has certainly not been free of criticism.

In this climate, the importance of critical actors should not be underestimated. In the 1960s and 1970s there was the enthusiasm of the French and British transport ministers Edgar Pisani and Barbara Castle (fleetingly); the unequivocal determination of Edward Heath's transport minister, John Peyton; and the positive approach shown by civil servants in the British transport ministry, such as Overy Gingell, John Barber, Peter Kemp, and Susan Fogarty. In the mid-1980s, the players were able to punch a more effective weight. There was the enthusiasm of the French ministers Pierre Mauroy and Jean Auroux, and the executive determination on the British side of Margaret Thatcher and her transport minister Nicholas Ridley; the effective civil service partnership of Andrew Lyall and Guy Braibant; the entrepreneurial response of large contracting firms such as Costain and Dumez; and the risk-taking support (if later regretted) of the major British and French banks. But the initiation of the Tunnel project in 1986 was only the start of the challenge. As *Construction*

*News* noted, when Thatcher and Mitterrand announced their support in January 1986, "many observers felt that they were watching little more than an elaborate public relations exercise" (*Construction News* 1988). There had been many of these in the past, a plethora of reports, reconsiderations, holding operations, "feet-dragging," and "playing it long." Even at this stage, the project would have foundered, as it had in the 1880s and the mid-1970s, without a continuity of political support from Thatcher and Mitterand, without the extraordinary drive inside Eurotunnel of Sir Alastair Morton, British co-chairman from 1987 to 1996, and the less strident but equally effective persistence of his French co-chairmen André Bénard and Patrick Ponsolle. Also important was the critical intervention of the Bank of England at key points, and the nerve held by the sponsoring banks, harassed contractors, and key bureaucrats in the British and French finance and transport departments. The two governments often pursued different agendas within the "quadripartite quilt" of decision making. For the French, the 1975 cancellation had been a major obstacle to a revival a decade later, but a determination to reverse economic decline and promote the regeneration of the Nord–Pas de Calais region was a major incentive. For the British, the insistence on full private sector financing proved the key to a change of heart, although, as we have seen, it often proved difficult to prevent the governments from being dragged into the support of private enterprise, and, in any case, the public support offered in the form of road and rail infrastructure was substantial (Mallaby 1994). Whether the Tunnel should have been built, or whether the Tunnel should have been built as a private sector venture, are legitimate questions to ask. However, the essential point to make is that it was built, and the history of the largest engineering project of the 20th century, chaotic as it has sometimes been, represents the supreme triumph of political will and entrepreneurial optimism over economic skepticism.

Finally, one might also challenge the notion that all of the owners necessarily lost out in supporting the project. The participating banks have of course experienced considerable losses if they held onto their investments, but many of them sold on the debt and could offset their putative losses with the lucrative commissions they enjoyed from placing the issues. Shareholders who held onto their investments made losses, it is true, but many British investors made considerable capital gains by selling when the price was high. Smaller shareholders, particularly those in France, who stayed loyal to the project, saw the value of the capital diminish substantially, but they were also offered generous travel concessions, and if these are priced at the average tariff charged, then one might argue that much of their capital investment was returned to them in the form of free or reduced travel tickets. Of course, it is more difficult to say that British and French taxpayers have benefited from the Tunnel. A conservative estimate of British government commitments indicates that at least £3 billion of public funds was invested prior to opening in 1994, and, with the Rail Link, around

£4 billion since then. However, now that the Rail Link has finally been completed, it seems likely that returns on a more realistic evaluation of the capital base will be healthier.

## NOTES

1. The only major railway scheme in the 1980s, apart from the Tunnel, was the electrification of the East Coast Main Line from King's Cross to Edinburgh, with an estimated cost of £306 million in 1984 (or £1.4 billion in 2009 prices).

## BIBLIOGRAPHY

Affuso, L., J. Masson, and D. Newbery 2003, "Comparing Investments in New Transport Infrastructure: Roads versus Railways?" *Fiscal Studies* 24(3): 275–315.

Anguera, R. 2006, "The Channel Tunnel—An ex post Economic Evaluation," *Transportation Research* Pt. A: 40: 291–315.

Anson, M. and G. Crompton 2009, "Predicting, Providing, Sustaining, Integrating? British Transport Policy since 1945," in *Business in Britain in the Twentieth Century*, eds. R. Coopey and P. Lyth, Oxford: Oxford University Press.

Binks, M. 1986, Letter to Al and Frank Davidson, 18 June, Technical Studies Inc. Archive, carton #13 f67, Boston: Harvard Business School.

Clifton, J., F. Comín, and D. Díaz Fuentes, "Privatizing Public Enterprises in the European Union 1960–2002: Ideological, Pragmatic, Inevitable?" *Journal of European Public Policy* 13(5): 736–756.

*Construction News* 1988, 10 March, 30.

Corbett, G. 1996a, *Project Finance International*, 100, 3 July.

Corbett, G. 1996b, "The Channel Tunnel—Managing the Financial Risk," Paper presented at the International Tunnelling Conference, Basel, 3–4 December.

*Daily Telegraph* 2008, 29–30 April, 29 May.

*Daily Telegraph* 2010, 13 February, 19.

Department for Transport (DfT) 2009, "£6 M for Humber Bridge Improvements," Press Release, 27 October.

Department of the Environment, Transport and the Regions (DETR) 1997, Cross Channel Passenger Traffic.

European Conference of Ministers of Transport (ECMT) 1999, Paper ECMT/CS(99)21, March.

*Financial Times* 1994, 1 January, xix.

*Financial Times* 2004, 16 September, 25.

*Financial Times* 2005a, 27 April, 22.

*Financial Times* 2005b, 18–19 June 2005, M1–2.

Florio, M. 2004, *The Great Divestiture: Evaluating the Welfare Impact of the British Privatizations 1979–1997*, Cambridge, Mass.: MIT Press.

Flyvbjerg, B., N. Bruzelius, and W. Rothengatter 2003, *Megaprojects and Risk: An Anatomy of Ambition*, Cambridge: Cambridge University Press.

Freud, D. 2006, *Freud in the City: 20 Turbulent Years at the Sharp End of the Global Finance Revolution*, London: Bene Factum Publishing.

Gourvish, T. 1986, *British Railways 1948–73: A Business History*, Cambridge: Cambridge University Press.

Gourvish, T. 2002, *British Rail 1974–97: From Integration to Privitisation*, Oxford: Oxford University Press.

Gourvish, T. 2006, *The Official History of Britain and the Channel Tunnel*, Abingdon: Routledge.

Gourvish, T. 2008, "Project Finance and the Archives of Entrepreneurship. The Channel Tunnel, 1957–1975," in *The Human Factor in Banking History: Entrepreneurship, Organization, Management and Personnel*, eds. E. Green and M.P. Fraser, Athens: Alpha Bank.

Grimsey, D. and M.K. Lewis 2002, "Evaluating the Risks of Public Private Partnerships for Infrastructure Projects," *International Journal of Project Management* 20: 107–118.

Grimsey, D. and M.K. Lewis 2004, *Public Private Partnerships: The Worldwide Revolution in Infrastructure Provision and Project Finance*, Cheltenham: Edward Elgar.

Group Eurotunnel 2008, Refrence Document for 15 April 2007.

Hall, J. 1998, "Private Opportunity, Public Benefit?" *Fiscal Studies* 19(2): 121–140.

Hay, A., K. Meredith and R. Vickerman 2004, "The Impact of the Channel Tunnel on Kent and Relationships with Nord-Pas de Calais," Canterbury: University of Kent Centre for European, Regional and Transport Economics.

Heslop, A. 2004, British Railways Board manager, interviewed by Terry Gourvish, London, 1 July.

House of Commons Select Committee on Environment, Transport and Regional Affairs 1999, Report on Regional Eurostar Services, P.P.1998–1999, xxvi, HC89.

Jackson, P.M. and C.M. Price, eds. 1994, *Privatisation and Regulation: A Review of the Issues*, London: Longman.

Kamel, K. and R. Matthewman 2008, "The Non-Transport Impacts of High Speed Trains on Regional Economic Development: A Review of the Literature," West Malling: Locate in Kent.

Kay, J., A. Manning, and S. Szymanski 1989, "The Economic Consequences of the Channel Tunnel," *Economic Policy* 8: 211–234.

Li, C. and B. Wearing 2000, "The Financing and Financial Results of Eurotunnel: Retrospect and Prospect," University of Essex Accounting Department Working Paper No. 00/13, November.

Mackie, P. and J. Preston 1998, "Twenty-one Sources of Error and Bias in Transport Project Appraisal," *Transport Policy* 5: 1–7.

Mallaby, Sir C. 1994, British Ambassador, Paris, letter to Douglas Hurd (Foreign Secretary) on "The Channel Tunnel," 24 May, Foreign and Commonwealth Office file ref. MDT178/3/94.

Martin, B. 1993, *In the Public Interest? Privatization and Public Sector Reform*, London: Zed Books.

Martin, S. and D. Parker 1997, *The Impact of Privatisation: Ownership and Corporate Performance in the UK*, London: Routledge.

Millward, R. 2007, "Review," *Enterprise and Society* 8(4): 970–972.

Monopolies and Mergers Commission (MMC) 1997, *The Peninsular and Oriental Steam Navigation Company and Stena Line AB: A Report on the Proposed Merger*.

Morrow, E.W., L.M. McDonnell, and R.Y. Arguden 1988, *Understanding the Outcomes of Megaprojects: A Quantitative Analysis of Very Large Civil Projects*, Santa Monica, Calif.: RAND Corporation.

Myddelton, D.R. 1987, *They Meant Well: Government Project Disasters*, London: Institute of Economic Affairs.

Myddelton, D.R. 2007, *They Meant Well: Government Project Disasters*, London: Institute of Economic Affairs.

Office for National Statistics (ONS) 2002, 2005, 2008, *Travel Trends*.

Parker, D. 2009, *The Official History of Privatisation, Vol. 1, The Formative Years 1970–1987*, Abingdon: Routledge.

Preston, J. and G. Wall 2008, "The *Ex-ante* and *Ex-post* Economic and Social Impacts of the Introduction of High-Speed Trains in South East England," *Planning Practice and Research* 23(3): 403–422.

Rail Freight Group 2002, "Cross-Channel Rail Freight Seeks £15 m Emergency Government Support," Press Release, 14 March.

*Sunday Times* 2003, 28 September, 30.

Szymanski, S. 2000, "*Nostrae Culpae*: Forecasts and Out-turns of Cross Channel Competition between the Ferries and the Tunnel," in *Privatization and Deregulation of Transport*, eds. B. Bradshaw and H. Lawton Smith, Basingstoke: Macmillan.

*Times* 2009, 21 December, 10–11, 20.

*Times* 2010, 22 February, 14.

Transport Statistics Great Britain (TSGB) 2009, London: DfT.

Wearing, R. 2005, *Cases in Corporate Governance*, London: Sage.

Wentworth, M.A. and A.K.C. Beresford 1998, "Major U.K. Tolled Road Crossings Reviewed," *Transport Policy* 5: 51–59.

Winch, G.M. 1996, "The Channel Tunnel: le projet du siècle," London: Le Groupe Bagnolet Working Paper.

Winch, G.M. 2002, Managing Construction Projects: An Information Processing Approach, Oxford: Blackwell.

# 7 Finance and Structure of the State-Owned Enterprise in Italy

## IRI from the Golden Age to the Fall

*Leandro Conte and Giandomenico Piluso*

The state-owned enterprise has had a first-rank place in Italian economic growth in the last century, although its ability to overcome gaps in technology and institutions proved to be somewhat insufficient. At a certain point, in the 1960s, it was so successful in coping with modernization processes that even in Britain it seemed reasonable to argue about the advantages of adopting the Italian model of public enterprise (Posner and Woolf 1967; Tomlinson 1999). The ensuing decline and, eventually, the dramatic fall of the Italian state-owned enterprise have been related to a vast array of factors. Some factors are typically endogenous, as when personal managerial capabilities are concerned or political mistakes are assumed to be responsible for capital misallocation and losses in profitability. In these cases, the analysis emphasized what are essentially degenerative processes within the model, also in relation to changes in the international context. Some factors are instead typically exogenous, as it may be when external price shocks are taken into account and the oil shock or the deregulation wave is considered. There is even a more radical interpretation of the end of the public enterprise, which emphasized the relevance of changes in technologies, namely, the underlying shift from investment-based strategies to innovation-based strategies, as the fundamental reason for its collapse (Acemoglu, Aghion, and Zilibotti 2006).

This chapter argues that all of these factors are better understood if attention is directed to the relationship between finance and structure within the state-owned enterprise in the long term. This approach suggests a new perspective on the causes of the sharp decline of the largest state-owned holding, Istituto per la Ricostruzione Industriale (IRI), by pointing out that a incoherent governance model failed to react to a rapidly changing environment, while a huge amount of debt undermined the financial position of the group. Thus, it was not possible to pursue appropriate investments in emerging technology, and financial weakness cut off the state-owned enterprise from the emerging stream of sectors and innovations.

This chapter is organized as follows: the first section presents in general terms the conceptual frame employed in the analysis; the second section deals with the capital structure of the top 200 manufacturing firms from 1952 to

1991, in order to assess to what extent corporate ownership has been relevant in determining different or similar degrees and dynamics of their capitalization; the third section addresses the specific financial structure of IRI as holding company over time in relation to the main changes which occurred within the domestic financial system; the fourth section considers the financial dynamics of sectoral sub-holdings in relation to investments, by estimating the relative weight of the individual sectors in driving the debt of IRI out of control; finally, in the last section, some conclusions will be drawn.

## FINANCING STATE-OWNED FIRMS IN ITALY: AN INTRODUCTION

The state-owned enterprise became established in Italy as a result of a series of rather erratic political choices, culminating in the early 1930s in the decision to employ public funds to finance enterprises which were capable of integrating the sectoral matrix of the second industrial revolution. Since the early 1930s, the state-owned enterprise has had a major role in shaping the Italian corporate landscape, and the largest state-owned holding, IRI, had a pivotal role in all of the capital-intensive sectors by supplying both physical capital and managerial capabilities. Following a parallel path in the 1920s and 1930s, the central authorities promoted the creation of special credit institutions which could avert financial instability phenomena frequently related to mixed banks, at least up to the mid-1930s, when universal banking was formally banned for several decades. These state-owned financial intermediaries should also have compensated imbalances caused by the lack of savings necessary to support long-term investments usually carried out via short-term bank loans, according to a scheme which in fact proved to be a source of inflation and instability. Thus, a coherent model emerged in the 1930s in which state-owned manufacturing firms and financial intermediaries had to foster capital formation processes in a highly regulated context of financial and monetary stability. The same conditions were once again present, in the form of a lack of appropriate industrial structures and a risk of financial and monetary instability, at the end of World War II. In the postwar recovery, the state-owned industry had a significant role in the institutional framework in which the Italian economy adjusted itself in the reconstruction of the international economy as a whole (Posner and Woolf 1967; Barca, 1997). This institutional model worked quite well, until the late 1960s, by enhancing investment rates, technological transfers, and organizational modernization in all of the sectors responsible for the high growth rates reached during the golden age (Rossi and Toniolo 1996).

During the recovery years, governments and economic policies assigned the task of investing in strategic sectors to IRI, as the major state-owned holding company, with the aim of adapting these sectors' production capacity to more advanced technological standards, attaining mass production by carrying out an "Americanization" of firms. Italy's joining the European Coal and Steel Community (ECSC)—which was rejected by the British government in order to protect its own state-owned enterprise—showed that this policy was based on those principles inspiring a state entrepreneurship which considered competition and the ability of public enterprises to be actually competitive as essential conditions (Ranieri 1999). According to this vision, the IRI group can thus be seen as a good example of the separation of ownership and control carried out in Italian history and public managers as architects of economic development (Amatori 2000).

The literature sets the end of the drive behind this mission in the decade between the early 1960s and the early 1970s, when the weakness of the public sector was characterized as insufficient coordination (Posner and Woolf 1967). The following factors contributed equally to this conclusion: the wearing out of the postwar impulse; the end of the managerial careers of that group of "nationalist" managers who had started in the 1920s and 1930s; and the necessity of launching a new cycle of industrial investments, or at least to reform and reorganize those industrial groups which had developed merely on the basis of economies of scale (De Cecco 1997).

The 1963 watershed, marked by the international economic slowdown, the raising of interest rates by the Bank of Italy, the nationalization of the electrical sector and the birth of the center-left governments, led to a relatively new role for the state-owned enterprise, in particular for IRI, which began to act as the main government agent. The planning policies pursued by center-left governments put IRI at the center of the scene by launching a new phase of public investments to counterbalance the fall in investment rates in the private sector (Lavista 2010). With the creation of the Ministero delle Partecipazioni Statali (Ministry of State Participations) (1956), IRI took on a new role, which became apparent in the early 1960s. The separation between ownership and control was less distinct. Investment decisions, especially in the iron, steel, and mechanical engineering sectors were no longer as focused on implementing a state entrepreneurship "completely similar" to the private entrepreneurship. They were instead rather increasingly focused on supporting the mainly political objectives of income redistribution and social cohesion, by coping with the reemergence of industrial conflict and the needs deriving from rapid urbanization and migration flows within the country.

The corporate finance framework thus stemmed from the idea that financing the enterprise meant financing the "industry," placing it in a condition of technological and productive excellence on a level with the average of its sector and ultimately raising incomes, especially the consumption of certain categories of goods, in a number of regional areas. This "new" IRI, therefore, was configured in the expectation of the ongoing of a long cycle of industrial growth in iron, steel, and mechanical sectors, an expectation subsequently thwarted by the international market turmoil which took place in the wake of the oil crisis, the end of dollar pegged payments, while stagflation phenomena were taking place on all national markets. These exogenous shocks hit rather harshly the finance structure of the state-owned enterprise and, in particular, IRI entered a long phase of decline in profitability and financial soundness as debt grew unbearably in comparison with its profit margins.

It should be emphasized that, although these analyses are, on the one hand, plausible and generally accepted, on the other hand, they are not completely on the mark as they interpreted the failure of the state-owned enterprise on the basis of economic policy categories. These analyses suggest the loss of profitability of state-owned enterprises was mainly due either to errors made in defining sectors and technologies in which to invest (on behalf of the ownership/government) or to the effect of allocative distortions introduced by the regulator (i.e., the Parliament). Though persuasive, therefore, they do not shed light on the methods or the relationships between structure and business strategy that gave rise to the phenomenon, thus ascribing its outcome to the obligations deriving from its public nature rather than to the choices made by its top management and the institutional contexts which they themselves created.[1]

Corporate governance, for the most part, is concerned with maintaining an adequate relationship between financing sources and industrial investment programs. This clear requirement is even truer in the case of firms with public capital rather than private capital. The objectives of these different shareholders can differ, in terms of the level of expected returns and, consequently, also in terms of investment plans. These conditions are subject to a natural increase in complexity if the state-owned enterprise is organized as a holding of companies, each in turn made up mainly of state-owned capital but sometimes of minority stakes provided by private investors or shareholders. The complexity in this case derives not only from the interaction of entrepreneurial agents but also from the possibility that the holding company management may 'supplement' the provision of capital destined for investment, or for its own running, and that of its controlled companies, through the raising of capital on both financial and credit markets (equity, bonds, and short-term loans). According to this perspective, the regulation of ownership rights might exert an influence on the profitability of companies and on investments to the point of affecting industrial growth, and different owners may have different expectations regarding the latter.

## FINANCIAL STRUCTURE AND OWNERSHIP OF THE TOP 200 MANUFACTURING FIRMS: EQUITY AND DEBT

Previous research has generated empirical evidence on the most important state-owned manufacturing enterprises, showing how their characteristic features did not stem exclusively from events regarding the availability or profitability of equity capital, but also, and in significant terms, from debt dynamics, at least from the mid-1960s onward (Conte and Piluso 2010). The main aim of this chapter is to use these research findings to analyze investment and capitalization choices, highlighting how the latter had profound repercussions on the governance of the state-owned enterprise. On the basis of the above approach, we examine the financing dynamics of IRI and its main sector sub-holdings (Finsider, Finmeccanica, Stet) in relation to the specific form of the corporate governance within the group.

Before analyzing the debt dynamics of IRI and its main sub-holdings, which coordinated controlled firms by sectors, we will first illustrate the results of a study of the top 200 Italian manufacturing firms from 1952 to 2001 as ranked by total assets (Conte and Piluso 2010). The study examined the top 200 manufacturing companies in terms of the composition of their capital structure (equity and debt), highlighting the main trends of the whole group as well as the particular trends of the state-owned enterprises within the sample.[2]

The analysis of the composition of sources of financing on the basis of equity and debt shows a rather significant undercapitalization of Italian enterprises for the entire period examined, with regard to both state-owned enterprises and private enterprises. The relationship between debt and equity shows a clear tendency on the part of the larger enterprises to collect most of their funds through debt rather than risk capital underwritten by shareholders. During the second half of the 20th century, from the early 1950s to the early 1990s, the overall debt amounted to two thirds of the entire resources, almost double the risk capital invested in the same companies (see Figure 7.1).

In the 1960s and 1970s, the gross debt-to-equity ratio reached particularly high levels (in 1971, the debt to equity ratio was 4.26), while in the latter half of the 1970s, the high debt level was associated with an increasing uncertainty generated by the upward movement of interest rates in nominal terms: both these conditions—high debt levels and high interest rates—penalized, to a growing extent, those enterprises that relied on external funds rather than

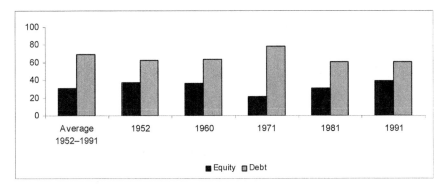

*Figure 7.1* Equity and debt of the top 200 Italian manufacturing enterprises (% shares).

Sources: *Notizie statistiche* and Imita.db; Mediobanca, *Le principali società italiane, ad annos.*

their own funds to finance activities and investments. Table 7.1 shows that the two sectors of the Italian manufacturing enterprise, the state-owned and the private, were not subject to radically different dynamics. The deterioration of the financial situation negatively affected all of the large manufacturing enterprises despite the partial recovery which can be noted in the last two benchmark years of the series (1981 and 1991) (Amatori and Brioschi 1997; Amatori 1999, 2000). The largest manufacturing firms became more dependent on external funding (especially on short-term bank lending) just as interest rates rose significantly. Although real interest rates were actually negative at some points, according to Ciocca and Nardozzi (1996), a higher nominal cost of money exerted a tight constraint as profitability and managerial efficiency declined. Thus, for about a decade, a macroeconomic variable—the interest rate—had a marked and negative influence on enterprises' activities and performance (Conte and Piluso 2010).[3]

The use of external financing has been attributed to sector variables in the general literature, mainly, capital intensity, the degree of technological maturity along the life cycle, and the average size of the enterprises (Rajan and Zingales 1995, 1998; Fisman and Love 2004). The Italian case has its own specific variables, namely, the governance model of the large enterprise (Barca 1994; Bianco and Casavola 1996; Bianco 2003; Bianchi et al. 2005), the feeble supply of capital interested in underwriting issuances of shares as a result of monetary policies which rapidly steered households savings toward substantial investment in public debt (Ciocca 2000), and the specific regulation of financial and stock markets that discouraged firms from listing (Pagano, Panetta, and Zingales 1996; Siciliano 2001).

Furthermore, these variables interacted with the economic cycle. The general trend appears to be toward a further worsening of these ratios as a result of the deterioration of the financial situation for the largest industrial enterprises at the end of the 1960s and along the following decade. The rapid increase in debt for major firms was also due to the reduced capacity of capital-intensive sectors in the wake of shocks in prices of raw materials

*Table 7.1*   Equity and Debt of the top 200 Italian Manufacturing Enterprises, 1951–1991 (% Shares)

|  | *Average 1952–1991* | *1952* | *1960* | *1971* | *1981* | *1991* |
|---|---|---|---|---|---|---|
| equity private enterprises | 29,59 | 31,71 | 37,62 | 16,55 | 32,52 | 34,96 |
| equity State-owned enterprises | 32,34 | 27,5 | 37,41 | 25,81 | 28,68 | 43,07 |
| debt private enterprises | 70,4 | 68,28 | 62,37 | 83,44 | 67,47 | 65,03 |
| debt State-owned enterprises | 67,65 | 72,49 | 62,58 | 74,18 | 71,31 | 56,92 |

Sources: *Notizie statistiche* and Imita.db; Mediobanca, *Le principali società italiane, ad annos.*

and energy products. In the 1970s, the severe financial crisis involving the most important industrial groups (both state-owned and private)—such as Ansaldo, Fiat, Montedison, Pirelli, and Ilva (Doria 1989; Brioschi et al. 1990; Marchi and Marchionatti 1992; Amatori and Brioschi 1997; Amatori 1999)—mirrors a more generalized tendency within the Italian industrial scene (Coltorti 1988; Frasca and Marotta 1988).

The relative position of the two sets of enterprises (the state-owned and the private) also varies noticeably by benchmark year, showing a moderate equivalence of the equity component in the first two years, close to the average for 1952–1991 or even higher. In 1952 and 1960, private enterprises in the sample are more capitalized than state-owned ones. Subsequently, there is strong contraction of the equity of private enterprises to 1971 (17%). The ratio for state-owned firms also contracts, but levels do not differ radically from the average for 1952–1991 and there is a return to fairly good levels of capitalization in the last two benchmark years. It is interesting to note the relative level of capitalization of state-owned enterprises just before the start of privatizations (see Figure 7.1).

In general, therefore, the composition of funds between equity capital and debt appears less unstable in the state-owned enterprises over time. This was probably due to the easier access to the risk capital component provided by the Parliament as fresh funds were injected through increases of the endowment funds (*fondi di dotazione*).[4] This option in fact was not available for private enterprises, which in some cases resorted to financial leverage which permitted the owning families to maintain the control of the firm even if they held minority stakes, as it happened to be, for example, in the cases of Fiat and Pirelli (Barca and Trento 1997).[5]

The difference between the two sets, at any rate, is consistent with the importance of Mediobanca in those years in assuring a certain stability in the ownership structure of the largest private firms (Colajanni 1991; Piluso 2005). The above point may be further explained by the analysis of the average and median values of the debt-to-net-worth ratio for the top 200 private and state-owned manufacturing enterprises. Table 7.2 shows the main differences in the relationship between corporate structure and finance. First, state-owned enterprises appear to be more dependent on debt than private enterprises. Having measured the net worth as the sum of equity (or the endowment fund) + reserve + profits—losses (i.e., the net worth might be inferior to the equity capital whereas losses exceeded the equity component), we observe that state-owned enterprises' debt/net worth ratios, relative to private enterprise, are higher than the relative debt/equity ratios in Table 7.1 as a likely consequence of reiterated losses in some sectors. Second, the net difference between average and median values, particularly evident for the group of public firms, shows that a small group of large state-owned firms tended to depend on debt to such an extent as to affect the entire group (also because of the increase of the state-owned component in the last three benchmark years).

The difference in the relative debt over equity ratio in the state-owned and private sectors is not consistent with the thesis of a complete similarity between the two sets (Giannetti and Vasta 2003, 2006). There is in fact a strong decline in the equity–debt ratio for the state-owned component as from the late 1960s and in the ensuing decade. Such a remarkable decline in the financial structure of the top state-owned enterprises appears to be connected to two negative phenomena: (1) a sharp drop in profitability rates for this group, and (2) increasing difficulties encountered by those capital-intensive sectors in which state-owned firms were particularly concentrated, due to the combined effect of the astonishing variations in the price of raw materials and intermediate goods, largely used in those sectors, and of the relative obsolescence of the technology employed by enterprises (Giannetti and Pastorelli 2007).

From the early 1970s until the beginning of the 1980s, there was a robust increase in the number of state-owned enterprises ranking among the top 200 manufacturing enterprises (there were 44 in 1971 and 58 in 1981). The average values in Table 7.2 show a rise in the debt/net worth ratio from 3.5 in 1960 to 9.7 in 1971, to a peak of 12.6 in 1981, followed by a drop to 8.1 in 1991. Once again, median values indicate that the financial decline of state-owned enterprises depends, primarily, on a set of companies, whose debt worsens to a greater extent. The set of enterprises that shows the greatest increase in debt over equity is made up of those firms included in the Ateco DI, DK, and DJ sections (iron, steel, and mechanical engineering). IRI's presence was predominant among the

*Table 7.2*   Ratio of Debt to Net Worth for the Top 200 Manufacturing Firms, 1936–1991

|  | 1936 | 1952 | 1960 | 1971 | 1981 | 1991 |
|---|---|---|---|---|---|---|
| Top 200 manufacturing enterprises (number) | 200 | 200 | 200 | 200 | 200 | 200 |
| debt/net worth ratio, average | 1,5 | 6,4 | 2,6 | 4,9 | 7,1 | 3,9 |
| debt/net worth ratio, median | 0,7 | 3,3 | 1,7 | 2,9 | 4,1 | 2,1 |
| State-owned enterprises (number) | 14 | 21 | 23 | 44 | 58 | 47 |
| debt/net worth ratio, average | 2,5 | 13,5 | 3,5 | 9,7 | 12,6 | 8,1 |
| debt/net worth ratio, median | 2,1 | 3,9 | 2,9 | 5,3 | 6,1 | 3,2 |
| Private enterprises (number) | 186 | 179 | 177 | 156 | 142 | 153 |
| debt/net worth ratio, average | 1,5 | 5,6 | 2,4 | 3,6 | 4,7 | 2,7 |
| debt/net worth ratio, median | 0,6 | 2,9 | 1,6 | 2,6 | 3,5 | 1,8 |

Sources: *Notizie statistiche* and Imita.db; Mediobanca, *Le principali società italiane, ad annos.*

state-owned component of the large enterprises in these sectors, and its industrial companies were grouped and organized into two of its sub-holdings (Finsider and Finmeccanica), while other state-owned firms were also operating in those sectors, even to a lesser extent, through the metal and mechanical Efim group (Conte and Piluso 2010).

## STRUCTURE AND FINANCE OF IRI
## AS HOLDING COMPANY

The ability of individual state-owned enterprises to raise capital for investments depended on the financial policies of the holding companies to which they belonged, whose asset structure in turn depended signifi-cantly on government and parliamentary decisions regarding the injection of additional capital in the holdings' endowment funds (Barca and Trento 1997; Amatori 2000). IRI's equity and debt dynamics reflect both a politi-cal resolve to increase the endowment funds of the major state-owned holding and the importance of the bond market for the state-owned enter-prises as a medium- and long-term debt provision, a market whose basic structure had been conceived and fine-tuned by Alberto Beneduce in the 1930s (Bonelli 1985).

Figure 7.2 illustrates IRI's capital raising dynamics. From the recovery until the mid-1970s, we can observe a relatively gradual progression of both equity and debt, obviously related to investment expansion and the parallel increase in the number of enterprises within the whole group.

As can be observed in terms of constant values (1970), IRI managed to collect resources through medium- and long-term debt through the bond market and special credit institutions (*istituti di credito speciale*). The mid-1960s mark a rapid drop in debt capacity, countered by an increase in equity provision until the first years of the 1970s. The oil shocks' decade sees, due to inflation, a progressive decline in IRI's assets, which in the 1980s leads to special support measures by the government. The access to risk capi-tal and to long-term debt was particularly good for IRI in the subsequent period, at least up to the early 1990s when IRI was quickly forced to reduce its debt. The amount of each of these main components at constant values (1970 lire) and their relations are plotted in Figures 7.3 and 7.4.

Figure 7.3 shows the provision of capital through the bond market. The fact that this provision was ample and on the increase until the second half of the 1970s allowed IRI to support industrial growth during the "eco-nomic miracle" years, but its rapid decline following the 1963–1964 crisis led to the need for tough choices in order to complete the industrial invest-ment programs. The growing difficulties encountered in the bond market from the beginning of the 1970s were caused by the declining interest of investors and savers in buying bonds issued by state-owned holding com-panies, and overlapped with the spread of the "double intermediation"

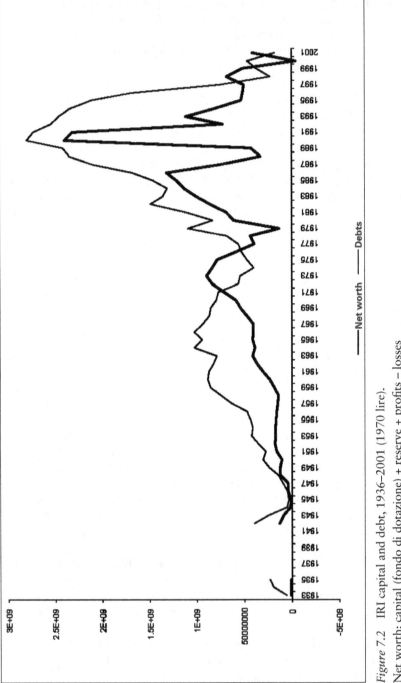

*Figure 7.2*   IRI capital and debt, 1936–2001 (1970 lire).

Net worth: capital (fondo di dotazione) + reserve + profits – losses
Debts: long-term debts (bonds and other long-term debts) + short-term debts
*Source:* IRI, *Official balance-sheets and financial statements, ad annos.*

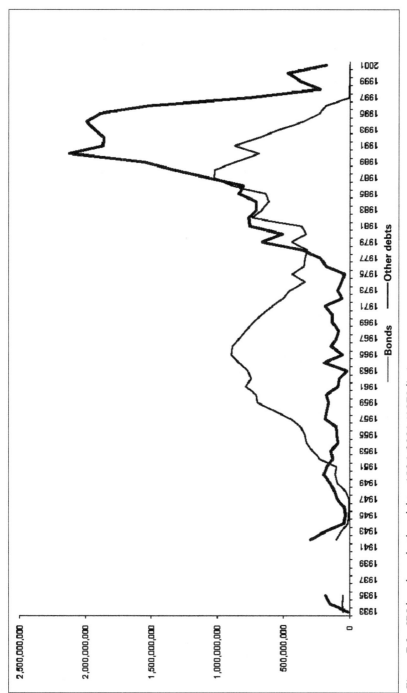

*Figure 7.3*   IRI bonds and other debts, 1936–2001 (1970 lire).
Other debts: long-term debts + short-term debts vs financial institutions and nonfinancial institutions
*Source*: IRI, *Official balance sheets and financial statements, ad annos.*

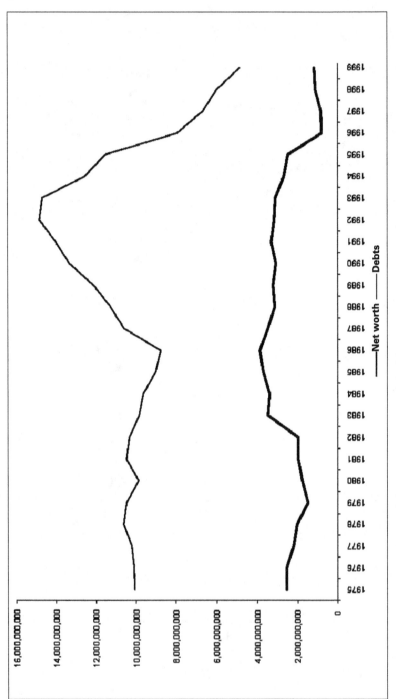

*Figure 7.4*   Net worth and debts of the IRI group (consolidated), 1975–1999 (in 1970 lire).

Net worth: capital ("fondo di dotazione") + reserve + profits - losses
Debts: long-term debts (bonds and other long-term debts) + short-term debts
*Source:* IRI, *Official balance-sheets and financial statements, ad annos.*

(*doppia intermediazione*) within the banking system. As the bond market sharply declined from the late 1960s, as a consequence of inflationary expectations, the so-called double intermediation took place. The "double bonds intermediation" originated in the fact that special credit institutions, such as Istituto Mobiliare Italiano (IMI), issued bonds which were not completely underwritten by investors or savers, so that the central monetary authorities were induced to force commercial banks to put such bonds in their portfolio as prudent reserves. As a consequence, the allocative efficiency of the banking system as a whole declined substantially in the 1970s, at the very moment when industrial firms needed a good response from the supply side. On the supply side, this loss of allocative effectiveness by the banking system might explain why financial intermediaries as a whole proved to be unable to act as a good selector of more dynamic and innovative industrial firms in the period (Piluso 1999).[6]

The increase of other debt components appears to be in line with the observations of Gian Lupo Osti, former manager at IRI, in a memoir on the Finsider group. From the beginning of the 1970s, IRI and in particular Finsider, due to the fact that they had to give up fund raising by means of bonds, had had to incur a growing amount of short-term debt at high interest rates levied by the commercial banks. The shift in maturity of debts and interest rate levels injected factors of instability into its own financial structure, thus making it vulnerable to political pressure on the management (Osti 1993, 276).

The data from the consolidated financial statements confirm the tendencies inferred from the firm-level balance sheets data. The consolidated financial statements, furthermore, also give indications as to the area actually controlled by the holding companies. As can be seen, IRI's undercapitalization appears persistent and uncontrollable until the mid-1990s (see Figure 7.4).

## STRUCTURE AND FINANCIAL CAPACITY OF THE SECTOR SUB-HOLDINGS

In agreement with Chandler, we assume as efficient a firm whose structure is consistent with its strategy, and we verify if the empirical evidence could confirm this assumption. To this end, we now consider the operating components of the holding IRI and its sectoral sub-holdings (Stet, Finsider, Finmeccanica, Fincantieri) from the beginning of the 1950s to the end of the holding's lifetime. In particular, variations in the financial structure of the balance sheets of the sectoral sub-holdings were compared to those of the entire holding's balance sheets and, as from 1975, to the consolidated balance sheets of the entire group, in order to highlight the dynamics created in the governance of IRI and the difficulties the latter incurred, particularly in the management of the processes of vertical integration, namely, the adoption of new roles both on the productive and the financial level. The composition of the liabilities of the holding company and its sub-holdings must also be correlated with the composition of the liabilities of the largest operating enterprises, in that these, given their industrial trajectories and their relative size, could affect the dynamics of the entire group substantially. In the current state of the art, we have reliable information on the financial structure of the state-owned industrial firms only for the second half of the century and only for three of the sub-holdings (Finmeccanica, Finsider, Stet), while there is still insufficient data for Fincantieri.[7]

At this point, a summary of the history of these sub-holdings is necessary to facilitate understanding of the findings attained through the quantitative approach.

Stet was created in October 1933 to manage the telephone shareholdings acquired by IRI after the bailout of the Sip-Stipel group and the Timo and Telve telephone companies. The task of this holding, therefore, was the management of telephone shareholdings accruing to IRI as a result of the bailout of the major German-style mixed bank, Banca Commerciale Italiana, which controlled Sip-Stipel. After World War II, Stet carried out its mandate mainly by investing in infrastructures and technology to foster the integration of individual regional networks into a national network. In the early 1960s, as a great change in the relationship between structure and financial capacity was arising, Stet became a complex multisector group with a presence in all of the telecommunications sectors (Bottiglieri 1987).

Finsider was formed in June 1937 to reorganize the iron and steel stakes (Ilva, Terni, Dalmine, Acciaierie di Cornigliano), which ended up in the IRI portfolio due to the mixed banks' bailout in the previous years. Finsider promoted the reorganization of its controlled manufacturing companies and restructured all major iron and steel plants in order to restore their profitability through substantial improvements in technical and managerial efficiency. The 1930s and the 1940s, under the leading drive of Agostino Rocca and then of Oscar Sinigaglia, saw the rationalization of existing plants and the creation of plants technologically more advanced than those of the steel sector. Finsider implemented productive efficiency strategies and an increase in production quantity, at first through the elimination of inefficient plants and then through the creation of integrated cycle iron and steel centers, such as the Cornigliano Ligure plant. The 1948 Piano Sinigaglia (Sinigaglia Plan) started off the rebuilding of the Cornigliano plant and the integration of the Piombino and Bagnoli plants. During the 1950s, Finsider embarked on considerable investments in the expansion of iron and steel production and raised profitability from the increasing efficiency of the iron and steelwork plants, especially that of Cornigliano. Another large iron and steel plant in Taranto was added to the three iron and steel works already in existence from the 1960s, while the main shareholdings were gradually united to form Italsider (Bonelli 1982, Balconi 1991, Carparelli 1982, Ranieri 1999).

Finmeccanica (1948) and Fincantieri (1959) were created after World War II as part of policies for the rationalization of investments in the mechanical and shipbuilding sectors. Figure 7.5 plots main trends in the relationship between debt and equity at the group level for the three above-mentioned sub-holdings, from the end of the 1940s to the early 1990s. In the case of the Stet, the debt–equity ratio appears relatively stable, whereas in the case of Finsider and Finmeccanica, it shows significant fluctuations and a tendency for growth but then stabilizes from the end of the 1960s for Finsider and from the end of the 1970s for Finmeccanica.

From the early 1970s, the deterioration of the Finsider's financial structure is evident, reaching a peak of almost 12.9 in 1974. Around the mid-1970s, the plans for the development of production capacity, via investments in the expansion of the Taranto plant and the creation of a new steel works in Gioia Tauro, began to conflict with the iron and steel market's difficult international situation. Furthermore, it should be noted that some of the stresses had been present, though to a lesser degree, even during the first phase of the industrial activities, or rather from the end of the 1940s to the middle of the following decade, evidently due to the investments made to increase the productive capacities of the iron and steel enterprises of the group.

From 1956 the debt–equity ratio for Finsider was lower, but levels were considerably higher than those of Stet and Finmeccanica, until the recovery of the cycle of investments in capital assets linked to the construction of the fourth iron and steel center at Taranto, the subsequent expansion of this plant and the start of the construction of the center at Gioia Tauro (in 1971 the investments for the fourth and fifth iron and steel centers amounted to approximately 2,650 billion lire of the approximately 3,650 billion lire planned by Finsider).[8] After the Bank of Italy increased interest rates in 1963, the ratio tended to increase at a constant rate and then returned to lower values following IRI's readjustment and refinancing of Finsider. As far as Finmeccanica is concerned, the ratio's trend is only partly linked to dynamics similar to those causing the variations of the equivalent Finsider indicator. The drop, though smaller, started at the end of the 1970s and lasted for the whole of the following decade (see Figure 7.5).

Stet's activity, on the other hand, was characterized by completely different conditions: acting in a monopolistic position, it was able to ensure a return on investments by revising tariffs and to resolve the tensions between state and private ownership components by "demanding and onerous" programs for the development and technical advancement of the telephone network.[9]

The dynamics of the relationship between debt and equity can only partly be attributed to the structure of the sector to which the operating companies, coordinated by the three sub-holdings, belonged.

While Stet operated in the telecommunications sector, which was a protected market segment and its profit margins were consequently sheltered by the absence of competition, Finmeccanica showed an even better overall performance until the end of the 1970s, even though it operated in sectors less sheltered from (private or foreign) competition and where public production orders were more common (Zamagni 2009).

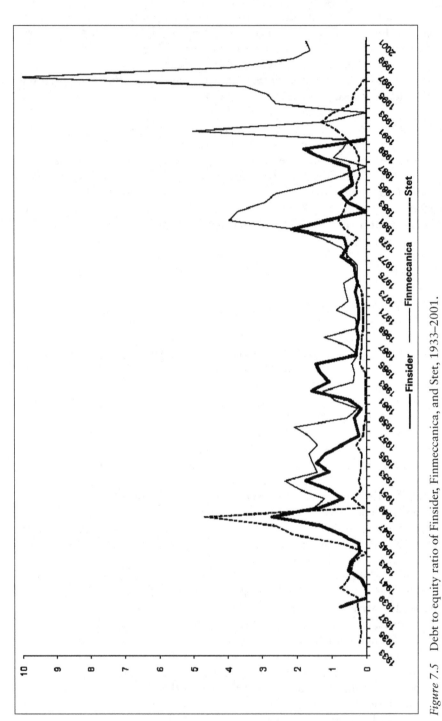

*Figure 7.5*  Debt to equity ratio of Finsider, Finmeccanica, and Stet, 1933–2001.

*Source:* IRI, Finsider, Finmeccanica and Stet, *Official balance-sheets and financial statements, ad annos.*

In any case, during IRI's great investment expansion phase, the holding supplemented the capital that the enterprises could raise directly on the market through the issue of bonds or through bank lending with staggered deadlines, the extent varying with the sector. The companies in the electrical and telecommunications sectors (34%) made little use of holding company financing, as did the mechanical enterprises (8.8%), whereas motorway construction (71.7%) and shipbuilding (67.7%) resorted to IRI financing to a greater extent. Finsider's requirements in 1961 amounted to 71 billion lire, and the support IRI provided was slightly less than that given to the sectors more indebted toward the holding company (46.1% versus 48.4%), but it represented approximately half of the total 148 billion lire that IRI made available to all of the group's enterprises.[10] Ten years later the total support provided by IRI for the group's financial requirements was considerably reduced; it was less than the enterprise's self-financing, which was dropping, and depended on the increase of the holding's endowment fund (220 billion over 1,313 billion lire).[11]

In the documents prepared by IRI to define the medium-term investment plan for the entire group, the deterioration of the financial structure is explicitly attributed to the industrial controlled companies' profit squeeze. In 1971, IRI's Industrial Plan explicitly acknowledged the dramatic deterioration of the companies' profits as the main cause of the reduction in the self-financing share of overall investments (estimated in 1971 at 320 billion lire, i.e., 24% of total liabilities).[12] At the beginning of the 1980s, the financial situation of the entire group became so critical as to induce IRI's management to exert a certain degree of caution regarding medium-term prospects for economic and financial recovery. In the preceding decade, the IRI group had lost its credibility on the financial markets and, therefore, there was no knowing, a priori, what the amount of the IRI's resources would be in the immediate future. IRI's 1981 Industrial Plan could not, therefore, exclude the possibility that in the ensuing years IRI would have to cut back on its investment programs because of a lack of sufficient equity or debt to finance their start or completion.[13]

The absence of an industrial strategy for the future was exposed to public opinion by a letter to the press in which the directors responsible for industrial policy declared their readiness to tender their resignations unless the government intervened with refinancing initiatives (Lavista 2006). The refinancing was finally obtained, but it was inadequate to support the already established industrial plans, and this caused—as depicted in Tables 7.3 and 7.4—a process of corrosion of the financial ties between the main holding and the sub-holdings. The tables show the correlation coefficients between the annual variation over time of the liabilities of IRI and those of the sub-holdings. Four sub-periods are identified between 1949 and 1992. Separate coefficients are calculated for IRI unconsolidated and consolidated and for each sub-holding as companies and as a group. The coefficients are necessarily partial, because they are sensitive to conditions outside the structure

*Table 7.3*   Correlation Coefficients between IRI Total Liabilities and the Liabilities of Sector Shareholdings (Company and Group), 1949–1992

| | IRI liabilities | IRI liabilities | IRI (consolidated) liabilities | IRI (consolidated) liabilities |
|---|---|---|---|---|
| | 1949–63 | 1964–74 | 1975–85 | 1975–92 |
| Finsider | 0,84 | 0,22 | 0,26 | |
| Finsider group | 0,94 | -0,1 | 0,05 | |
| Finmeccanica | -0,26 | 0,33 | 0,26 | -0,01 |
| Finmeccanica group | | 0,23 | -0,45 | 0,85 |
| Stet | 0,98 | 0,04 | 0,61 | 0,79 |
| Stet group | 0,67 | -0,29 | -0,16 | -0,05 |
| Fincantieri | | -0,29 | 0,36 | 0,85 |

*Sources*: *Notizie statistiche* and Imita.db; Mediobanca, *Le principali società italiane, ad annos*; IRI, Finsider, Finmeccanica and Stet, *Official balance-sheets and financial statements, ad annos.*

*Table 7.4*   Correlation Indexes between IRI Total Liabilities and the Liabilities of Sector Shareholdings (Company and Group), 1949–1992

| | IRI liabilities 1949–63 | IRI liabilities 1964–74 | IRI (consolidated) liabilities 1975–92 |
|---|---|---|---|
| Finsider—equity | 0,96 | 0,17 | -0,43 |
| Finmeccanica—equity | 0,28 | 0,35 | 0,17 |
| Stet—equity | 0,99 | 0,47 | 0,53 |
| Fincantieri—equity | | -0,41 | 0,59 |
| Finsider—debt | 0,56 | 0,04 | -0,24 |
| Finmeccanica—debt | -0,41 | 0,23 | -0,08 |
| Stet—debt | 0,29 | -0,52 | 0,71 |
| Fincantieri—debt | | 0,09 | 0,84 |
| Finsider group—equity | 0,97 | 0,25 | -0,69 |
| Finmeccanica group—equity | | 0,35 | 0,63 |
| Stet group—equity | 0,66 | 0,43 | 0,17 |
| Fincantieri group—equity | | | |
| Finsider group—debt | 0,9 | -0,05 | -74 |
| Finmeccanica group—debt | | 0,1 | 0,86 |
| Stet group—debt | 0,58 | 0,01 | 0,14 |
| Fincantieri group—debt | | | |

*Sources*: *Notizie statistiche* and Imita.db; Mediobanca, *Le principali società italiane, ad annos*; IRI, Finsider, Finmeccanica and Stet, *Official balance-sheets and financial statements, ad annos.*

of the entire IRI group, but they are highly effective in revealing the difference in the strength of ties between the components:

1. The absolute importance of the IRI–Finsider relationship in the period from 1949 to 1963 and, subsequently, the difficulties and the crisis which affected this relationship during the following two phases of economic and industrial policy;
2. The importance of Finmeccanica; that is, though it never in absolute terms equaled that of Finsider in the financial commitments of the holding, it was highly relevant in the emergence of budgetary constraints; in other words, it is conceivable that the Finmeccanica sub-holding was unable to manage the debt flow between the controlled companies and the liabilities of IRI, the reason for the minus sign, thus causing tension within the debt structure of the entire group;
3. Stet was substantially important with regard to the holding company.

The investment financing capacities were therefore connected to IRI obtaining additional capital from the state to recapitalize the group, to be used to counter strong imbalances due in part to macroeconomic shocks.[14] As the years went by, the sector holdings were assigned industrial policy and economic policy tasks which affected the size, the localization, and the quality of investments (Federico and Giannetti 1999).[15] The difficulties encountered by the iron and steel company Ilva are emblematic of the trends common to Finsider and Finmeccanica sector holdings during the benchmark years 1971–1991. In those years, Ilva's return on equity and return on assets were markedly negative and, simultaneously, there was a marked growth in debt, while Finsider's debt increased in relation to equity (Balconi 1991; Osti 1993). During the 1980s, the reduced efficiency of the industrial plants in the southern regions and the oversizing of the group's overall production capacity had a negative effect on Finsider's asset and liability structure and caused IRI to place it in voluntary winding-up in 1988, in an attempt to recover its debt exposure.

## CONCLUSIONS

IRI's creation of a divided structure by organizing the group according to three distinct levels—parent company holding, sector sub-holding, operating companies—fulfilled a similar purpose to the devolution of responsibilities pursued by the large U.S. enterprises by means of the M-form.[16] After the initial success of this division during the 1950s, IRI's balance sheets data, however, showed a progressive decline in the advantages of this structure with regard to debt management at the infra-group level. From the 1960s onward, the intermediate level of coordination and management responsibility, represented by the sector sub-holdings, became less and less relevant in the management of infra-group flows.

Between the late 1960s and the early 1990s, the group of enterprises that registered the most robust increase in debt–equity ratios was that of the enterprises belonging to the iron and steel and mechanical manufacturing sectors, in which IRI's shareholdings, via Finsider and Finmeccanica, were particularly well represented. The capital collected by IRI was directly used by the manufacturing companies, and the debts of the latter were thus rapidly transposed into the holding company's liabilities, while the various sub-holdings lost intermediation and capital raising capacity on the bond market. The top IRI group enterprises, which were active in these manufacturing segments, followed and reinforced these trends.

It must be concluded then that the progressive and consequent deterioration of the IRI's asset and liability structure was a joint consequence of government economic policy errors and of the corporate governance structure, which was incapable of making efficient choices on the capital market, thus causing an irreversible weakening of the group's capacity for industrial growth.

We express our special gratitude to Robert Millward for his invaluable guidance and assistance in revising the text. Usual disclaimers apply.

## NOTES

1. This observation is in line with the core lesson of Chandler 1962.
2. Balance sheets data on the top 200 manufacturing companies here analyzed are from *Notizie Statistiche*, edited by Assonime, as digitalized in Imita. db, and from *Le principali società italiane* published yearly by Mediobanca-R&S. These sources are discussed in Conte and Piluso 2010.
3. Sources are presented and discussed in Colli and Vasta 2010, and, for our specific purposes, in Conte and Piluso 2010.
4. IRI was a state-owned conglomerate, a holding company whose capital was not represented by equity but by an endowment fund provided by the Treasury.
5. There were, on the other hand, families who were forced to abandon the ownership since they did not have adequate financial resources, as it was, for example, for the Olivetti family in the mid-1960s, after the death of the influential Adriano (Bricco 2005).
6. This was a typical second best solution within a highly regulated banking system in which central banks could manipulate credit intermediation, generally in order to meet inflation policies.
7. Problems regarding sources provided by *Notizie Statistiche* and a possible integration with data collected by Mediobanca and by R&S, a company entirely controlled by Mediobanca, are discussed in Conte and Piluso 2010.
8. Archivio Storico IRI (henceforth, AS IRI), Rome, Ufficio Studi, IRI, *Piano quadriennale*, 1971.
9. As is written, for example, in AS IRI, IRI, *Piano quadriennale*, 1961, p. 15.
10. AS IRI, IRI, *Piano quadriennale*, 1961.
11. AS IRI, IRI, *Piano quadriennale*, 1971.
12. "The drastic drop in the self-financing quota . . . must in fact also be attributed to the significant deterioration of the economic performance of the

firms," due to the joint effect of the underutilization of the plants and the increase in factor prices: AS IRI, IRI, *Piano quadriennale*, 1981, p. 4.

13. AS IRI, IRI, *Piano quadriennale*, 1981.

14. The long-term sustainability of the total liabilities accumulated during the 1960s, especially by Finsider, owing to investments aimed at increasing total productive capacity (also with reference to economic policy objectives, such as the re-equilibrium of the trade balance), depended on IRI's access to cash endowment funds, as was clearly stated in the 1982 Industrial Plan. On the same occasion it was made clear that improving the financial structure depended on two conditions: recapitalization by means of an increase in the cash endowment fund, and thus the reduction of debt plus a drop in interest rates which would have permitted the containment of the debt burden. The interest paid did in fact drop from 15.4% of revenue in 1981 to 9.8% in 1982.

15. Finsider, for example, was assigned the objective of realigning the Italian iron and steel balance between the 1960s and the 1970s. The expansion of the Taranto center and the building of the Gioia Tauro center would have permitted the achievement of the double aim of starting off the growth process in the southern regions and of reducing the burden of the import of steel and other intermediate goods on the Italian trade balance.

16. In his overview of the Italian state-owned enterprise, Amatori is rather critic about this process, arguing that IRI lacked of a fitting guidance as a conglomerate structure (Amatori 2000). Such an assessment echoes what Posner and Woolf argued about IRI's weaknesses in the late 1960s (Posner and Woolf, 1967).

## BIBLIOGRAPHY

Acemoglu, D., P. Aghion, and F. Zilibotti 2006, "Distance to Frontier, Selection, and Economic Growth," *Journal of the European Economic Association* 4: 37–74.

Amatori, F. 1999, "La grande impresa," in *Storia d'Italia* 15, *L'industria*, eds. F. Amatori et al., Turin: Einaudi.

Amatori, F. 2000, "Beyond State and Market: Italy's Futile Search for a Third Way," in *The Rise and Fall of State-Owned Enterprise in the Western World*, ed. P.A. Toninelli, Cambridge: Cambridge University Press.

Amatori, F. and F. Brioschi 1997, "Le grandi imprese private: Famiglie e coalizioni," in *Storia del capitalismo italiano dal dopoguerra a oggi*, ed. F. Barca, Rome: Donzelli.

Balconi, M. 1991, *La siderurgia italiana (1940–1990). Tra controllo pubblico e incentivi di mercato*, Bologna: Il Mulino.

Barca, F. 1994, *Imprese in cerca di padrone*, Roma-Bari: Laterza.

Barca, F., ed. 1997, *Storia del capitalismo italiano dal dopoguerra a oggi*, Rome: Donzelli.

Barca, F., et al. 1997, "La trasformazione proprietaria di Fiat; Pirelli e Falck dal 1947 a oggi," in *Storia del capitalismo Italiano dal dopoguerra a oggi*, ed. F. Barca, Rome: Donzelli.

Barca, F. and S. Trento 1997, "State Ownership and the Evolution of Italian State Corporate Governance," *Industrial and Corporate Change*, 6: 533–559.

Bianchi, M., et al. 2005, *Proprietà e controllo delle imprese in Italia*, Bologna: Il Mulino.

Bianco, M. 2003, *L'industria italiana*, Bologna: Il Mulino.

Bianco, M. and P. Casavola 1996, "Corporate Governance in Italia: Alcuni fatti e problemi aperti," *Rivista delle società* 41: 426–439.

Bonelli, F. 1982, "La riforma siderurgica Iri tra autarchia e mercato," in *Acciaio per l' industrializzazione. Contributi allo studio del problema siderurgico italiano*, ed. F. Bonelli, Turin: Einaudi.

Bonelli, F. 1985, "Alberto Beneduce, il credito industriale e l'origine dell'Iri," in *Alberto Beneduce e i problemi dell'economia italiana del suo tempo*, Rome: Edindustria.

Bottiglieri, B. 1987, *STET. Strategie e struttura delle telecomunicazioni*, Milan: Angeli.

Bricco, P. 2005, *Prima e dopo Adriano*, Naples: L'Ancora del Mediterraneo.

Brioschi, F., L. Buzzacchi, and M.G. Colombo 1990, *Gruppi di imprese e mercato finanziario*, Rome: La Nuova Italia Scientifica.

Carparelli, A. 1982, "I perché di una mezza siderurgia. L'Ilva, l'industria della ghisa e il ciclo integrale negli anni Venti," in *Acciaio per l' industrializzazione. Contributi allo studio del problema siderurgico italiano*, ed. F. Bonelli, Turin: Einaudi.

Chandler, A.D., Jr. 1962, *Strategy and Structure: Chapters in the History of the American Industrial Enterprise*, Cambridge, Mass.: MIT Press.

Ciocca, P. 2000, *La nuova finanza in Italia. Una difficile metamorfosi (1980–2000)*, Turin: Bollati Boringhieri.

Ciocca, P. and G. Nardozzi 1996, *The High Price of Money*, Oxford: Clarendon.

Colajanni, N. 1991, *Capitalismo senza capitali. Storia di Mediobanca*, Milan: Sperling & Kupfer.

Colli, A. and M. Vasta, eds. 2010, *Forms of Enterprise in 20th Century Italy: Boundaries, Strategies and Structures*, Cheltenham: Edward Elgar.

Coltorti, F. 1988, "Note sulle modificazioni della struttura finanziaria delle imprese italiane negli ultimi venti anni," in *Ristrutturazione economica e finanziaria delle imprese*, ed. Banca d'Italia, Rome: Banca d'Italia.

Conte, L. and G. Piluso 2010, "Financing the Largest Italian Manufacturing Firms. Ownership, Equity, and Debt (1936–2001)," in *Forms of Enterprises in 20th Century Italy: Boundaries, Strategies and Structures*, eds. A. Colli and M. Vasta, Cheltenham: Edward Elgar.

De Cecco, M. 1997, "Splendore e crisi del sistema Beneduce: Note sulla struttura finanziaria e industriale dell'Italia dagli anni venti agli anni sessanta," in *Storia del capitalismo italiano dal dopoguerra a oggi*, ed. F. Barca, Rome: Donzelli.

Doria, M. 1989, *Ansaldo. L'impresa e lo Stato*, Milan: Angeli.

Federico, G. and R. Giannetti 1999, "Le politiche industriali," *Storia d'Italia, Annali, 15, L'industria*, eds. F. Amatori et al., Turin: Einaudi.

Fisman, R. and I. Love 2004, "Financial Development and Growth in the Short and Long Run," *NBER Working Paper* 10236.

Frasca, F.M. and G. Marotta 1988, "La ristrutturazione finanziaria delle grandi imprese," in *Ristrutturazione economica e finanziaria delle imprese*, ed. Banca d'Italia, Rome: Banca d'Italia.

Giannetti, R. and S. Pastorelli 2007, "Il sistema nazionale di innovazione negli anni Cinquanta e Sessanta," in *Innovazione tecnologica e sviluppo industriale in Italia nel secondo dopoguerra*, eds. C. Antonelli et al., Rome-Bari: Laterza.

Giannetti, R. and M. Vasta, eds. 2003, L'impresa italiana nel Novecento, Bologna: Il Mulino.

Giannetti, R. and M. Vasta, eds. 2006, *Evolution of Italian Enterprises in the 20th Century*, Heidelberg: Physica Verlag.

Lavista, F. 2006, "Considerazioni sul ruolo e le funzioni dell'Iri. Il 'documento dei funzionari' del 26 marzo 1975," in *Annali di storia dell'impresa*, 17: 489–533.

Lavista, F. 2010, *La stagione della programmazione. Grandi imprese e Stato dal dopoguerra agli anni Settanta*, Bologna: Il Mulino.

Marchi, A. and R. Marchionatti 1992, *Montedison 1966–1989. L'evoluzione di una grande impresa al confine tra pubblico e privato*, Milan: Angeli.

Osti, G.L. 1993, *L'industria di Stato dall'ascesa al degrade. Trent'anni nel gruppo Finsider*, interviewed by R. Ranieri, Bologna: Il Mulino.

Pagano, M., F. Panetta, and L. Zingales 1996, "The Stock Market as a Source of Capital: Some Lessons from Initial Public Offerings in Italy," *European Economic Review* 40: 1057–1069.

Piluso, G. 1999, "Gli istituti di credito speciale," in *Storia d'Italia 15, L'industria*, eds. F. Amatori et al., Turin: Einaudi.

Piluso, G. 2005, *Mediobanca. Tra regole e mercato*, Milan: Egea.

Posner, M.V. and S.J. Woolf 1967, *Italian Public Enterprise*, London: Duckworth.

Rajan, R. and L. Zingales 1995, "What Do We Know about Capital Structure? Some Evidence from International Data," *Journal of Finance* 50: 1421–1460.

Rajan, R. and Zingales 1998, "Financial Dependence and Growth," *American Economic Review* 88: 559–586.

Ranieri, R. 1999, "Steel and the State in Italy and the UK. The Public Sector of the Steel Industry in Comparative Perspective (1945–1996)," *European Yearbook of Business History* 2: 125–154.

Rossi, N. and G. Toniolo 1996, "Italy," in *Economic Growth in Europe since 1945*, eds. N. Crafts and G. Toniolo, Cambridge: Cambridge University Press.

Siciliano, G. 2001, *Cento anni di borsa in Italia*, Bologna: Il Mulino.

Tomlinson, J. 1999, "Learning from Italy? The British Public Sector and IRI," *European Yearbook of Business History* 2: 109–124.

Toninelli, P.A., ed. 2000, *The Rise and Fall of State-Owned Enterprise in the Western World*, Cambridge: Cambridge University Press.

Zamagni, V. 2009, *Finmeccanica. Competenze che vengono da lontano*, Bologna: Il Mulino.

# Part II

# State-Owned Enterprises in Different Sectors

# 8 Property Rights, Economic Rents, BNOC, and North Sea Oil

*Martin Chick*

## INTRODUCTION

The British National Oil Corporation (BNOC) was established in 1976, formally with the passing of the 1975 Petroleum and Submarine Pipelines Bill and practically as the result of negotiations between the UK government and the oil companies. Established with an initial capital of £600 million, BNOC was required to pay all of its revenues into a new account, the National Oil Account, and it was able to draw on this account to finance its activities. Potentially, the Petroleum and Submarines Pipelines Act gave the UK government virtually total control over the exploration and development of North Sea oil resources. In fact, the government chose to confine BNOC's interest to 51% of new commercial discoveries and, as in Norway, it opted for a so-called carried interest system of participation. The oil companies were licensed to explore particular blocks in the North Sea on the understanding that in the event of oil being discovered, the government could take a 51% interest in the project. The state thereby specifically arranged that it would not bear any of the costs of 'dry holes' discovered during exploration. In Norway, Statoil, and in the UK, BNOC, were established to oversee the state's interests in the offshore projects. BNOC was, in a sense, the government's eyes and ears in the North Sea. The main use made of licenses was as a means of controlling the rate of output, both by means of the rate at which licenses were issued and then, when oil was found, through BNOC's 51% equity interest. The task of extracting economic rent was assigned to taxation, notably the petroleum revenue tax (PRT) which was introduced in the 1975 Oil Taxation Act and from which BNOC was exempt. The PRT was levied prior to corporation tax, initially at a rate of 45% on the assessable profit from each oilfield (Webb and Ricketts 1980, 172; Millward 2005, 227–228).

Although BNOC was a nationalized public corporation, its establishment was not a traditional act of nationalization, as no existing privately owned assets were transferred into public ownership. By means of the Petroleum and Submarine Pipelines Bill, BNOC was to acquire the equity capital, staff, and stakes in the Thistle, Dunlin, and Hutton oilfields of National Coal Board (Exploration) Ltd. Fortuitously for BNOC, the government's financial rescue of the Burmah Oil Company in late 1975 also provided an opportunity for BNOC to acquire Burmah's 16% interest in the Ninian field and 20% of its interest in the Thistle field. In addition to gaining a 51% stake of the 86 blocks allocated in the fifth and sixth licensing rounds, in 1978 BNOC was given first right of refusal to buy stakes in blocks previously awarded to private companies as and when such stakes came up for sale. By 1979, BNOC had become a major trader in oil, able to buy oil from other producers under its various participation agreements and then able to sell this oil into competitive markets (Vickers and Yarrow 1988, 320). BNOC's main practical role was as a privileged buyer of North Sea oil. A condition of its having the first option to purchase 51% of oil output was its guaranteeing to the companies that they would not suffer financially, that is, that they would receive the market price for the oil (Shonfield 1976; Cameron 1983, 142–143). What BNOC was not was an instrument of national ownership and control over all of the North Sea oil activities. This very limited role disappointed the early hopes of the BNOC's supporters, and the corporation's subsequent aspirations to participate directly in exploration and development activities were stymied by the Treasury. In one sense, the creation of BNOC was a curiously old-fashioned, last, weak flicker of the flame of nationalization before it was doused by the privatization program of the 1980s.

Yet, from another perspective, the establishment of BNOC was part of government's increasing involvement in issues concerning the ownership of common resources, be they in or under the sea, or in the air. Since the end of World War II, there had been increasing interest in the extent of national property rights at sea, and these had required negotiated settlement at an international level, such as at the Law of the Sea Conferences. The rights to extract North Sea oil derived from the continental shelf legislation, which gave authority to the sovereign state to allocate exploration and production licenses. The sovereign state also enjoyed the ability to charge royalties and to tax the profits and economic rents from off-shore oil-drilling activities. In the United Kingdom, the discovery of oil brought with it a challenge, notably from the Scottish National Party, to the existing boundaries of the sovereign state. The establishment of an independent Scotland would provide the basis for the government of Scotland to exercise those same sovereign rights of taxation over its own newly defined territorial waters and continental shelf. The purpose of this chapter is to examine the establishment and thwarted ambitions of BNOC and to set them within the wider framework of the discussion and negotiation over the definition, enforcement, and allocation of property rights. In so doing, it mixes the past with the future, hailing back to the spirit of post-1945 nationalizations and looking forward to the issues of natural resources and property rights that were to form a central thread in the development of modern environmental economics.

## PROPERTY RIGHTS

The right to allocate licenses had its recent basis in the 1958 Geneva Continental Shelf Convention, which formed part of the wider negotiations on the extent and depth of national territorial rights over (and in and under) the sea. Like many other governments, in the UK since 1934 the Crown had enjoyed exclusive property rights over all natural gas and oil found on shore and within UK territorial waters. The passage of the Continental Shelf Act in 1964 amended UK law to allow for the implementation of the Continental Shelf Convention. It also extended the licensing provision of the Petroleum (Production) Act of 1934 to the area beyond territorial waters (Cameron 1983, 73). However, what had become a matter of protracted international negotiation was the extent of such territorial limits. Claims over territorial waters varied from 3 miles in Australia to 200 miles in the case of some Latin American countries, and any decision clearly carried implications for each country's deep-sea fishing industry, although not always as obviously as might be thought. While in some countries—notably Iceland, with whom Britain became involved in a 'Cod War'—the sea fishing industry supported an extension of territorial limits, in Britain the government was generally opposed to any such extension, because any gains in inshore fishing would be more than offset by the closing to them of previously open waters around other countries. For countries with off-shore oil interests, improvements in off-shore technology and the general growth of interest in oil extraction prompted moves to lay claim to the natural resources of the seabed adjacent to their coasts. Venezuela had advanced such claims in the Gulf of Paria in 1942 and, from 1945, the U.S. noticeably increased its interest in laying claim to what it considered to be its offshore continental shelf. In the UK, the perceived growing value of the North Sea oilfields was to lead to the interests of the oil companies being given priority over those of the distant-deep-water fishing industry. However, before that, the precise boundaries of the UK's share of the North Sea still required negotiation. The North Sea was bounded by seven littoral states (the UK, Norway, Denmark, West Germany, the Netherlands, Belgium, and France) and the necessitous negotiations concerned not only the horizontal extent of territorial waters but also their vertical depth. As far as the continental shelf was concerned, what eventually emerged after years of negotiation was the 1958 Geneva Continental Shelf Convention. This extended the sovereign rights of the littoral states to include the exploration and exploitation of the natural resources of the seabed on the continental shelf to a depth of 200 meters or 'to where the depth of the super adjacent waters admits of the exploitation of natural resources'. The extent of each state's rights depended upon its reaching agreement with other bordering countries, and given mutual agreement, the boundary line could be determined by any set of principles. However, failing such agreement, Article 6 of the Convention established the principle of equidistance to guide countries that were partners to the Treaty. Between two coastal states, such as the UK and Norway, the boundary line was the median line between them, and indeed the line demarcating the UK sector of the North Sea was the result of five separate agreements, each of which was consistent with this principle of equidistance (MacKay and Mackay 1975, 20). The principle of equidistance favored countries like Norway with a long coastline (and a small population).

## ALLOCATING LICENSES

Once the principles underpinning property rights had been more or less settled, the subsequent practical issue concerned the basis on which to divide the UK section of the North Sea. One approach to the division of development and exploitation rights in the sea was to adopt the 'checkerboarding' approach, in which blocks were allocated on the diagonal. The checkerboarding principle was pioneered in Alberta, Canada, and a variant was subsequently adopted in Saskatchewan (TNA 1969d). The principal objective of a checkerboarding scheme was to ensure that the licensing authority had an equal (or near equal) share in any territory found to have oil and gas reserves.

The UK government opted for neither approach to dividing up the North Sea and its potential oil reserves, choosing instead to allocate licenses to develop and exploit designated blocks of 100 square miles. Checkerboarding was rejected in favor of the more usual surrender provisions on the grounds that the latter would be more acceptable to the companies, more flexible to administer, and would probably lead to a more rapid development of the UK's continental shelf resources. Licenses were distributed in rounds with the first four rounds occurring in 1964, 1965, 1970, and 1971–1972. Whereas the first licensing round concentrated heavily on the southern North Sea (the English sector), the subsequent three rounds all concentrated on the northern (Scottish) sector. Of these rounds, the fourth round was the most important, resulting in a total area licensed of 24,000 square miles. The rate at which licenses were issued was the main determinant of the subsequent rate of development and extraction (The National Archives, Kew, TNA 1969c, paras. 5, 7, 9; MacKay and Mackay 1975, 27). From the start, the UK government was keen to strike a balance between maximizing its possible take of economic rents and promoting the development of the North Sea oil and gas resources. Inasmuch as rent was concerned, it explicitly undertook calculations of the likely returns on investment available to companies in the North Sea compared with other, usually OPEC, projects. In 1972, during a review of the Continental Shelf Licensing Policy, the Ministry of Power compared the prospective post-rent returns for companies in the North Sea and the Middle East. On central price assumptions, in 1980 the companies' returns in the North Sea were thought likely to be £7 per ton, with a UK government take of about £8 per ton (assuming 50% corporation tax and no depreciation or interest) compared with just over £1 in the OPEC case, with the OPEC governments' take of £11. On the basis of 1972 prices (i.e., assuming no real increase in the price of oil), the comparable figures for the North Sea were £3.5 and £4.6, and for OPEC £1 and £4.86. Although these estimates indicated that North Sea investment could be significantly more attractive than OPEC investment, investment in the North Sea required much greater capital investment. A field of the Forties size in the North Sea could require investment of £325m; in OPEC the same production might be obtained for £100m (although the companies would also have to invest £66m in tankers to get the oil to the UK). Using a 10% rate of discount to estimate the net present value of investment projects in the North Sea and OPEC, for a field of Forties size the net present value of a North Sea project was about £600–£700 million, and of an OPEC project about £130 million (the former figure assumes corporation tax at 50% is paid). Nonetheless, the initial capital risk was larger and working conditions more difficult. Returns on fields smaller than Forties were themselves likely to be commensurately smaller (TNA 1972c, para. 8).

In the first three rounds, discretionary licensing was favored, principally because it gave the government some influence as to who would enjoy the direct benefits of North Sea oil. The emphasis was on the rapid development and maximization of output, a concern which was underlined further by the requirement that each licensee surrender one half of its area after a 6-year period, thus providing a strong incentive to determine which part of any area offered the best commercial prospects. The licensee then had the option to continue the license for the remaining half of his area for a further 40 years. The early development of North Sea oil resources was also intended to be encouraged by the UK government's decision to take a low annual rent for each block allocated, this being fixed in price for the first few years and then increased to a stipulated maximum. The Exchequer was to receive 12.5% of the wellhead value of any petroleum produced, and profits were subject to UK tax (MacKay and Mackay 1975, 31). Not only was the rapid extraction of oil favored for the boost which it could give to government revenue, but also for the contribution which it could make to the balance of payments, both in itself as an import substitute and also from the contribution which North Sea oil could make to export earnings (TNA 1973b, para. 1). The high-quality North Sea oil, with its low sulfur content and high yield of lighter fractions (e.g., gasoline, naphtha) suitable for use in petrochemicals, appeared to have a large potential market in the U.S. Its heavy-fuel yield was thought likely to be low, so that whereas much of North Sea oil would be exported, particularly to northern Europe but also to the U.S. market, the UK would continue to import heavy crude from

Middle East producers so as to satisfy its large requirement for fuel oil. Moreover, projections made in 1972 suggested that whereas the foreign-exchange cost of oil drilled from the UK shelf by a foreign-owned company in 1980 (on future price assumptions) would be nearly £8 a ton, it would only be £1 per ton for production by a British-owned company. Every extra 10% share of total production in 1980 by a British company would therefore save the balance of payments about £50 million. It was perhaps not so surprising then that when allocating licenses, the government appeared to favor British-owned companies, whose balance of payments and employment benefits the government was keen to capture.

From the second round of licensing in 1965, the new Labour government explicitly signaled its intention to pay particular attention to the contribution made by applicants to the balance of payments and to the creation of employment in the UK, and most especially in the regions (TNA 1972c, para. 41; MacKay and Mackay 1975, 3, 25). It was a requirement that an applicant should be incorporated in the UK, where the profits of the operation would be taxed. UK companies seemed to obtain a relatively higher proportion of the more promising areas and over the first three rounds, the share of UK interests tended to rise. Yet while preference was shown to British-based companies, given the emphasis on speed of development, and the view that the two UK, or partly UK, majors, British Petroleum and Shell, did not have the necessary resources to develop all the licensed areas as quickly as was desired, reliance had necessarily to be placed on foreign, often U.S.-controlled, companies. Foreign interests never accounted for less than 62.5% of the areas licensed and in this, U.S. interests predominated. According to MacKay and Mackay, in November 1974, U.S.-based companies controlled 38% of the estimated production potential from established North Sea oil fields, compared with 44% by UK-based companies and 18% controlled by companies of other nationalities. In 1972, the view of the Petroleum Division was that there had been greater emphasis on showing a preference for British companies than in placing pressure on licensees to buy British (TNA 1972c, para. 40; MacKay and Mackay 1975, 25). Internationally, practice varied. The Norwegian government appeared not to have preferences among applications for licenses other than requiring all applicants to be domiciled or to have permanent branches in Norway. In Italy, the licensing system was highly discriminatory in favor of ENI (Ente Nazionale Idrocarburi), which had prior rights to survey the whole of the area to be awarded and an option to take out exclusive title to 25% of the area before other applicants were considered (TNA 1969b).

For the first three rounds, discretionary licensing was favored. In the fourth round, a measure of auctioning was admitted. The formal invitation to apply for blocks was published in June 1971, and the limited auction of 15 of the 286 blocks was in the following August. Discretionary blocks were allocated in December 1971 and March 1972 (TNA 1973a). This limited experiment in auctioning reflected a growing interest among economists in using this form of allocative mechanism. Indeed, Kenneth Dam of the University of Chicago Law School and the author of one of the better-known articles advocating the auction of North Sea oil licenses had worked with Mr. Scholes of the Ministry of Power while conducting some of the research for his article on the pricing of North Sea gas in Britain (Coase 1970; Dam 1965; Dam 1970; TNA 1970). The auctioning of some licenses was also in part a response to criticism that the UK government was not maximizing the financial benefits of its control of license allocation. Typical of this view was an article by the consultant petroleum geologist, James Law, which appeared in *The Guardian* of 28 December 1971 under the heading of 'Britain's giveaway petroleum policy' (TNA 1971, para. 3). Whereas in the early uncertain days of North Sea oil and gas exploration a discretionary system might have been well suited to encouraging the development of uncertain new territory, by the time of the fourth round it was felt that the prospects of finding and extracting oil had become sufficiently less uncertain to favor the auctioning of at least some licenses. The major Ekofisk oil strike had been made in November 1969, just over the median line in the Norwegian sector. In the UK sector, the discovery of the Forties field was announced in 1970; the more minor discoveries of Argyll and Auk were in 1971; and in the Brent field, the discovery of what later turned out to be a major field had been drilled before the fourth round. By the spring of 1971, the Northern basin was looking attractive to the oil companies who had done extensive seismic work there and who, like the government's Petroleum Division, had access to an encouraging study carried out in 1969–1970 by the consultants Seiscom (TNA 1973a, para. 2).

In the event, altogether the companies bid £135m for the 15 blocks put out to auction in August 1971 (of which £37m was on winning bids). In comparison, the blocks allocated through the discretionary system brought in an income of only some £3 million (TNA 1973a, para. 2; MacKay and Mackay 1975, 29). One effect of auctioning was to transfer risk to the successful bidder with the government taking its share through royalties and other payments, in addition to the taxation of the profits of successful ventures (TNA 1968b, para. 7). An argument against transferring risk in this way was that the need for the oil companies to put more money up-front would significantly reduce their working capital and thereby slow development. However, having once invested capital in buying a license, the rational licensee could be expected to seek a return on that capital as quickly as possible.

## A NATIONAL HYDROCARBONS CORPORATION

The rumbling concern that the UK was not maximizing the potential benefits of North Sea oil, and that the oil companies were stealing a march on the government, provided the general background to the eventual establishment of BNOC. During the 1967 Labour Party Conference, calls were made for the creation of a national hydrocarbons corporation charged with handling future exploration and exploitation. Comparisons were drawn with the Italian ENI and French ERAP (Entreprise de recherches et d'activités petrolières). Thus provoked, the Labour Party endorsed a proposal by the Party's North Sea Study Group that the National Hydrocarbons Corporation (NHC) should be set up with the power to search for and produce oil and gas in the North Sea (TNA 1968a, paras. 1–2). The NHC would take over the existing concessions held by the Gas Council and the National Coal Board and all unallocated areas, including those to be relinquished by the existing licensees. It would also act as a monopsony purchaser of gas. It was envisaged that the NHC might assume responsibility for the distribution of gas to Area Boards and bulk sales to large industrial consumers; develop internationally on the lines of the Italian ENI or French ERAP; and form an instrument for the regulation of the oil industry in the UK (TNA 1968b, paras. 1–2). The idea gained a particular bite and urgency as half of the areas originally licensed in 1964 would revert to the government in the autumn of 1970, and if no NHC had been set up by then, the opportunity to do so might have been lost (TNA 1968c, para. 2).

What was popular in the fevered enthusiasm of a Labour Party conference drew a more ambivalent response along the corridors of the Labour government. The 1966–1970 Labour government ministers avoided committing themselves one way or another on the issue. The staffing and finance of an NHC and its relationship with the Gas Council was discussed between Mr. Gunter, the incoming but short-lived Minister of Power, and the Labour Party's Home Policy Committee on 10 June 1968. Neither Gunter nor Richard Marsh, the outgoing Minister of Power, reached any conclusion on the proposal, and it was never considered by Ministers collectively (TNA 1968c, para. 1). However, by the mid-1970s, following the first OPEC oil price hike of 1973–1974, the issue had gained in urgency and pertinence. The government began negotiating for a 51% share of each license, a move that unsurprisingly was resisted by the oil companies. One possibility raised was that some form of sweetener or offset payment might be made to those companies who accepted participation. When this possibility was raised on 30 October 1974 at the first meeting of the group charged with 'North Sea Oil Renegotiation', it received short shrift from Harold Lever and Edmund Dell, the Paymaster General. Harold Lever had chaired the Committee of Public Accounts inquiry into the North Sea oil and gas fields. The Lever Inquiry itself came in response to the economist Thomas Balogh's criticisms in an article in *The Sunday Times* in February 1972 of the government's failure to maximize its revenue from, and participation in, the North Sea oil fields. The Committee of Public Accounts report was published in 1973 and was of the view that the terms of the licenses issued in the first four rounds were insufficiently demanding of the companies, while also noting that, in general, the Exchequer was likely to receive a smaller share of oil revenues than other oil-producing countries. Something of Lever and Dell's view of oil companies was captured in their response to the suggestion that sweeteners be offered to the companies. As noted in the summary of the meeting:

> Mr. Dell said firmly that as a negotiating tactic this (the offer of a sweetener) would not work and financially it would be highly disadvantageous. Mr. Lever concurred. Any sweetener likely to be of effect with the oil companies would have to be too big to be acceptable. Either they would do it for love or not at all. A few hundred pounds meant nothing to girls who were used to going to bed with the Shah. (TNA 1974c, para. 1)

## RISK, PUBLIC EXPENDITURE, AND THE TIMING OF BNOC INVESTMENT

The idea that government might become involved in oil exploration and development in the North Sea had been at the core of the earlier calls for the establishment of an NHC. The NHC could handle the future exploration and development of the North Sea, thus securing a greater degree of direct public involvement at a growth point in the economy without the heavy compensation that would be involved in outright nationalization. Yet, the NHC could obtain all the profits from future successful ventures only by putting up the necessary investment and carrying the risks of failure. Since the beginning of 1965, 87 exploration wells had been drilled in the North Sea at a total cost of about £60 million, and four important gas fields had been discovered. There was some concern that because all of the big discoveries had been made early on, the NHC would be operating under a double disadvantage. Not only would it have to build up a new organization from scratch and compete with the oil companies for skilled staff, but it would also be left with territory that the present licensees, after 6 years exploration work, considered to be the least attractive. A moderate exploration effort comprising seismic work and the drilling of four or five wells per year would cost around £3–4 million a year, and at this rate it could easily take several years to find a commercially exploitable field. In the meantime, the finance would have to be found either from the Exchequer or from the profits on the Gas Council's existing fields, which would otherwise go to benefit gas consumers (TNA 1968b, paras. 1–6). If the NHC wished to limit its risk and financial commitment, then it might negotiate some kind of arrangement with private oil companies under which the companies bore all or part of the costs of exploration in return for a share in the profits of any successful ventures. Insofar as it did this, it would in effect be acting as a licensing authority, and any change from the existing arrangements would be of form rather than of substance. Moreover, to the extent that the risks were limited, so would be the potential profits. Once established, however, the NHC would inevitably come under pressure to invest money and explore on its own account, thereby incurring at least some risk (TNA 1968b, paras. 6, 11a).

The issue of whether or not BNOC should actively engage in exploration and development activities came to a head following the establishment of BNOC. Understandably perhaps, BNOC's first chairman, Lord Kearton, thought that for BNOC to have any credibility, it ought to be at least a 51% contributor to the costs of exploration and development from the start. That BNOC would contribute 51% of the costs of successful ventures was not in doubt. What was in dispute was when this contribution would be made. Kearton wanted BNOC to put in up-front capital from the start, and thereby, in his view, gain experience more quickly and act in a commercial manner. The Treasury disagreed. It preferred that BNOC be 'carried' during exploration and development, with its share of capital costs being contributed

*Table 8.1*   British National Oil Corporation Contribution to Estimated Expenditure under Fifth Round Licenses (Net Exchequer Cash Flows under Alternative Routes of Contribution)

| Year | 'Pay as you go' route (£ million) | Carried at 7% interest rate (£ million) |
|------|-----------------------------------|------------------------------------------|
| 1977 | -2 | |
| 1978 | -2 | |
| 1979 | -5 | |
| 1980 | -17.8 | |
| 1981 | -66.1 | |
| 1982 | -122.3 | |
| 1983 | -127.1 | 9.0 |
| 1984 | -70.3 | 24.1 |
| 1985 | 76.3 | 66.1 |
| 1986 | 278.4 | 187.3 |
| 1987 | 430 | 254.7 |
| 1988 | 542 | 399.3 |
| 1989 | 581.1 | 483.9 |
| 1990 | 558.9 | 497.2 |
| 1991 | 510.2 | 499.1 |
| 1992 | 436.6 | 436.6 |
| Total | 3000.9 | 2857.3 |

*Source*: TNA POWE 29/963, BNOC Contributions, April 1976.

retrospectively out of revenue. The company would be entitled to interest on the repayment of the capital contribution that it made on behalf of BNOC. Illustrative estimates were made of the comparative costs of the 'pay as you route' and that of being 'carried' at 7% interest, the comparisons being made for four medium-sized fields discovered under the fifth round licenses.

In this way, payments from the North Sea Oil Account would be deferred, albeit at a cost to the account in the longer term (TNA 1976b, paras. 3a, 3b). The Chancellor of the Exchequer, Denis Healey, informed the new Prime Minister, James Callaghan, in April 1976 that he could

> see no case for a Government contribution to exploration . . . [as] . . . we can secure access to information and the decision-making powers that we need through the ordinary licensing process during the exploration phase, and through participation at the development stage. Participation will also give us half the oil. Provided BNOC has a "carried interest" option to join in once a field is declared commercial, I think the public interest is safeguarded. (TNA 1976a, paras. 2, 3, 5)

Certainly, Healey's perspective was shaped by the public finance difficulties assailing the government at the time. Healey was nervous of the prospective calls on public expenditure and the public sector borrowing requirement if the government were required to finance 50% of BNOC's future development costs.

Fashionable arguments of the day that the UK should ape the example of Norway, and of Norway's Statoil, were muddied by the Treasury's view that it was not clear as to whether Statoil was carried until development or until production. As for Treasury perceptions of behavior elsewhere, the understood practice in Ireland was that the licenses issued recently were on a 'deferred' basis, the state being liable for its share of both exploration and development costs, paying later with interest on outstanding debt. In Greenland, provisions were also on the Treasury preferred route, and provided for interest. Ireland's and Greenland's full packages were regarded as being less onerous than that of the UK, as neither country had a special oil tax (TNA 1976b, para. 4).

## PROPERTY RIGHTS AND AN INDEPENDENT SCOTLAND

Even if government involvement in both North Sea oil exploration and development were to be confined to the extraction of royalties and taxes, the ability to so do so depended on its position as the sovereign government of the United Kingdom. As the prospect of oil revenues increased in size and attractiveness, so, too, did the resonance of the Scottish National Party's (SNP) criticisms of the management of the North Sea oil reserves increase. In part, there was an impatience to enjoy the benefits of this stream of income. Early on there was criticism that the Scottish economy had not derived sufficient benefit from the construction of rigs, although the benefits to the local economy of Aberdeen were apparent. On 29 January 1972, the leading article in the business section of *The Economist* was titled "Texas of the North" and accused a government "with 1 million unemployed on its back, . . . [of] . . . making too little of the thousands of jobs and the millions of pounds that North Sea oil is going to bring to some of the poorest parts of the country, from Scapa Flow to Teesside."

However, there was more to Scotland than Aberdeen, and the SNP began to exploit a growing sense of frustration that insufficient benefits from oil revenue were being enjoyed across Scotland. In 1978, SNP leaflets accompanying the campaign slogan 'The Boom that Never Was' claimed that North Sea oil was now worth £150 billion, or £30,000 for every man, woman, or child in Scotland. Yet since 1969, when the first discoveries had been made, Scotland had suffered from rising unemployment, growing poverty, and a deterioration in its health and housing provisions (TNA 1978). This sense that Scotland was missing out could be exploited by the SNP in support of their core pursuit of independence for Scotland. If Scotland had missed out on the early benefits of oil rig construction, as well as the initial phase of exploration and development, then what was to stop it missing out on the real benefits of oil extraction, namely, the years of oil taxation revenue? That, in the view of the SNP, would be 'unfair'.

Crucially this line of argument relied on the assumption that people living in Scotland should enjoy a higher per capita income from North Sea oil revenue than people living in, say, Wales and Cornwall, because the oil was under waters off the coastline of Scotland. Obviously, such a line of argument was consistent with the SNP's wish for an independent Scotland. As an independent sovereign nation, Scotland would enjoy the ability to collect economic rents from activities undertaken in its continental shelf and territorial waters. On rough Treasury estimates, oil revenues were likely to equal 50% of the GDP of Scotland, thereby offering an independent Scotland a very high per capita income (TNA 1975b). However, the fact was that in the 1970s, Scotland was not an independent nation but an un-devolved constituent part of the United Kingdom. Under international law, the state was therefore the UK, and Scotland had no separate international status. Rights over the continental shelf derived from the 1958 International Convention on the Continental Shelf which gave the coastal state (i.e., the UK) sovereign rights over the continental shelf for the purpose of exploring it and exploiting its natural resources (TNA 1974b, para. 3). Unless and until Scotland became independent of the rest of the UK, it was difficult to see on what basis it could claim ownership of the oil resources off the coast of Scotland. Two of the many questions to arise from this mismatch of aspiration and actuality were, first, what, if any, special considerations should be made for Scotland in the use of oil revenues, and, second, were Scotland to become independent, where exactly would the boundaries of its territorial waters and continental shelf lie?

The political advantage of allowing Scotland to enjoy a greater per capita benefit from government oil revenues was recognized within government. In the Prime Minister's Office in 1972, Robert Armstrong noted the advantages of allowing the benefits of North Sea oil to

> accrue, and be seen to accrue, to the Scottish economy . . . [since] . . . it would be difficult to stress too highly the psychological gains which would come from the revival of the Scottish economy being seen to be something which Scotland was achieving from its own resources, not just by the grace and favour of the Government at Westminster or of English industry. (TNA 1972a)

Certainly, in Scotland there seemed to be emerging a widely held view that Scotland had been neglected by London and the Heath government, preference being shown instead to the South East and Midlands. Even within the Scottish Office, the view was advanced that Scotland had had a raw deal for well over 50 years while the South East has hugged the honey pot and that it was not unreasonable for Scotland to get a bonus for the next decade or two (TNA 1974a). Against this could be set the Treasury's view that it was time Scotland put something back into the pot. In 1969, the Treasury had produced a separate 'Scottish budget', which indicated that Scotland took a larger share of public spending than it contributed to public revenue and that an independent Scottish Exchequer would be left with a borrowing requirement, in 1967–1968, approaching £350m. At that time, oil revenues were relatively small compared with this figure and would be too late in arriving (being based on actual oil production) to be really useful in giving early support to building up an appropriate oil industry infrastructure within Scotland. Even if Scotland moved to enjoying much higher oil revenue, a view was that Scotland should then take its turn in contributing to any 'deficit' in the public expenditure account suffered by other areas in the UK (TNA 1972b, para. 24).

However in 1974, not least around the time of the two general elections of that year, the growing strength of the SNP made life difficult for the Scottish Office which felt "under pressure to demonstrate that 'Scottish' oil is bringing recognisable *additional* benefits to Scotland" (TNA 1974a). Because it was estimated in 1974 that by 1980, North Sea oil revenues could total £3,000m a year (more than the existing corporation tax and almost half as much as income tax), this was a significant amount of revenue which seriously weakened the economic arguments against a separate Scotland (TNA 1974b, para. 4). A shift in the mood of Scottish opinion seemed to be occurring. At least one official in the Scottish Industrial Development Office thought that there had been "a major change in political attitudes in Scotland in the last 2 years and that the claims being made about 'Scottish' oil cannot be dismissed as a noisy clamour by a few extremists" (TNA 1974a).

Unsurprisingly, hypothecation raised its head in relation to revenue from oil license fees, royalty receipts, and corporation tax. Government has always resisted hypothecation as restricting its ability to allocate resources, quite apart from the difficulties in identifying taxable profits with trading activities in a particular area. One suggested approach to this last difficulty was to require companies undertaking off-shore exploration and production to be incorporated in Scotland so that their 'Scottish activities' might be identified for the purposes of hypothecation (e.g., royalty income) (TNA 1972b, para. 17). Even if hypothecation was rejected, there was growing pressure for Scotland to receive increased regional assistance and for a Scottish 'shopping list' to be sent down to Whitehall (TNA 1974a). For her part, in 1978 Margo MacDonald demanded an economic plan for Scotland which set out the targets for full employment; industrial modernization; retraining; the upgrading of schools, hospitals, and roads; and the establishment of a Scottish oil fund; with £1 billion to spend in Scotland every year and full economic powers for the proposed Scottish Assembly. Arguably by 1978, when the SNP's rating in the opinion polls was half of what it had been in 1974, the SNP's moment had passed—for the time being at least (TNA 1978).

Yet, even if Scotland were to gain independence, it was not entirely clear as to what North Sea oil resources she would own. While questions arising out of the exploration or exploitation of all North Sea oil were subject to Scottish jurisdiction under existing domestic legislation, it was not clear that the self-same area would belong to Scotland if it became independent. A dividing line had been drawn between Scottish and English waters in the North Sea because of the substantial differences between Scottish and English civil law. As it was therefore necessary to decide which system of law would prevail for cases arising out of activities on the continental shelf, for this purpose the Continental Shelf (Jurisdiction) Order of 1968 laid down that the division should be a line running due east from the eastern end of the Scottish/English border. As was evident from a glance at the map, all of the oil reserves lay to the north of this line, but the UK government had always maintained that the line was only relevant to jurisdiction areas and was irrelevant with regard to oil reserves for which there were no subdivisions of the continental shelf. The international law on the delimitation of maritime boundaries was sufficiently uncertain at the time for anyone to be completely confident as to the outcome of any arbitration as to where the median line between England and Scotland in the North Sea would be drawn. On normal median line principles, it seemed likely that it would run north eastward rather than due east, thus placing a number of fields like Argyll, Auk, and perhaps Montrose in the English sector. This argument might be countered by the suggestion that on geophysical grounds the boundary should run more or less east along the 'high' line dividing the northern and southern basins of the North Sea (the approach which Lord Balogh always believed should have been adopted in negotiations with the

Norwegians) (TNA 1976c). An independent Scotland might have grounds for claiming that it was no longer bound by the 1958 Continental Shelf Convention, so that any delimitation would have to be effected on the basis of 'equitable principles' rather than on the basis of the automatic application of the true median line (which would cut substantially across Scotland's coastal front) (TNA 1977a, para. 2). Nonetheless, whatever definition was used, most of the oil would still be in Scottish waters.

However, quite what would constitute Scotland was also open to speculation. Mr. Grimond of the Shetland Islands was happy to raise the possibility that should Scotland gain its independence, the Shetland Islands might wish to remain in the UK. If the Shetlands (plus possibly the Orkneys) stayed in the UK, a large part of the northern North Sea which then counted as Scottish waters, including substantial reserves of oil, would no longer be Scottish under international law (TNA 1977a, para. 3). If Scotland and the Orkney and Shetland Islands were to be separate states from the rest of the United Kingdom, median lines would be drawn to divide the UK continental shelf between Orkney and Shetland/Scotland and between Scotland/England. On that basis, one estimate was that, of the known oil reserves in 1975, 53% would 'belong' to the Orkney and Shetland Islands; 46% would belong to Scotland; and the remaining 1% to England (TNA 1975a, paras. 33–34). While the Shetland Islands were tactically maneuvering to maximize their own benefits from North Sea oil, the uncertainty of the Shetland issue and of the angle of any dividing line between England and an independent Scotland was used in Whitehall to niggle the SNP. "Indeed, it is part of my standard 'sales patter'" remarked Bernard Ingham. Similarly, government departments in the form of the Department of Energy Press Office had also put a lot of energy into a *Sunday Times* article of 5 December which was triggered by Mr. Grant's book in which such fears were stirred up again (TNA 1977b).

## CONCLUSIONS: THE SLOW DEATH OF BNOC

The public expenditure concerns of the mid-1970s which influenced the Treasury's decision not to allow BNOC to invest up-front capital in oil exploration continued to shape government relations with BNOC for the rest of its short life. Had it not been for the heightened concern with the security of oil supply caused by the revolution in Iran in 1979, then BNOC might well have been privatized in that year. That the Labour government in 1977 and the Conservative government in October 1979 sold shares in B.P. reflected the greater political importance attached to raising money rather than with perpetuating partial ownership of an oil company in the vague hope of enhancing the national security of oil supply. As it was, BNOC only had to wait until August 1982 to see its production assets, but interestingly not its trading assets, transferred to a new company called

Britoil. In November 1982, in the largest act of privatization in Britain up to that date, 51% of Britoil's shares were sold to the public, producing net proceeds of £536 million. In August 1985, the government sold its remaining 49% stake in Britoil for £450 million (gross). In 1985, the trading rump of BNOC was abolished and the mainly security aspects of monitoring pipelines and storage were transferred to the Oil and Pipelines Agency. None of these developments prevented economic rent being collected. By 1983, the PRT, which had been set initially at 45% in 1975, had risen in stages to 75% (Vickers and Yarrow 1988, 318); Millward 2005, 228).

That the Thatcher government felt able to abolish BNOC raises the questions of what BNOC did, and what it might have done. That it became more important as a privileged purchaser and trader of oil rather than as an active participant in its exploration and development disappointed its more ambitious supporters. To the early advocates of the case for a National Hydrocarbons Corporation and then for the BNOC, one potentially important role was as an active participant in the exploration and development of oil supplies. Some even argued that such a role need not be confined to the North Sea, but might, like the Italian ENI or the French ERAP, traverse beyond its domestic national boundary. When any such aspirant possibility was put to the Treasury, it was dismissed as not being germane to its current concerns (TNA 1969a). That such ideas were stymied by the Treasury was not so much because of any intrinsic risk, but rather because of the Treasury's overwhelming preoccupation with the specific and wider implications for public expenditure of any such initiative. The Treasury's response to Kearton's ambitions in the mid-1970s was in line with its consistent and developing approach toward nationalized industries since the mid-1950s. Obvious signposts on the Treasury's journey toward its stance by the mid-1970s are the 1961 and 1967 White Papers on the nationalized industries, the first of which required nationalized industries to earn a required rate of return on existing assets, while that of 1967 insisted that all proposed capital investment projects clear a test discount rate hurdle set by the Treasury. This was in sharp contrast with the early days of the nationalized industries when, exploiting the government's ability to raise low-cost finance, the vaunted concerns had been with average cost pricing, improving working conditions in coal mining, and extending the electricity system to those who, for reasons of geography or income, had never previously been connected. While economists rightly criticized the criteria and mechanisms of resource allocation to and within nationalized industries, as instruments of wider social policy, the aims and practices of nationalized industries cohered well with the optimism and ambition of early post–World War II governments. As concern with international comparative growth rates developed and, more particularly, as public expenditure concerns grew from the mid-1950s, then so did the Treasury selectively employ the language and arguments of welfare economics to rein in the more socially ambitious aspects of the nationalized industries' programs.

That by the mid-1970s the Treasury was reluctant to put capital up-front for oil exploration was consistent with the drift of its approach toward the nationalized industries since the later 1950s.

Not that BNOC was a typical nationalized public corporation. It was not a monopoly: it traded rather than produced, and it was a taker and not a maker of prices. It spent no time worrying over the comparative merits of marginal and average cost pricing, and it never fretted as to how pricing behavior might be squared with the statutory requirement to break even taking one year with another. As a national corporation, its origin and workings reflected a much older concern, that the country's natural resources were being exploited by the seven sisters of international capitalism and the government was not getting its fair share. Technically, the introduction of PRT addressed many of these concerns, and with the Treasury refusing to allow BNOC to put capital up-front, BNOC became a trading arm of government and a conduit for supplying Whitehall with more and better information on the exploitation of the UK continental shelf than it would otherwise have enjoyed. In a sense, BNOC was both an equity participant and a regulator at one and the same time. The value that the Thatcher government attached to BNOC's performance of these functions was reflected in its abolition.

During what for practical purposes was BNOC's short life, from its establishment in 1976 until the removal of its production assets in 1982, the corporation managed to encompass the last haltering gasps of the old spirit of nationalization, the mid-1970s fixity of the Treasury's concentration on public expenditure, and the early steps toward a substantial program of privatization in the 1980s. It also coexisted with the emergence in the 1970s of a serious concern with the environmental implications of the rate of use of natural resources and the nationalistic concern for how and for whose benefit such resources were exploited. The concerns of both environmentalists and nationalists were to place the issue of property rights at the center of political and academic debate. Potentially, BNOC could have played a role in limiting the rate of oil production. Certainly, the economics of conservation and depletion were read and understood within government, but the dominant concern was always that oil should be extracted as quickly as possible. There is little sense of any government calculating the comparative benefits of current production plus interest on income earned against the benefit of postponed production at future, potentially higher, prices. While an independent Scottish government may have sought to restrict production so as to conserve its oil reserves, the Treasury's concern to maximize output disposed it to leaving the oil companies free to push on with exploiting the oil fields. Yet if this aspect of the emerging work on environmental economics was ignored, the involvement of successive UK governments in the exploration and development of its North Sea oil fields did necessarily involve them in international negotiations on the extent of property rights at sea and on the continental shelf. That in the UK these international negotiations over property rights also extended downward below the level of national government to include arguments over the possible future sovereign structure of the United Kingdom itself gave a very modern edge to this last pre-privatization expression of the spirit of public ownership and the nationalized industries.

## BIBLIOGRAPHY

Cameron, P.D. 1983, *Property Rights and Sovereign Rights: The Case of North Sea Oil*, London: Academic Press.

Coase, R.H. 1970, "The Auction System and North Sea Gas: A Comment," *Journal of Law and Economics* 13(1): 45–47.

Dam, K.W. 1965, "Oil and Gas Licensing and the North Sea," *Journal of Law and Economics* 8: 51–75.

Dam, K.W. 1970, "The Pricing of North Sea Gas in Britain," *Journal of Law and Economics* 13(1): 11–14.

MacKay, D.I. and G.A. Mackay 1975, *The Political Economy of North Sea Oil*, London: Martin Robertson.

Millward, R. 2005, *Private and Public Enterprise in Europe: Energy, Telecommunications and Transport, 1830–1990*, Cambridge: Cambridge University Press.

Minister of Power, *Hansard (Commons)*, 12 July–23 July 1964–1965.

Shonfield, A. 1976, "Enfeebled Government," *The Listener* 95: 326–328.

TNA 1968a, (The National Archives, Kew, London) POWE 63/208, Note of Meeting between Ministry officials and the Labour Party's North Sea Study Group, 19 June.

TNA 1968b, POWE 63/208, Draft paper, "A National Hydrocarbons Corporation," Petroleum Division, 5 July.

TNA 1968c, POWE 63/208, Draft minutes, H. Scholes, Petroleum Division, 5 July.

TNA 1969a, POWE 63/518, Proposals for a National Hydrocarbons Corporation, January.

TNA 1969b, POWE 63/518, "Preference for National Companies," January.

TNA 1969c, POWE 63/519, Paper on 'Checkerboarding', 2 May.

TNA 1969d, POWE 63/519, Paper, "Oil and Gas Leasing in Alberta and Saskatchewan," Annex 1, 5 May.

TNA 1970, POWE 63/350, "The Pricing of North Sea Gas," Derek Eagers, 18 June.

TNA 1971 POWE 63/867, Summary of *The Guardian* article, 1971, "Britain's Giveaway Petroleum Policy," by James Law, 28 December.

TNA 1972a, POWE 63/854, Letter to Eric Wright, Department of Trade and Industry, from Robert Armstrong, Prime Minister's Office, 18 January.

TNA 1972b, POWE 63/854, "North Sea Oil and the Scottish Economy," 23 February.

TNA 1972c, POWE 63/835, "Synopsis of Review of Continental Shelf Licensing Policy," Petroleum Division, 11 October.

TNA 1973a, POWE 63/954, "The Fourth Round Terms," Petroleum Division, 27 February.

TNA 1973b, POWE 63/1027, DTI, "North Sea Oil Depletion Policy," 8 October.

TNA 1974a, POWE 63/1151, Letter to Raymond Prosser from E.J.D. Warne, Department of Trade and Industry, Scottish Industrial Development Office, 18 February.

TNA 1974b, POWE 63/1151, "North Sea Oil—British or Scottish," Note by G.W. Monger, 12 March.

TNA 1974c, FCO 96/178, "North Sea Oil Renegotiation, First Meeting," Summary, A.J. Wilton, 30 October.

TNA 1975a, T319/2929, "Scottish Devolution and North Sea Oil," May.

TNA 1975b, T319/2929, "Devolution: Economic Advantages to Scotland of the Union," Note by M.S. Buckley, Treasury, 19 May.

TNA 1976a, POWE 29/963, "Fifth Round North Sea Licenses—Government Contribution to Capital Costs," Letter from D.W. Healey, Treasury Chambers, to Prime Minister, 9 April.

TNA 1976b, POWE 29/963, Fifth Round of Licensing, Brief for Secretary of State, 13 April.

TNA 1976c, POWE 63/1259, "Scottish and English Oil," undated but probably 1976.

TNA 1977a, POWE 63/1259, "Scotland's Oil," Paper by Foreign and Commonwealth Office, 17 January.

TNA 1977b, POWE 63/1259, "Scotland's Oil," Note by Bernard Ingham, Director of Information, 27 January.

TNA 1978, POWE 63/1259, Newspaper cuttings, probably 3 October.

Vickers, J. And G. Yarrax 1988, *Privatization: An Economic Analysis*, Cambridge: Cambridge, Mass: The MIT Press.

Webb, M. and M. Ricketts 1980, *The Economics of Energy*, London: Macmillan.

# 9 Capabilities, Entrepreneurship, and Political Direction in the Italian National Oil Company
## AGIP/ENI (1926–1971)

*Daniele Pozzi*

State-owned enterprise (SOE) was one of the most important instruments of oil policy in the European industrialized countries from the 1920s onward, and in the 1970s, national oil companies were protagonists in the shift of power from consuming to producing countries. Even the more recent evolution of the oil industry, the rise of new giant-consumer countries in Asia, saw SOE as a crucial player in the new scenarios.[1] The oil industry is a complex sector that requires a high level of technical and managerial capabilities. Business strategies should consider technological changes, the evolution of producing and consuming economies, geopolitical issues, social and environmental problems, and more. It is possible, to some extent, to see oil business as a test field, where the interaction between economic and noneconomic goals of the SOE is dramatically exposed. The case of the oil industry in Italy is even more significant because it underlines the role of SOE in the development process, the difficulties in developing competencies adequate for a modern business in a latecomer economy, and some of the limits of the Italian model of SOE.

This chapter suggests that the evolution of the Italian national oil company, Azienda Generale Italiana Petroli (AGIP) and, after 1953, Ente Nazionale Idrocarburi (ENI), was a result of an interaction among the goals assigned to the SOE, its development as a collector of very specific competencies, and the power balance between the company and government in different periods of its history. The effectiveness of core competencies embedded in the firm, the capability to translate them into economic results, and information asymmetry between the company's techno-structure and the public shareholder explain AGIP/ENI's performance better than the institutional context and formal organization of the firm.

Entrepreneurship was a relevant driving force, mainly after World War II, when Enrico Mattei (1906–1962) led the company. This was not a self-sufficient element, but acted as a catalyzer, directing the capabilities of the firm toward a coherent strategic aim. Besides relying on AGIP/ENI's industrial successes, Mattei exploited his position inside the Italian ruling elite to back the development of the company to an extent not possible for his predecessors. This final result was the outcome of a relationship between the state and national oil company defined during half a century as more of a continuous bargaining process rather than as a set of shared formal rules and practices.[2]

## AGIP UNDER PRIVATE CORPORATE LAW

Oil became a strategic issue after World War I (Clark 1991, 41ff.; Yergin 2003, 167ff.); however, despite the fierce struggle among the Powers to gain control over oil resources, the European energy consumption relied almost entirely on coal: in 1925, solid fuels accounted for 74.2% of total energy use in the U.S., while they rose to 96.2% in the United Kingdom, 95.5% in France, and 98.7% in Germany. Italy, a coal-poor country, relied much more on oil (9.2% vs. 83.9% of solid fuel) even though Italian national consumption was only 792 thousand tons, against 4,561 in the UK, 1,870 in France and 1,174 in Germany (Darmstadter 1971).[3]

Even so, during the 1920s, European states became more and more committed to oil policy. The involvement of the British government in the Anglo-Persian Oil Company (APOC) began in 1914 as a *mariage de convenance* (Ferrier 1982, 202ff.). It saved the enterprise started by William D'Arcy and guaranteed the interest of the admiralty in the development of a new and promising source of fuel for the navy. Compagnie Français des Pétroles (CFP) was born in 1924 as a government tool to obtain a representation in the international consortium allowed to exploit the Iraqi oil (Turkish Petroleum Company [TPC]). In 1927, Spain established complete state monopoly of oil supply—more for fiscal rather than industrial aims—promoting the creation of the national company Compañía Arrendataria del Monopolio de Petróleos Sociedad Anónima (CAMPSA) to manage it. The creation of the Italian oil company AGIP shared some elements of the wave of "oil nationalism" which affected other European countries after World War I, representing an important step in the evolution of state intervention during the 20th century.

AGIP was created in 1926 as a company subject to private corporate law. Its share capital was entirely owned by the state: 60% belonged directly to the Ministry of Finance, 20% to Istituto Nazionale Assicurazioni and 20% to Cassa Nazionale Assicurazioni Sociali, two insurance public concerns. A royal decree—r.d.l. 03/04/1926, no. 556—sanctioned the creation of the enterprise, allowing the three shareholders to pay the 100 million lire capital, but otherwise, AGIP was born as a privately owned company. Its administrative structure was typical of the Italian privately owned companies (president, deputy president, delegate administrator, board of directors), and the public shareholders had no special prerogatives (Pizzigallo 1984, 12–14).

## A Fragile Newborn

Comparing AGIP to the previous intervention of the Italian state in the economy, the company represented a significant novelty: it was neither a case of nationalization directly managed by the public administration nor a state concern, to which the national purpose gave special guarantees and a statute different from private companies. The original AGIP's character was in fact a mix of different and often ill-compatible aims: the SOE was intended to overcome the previous poor attempts of state intervention in oil supply policy (Pizzigallo 1981), but it also had to take care of private enterprise failures in the industry and offer the government a tool to take part in the oil chessboard of the 1920s.

AGIP's first chairman was Ettore Conti, a prominent electricity entrepreneur, deputy-chairman of Banca Commerciale Italiana (COMIT, the most important Italian universal bank), senator of the Kingdom, and very close friend of Giuseppe Volpi. This latter was, at the same time, the powerful Minister of Finance and an electricity industry tycoon (Armanni 1996). Conti was thus one of the pivotal "big-linkers" in the network that bonded finance, politics, and business in interwar Italy since the liberal era (Amatori 1997). AGIP too was designed as a node of this network, taking the shape of a holding company that received its share capital from the state and used it to acquire participation in businesses previously set up by the state or by private entrepreneurs.[4]

During the 1920s, the core of AGIP's activity was limited to import and retail of refined products from the Soviet Union. Almost every facility, personnel, and even the management were inherited from Società Nazionale Olii combustibili (SNOM). This trade company, acquired by AGIP between 1926 and 1927, was created in 1920 by a group of private entrepreneurs. Among them were Giovanni Agnelli (FIAT founder), Piero Pirelli (owner of Pirelli tire company), and some important electricity industrialists.[5] The enterprise was created as a futile attempt to undermine the position of the local branches of the main multinational oil companies that dominated the Italian market (Società Italo-Americana pel Petrolio [SIAP] for Standard Oil New Jersey, and Nafta for Royal Dutch-Shell). SNOM's founders had underestimated the capability of the majors' affiliate to push down prices defending their market share, and in 1926, the company was on the verge of bankruptcy. State intervention guaranteed the survival of the only relevant national player in the Italian oil business and also saved the investment of the well-connected shareholders.

On the other hand, expansion abroad—a necessity for a country lacking relevant oil-producing areas—was driven by diplomatic ambition over Eastern Europe. Both Conti and Volpi had been deeply involved in the futile attempt to gain Italian control over regions "freed" after World War I and remained important players in the Italian *ostpolitik*. Also abroad, AGIP relied entirely on acquisition and indirect financial control of already existing businesses. In 1927, AGIP acquired a majority share in Raffineria Oli Minerali Società Anonima (ROMSA), a small refinery in the Italian enclave of Fiume (Rijeka, Croatia) and in a group of Romanian companies (the main was Prahova AG), previously connected to COMIT's interests in the Balkans (Pozzi 2008).

In fact, AGIP's reality was very far from the pretended harmonious mix of private competences and public funding. First of all, AGIP inherited some private enterprises near to collapse without introducing any significant improvement with respect to their previous administration. The holding structure neither achieved a significant degree of integration among the subsidiary companies nor designed a coherent strategy of development. Very often, AGIP's branches competed among themselves or pursued their aims in complete isolation, as in the case of the Romanian affiliates, which did not export their products to Italy (AGIP was merely interested in financial revenues). Finally, despite its "private" statute, AGIP lacked autonomy from the government, and every strategic issue was resolved outside the company. Conti often truncated any board debates, announcing that a key decision was already made by Volpi or another member of the government (sometime by Mussolini himself), and AGIP had to put it into action.

Other national companies shared some of AGIP's weaknesses, but it is difficult to find an analogue of the undefined position between public and private enterprise of the Italian company. APOC, for instance, was born to save the only viable supplier of oil fuel for His Majesty's Navy at the eve of the World War. Since 1912, APOC had serious financial difficulties, and production and refining facilities reached an acceptable level of efficiency only during the war. Despite the troubled start as an SOE, APOC took advantage of its position as supplier of the British war machine, building the basis for a vigorous postwar growth (Yergin 2003, 173–174). CFP was set up with insufficient financial resources, lacking a supply of crude immediately available and burdened with the interdiction to refine or directly sell its production. Nevertheless, the French company enjoyed a strong legitimation and a relevant pool of expertise, as it had among its private shareholders almost all the companies already operative in France (even some representatives of the foreign majors). Furthermore, in the following year, the state never denied its diplomatic and financial support to improve the position of the company (Nouschi 2001, 33–35). The Spanish monopoly was managed by a new company without any background in the business, like AGIP. CAMPSA's shareholders were bankers, and almost all the share capital of the company was used to acquire already existing plants, expropriated by the state. Even though CAMPSA was guaranteed freedom from competition by the very nature of the monopolistic Spanish oil law, it excluded foreign players from the domestic market (Tortella, Ballestro, and Díaz Fernández 2003, 68 ff.).

The Italian state, conversely, allowed AGIP only petty privileges with respect to its private competitors, such as some advantages in opening new gas stations. Hence, the SOE had to compete against the majors' affiliates in a free market context, lacking the needed activities, competences, and assets. As a result, AGIP's economic situation was deteriorating even more by the end of the decade. When Volpi left office in the summer of 1928, Conti's position weakened and he had to resign after an unsuccessful attempt of agreement with APOC.[6]

## A Strong Leader in a Weak Company

In September 1928, a new board of directors was chaired by Alfredo Giarratana, a 39-year-old publicist and engineer who came from the chairmanship of the municipality-owned utility company of Brescia, a large industrial town in northern Italy (Zane 2001). Giarratana, a very close friend of Augusto Turati, general secretary of the National Fascist Party, belonged to a generation of young technocrats who thought fascism had to act as a renovation force to transform Italy into a modern industrial country. To achieve progress, he favored a stronger involvement of the state in the economy and was hostile toward the industrial-financial liberal oligarchy to which Conti and the previous top management belonged.

Giarratana's leading idea was that the SOE must be managed like— or better than—private-owned companies, and that AGIP had to compete with the latter but aiming toward the national interest. The immediate consequence was to overcome the holding model and transform AGIP into a more integrated company. The rationalization involved the Italian retail facilities; the refining plant in Fiume; and new negotiations with the main AGIP's supplier, the Soviet oil syndicate. In addition, for the first time, AGIP gave some attention to its mining activities (the so-called upstream).[7] Since its foundation, the SOE was entrusted with exploration duties in Italy and in the colonies, but very few had been done. Besides, AGIP managed upstream in an ambiguous legal frame. To avoid involvement of the shareholder insurance companies in a risky activity, mining was handled by a *Gestione Separata* (Autonomous Exploration Department), which acted on behalf of the state, using funds provided by some Ministries. During Giarratana's chairmanship, mining activities remained in a blurred zone between company and public administration, but AGIP promoted better cooperation with the technical bodies of the Ministry of Industry. It started to enlist directly, train young mining technicians, and adopt new techniques imported from abroad.[8]

Giarratana tried to make AGIP the center of the Italian oil policy, but he could not overcome the pitfalls that limited the operative freedom of the company. AGIP's main weakness was that the company—despite Giarratana's vigorous recovery program—could not gather a strong core of profitable activities and did not have bargaining power against political influence that could undermine its long-term investments. Giarratana's efforts were only partly successful, and he was dismissed in 1932, because of the opposition of the majors against his attempt to reach an alliance with the Soviet oil industry and for the political animosities against him after Turati left his office in 1931 (Pizzigallo 1984, 238ff.). Giarratana's successors—usually retired ministers without any experience in oil business—delegated many functions to the technical management the former president had put in a position of control. Thus, AGIP's strategy maintained some continuity after the end of his chairmanship, even though AGIP's performance during the 1930s was varied, as a result of the effects of the international crisis and the political interferences that distorted the resources allocation process of a company too weak to claim real autonomy.

During the 1930s, AGIP was becoming a tool of the public bureaucracy rather than an industrial company, even though its formal structure remained unmodified. Abandoning its "free market" oil policy around 1933, Italy created a system of import quotas and administrative authorizations that mirrored, to some extent, the apparatus existing in France since 1928 (Grayson 1981, 24–26). However, whereas in France the quotas guaranteed state control of the development of a national refining industry, the Italian institutions—answering to the international crisis—mostly aimed to limit the expenditure of hard currency, even reducing production and consumption.[9] Under the quotas system, AGIP enjoyed, for the first time in its history, a relevant and stable share of the Italian market (around 30%), but the company had to renounce progressively to control many variables of its strategy (prices, production level, choice of the suppliers) which passed to the civil and, after 1940, military administration.

Political interference brought some important consequences. The "autarky campaign," started in 1935, gave AGIP progressively more control over many resources to improve its mining activity. Despite few immediate achievements, AGIP was creating a relevant core of technical competence in upstream, thanks to internal growth and contact with the U.S. oil industry.[10] As a result, by the 1940s, the new Mining Department—directed by drilling engineer Carlo Zanmatti—embodied a capital of knowledge and capabilities unequaled in Italy, neither in universities nor in the technical bodies of the administration. In 1943, AGIP began work at Caviaga's giant gas field, near Milan.

## AGIP, MATTEI, AND THE MONOPOLY ON METHANE

In the new democratic Republic of Italy, the plethora of economic institutions, agencies, and public concerns created by fascism led to suspect and unfavorable feelings. The new political class had neither the will nor the economic possibility to sustain entities that supposedly gave an advantage only to the personnel they employed. The conventional wisdom judged AGIP as one of these parasites, because of its ineffective commercial activities and the lack of evident results in upstream.

During the war, AGIP's import and commercial branches had become part of the supply administration, and after the ceasefire, the company facilities and personnel remained framed as a bureaucratic body in 1948, serving first the Allied occupation authority and then the new Italian government.[11] Mining activities continued even during the war. The area of operation was reduced to the Caviaga field, where Zanmatti gathered the best technicians and devices AGIP could retain. During 1944, the rig reached a deep reservoir of methane, but the relevance of the success was difficult to appreciate outside the technical experts, and they were little known outside AGIP's northern offices. In addition, the Treasury refused to allow new funds for mining exploration, denying even to refund the amount AGIP had already spent from its own resources during the previous years.[12]

Enrico Mattei was entrusted by the Partisans' provisional authorities[13] to superintend AGIP's northern units until they could be merged with the main body of the company, under a new board of directors appointed in Rome. His main duties were to preserve the assets of the company and fire the personnel closest to fascism.[14] This brought Mattei in continuous contact with the operating units of the company. The commissioner realized the relevance of Caviaga's field and the pool of competences gathered by the mining branch of the company. In the late 1940s, Mattei became the main supporter of a reconstruction of AGIP based on the capabilities of the technicians in the mining branch. Zanmatti became one of Mattei's right hands, even if he was still facing trial as a fascist collaborator.

While AGIP's commercial activities and refining recovered slowly and partially, the natural gas industry became a new, fast-growing and high-profitable area of business. By 1953, AGIP located four main methane reservoirs (Caviaga, Ripalta, Cortemaggiore, and Ravenna) in the Po Valley, built pipeline facilities to connect the field to the main industrial cities in northern Italy, and gained some important customers (among them, Dalmine, Italcementi, FIAT, and Edison). AGIP's gas production rose from 12 million cubic meters in 1946 to over 3,300 million in 1955, accounting for 13% of the national energy balance.[15] In Italy, there was no relevant competitor already established in the natural gas industry, even though AGIP's successes compelled many small private investors to start enterprises to exploit reservoirs in the Po's delta or to enhance some cottage businesses created there during autarky. Despite the lack of a real alternative to AGIP's already established pool of activities, private-owned enterprise supporters started a fierce campaign against the SOE, blaming AGIP for the backwardness of private methane business.

In fact, AGIP was still keeping its "private-like" nature. The Autonomous Exploration Department, on behalf of the state, was officially responsible for AGIP's upstream, but the company managed it by itself and financed its investments through earnings from methane or borrowing from its machinery suppliers (IRI group, but also some U.S. companies). The old and inefficient Italian mining law did not allow any special treatment to the SOE, but AGIP already owned large exploration permits since the 1930s, while its competitors had to pass through a tiring and uncertain procedure to gain their first fields.

Persisting, Mattei threw all his personal political weight into the struggle to guarantee that AGIP technicians could continue working on the Po Valley fields. The positive results from the fields strengthened Mattei's position inside the company, toward the government, and inside the Christian Democrat Party. In 1948, Mattei became Member of Parliament, tidying up his relationship with the Leftist wing of the Christian Democracy and with the new Minister of Finance, Ezio Vanoni, economic adviser to Alcide De Gasperi, the Prime Minister. Consequently, Mattei's position inside the company became stronger: in June 1948, he was deputy president of a new board of directors, chaired by Marcello Boldrini, a prominent economic scholar and Mattei's close friend.

Mattei progressively rid AGIP of the old management, who were less favorable to a development program based on natural gas, and promoted managers from the mining branch to the highest ranks in the company. As a result, AGIP overcame its legacy as bureaucratic tool of the national supply administration, developing a company culture rooted in the work experience of drilling engineers, geologists, and geophysicists. The new management went beyond the traditional relationship that linked AGIP's upstream to the technical offices of the Ministry of Industry. Under Giarratana, the cooperation with bodies of the ministerial administration had been a valuable asset for the beginning of the exploration, but after World War II, it was just an anachronistic burden. At the beginning of the 1950s, AGIP's technicians dealt with suppliers and contractors from the U.S. oil industry, while Ministry officers had little or no experience with the business and the most updated techniques.

AGIP's upstream was still living in a sort of juridic limbo. Theoretically, an arbitrary decision of the Minister of Industry could halt the whole AGIP program of exploration and exploitation of natural gas. Mattei allowed AGIP to bypass its formal dependence on the administration of the state, taking advantage of personal connections with members of the government and prominent representatives of the Christian Democracy. In 1949, a fierce debate about the role of the SOE in the new Republic arose from AGIP's claims for exclusive rights of exploitation in the area where the company achieved its first successes. In the opinion of those who supported a stronger intervention of the state in the economy, AGIP demonstrated the efficiency of SOEs in a business where private companies failed or did not invest with real commitment. In this opinion, only a coherent strategy, managed by a single center of decision, could efficiently exploit the natural resources of Po Valley, and this actor had to be controlled by the state to guarantee the national interest and to collect tax revenue from the mining activity. Vanoni was particularly sympathetic with this last point.

In fact, in Mattei's vision, AGIP's growth contributed to the development of the country; thus, the company deserved to be guaranteed continued control over its assets. This meant not only the end of the ambiguous position of the upstream between company and administration, but also a legitimation of the hegemony that AGIP maintained de facto over the Po Valley fields. The last point implied putting this area officially outside the control of the ordinary mining law, and therefore out of the Ministry of Industry's ability to interfere in the SOE.

The creation of ENI represented a sort of paradox. The rise of AGIP in the natural gas business was the first opportunity in the history of the SOE in which the company could follow a strategic path consistent with being a private-like company as specified in its statute. The new area of business was developed starting from the only branch of AGIP that was clearly recognized as a part of the administrative body of the state. The final result of building a self-sustaining strategy was the claim for a right of monopoly over Po Valley's gas and the merge with AGIP in a new public concern, ENI, which became a holding company over AGIP and other minor SOEs that operated in hydrocarbons-related industries (Azienda Nazionale Idrogenazione Combustibili [ANIC], Società Nazionale Metanodotti [SNAM], Ente Nazionale Metano [ENM]). The ownership and all the rights of the *Gestione Separata* passed from the Ministry to ENI; finally, it was endowed with monopoly rights to explore and exploit the Po Valley hydrocarbons (Pressenda 1978, 46ff.).

## A PRIVATE INITIATIVE OF A PUBLIC ENTREPRENEUR

The creation of ENI could be seen as an offspring of the general debate on the role of the SOE that was taking place both in Italy and in other European countries after World War II (Amatori 2000, 145–147). After the war, the national oil companies appeared more committed toward the development of their home countries. The evolution of the international geopolitical frame reduced the relevance of oil SOEs as devices of the colonial empires, while the growing weight of hydrocarbons in the European economies created a strong connection between oil and development policy.[16] For AIOC,[17] the end of the war implied stricter bureaucratic burdens and the attempt of the government to interfere in the strategies of the company, as in the case of the 1947–1948 coal-to-fuel oil conversion campaign (Bamberg 1994, 308ff.). Other national companies became more involved in the energy policy of their countries. For instance, from 1945 onward, France reorganized its regulatory system around the Bureau de Recherches de Pétrole (BRP), a public concern entrusted with the coordination of research and development of the industry (Grayson 1981, 26ff.). Oil became a part of the economic planning also in Spain, since Instituto Nacional de Industria (INI, the public concern created based on the model of the Italian IRI in 1941) replaced CAMPSA as a main player in the hydrocarbon national industry (Tortella et al. 2003, 223ff.).

The creation of ENI seemed to mark a stronger involvement of the Italian state in the activities of its national oil company, but in fact, ENI maintained the autonomy Mattei gained for AGIP: the Italian SOE remained "a private initiative of a public entrepreneur" (Amatori 1980, 379).

## The Unbounded SOE

IRI's model clearly inspired ENI's formal structure. Like IRI, the new state concern was a holding company controlling different operating businesses that were still shareholding companies subjected to the private corporation law.[18] To ensure the political direction, ENI was supervised, like IRI, by a committee composed of the Ministries of Industry, Finance, and Treasury, which elected their representatives to the board of directors (5 out of 14 members, unlike IRI, that had 12 directors). At ENI, the board had only a supervising function, while the main administrative body was the Executive Board (*Giunta*), consisting of a president, deputy president, and three directors from the board. ENI's president, just like IRI's, was directly appointed by the government, and the budget of the holding had to be approved by the three Ministries and then presented to the Parliament (Pressenda 1978, 57ff.).

However, ENI was significantly different from IRI. First, taking into account the formal composition of the group, ENI was different because it incorporated companies that were more homogeneous than IRI's, which operated in different branches of the same industry (in this respect, ENI was more similar to IRI's sector sub-holdings, like Finsider or Fincantieri). The homogeneity of ENI was recognized in its statute, which clearly indicated the hydrocarbon-related businesses as the object of its activity. Also, ENI had complete control of its subsidiaries, because the presence of private shareholders in the operating companies was minimal or nonexistent (where it was significant in 1953, as in ANIC, ENI managed to reduce it very soon).

Even more important were some "informal" differences rooted in the previous experiences and the company culture of the oil SOE. Even though the group also embraced some other operating companies, AGIP's legacy was ENI's distinctive character. The struggle for control of Po Valley's natural gas created strong personal bonds between Mattei and the technical management; hence, the company developed a steely *esprit de corp*. The technical community, whose capabilities boosted the growth of the natural gas business, saw themselves and the company as a sort personal army of Mattei's, even after the monopoly control of the Po Valley resources was guaranteed by law. The creation of ENI changed the scale of intervention of the "state entrepreneur," but from a perspective internal to the SOE, changes from Mattei's AGIP were minimal. Mattei was president of all the subsidiaries, and he—or a very small group of his trusted high officers— directly managed all the main issues at a strategic and then operative level. The ENI holding company itself was a sort of enlarged secretariat of the president, who operated like a chief executive officer in all of the operating companies. The coordination among the branches of the group was hence stronger than it appeared on paper—they were formally pictured as independent companies, but coordination was achieved only through a network of personal trust gathered around Mattei.

Probably the most important function of the ENI parent company was to act as a shield between the political shareholder and the operating companies, preserving them from direct contact with the politics and making the activities of the group less visible for their would-be supervisors. To guarantee ENI's autonomy, Mattei exploited his position in the Christian Democracy Party, taking advantage of the lack of a clear economic policy line inside the majority party and the information asymmetry that shielded ENI from political interferences.[19] With regard to issues of investment abroad or development of petrochemical plants, it was very difficult for the three Ministries who "supervised" ENI to really understand what the company was doing, and it was almost impossible for them to agree on a strategy alternative to Mattei's. Left by itself, ENI was achieving impressive results that contributed to the economic development of the country; thus, there was no strong motivation for a clash between the shareholders and the powerful public entrepreneur.

At the end of 1956, it seemed that politics was tightening its control over SOEs, thanks to the creation of the Ministry of State Holdings (Ministero delle Partecipazioni Statali [MINPASTA]). The institution of MINPASTA was a result of the debate over the role of SOEs in the democratic Italy started just after the war and was triggered by the confrontation between AGIP and private enterprise supporters since 1949. MINPASTA fulfilled the expectation of some Christian Democracy wings for direct control over the SOEs by the government, bypassing already well-established and politically neutral bureaucracies (e.g., technical bodies in Ministry of Industry or Treasury). For almost 30 years, the MINPASTA was firmly controlled by Christian Democrat ministries, strengthening the dependence of SOEs from the majority party. As a matter of fact, the approach of Mattei's ENI to its political overseer—MINPASTA assumed the duties previously assigned to the committee of Ministries—did not change significantly. In some respect, MINPASTA freed even more of ENI from administrative controls. ENI benefited from a privileged position between 1960 and 1968 as Giorgio Bo held the office of chief of MINPASTA. Bo, portrayed as Mattei's yes-man by some commentators, was very close to ENI's top management and shared its idea of the role of a strong national oil company as a key factor in the development of the country (Colitti 2008, 32–33).[20]

## A Double-Edged Weapon

The fact that the political class that governed Italy during the 1950s and 1960s was incapable or unwilling to choose a coherent line of economic policy gave ENI *carte blanche* in many respects, but it also meant that its investments were not backed by sound political decisions or by a stream of financial resources sufficient to reach the goals stated for the company. The very nature of ENI was still somehow ambiguous. In some respect, the SOE was considered the administrator of revenues coming from the national subsoil, at least in the Po Valley. On the other hand, the Ministries were supposed to be supervising investments typical of a modern competitive oil company, often without understanding the logic of the business.[21] The more controversial topic was the right of the company to start exploration abroad, to reach the complete vertical integration in its liquid fuel business.

Even though by the mid-1950s it was becoming clear that no significant oil field existed in the Italian subsoil, Mattei had to defend the legitimacy of ENI investing outside Italy to the committee of supervisor ministries.[22] The main argument that Mattei had to face was that ENI's "national purpose" referred only to the administration of the Po Valley's natural gas. Thus, the aim of the SOE's investment had to be the creation of jobs in Italy, possibly locating new fields in the southern regions, because the area badly needed new industrial activities. The only solution to soften the Ministries' opposition was to pretend that investment abroad would bring only limited expenditure, with sure revenue. This generated exaggerated expectations and deprived ENI of the possibility of gaining sound diplomatic and financial support in the future. Information asymmetry also became a double-edged weapon in other cases of investment abroad, especially when ENI, without any significant support from the Italian diplomacy, had to tackle strong competition and criticisms because of some controversial agreements in Iran, Libya, and the USSR (Frankel 1966, 119ff.).

The trade-off between autonomy and support from its shareholders affected ENI mostly with respect to the mismatch between available resources and investment needs. After Mattei's death, his successor, Eugenio Cefis,[23] had to cope with a large set of recently started investments in different countries and business areas. In the short run, most of them could not give any revenue but needed new resources to be completed. This is a situation quite typical in the oil companies, which need a well-balanced pool of activities and strong financial stability to survive the low conjuncture periods, fulfilling, at the same time, their long-term investment programs (Frankel 1946).

At the beginning of the 1960s, ENI was growing heavily indebted as a result of a terrific expansion sustained mainly by borrowings. In fact, the sole area of business that continued to give significant profits was still natural gas in northern Italy. ENI's share capital remained almost the same as what the company owned in 1953 (between 30 and 37 billion lire).[24] In fact, ENI could find fresh share capital only through a political directive that would allow an increase of its endowment fund (*fondo di dotazione*).[25] Mattei always refused to take this step, to grant the politicians any "credit of reconnaissance" that could put the autonomy of the company in danger.

The new chairmanship began in a period of internal difficulties, because of the high need of investments and more hostility toward ENI. For instance, the oil market was becoming more competitive, and the Italian high growth rate began to cool down (in 1963, the Bank of Italy raised the interest rate, making borrowing even more costly).The worsening situation compelled ENI to adjust its share capital to the scale of its investment, and Cefis had to open a wider bargain with the political parties to obtain a more significant commitment from the shareholder to the development of the SOE.[26] During 1964, ENI was allowed to raise its endowment fund from 36.9 to 161.9 billion lire, and in 1968, it rose to 778.9 billion. New investments were 236.5 billion in 1963, became 393 billion in 1968, and more than 701 billion in 1970. During Mattei's chairmanship (1953–1962), new investment had reached just 910 billion. In addition, Cefis strengthened the company, implementing new tools for investment planning and control, promoting a severe reduction of some expenses, and expanding the availability of capital by issuing new company bonds (also on the international markets).[27] Thanks to the new investment, ENI could consolidate its position as "junior member" in the international oil business.[28]

The large injection of fresh financial resources did not imply a real understanding of the needs of the business by the public shareholder, while the political class felt the increase of the endowment fund was a counterbalance that overloaded the company with "improper financial burdens" (*oneri impropri*). In his relationship with politics, Cefis acted with some continuity with regard to Mattei's chairmanship. Even if he never officially held any political office, Cefis maintained a strong personal influence inside the Christian Democracy (e.g., financing different wings of the party); he could present himself as the only legitimized interface between the company and the political parties, preserving ENI from direct involvement with politics. Even if the SOE had to allow some costly *oneri impropri*, the political interferences did not distort the main investment programs (Briatico 2004, 119ff.).

The SOE remained dependent on the strategy it had developed successfully since the 1950s: the bargain remained essentially based on a confrontation of power—the power of ENI to generate profits to sustain its own investment, and the power of the leadership of the SOE to reduce political interferences to a minimum. At the beginning of the 1970s, Cefis perceived that both forces that had shielded ENI were growing feeble, and, not trusting that ENI could keep its independence in the future, he left the national oil company in 1971 to become Montedison's president.

## CONCLUSIONS

It could be possible to frame the evolution of the Italian national oil company as a two-entry matrix, putting on one axis the strength of the leadership and on the other the effectiveness of the organizational capabilities embedded in the company to reach its economic goals. During AGIP's prewar period, the main constant element was the lack of a strong core business: the refining and commercial activities of the SOE did not retain any competitive advantage, and the company remained a follower, very far from its foreign competitors. A chairmanship with few committed to the development of the SOE brought it to the verge of bankruptcy, but even Giarratana's energetic leadership could not stop the interference of politics, lacking any significant economic weight. A clearer strategic program could at least set in motion the process of accumulation of organizational and technical capabilities that sustained the postwar growth in the mining business. After 1945, for the first time, entrepreneurial skills introduced concrete possibilities of translating AGIP's competences into profits.

The transformation of a company theoretically "private-shaped" into a state concern was more significant because it made certain the control of the SOE over AGIP's main source of profits (and influence) rather than because the creation of ENI changed the relationship between the company and its shareholder. In fact, when AGIP was still operating under the private corporate law, the possibility of political interference was enormous, mostly because the nature and the aims of the company were ill defined or did not have an operative concreteness. Only the monopoly on the Po Valley gave AGIP a legitimized role and, at the same time, an economic weight that could be translated into bargaining power with the state to guarantee a wider sphere of autonomy.

Despite being a state-owned concern, ENI worked like private international oil companies until it could express a strong leadership with a specific political power and a positive economic performance. The independence of the strategic decision process was guaranteed, limiting contact with the political shareholder except when strictly necessary. This solution allowed ENI a large autonomy but deprived the company of the possibility to interact with its supervisors in a more constructive manner. Mattei and Cefis maintained the autonomy of their strategy on the basis of continuous power bargain. At the time, this solution worked efficiently because the company and its leaders were the stronger players, but they did not take advantage of this position to establish a permanent equilibrium that could survive in less favorable conditions.

In fact, even during Mattei's and Cefis' chairmanships, some processes were put in motion that could interfere with the evolution of the SOE, but they remained ineffective because ENI was able to maintain a favorable position. In 1956, the creation of MINPASTA was the first attempt to control the SOEs. The Ministry did not interfere significantly with ENI's strategies, mostly because Mattei, Cefis, and Bo shared similar goals. More relevant was, in 1967, the creation of Comitato Interministeriale per la Programmazione Economica (CIPE, Interministerial Committee for Economic Planning), a committee of Ministries and experts from the administration that had the authority to plan and coordinate the goals of the national economic policy. CIPE was sponsored by the Socialist Party to limit the Christian Democrat influence. As a result, the position of MINPASTA diminished and the SOEs were cut off from the planning process. Cefis, however, was influential enough to limit the CIPE's interference to a minimum.

Raffaele Girotti (1971–1974) and the following ENI presidents operated under the same institutional pattern as Cefis, but in a weaker position. They did not express a strong leadership—some of them even lost the loyalty of ENI's management (Colitti 2008, 229ff.)—and could not rely on personal political influence. After the 1973 oil crisis, the company was no longer able to find a strong strategic coherence among its branches of activities. Only businesses based on a strong core of technical capabilities (mining, engineering) could maintain a positive performance; meanwhile, the interference of political parties began to severely distort investment in businesses less firmly established (e.g., petrochemical). The order that was able to preserve the independence of the company—not by a pattern of formal rules and institutions, but only by personal capabilities, commitment, and contingency—was doomed to collapse during the following years.

## NOTES

1. An exhaustive comparative research study of different experiences of SOEs in the oil business does not exist. Partial insight can be retrieved for European cases in Grayson (1981) and Beltran (2010); for producing countries' cases in Marcel (2006); and for recent Asian cases in Goldstein (2009).
2. The reconstruction of AGIP/ENI's evolution is based on the primary sources and literature used in Pozzi (2009). See the book for the complete references in the Italian language.
3. It is important to note that until after World War II, an intensive consumption of liquid fuels remained an American prerogative: in 1925, Western Europe used 11,103 million tons of oil, while the U.S. used around 91,743.
4. The following reconstruction is based on Meetings Cda AGIP (1926–1928), f.11/b.1/Exploration & Power/Archivio Storico ENI.
5. Some documentation on SNOM survives in CdA CUN (1920–1929), f.1b9/ b.38/E&P/AS ENI.
6. The negotiation aimed to make AGIP a sort of agency of the British major. APOC withdrew the agreement when it realized that AGIP didn't have control of its own strategic variables (e.g., the Italian SOE had to adopt a price discount imposed by the government). In fact, the international position of the British company ("As Is" agreement) discouraged the alliance with AGIP. Meetings 26/09/1928 and 15/10/1928 Cda AGIP (1926–1928), f.11/b.1/ E&P/AS ENI; see also Bamberg (1994, 115–116).
7. According to the Schlumberger Oilfield Glossary, the adjective refers to facilities or systems located in the wellbore or production train above the surface choke (http://www.glossary.oilfield.slb.com). In the oil business jargon it is often used as a noun, indicating the whole upstream activity (conversely, downstream indicates refining, marketing and distribution operations).
8. Giarratana's line of action is documented by Cda AGIP (1929–1931), f.12/ b.1/E&P/AS ENI.
9. R.d.l. 02/11/1933, no. 1741.

10. Documents 1775 sc. 19, 8596 sc. 123, 47781 sc. 553, Scatole Rosse/E&P/ AS ENI.
11. War brought Italy to a sort of "energy starvation." In 1938, 515,000 tons of gasoline were available in the country, and in 1943, the figure collapsed to 98,000. Data from Dir. Gen. Miniere (1951, 310)
12. Documents on the tense relationship between AGIP and Treasury during 1945–1946 are in sf.11/f.6/b.314/Permessi e Concessioni/Dir. Gen. Miniere/ Ministero Industria/ACS.
13. At that time, Enrico Mattei (1906–1962) was a young chemical industrialist who came from a middle-class family from Marche (a rather poor region in central Italy). He had started, with his brothers, a small factory of tanning products in Milan during the 1930s. During the war, he joined the Christian Democrat clandestine party and became one of the leaders of the Resistance movement. He died in 1962, in a plane crash that some commentators claim was caused by sabotage.
14. Reconstruction of Mattei's first period at Northern AGIP is based on documentation in sc. 19 and 21/Scatole Rosse/E&P/AS ENI.
15. France—the only Western European country that relied significantly on natural gas—produced just 256 million cubic meters in 1955 (in 1946, the French production was 100 million). In the mid-1950s, natural gas accounted for 0.4% of the French energy consumption (Darmstadter 1971; Grayson 1981).
16. By 1960, Western Europe depended on liquid fuels for around 32% of its energy consumption (United Kingdom 25.8%, West Germany 22.5%, France 34%, Italy 56%). Before the war (1938), the European average was 7.7% (Darmstadter 1971).
17. In 1935, the Anglo-Persian Oil Company changed its name to Anglo-Iranian Oil Company Limited (AIOC). The name British Petroleum Company Limited (BP) has represented the whole group since 1954.
18. Law 10/02/1952, no. 136.
19. The political position of Mattei and his role in the complex balance among the many Christian Democracy wings is explained by Galli (1976).
20. ENI's autonomy and political unresponsiveness was a usual topic for the opponents of the SOE worried about the rising of Mattei's power (see Votaw 1964).
21. It is also possible to say that in ENI there was a coexistence between the nature of the national oil companies typical in the producing countries (Marcel 2006) and the character of the multinational oil companies (SOEs or privately owned) established in consuming countries. British government created instead a new SOE to manage domestic oil exploitation in the North Sea (see Chick, Chapter 8).
22. Report of the meetings held in 1955 is in f.1810/b.55/Direzione Estero/ENI/ AS ENI.
23. Cefis had been partisan commander and Mattei's companion in arms during the war. He became Mattei's right hand in ENI, supervising mostly the petrochemical branch and the most delicate international negotiations. He was trusted by the technical management of the group as Mattei's "lieutenant," thus recognized as a legitimate successor of the founder by the majority of the company. He led ENI as deputy president in 1962 (with Boldrini as president) and as president from 1967 to 1971.
24. From 1955 to 1963, total assets rose from 48,631 to 375,575 million lire, around 7.7 times. During the same period, borrowings multiplied 34 times (from 9,459 to 324,933 million) while net worth increased just 1.3 times (from 39,172 to 50,642 million). Data from ENI Holding's official balance sheets, analyzed in Pozzi (2004, Appendix A).

25. See Chapter 3.
26. The Socialist Party supported the Christian Democracy in 1963 and this further complicated the "extraordinary compromise" equilibrium of the Italian economic policy (Barca 1997).
27. Data from ENI Holding official balance sheet 1970. See also documents in Giunta ENI (1963–1966), f.2501/b.6/ENI/AS ENI.
28. In the mid-1960s, AGIP produced little more than 18,000 tons of refined products, against around 218,000 tons by Standard NJ, and 84,000 tons produced by BP. In any case, this result was impressive: ten years before, the Italian SOE produced just 5,000 tons, against 127,000 tons produced by Standard (ENI official balance sheet 1967; Penrose 1968).

## BIBLIOGRAPHY

Amatori, F. 1980, "Entrepreneurial Typologies in the History of Industrial Italy (1880–1960): A Review Article," *Business History Review* 54(3): 359–386.

Amatori, F. 1997, "Italy: The Tormented Rise of Organizational Capabilities between Government and Families," in *Big Business and the Wealth of Nations*, eds. A. D. Chandler, F. Amatori, and T. Hikino, Cambridge: Cambridge University Press.

Amatori, F. 2000, "Beyond State and Market. Italy's Futile Search for a Third Way," in *The Rise and Fall of State-Owned Enterprise in the Western World*, ed. P. A. Toninelli, Cambridge: Cambridge University Press.

Armanni, V. 1996, "Ettore Conti tra industria elettrica e banca mista," in *Storie di imprenditori*, ed. D. Bigazzi, Bologna: Il Mulino.

Bamberg, J. H. 1994, *The History of the British Petroleum Company: The Anglo-Iranian Years, 1928–1954*, Vol. 2, Cambridge: Cambridge University Press.

Barca, F. 1997, "Compromesso senza riforme," in *Storia del capitalismo italiano*, ed. F. Barca, Roma: Donzelli.

Beltran, A., ed. 2010, *A Comparative History of National Oil Companies*, Bruxeles: Peter Lang.

Briatico, F. 2004, *Ascesa e declino del capitale pubblico in Italia*, Bologna: Il Mulino.

Clark, J. G. 1991, *The Political Economy of World Energy*, Chapel Hill: University of North Carolina Press.

Colitti, M. 2008, *ENI. Cronache dall'interno di un'azienda*, Milano: Egea.

Darmstadter, J. 1971, *Energy in the World Economy. A Statistical Review of Trends in Output, Trade and Consumption since 1925*, Baltimore: Johns Hopkins Press.

Dir. Gen. Miniere 1951, *Relazione sul servizio minerario per l'anno 1945*, Roma: Istituto poligrafico dello stato.

Ferrier, R. W. 1982, *The History of the British Petroleum Company: The Developing Years, 1901–1932*, Vol. 1, Cambridge: Cambridge University Press.

Frankel, P. H. 1946, *Essential of Petroleum*, London: Chapman & Hall.

Frankel, P. H. 1966, *Mattei. Oil and Power Politics*, London: Faber & Faber.

Galli, G. 1976, *La sfida perduta*, Milano: Bompiani.

Goldstein, A. 2009, "New Multinationals from Emerging Asia: The Case of National Oil Companies," *Asian Development Review* 26(2): 26–56.

Grayson, L. E. 1981, *National Oil Companies*, Chichester: John Wiley and Sons.

Marcel, V. 2006, *Oil Titans. National Companies in the Middle East*, London: Chatham House.

Nouschi, A. 2001, *La France et le pétrole de 1924 à nos jours*, Paris: Picard.

Penrose, E. T. 1968, *The Large International Firm in Developing Countries. The International Petroleum Industry*, Cambridge, Mass.: MIT Press.

Pizzigallo, M. 1981, *Alle origini della politica petrolifera italiana*, Milano: Giuffrè.

Pizzigallo, M. 1984, *L'AGIP degli anni ruggenti*, Milano: Giuffrè.

Pozzi, D. 2004, *L'affermazione delle capacità tecnico-manageriali nell'AGIP di Enrico Mattei come sviluppo di un processo di lungo periodo (1930–1965)*, Ph.D. thesis, Università commerciale Luigi Bocconi, Milano, XVI ciclo.

Pozzi, D. 2008, "AGIP in Romania: The Prahova's Venture (1926–1943)," *Bulletin of Petroleum-Gas University of Ploiesti* 60(1): 29–39.

Pozzi, D. 2009, *Dai gatti selvaggi al cane a sei zampe*, Venezia: Marsilio.

Pressenda, A. 1978, "L'ENI nello sviluppo economico italiano," in *Ricerca sulle partecipazioni statali*, Vol. 2, ed. G. Cottino, Torino: Einaudi.

Tortella, G., A. Ballestro, and J. L. Díaz Fernández 2003, *Del monopolio al libre mercado. La historia de la industria petrolera española*, Madrid: LID.

Troilo, C. 2008, *1963–1982. I venti anni che sconvolsero l'IRI*, Milano-Roma: Bevivino.

Votaw, D. 1964, The Six-Legged Dog. *Mattei and ENI*, Berkeley: University of California Press.

Yergin, D. 2003, *The Prize*, New York: Free Press.

Zane, M. 2001, *Alfredo Giarratana*, Brescia: Grafo.

# 10 Iron and Steel State Industry in the UK and Italy

*Ruggero Ranieri*

In Italy, during the 1930s, a large part of the steel industry was incorporated in IRI-Finsider, a publicly owned conglomerate. After roughly 60 years, between 1993 and 1996, all steel state-owned enterprises (SOEs) in Italy were privatized (Balconi 1991, 1998). In Britain, after 1945, the industry became the object of party political controversy. Two successive nationalizations were carried out by Labour governments: the first one, short lived, in 1951, and the second, more enduring, in 1967. Each of these was followed by a return to the private sector (Vaizey 1974; Beauman 2000).

The nature of the public sector was quite different in the two countries. There are, however, some broad similarities. First, the rationale for public ownership was the need to modernize and rationalize the industry, by injecting a measure of technocratic leadership into it. Second, once the public sector had been set up, it faced the dilemma of reconciling efficiency and competitive strength with being part of the state-owned sector (Ranieri 1999). Also, the actors involved in the debate were basically the same in the two countries: they were corporatists, modernizers, and liberals (Ranieri 1995). Especially the former two—as the importance of the liberals was marginal—were active within industry and government. The corporatists were entrenched in the powerful steel employers' associations: the British Iron and Steel Federation (BISF) and Assider in Italy. The modernizers were essentially technocrats, and their point of view should not be mistaken with that of the nationalizers belonging to the Left, for whom political and ideological motivations were clearly stronger than industrial ones. In Britain, modernizers and nationalizers interacted uneasily, with the latter briefly gaining the upper hand in 1949 and in 1967. In Italy, the modernizers coalesced in the public sector, making the influence of nationalizers negligible.[1]

## ITALY: FINSIDER AND THE SINIGAGLIA PLAN (1933–1960)

In Italy, the public sector was a result of the Great Depression, when the state stepped in to salvage the large 'mixed' banks, particularly the Banca Commerciale and the Credito Italiano, taking them over, together with all their industrial assets. As a result, when the Istituto per la Ricostruzione Industriale (IRI) was created in 1933, it was saddled with a number of important steel companies, accounting for about half of the industry's capacity. The old company structure was left intact but, a few years later, all of IRI's steel SOEs were placed within Finsider, a newly formed public holding, accounting for 77% of Italy's pig iron production, 45% of crude steel, and 38% of hot rolled products.

What lay behind the creation of IRI-Finsider? Some have pointed to the fact it was not intended as a deliberate attempt at nationalization; rather, it was the result of particular economic circumstances. Furthermore, state intervention in the industry, in the form of subsidies and bailouts, went back to the early years of Italy's rise as an industrial nation. Others have stressed that the creation of IRI was, in fact, a turning point, as the state, for the first time, became the direct owner of a number of major steel companies (Amatori 2000, 142ff.). With the prospect of state ownership beckoning, as early as 1931 there was a conscious attempt by a group of state technocrats to acquire a role in reorganizing the industry and in pursuing its modernization and expansion. Some of the best managers and technicians, including Oscar Sinigaglia, Agostino Rocca, and many others, who were later to play a key role in Finsider, coalesced around Sofindit, the financial arm managing in trusteeship all steel assets belonging to the Banca Commerciale Italiana, and started planning for expansion and rationalization (Barca 1997; Petri 2002).

A similar drive for modernization and efficiency emerged, even more clearly, in the post–World War II (WWII) years, despite the prevailing free market rhetoric. As Amatori observes, "in this period strategy—or more precisely a series of strategies—clearly emerged" and "thanks to the efforts of nationalistic entrepreneurs, sincere development ideologists, and ambitious party leaders, Beneduce's creation [i.e., the IRI] was solidified and expanded." A key role was played by Oscar Sinigaglia: Amatori calls him an example of an Italian "samurai." Having started his career in steel as a small private entrepreneur, he had come to believe that modernization and technical progress in the steel industry could be achieved only through the intervention of the state and, accordingly, he was influential in designing a national strategy for the industry, in competition with the private sector (Amatori 2000, 147ff.).

Although the creation of Finsider gave the planners and modernizers an important advantage, they still faced formidable resistances on the part of the tightly cartelized, and heavily protected, industry's private sector, organized around Assider, composed mainly of small firms, based in northwest Italy. The two largest private steelmakers were Fiat, an automobile maker that had integrated backward into steel during the 1920s, and the family-owned Falck group. The dispute between Finsider and the Falcks on the terms of post–WWII Reconstruction is regarded as a classic. Oscar Sinigaglia, the chairman of Finsider, insisted on rebuilding large integrated coastal plants based on standardized mass production, whereas the Falcks believed that Italy should concentrate on high value-added small-batch production. In that instance, Fiat broke ranks with its private sector partners to support Sinigaglia's plans, which included installation of a wide strip mill at Cornigliano. Sinigaglia won the argument and the government and IRI committed themselves fully to funding his plan. The contrast between private and public sector was renewed at the time of the second wave of postwar investment, in the late 1950s, when private producers tried to stop Finsider from building a large greenfield plant at Taranto, in the South. Once more, however, they were forced to give way to IRI's, government-backed, investment plans (Sinigaglia 1948; Osti 1993; Ranieri 2002).

The corporatist wing of the industry was influential not just in the private sector but also in the public sector, especially in the older companies, for whom becoming part of IRI had not implied any substantial change in management or strategy. Because the IRI system was supposed to operate according to private company law, they could, to some extent, resist outside interference. Recent research on Dalmine—a company specializing in seamless tube, which enjoyed a quasi-monopolistic position on the home market, well sheltered by tariffs as well as by quotas in the international tube-makers cartel—has shown how reluctant management was to follow Finsider-led plans for expansion and nationwide rationalization of the tube sector (Amatori and Licini 2006). The result was a compromise, unsatisfactory for both sides. Equally, Ilva, one of Finsider's largest companies, was still firmly embedded in a corporatist, conservative culture far removed from Sinigaglia's reforming program. Sinigaglia and his followers had no choice but to carry out their plans by creating a new company, Cornigliano, making it the focus of their strategy and eventually seeking to reshape Ilva by merging it with Cornigliano into a new company by the name of Italsider.

## BRITAIN: THE FIRST AND SECOND
## NATIONALIZATION OF STEEL (1945–1967)

Nationalization of the steel industry was obviously a sensitive and important political issue. But there was another issue, in many ways separate from the first, about how the state could contribute to the industry's modernization and, thus, confront the dominant corporatist model, with steel entrenched as a self-governing national cartel. A number of intermediate solutions were explored, all proving unsatisfactory, until the industry's self-governing body was dismantled and the main bulk of the industry was turned into a public corporation, working under constraints of efficiency, with a strong technocratic leadership. This, however, did not happen until 1967, in occasion of the second steel nationalization. The first public body to play a role in the UK steel industry was the Imports Duties Advisory Committee (IDAC), which was set up in 1932 with the task of enforcing tariff protection and reorganizing the industry (Tolliday 1987). It acted in conjunction with BISF, with a clear mandate to speak for the whole trade. Thereupon, a complex web of trade barriers, price fixing arrangements, cost spreading measures, and domestic and foreign quota allocation was spun around the industry, with the primary objective of fending off competition by Continental European producers (Burn 1958; Millward 2000, 164). One of the first tasks the IDAC undertook was, in fact, to negotiate a satisfactory agreement with the European Steel Cartel, based on reciprocal market share allocation (Wurm 1993).

The officially sanctioned cartel was further consolidated during WWII. The industry was effectively self-governed, but, at the same time, it worked in close cooperation with the government, either through the machinery of the relevant Ministry or through special public supervisory bodies, acting on the government's behalf. Thus, during the war, the Iron and Steel Control of the Ministry of Supply absorbed most of the BISF staff. After the war, a new public body, the Iron and Steel Board, was set up to advise the government and oversee the industry, with BISF resuming a key role in setting prices, planning investment, and managing foreign trade.

BISF epitomized the corporatist style of government. It was a formidable body, with a large staff and an influential and commanding leadership. The largest companies controlled its key committees. There was little room for outsiders, however innovative or successful. The example of Sir William Firth, the head of Richard Thomas and Co. has been extensively covered in the literature (Tolliday 1987, chap. 5). Firth was an innovator who understood the potential of new U.S. mass production technology, which, on the other hand, most of the industry was reluctant to embrace. In the 1930s, he had sought to reorganize the highly cartelized tinplate industry through amalgamations, restructuring, and takeovers, thus achieving a sufficient to hold on the market to justify installing a wide strip mill at Ebbw Vale. This was a suboptimal location, which Firth was compelled to choose because of political pressure. What is more important, however, was that when a downturn in the market in 1938 compelled Firth to ask for external financial help, BISF promptly stepped in, gaining a foothold in the management of Firth's business and, soon after, pushing him out.

After the Labour victory in 1945, BISF faced the prospect of nationalization. The literature suggests a certain amount of reluctance on the part of the Labour Party toward extending nationalization in the manufacturing sector (Millward 1997, 227). However, some Labour politicians considered steel as a kind of a service, a "means of production" (as mentioned in Clause 4) supplying other industries semi-finished inputs. Moreover, it was a candidate for rationalization and amalgamation, as its structure compared poorly, in terms of size of plant and units, to U.S. and German giants. Be is as it may, iron and steel had appeared as a candidate for nationalization in the Labour Party's 1931 Election manifesto, in the 1934 *For Socialism and Peace* publication, and in the 1945 *Let Us Face the Future* election manifesto (Tomlinson 1994, chap. 8).

BISF tried to make the case that it was able to deliver enough expansion of output, rationalization, and modernization to make nationalization unnecessary. Its case rested on the fact that steel, as opposed to coal, had had a relatively good war. Furthermore, its vicinity to the government had given ministers and officials an opportunity to take a close look at the industry and map out future plans (Chick 1988). An investigation on the industry's prospects, the Franks-Chester report, was carried out in 1944 under the auspices of the Ministry of Supply and of the Board of Trade. Much of it was devoted to modernization, a switch to mass production, the exploitation of economies of scale. Significantly, however, it did not challenge the corporatist pattern of management. The 1944 report was, therefore, an uneasy compromise between the modernizers and the corporatists, which gave the latter room for maneuver in their dealings with the government, not least because many influential Labour ministers were not fully convinced about the need for full-scale government ownership (Ranieri 1995).

In the following years, the compromise unraveled. In 1945, BISF duly produced an apparently ambitious Five-Year Plan. It then proceeded to sell its case to the government. Why, BISF demanded, should the government want to own an industry that was delivering the goods, and with which, anyway, it enjoyed such a close and intimate relationship? The Labour government, at least for a time, dithered, as was revealed in the discussions that Morrison and Dalton had with the chairman of BISF, Andrew Duncan, in the spring and summer of 1947. Were they seeking to control the industry more closely? Did they want it to modernize more quickly? Did they want to take over some of its most important investment projects? All of these objectives were within their reach, but none seemed to convince them. They settled, instead, for an arrangement which would give them a large amount of ownership rights, just short of a full takeover. This, however, the industry was not prepared to concede. Thus, the talks stalled, the Labour Party and the trade unions complained vociferously about backhand deals, and the government finally decided to nationalize (Ranieri 1995, 285ff.).

The Nationalization Bill was first introduced before Parliament in November 1948 and after a prolonged and often fierce debate, it became law in November 1949. The drafting of the bill had revealed the confusion and indecisions that surrounded the takeover of the industry. It became evident that nationalizing the steel industry meant nationalizing companies engaged in many other manufacturing activities, from engineering to chemicals. This had not been foreseen and was greeted as a nuisance, but there seemed to be no alternative solution. After much soul searching, the existing company structure was left intact, while a public holding—the Iron and Steel Corporation of Great Britain—took over all the companies' shares on 15 February 1951 (Ross 1965; Millward 1997, 211; 2000, 169). Still, the companies' boards were able to retain most of their powers, while BISF, formally empowered to represent the smaller firms which had escaped the net of public ownership, continued to play an important role (Tivey 1966, 58). If the idea was to modernize and rationalize the industry, this form of nationalization would not have been of much help. In the event, there was very little time for it to be tested, because, as soon as the Conservatives came back to power, in October 1951, they passed the Iron and Steel Act, to bring the industry back into the private sector (Tivey 1966, 57–59; Burk 1988).

Discussions between 1945 and 1951 point to the fact that nationalization was not a carefully planned strategy and that it diverted energies from the only other strategy that might have worked—that is, to ensure, through controls, financial levers, market liberalization, and even piecemeal public ownership, that the industry be forced to modernize and break out of its sheltered, subsidized, and cartelized existence. Not only, therefore, was nationalization mismanaged, but the corporatists' bluff was not called, and the outmoded and inadequate corporatist arrangement enveloping the industry was allowed to survive (Ranieri 1995).

The BISF regime was particularly damaging in the industry's commercial and foreign policy. Between 1952 and 1955, it might have been possible to reach an agreement with the European Coal and Steel Community (ECSC), accepting common rules over pricing and dismantling reciprocal tariff barriers, in order to boost trade between Britain and the Continent. After a fractious internal debate, the industry turned its back to such a solution: the UK market remained practically cut off from the Continental one, protected by quotas and tariffs and screened by its baroque cross-subsidies and artificial pricing rules. Whereas preferential access to Commonwealth markets could be raised as a justification for this state of affairs in the short term, in the long term, given that those markets were becoming self-sufficient in steel, this meant postponing inevitable choices (Ranieri 1993; Owen 2000, 129ff.; Milward 2002, chap. 5). Equally, the investment plans laid out by BISF proved to be little more than a smokescreen. The industry, left to its own devices, failed to rationalize.

There was of course a second opportunity for Labour, when it came back to power in 1964. Conditions had become more favorable, essentially because the corporatist model was, by that time, largely perceived to have failed. In the previous years, privatization had been carried out fairly rapidly so that by 1957 companies accounting for 85% of total steel output had been brought back into private ownership, mostly into the hands of former shareholders. The only major firm still waiting to be sold was Richard Thomas and Baldwin's, whose prospects, pending the construction of a new controversial strip mill in South Wales, were seen as uncertain.

A new Iron and Steel Board was set up in 1953 to supervise the industry. It remained in existence for 14 years. Its powers over investment and prices were not negligible, but they were not enough to make it an effective planning or regulatory body. On many issues it found itself dependent on BISF, which remained a major force, with its influential leadership and its powerful and pervasive bureaucracy. By 1966, BISF employed 600 officials, as compared to the Board's 140 (Ovenden 1978, 18, 214). The government, on the other hand, showed that it was prepared to overstep the Board, whenever a major investment decision with electoral implications came up. This proved the case in 1958 when the Cabinet, against the Board's advice, decided to built two new strip mills, rather than one—the first going to South Wales and the other to Scotland. Increasingly the Board vented its frustration at being prevented from rationalizing the industry (Burn 1961, chap. 10).

Much effort went into laying out Five-Year Development Plans, but the effort was clearly not enough to keep the industry in the top league. Particularly marked was the failure to reduce the number of plants and concentrate production. Investment tended to be of the patch-up kind and it peaked at the end of the 1950s, just as major new technological innovations, such as the basic oxygen steelmaking process and continuous casting, beckoned for the industry. Macroeconomic factors did not aid either, with domestic demand subject to considerable fluctuations. Labor productivity in the UK grew by about 25% between 1955 and 1965, whereas in Italy and Japan it grew by 150% and in West Germany by 58%. This meant that by 1965, the UK ranked below major competitors. During the early 1960s, although some parts of the industry were well managed and healthy, total profitability of the largest companies consistently declined (Aylen 1980, 1982).

The period between 1964 and 1966 witnessed a new debate over the future of the industry, with counterproposals put forward by the BISF for reorganization under private ownership (the Benson Report) or alternatively for mixed ownership. Some of the arguments already heard in the late 1940s were given a new airing. The Labour Party's attitude toward nationalization, however, under the leadership first of Gaitskell, then of Wilson, had become more pragmatic, stressing the fact that public corporations were to be set up not as vehicles for administering a whole industry, but as public firms in their own right. Having won a second general election in 1966 with a clearer mandate, Wilson's Labour government put forward an Iron and Steel Bill to nationalize the industry; the bill became law in March 1967.

A few lessons from the past were learned. Whereas in 1951 all but the smallest steel companies were nationalized, in 1967 only the 14 largest companies were nationalized. This left a sizeable private sector in existence, accounting for about 10% of crude steel production and 30% of finished steel, ensuring that there would be a measure of competition. Furthermore, one year before nationalization, in the autumn of 1966, an Organizing Committee was set up, composed of government officials, industry leaders, and other prominent businessmen and supported by the staff of the Iron and Steel Board. Its mandate was to prepare the details of the takeover, including the selection of the top management of the new public holding, and think through some of the measures that needed to be taken (Abromeit 1986, 116ff.). This too was a new departure, as the 1949 nationalization had not been preceded by any amount of industrial and organizational planning.

Thanks to the work of the Organizing Committee, the British Steel Corporation (BSC) was not simply a grouping of the industry's different sections. It was meant to be a single business organization, with a centralized management structure, allowing it to pursue a coherent strategy and to achieve its objectives, which were set out as being mainly of a commercial nature. As a consequence, it was agreed that BISF would be dissolved and that its remaining functions to represent the private sector would be taken over by a new, far less influential body, the British Independent Steel Producers' Association (BISPA). BSC, moreover, was able to draw on the best professional management within the industry, main areas of strength being the United Steel Company and the companies running the large wide strip mills in South Wales and in the Northwest: that is, the Steel Company of Wales, Richard Thomas and Baldwin's, and Richard Summers' at Shotton. These were to provide BSC with most of its management expertise. BSC's first achievement was to bring together the various companies (it had inherited 22 integrated plants together with 47 other units, with an inflated workforce of over 250,000) and subject them to centralized management along technocratic lines. This was accomplished progressively, through a sequence of internal reforms, moving from regional groups, which still reflected the old company structure, to six product divisions (Heal 1974, 174–181; Bodsworth 2000; Aylen 2008).

The first two chairmen of BSC, Lord Melchett and Monty Finniston, inherited the recommendations included in 'Benson Report', the so-called heritage strategy, of upgrading and enlarging the five largest integrated existing sites (Beauman 1998, 2000). Furthermore, there would be enlarged port facilities at Teesside and Port Talbot. To this they added a sixth new plant on Teesside, to be built on Japanese lines. They were working on what proved to be largely fallacious assumptions of large increases in output, fueled by a rise in exports and in domestic demand. Technocratic planning and modernization had come to the British steel sector at last, although at the wrong time in the economic cycle.

## THE RISE AND FALL OF THE PUBLIC SECTOR IN ITALY (1960–1990)

There is broad agreement in the literature that Italy's public sector steel enjoyed a very successful spell until the late 1960s. After having secured government approval for the Sinigaglia Plan, Finsider's leadership rose to the challenge and secured a dominant position in the industry for the state sector by expanding output and rationalizing and concentrating capacity within the larger, integrated coastal plants, where much of the investment was channeled. In 1962, the Finsider group accounted for 90% of the country's pig iron, 55% of crude steel, and 57% of hot rolled products. Italy was on the way to becoming a major, competitive steel producer. Finsider's managers succeeded in cutting costs, closing marginal plants and units, and thereby increasing productivity. Although starting with costs and prices as much as 70% higher that the corresponding German and Belgian ones, by the early 1960s Italian steel producers were able to command a premium over most of their European competitors (Ranieri 2004–2005).

Oscar Sinigaglia's first-class managerial team, largely drawn from the private sector, was able to provide dynamic leadership. Foremost among their achievements was the construction of the second Cornigliano works (the first had been built and then destroyed during WWII), at the outskirts of Genoa. It was endowed with a wide strip mill, a cold strip mill, and modern coating facilities. It was an 'Americanized' plant: built with American equipment, with the aid of American engineers and consultants; its personnel trained by the American firm, ARMCO; and its management structure, organizational design, and industrial relations modeled on what was understood as best 'U.S. practice'. Deciding to install a wide strip mill in Italy in the precarious conditions of the late 1940s was a risky gamble, but it paid off and Cornigliano stood out for many years as the largest, fastest growing, and most profitable plant in the industry (Ranieri 2000).

The completion of Cornigliano brought with it a vast rationalization, with many plants either closing down or refocusing to process coil rolled in Cornigliano. Markets for long products, however, were not streamlined in the same way, and much duplication of plant within Finsider and between the private and public sector persisted. Nevertheless, the main goals behind the Sinigaglia Plan were achieved and were further developed when it was decided to build a large new coastal works at Taranto. Also important was the commercial success enjoyed, at this stage, by Dalmine, as well as the launching of Terninoss, a joint venture between Terni and U.S. Steel in the field of stainless and electrical cold rolled sheet. Finally, Finsider was able to secure very favorable terms for Italy within the ECSC. When the Schuman Plan was launched in 1950, there was a danger that Italy, as often in the past, would be at the mercy of a strong Continental combination and be forced to accommodate increasing steel imports. However, Italy was able to set its own conditions for membership, including a guarantee of being able to complete Finsider's investment plans, temporary tariff protection for domestically produced common and special steel, and favorable arrangements for supplies of iron ore, coke, and scrap. Contrary to assumptions commonly held in the literature, membership in the ECSC was a key factor in the success of Italy's steel industry (Ranieri and Tosi 2004).

It is important to underline the mixture of cooperation and competition established by Finsider with the private sector. Fruitful partnerships were struck with final users: for example, Fiat contracted to purchase coil produced in Cornigliano—which gave Finsider a considerable captive market. In some cases it was a question of bullying smaller private producers to buy Finsider's products, whereas in others the aim was to undercut rivals in their hitherto most profitable market niches. Sinigaglia was clear on the fact that Finsider should not be supplying private companies with semi-finished goods; on the contrary, it should compete with them by developing its own finishing units. Sinigaglia believed in mass production not just for the sake of raising output, but because it allowed higher productivity and profits. Therein lay the reason for his irreconcilable differences with the Falck group and with others in the trade, wedded to more traditional market sharing practices (Sinigaglia 1948; Osti 1993).

By the early 1970s, however, the picture had changed dramatically. Overoptimistic capacity expansion impacted severely with the European steel crisis, opening up in 1975. Although the recession was, clearly, an important factor, there was still a distinctive failure to meet the challenge and mitigate its effects. Steel SOE was characterized by crippling financial losses, due to overinvestment and poor capacity utilization as well as poor industrial relations and declining productivity. Finsider's labor productivity, for example, failed to show any progress between 1968 and 1980, despite massive new investment, particularly in the huge Taranto works, which had been brought to a capacity of over 10 million tons per year. The number of employees in the group, in fact, continued to grow, reaching a record number in 1976. The first cutback had to wait until 1981. In no year between 1975 and 1988 did Finsider make a profit, and huge sums of public money were poured into it (Balconi 1998).

During the early 1980s, retrenchment and cuts under the auspices of the European Commission were designed to meet this crisis. Despite sizeable cuts in capacity and personnel (from over 120,000 in 1980 to 76,000 in 1987); Finsider's financial situation remained precarious. By 1987, Finsider was unique within the European Economic Community for still being unable to stand on its own feet. At the beginning of 1989 the group's assets, after a government debt write-off, were handed over to a new public company by the name of Ilva. A few years later, in 1993, against poor performance and heavy losses, and in the face of mounting debt in the state sector, Ilva was broken up into three new companies, each of which was then hurriedly sold off to a number of Italian and foreign buyers (Parker 2003, 107).

Various explanations of this debacle have been advanced. One of the most common ones relates to the increasing interference of politicians in Italy's public sector management, starting with the creation of the Ministero delle Partecipazioni Statali, designed to manage all public sector assets, in 1956. Amatori, quoting the expansion of the Taranto steel works, beyond what most of the management thought viable, talks of a "Soviet-style expropriation of top management" (Amatori 2000, 151–152).

In the early postwar period, steel SOEs were able to enjoy the privileges of being state-owned, without the burden of having to submit to any substantial external interference, given that Italy's new political ruling class needed time to establish itself. It seemed, in this respect, that the IRI system was able to capture the best of the state and the market. What happened, however, was that gradually the holdings, Finsider and IRI, became more prone to politicians and exercised more power. There is a whole record of corrosive day-to-day encroachments on company management, backed up by financial blackmail and pressure on appointments (Balconi, Orsenigo, and Toninelli 1995).

This needs to be considered against a background of rising costs, low demand, and a managerial culture struggling to overcome a supply-oriented culture, fostered by a long period of rising output and a sellers' market. Most European companies posted huge losses. Some were able to ride out the storm, whereas others were not. Even within Finsider, there were exceptions. Dalmine, for example, decided to refocus on its core business of seamless tubes and was able to regain profitability by investing in a new, revolutionary, rolling mill. On the whole, however, it was the inability, or even the unwillingness, to find a strategic response to the changing market situation that eventually brought Finsider to its knees.

In Finsider's case, one more factor, often overlooked, needs to be considered: the rise of powerful new domestic competitors in the mini-mill sector. The mini-mills (also known as 'bresciani', from the Brescia district, where they were clustered) were originally very small electric steelmakers and scrap re-rollers involved in the production of concrete reinforcing bar (rebar) and other long products. Faced with very favorable market opportunities during the 1950s and 1960s, such as a strong demand for rebar by the construction industry and comparatively low scrap prices, they became larger and more aggressive. During the 1970s, they captured most of the domestic market for long products. Their flexibility and their low cost structure were particularly suited to a period of economic fluctuations. They were also effective in flouting most of the regulations imposed by the European Commission during the steel crisis. Some of them, such as Riva, Leali, Lucchini, grew into large multinational groups, capturing important shares of the European market for long products, and eventually, in the mid-1990s, were able to acquire some the largest plants put out for sale as a result of the liquidation of the public sector. In particular, Riva acquired the Ilva Laminati Piani (ILP), which included the strip mill section of the former public sector, including the huge Taranto plant (Balconi 1993; Pedrocco 2000).

## BRITISH PUBLIC SECTOR STEEL REAPPRAISED: THE BRITISH STEEL CORPORATION (1967–1988)

The performance of the UK public steel sector in the 1970s suggests it was beset by some of the same weaknesses that brought the Italian public sector to its knees. BSC had been saddled with much antiquated capital, overmanned plants, poor product quality and service, and bad labor relations (Houseman 1991, 24). The first plans, moreover, were far too ambitious; they were trimmed down to some extent by the Heath government elected in 1970 and were, then, overcome by the slump in the steel market, triggered by the oil crisis in 1974 and lasting for over a decade. Restructuring, therefore, had to be carried out in unpropitious circumstances; large losses were posted, which eventually required huge injections of public money just to keep the company alive. Serious strategy mistakes were made and were compounded by damaging political meddling on the part of both Conservative and Labour governments (Dudley and Richardson 1990).

While new projects were being launched, BSC lost significant market share to imports, particularly after UK membership in the European Communities, at the start of 1973, brought to an end the cozy arrangements that had protected the industry since the 1930s. Attention to the needs of final users seems to have slackened, and BSC was found wanting in commercial clout. Local pressures from trade unions and politicians crucially delayed closures of redundant plants.

The private sector of the industry, which, during the 1970s, was boosted by the entry of foreign-owned mini-mills, succeeded, at first, in exploiting BSC's weaknesses and was able to cut into its market share, particularly for semi-finished goods. Private firms based in Sheffield and Rotherham held on to their profitable business in special steel products. On the whole, however, the private sector never posed the same challenge as in Italy. Private companies were hit by the recession and, particularly in the Sheffield area, were forced to merge defensively and seek joint ventures with BSC. The division between the private and the public sectors, thus, became blurred. For example, in 1986 BSC was responsible for 76% of crude steel, with another 15.8% provided by the so-called Phoenix companies, joint ventures in which BSC was the dominant partner. This left less than 10% of crude steel output entirely in private hands (Cockerill 1980, 141ff.; Jones and Cockerill 1984).

Despite the setbacks, the 1970s also brought some achievements, the importance of which became clear in the following decade. There was, in particular, an effort to pursue a coherent investment strategy. Technocracy, on the whole, was able to assert itself: a BSC leadership emerged with a strong sense of purpose and an equally strong *esprit de corps*. Whereas Ministers retained considerable statutory powers over BSC, in actual fact, inside knowledge and technical expertise gave BSC's executives an edge (Dudley and Richardson 2001, 142). In their negotiations with the government, management occasionally had to give ground, but it did not revert to short-termism. Gradually, therefore, most of the original plans drawn up at the time of nationalization were carried out: concentration of operations in five major coastal centers, flanked by a number of more specialized works, was finally achieved. Furthermore, by 1980 all major works were based on large-scale oxygen steelmaking plants, and a massive switch had taken place away from low-grade expensive domestic ores to high-quality foreign ones.

The turnaround in BSC's performance did not happen overnight. Between 1979 and 1985, losses totaled around £2.5 billion, and the difficulties of the early 1980s were compounded by a bitter 3-month strike over pay in 1980, the collapse of which, however, allowed management to push through radical reform of outmoded and inflexible working practices. A first turnaround took place around 1980–1981, under the chairmanship of Ian MacGregor, appointed by the newly elected Thatcher government (Aylen 1988). The Conservatives had pledged to prepare the industry for privatization, by cutting back on public subsidies. In the short term, however, this proved impossible, and large sums were still needed to bail BSC out of its grave financial difficulties (Owen 2000, 144; Dudley and Richardson 2001, 143). Crucially, however, the government was prepared to leave BSC's top management a free hand. The strategy of shutting down all plants except for a few large works was, basically, the same that had been outlined in the 1970s; the difference was that now most, if not all, compromises and delays were ruled out. Between 1980 and 1983, there were about 100,000 redundancies, and BSC's total workforce in 1985 fell by 60%. Labor productivity gains of 19.5% a year were posted between 1981 and 1985 while the BSC value added was even more impressive (Martin and Parker 1997, 208). The industry was back to levels of international excellence. It was helped by the ECSC regime of 'manifest crisis', which, during the early 1980s, when the company was at its most vulnerable, helped to stem imports from the Continent, avoiding damaging price wars.

Significantly there was a "culture shift" within BSC itself, with an increasing focus on commercial efficiency and profitability. By the early 1980s, it was senior management, rather than the government, that was pushing for privatization. This was particularly evident through the actions of Sir Robert Scholey, who was chairman of the company from 1986 to 1992 and steered it first back to profit in 1986 and then into the private sector, in December 1988, for the sum of £2.5 billion. Once in the private sector, British Steel PLC, as it came to be called, developed a strongly adversarial attitude toward any form of state, or indeed EC intervention, to the point of antagonizing, on several occasions, the UK government. In a way the pupil was outshining the master (Dudley and Richardson 2001, 148).

## STEEL AND THE STATE: A BYGONE PARTNERSHIP

Issues relating to the state-owned sector in steel can of course be dealt with from many different angles (Tomlinson 1994, 187ff.). The choice made here was to look at them, mainly, from the point of view of the performance of the industry itself. One of the first conclusions that can be drawn relates to the nature of the public sector. Wholesale nationalization, as attempted in the UK between 1945 and 1951, proved impractical in the context of a complex and diverse industry. The ideas behind nationalization related, primarily, to controlling the commanding heights of the economy; at the same time, there was an understandable reluctance to move this exercise deep into the manufacturing sector (Millward and Singleton 1995, chaps. 1, 2, 14). Steel, however, was considered a basic industry, in that it provided semi-finished inputs to other industries. This idea, probably always flawed, by 1945 was utterly unrealistic, because the steel industry was very diverse, including different trades and technologies, while companies making steel were often vertically integrated into other areas of manufacturing activity. The concept that steel could be taken over as a sector and run as a single operation, as advocated by the Morrisonian public corporation, was basically a non starter. On the other hand, it was clear that inadequate size of plant and unit, the existence of a cartelized monopolistic industry, and the need to direct new investment to achieve economies of scale called for some form of state intervention.

At this point it is worth coming back to the three main contending groups at work in the steel industry: the modernizers, the corporatists, and the liberals. The arguments developed here have been (a) that public sector steel could, under certain circumstances, provide a useful framework for the modernizers; and (b) that the corporatist model was largely inefficient.

The first argument, of course, is easier to prove for Italy in the period 1945–1970. The development of a successful technocracy in SOE (steel, oil) was a concrete step toward managerial capitalism in Italy (Balconi et al., 1995). Clearly, the rather unique nature of the IRI model in Italy has been the subject of much discussion, for whereas it is seen to have unlocked, or at least enabled, the process of modernization, it is blamed for engendering failure after 1970. The issue becomes simpler, if attention is placed on the quality of top management: a good managerial team, following a sound strategy and responding to a far sighted mission, both corporate and national, can make good use of being part of an SOE, provided certain conditions of flexibility, market-based signals, and lack of blatant political interference are met.

This allows us to briefly consider why, in the UK an IRI-like model was not adopted for steel. In truth there was no lack of plans or suggestions: in 1964, the Liberal Party produced a report seeking a "third way" for steel, suggesting state shareholding in four "pacesetting" firms, which would be in competition with privately owned ones (Tivey 1966, 194). Ideas about a state holding agency with wide powers of investment were entertained within the Labour Party and even tried out, to some extent, in the case of the National Enterprise Board in the 1970s (Tomlinson 1999). It has been stressed that IRI was more appropriate to a country engaged in a big developmental spurt, but, as far as Finsider is considered, one of its main successes was in restructuring and focusing investment on key plants, exactly what was needed in the UK (Holland 1972). However, while interesting in highlighting the differences in political culture between the two countries, this debate is not really of crucial significance for steel, because, probably, we need to go no further than what was actually achieved. The creation of BSC in 1967 was centered on a "company," not a sector, and it succeeded in promoting a managerial team with a strong focus on restructuring and modernization.

The second argument about the inability of the corporatist system to deliver results in terms of efficiency is best proven by failure of the BISF 'regime' in Britain, especially in the decade after denationalization. The industry at the time offers a particularly striking example of a coherently organized and protected cartel with a poor performance record (Keeling and Wright 1964). It might be useful here to compare the UK with West Germany, where the postwar corporatist system worked quite well, with larger companies achieving adequate economies of scale and engaging in defensive mergers during the crisis. Clearly, the process of deconcentration and decartelization after the war followed a U.S.-inspired philosophy, which some believe might have allowed a successful private steel industry to emerge in the UK (Owen 2000, 139).

It is useful, finally, to consider the issue of competition. The steel industry was (and remains) oligopolistic and prone to cartelization. We can examine various national systems, but we come down to similar conclusions: price leadership, dominant players, national and international cartels. Competition was therefore limited, at best taking place between a few dominant players. A new departure was ECSC, a supranational regime of governance, introducing "regulated competition with provisions for central crisis management" (Dudley and Richardson 2001a). Although ECSC did not introduce full liberalization, it did, however, provide for a more open internal market. Arguably, the competitive pressures of ECSC on the Italian market were crucial, just as much as the ability of Finsider's managers, in reorganizing Italy's public steel sector. Conversely, the steadfast refusal to liberalize trade with the Continent became the raison d'être of BISF, nurturing complacency, whereas BSC was faced with an altogether different set of pressures emanating out of Europe. So whereas the liberal argument for steel, in a 'pure' form, was always misplaced, the variable performances of the public sector in the UK and Italy speak in favor of a mixture of modernization, competitive pressures, and effective management empowerment.

The demise in the public sector after 1970 needs to be discussed in terms of crisis management and decline management, that is, managing output cuts, financial decline, and especially the fall of employment (Dudley and Richardson 2001a, 14ff.). Here the UK did much better than Italy and was, thus, better placed to meet the challenges of the 1990s, when the steel industry faded away from its previous strategic and political significance, and ECSC, which had provided the interventionist framework until the end of the 1980s, was wound down. In the Italian case, ECSC had provided a minimum of external discipline on the failing public sector, not sufficient to reverse the trend, but enough to stop the slide in the 1980s. It was, however, the fiscal crisis of the Italian state at the start of the 1990s which generated the domestic and international pressure needed to trigger the privatization process that followed (Balconi et al., 1995, 312), with the assets of the former Ilva handed over to a number of domestic private companies (Riva, Lucchini) and multinational subsidiaries (ThyssenKrupp, Techint, etc.) (Balconi 1998). In the UK, management continuity ensured BSC a smooth progression from publicly owned corporation to public company and private national champion. In 1995, British Steel was Europe's third largest steel company and appeared to be one of the most successful (Beauman 1998).

Since the mid-1990s, a wave of globalization has swept the steel industry, making previous paradigms discussed in this chapter somewhat obsolete. The very concept of a national steel industry, or even of cross-national alliances, has been undermined by the emergence of global corporate players, with plants scattered across many countries, and a particular focus on rapidly emerging East and South Asian markets. Moreover, the diversification within steel has rapidly progressed: a multiplicity of highly specialized branches, catering to different markets have emerged (European Commission 2006). National champions, even when fertilized by cross-European alliances—as in the case of Corus, a 1999 merger of British Steel and Hoogovens, or of the Franco-Spanish Arcelor—have been fair game for globally based players, such as Tata and Mittal. Clearly, the market has prevailed over the state.

## NOTES

1. Some attention needs to be drawn to the nature of the cycles in the development of steel. Between the 1930s and the 1960s, the 'American model' was widely regarded as the most successful. It consisted of a package of new thin flat rolling technologies; of economies of scale, at both plant and unit level; of standardized production in large batches; and of new organizational methods, designed to maximize management control, workforce productivity, and company profitability. In Italy, during the 1930s, the attraction of the German model had been paramount, and there had been strong links with German firms. However, the German model, although in a different way (less specialization, more vertical integration, more craft-based skills), was also based on large integrated firms, resulting from a process of consolidation. After the war, modernizers in the Italian steel industry enthusiastically embraced the American package of technologies and business organization (Osti 1993; Amatori 1997). In the UK, the 1952 report on the steel industry of the Anglo-American Council for Productivity discussed the reasons for the higher productivity of U.S. steel and found them, mainly, in the greater size of plants and units of production and smaller range of specifications (Ranieri 2002).

    The upward trend in the steel market, in all industrialized countries, came to an end in 1974, followed by a prolonged and structural fall in demand, calling for major readjustments in capacity. Both in Italy and in the UK (Britain having joined the EC Treaties in 1973), between 1978 and 1986, steel policy was managed mainly at the European level, by national governments acting in conjunction with the European Commission and national trade associations. From 1981, steel was subjected to the "manifest crisis" ECSC (European Coal and Steel Community) regime, which consisted of restricting output, preventing price cuts, and encouraging cuts in capacity in return for public subsidies under the Steel Aid Code. The public sector in the two countries acted as a lifeboat for the rest of the industry. Enduring widescale losses prompted a radical change in steelmaking culture, the emphasis shifting toward recapturing profitability, higher product quality, and better marketing (Meny and Wright 1987; Jörnmark 1993, 233ff). Performance, however, was very different.

## BIBLIOGRAPHY

Abromeit, H. 1986, *British Steel: An Industry between the State and the Private Sector*, Leamington Spa, UK: Berg.

Amatori, F. 1997, "Growth via Politics: Business Groups Italian-Style," in *Beyond the Firm: Business Groups in International and Historical Perspective*, eds. T. Shiba and M. Shimotami, Oxford: Oxford University Press.

Amatori, F. 2000, "Beyond State and Market: Italy's Futile Search for a Third Way," in *The Rise and Fall of State-Owned Enterprise in the Western World*, ed. P.A. Toninelli, Cambridge: Cambridge University Press.

Amatori, F. and S. Licini, eds. 2006, *Dalmine 1906–2006: Un secolo di storia*, Bergamo: Fondazione Dalmine.

Aylen, J. 1980, "Innovation in the British Steel Industry," in *Technical Innovation and British Economic Performance*, ed. K. Pavitt, London: Macmillan.

Aylen, J. 1982, "Plant Size and Efficiency in the Steel Industry: An International Comparison," *National Institute Economic Review* 100(May): 65–76.

Aylen, J. 1988, "Privatization of the British Steel Corporation," *Fiscal Studies* 9(3): 1–25.

Aylen, J. 2008, "Construction of the Shotton Wide Strip Mill," *Transactions of the Newcomen Society* 78(1): 57–85.

Balconi, M. 1991, *La siderugia italiana (1945–1990): Tra controllo pubblico e incentivi del mercato*, Bologna: Fondazione Assi.

Balconi, M. 1993, "The Notion of Industry and Knowledge Bases: The Evidence of Steel and Mini-Mills," *Industrial and Corporate Change* 2(3): 471–507.

Balconi, M. 1998, "The Privatization of the Italian State-Owned Steel Industry: Causes and Results," in *The Steel Industry in the New Millennium, Vol. 2, Institutions, Privatisation and Social Dimensions*, eds. R. Ranieri and E. Gibellieri, London: IOM Publications.

Balconi, M., L. Orsenigo, and P.A. Toninelli 1995, "Tra gerarchie e mercati: Il caso delle imprese pubbliche in Italia (acciaio e petroli)," in *Potere, mercati e gerarchie: Storici, economisti e sociologi a confronto*, ed. M. Magatti, Bologna: Il Mulino.

Barca, F. 1997, "Compromesso senza riforme nel capitalismo Italiano," in *Storia del capitalismo italiano dal dopoguerra ad oggi*, ed. F. Barca, Roma: Donzelli.

Beauman, C. 1998, "The British Steel Case: How History Determines Strategy," in *The Steel Industry in the New Millennium, Vol. 2, Institutions, Privatisation and Social Dimension*, eds. R. Ranieri and E. Gibellieri, London: IOM Publications.

Beauman, C. 2000, *Privatizzazione e nuove strategie di impresa. Il caso della British Steel*, Quaderni Steelmaster, Terni: ICSIM.

Bodsworth, C., ed. 2001, *British Iron and Steel, AD 1800–2000 and Beyond*, London: IOM Communications.

Burk, K. 1988, *The First Privatization: The Politicians, the City and the Denationalisation of Steel*, London: Historians Press.

Burn, D.L. 1958, "Steel," in *The Structure of British Industry*, Vol. 1, ed. D.L. Burn, London: Cambridge University Press.

Burn, D.L. 1961, *The Steel Industry 1939–1959: A Study in Competition and Planning*, London: Cambridge University Press.

Chick, M. 1988, *Industrial Policy in Britain 1945–1951: Economic Planning, Nationalisation and the Labour Governments*, Cambridge: Cambridge University Press.

Cockerill, A.J. 1980, "Steel," in *The Structure of British Industry*, ed. P.S. Johnson, London: Granada.

Dudley, G.F. and J.J. Richardson 1990, *Politics and Steel in Britain 1967–1988*, Aldershot: Dartmouth Publishing.

Dudley, G.F. and J.J. Richardson 2001, "British Steel and the British government: Problematic Learning as a Policy Style," in *Success and Failure in Public Governance: A Comparative Analysis*, Part II, eds. M. Bowens, P.T. Hart, and G.B. Peters, Northampton: Elgar.

Dudley, G.F. and J.J. Richardson 2001a, "Managing Decline: Governing National Steel Production under Economic Adversity," in *Success and Failure in Public Governance: A Comparative Analysis*, Part II, eds. M. Bowens, P.T. Hart, and G.B. Peters, Northampton: Elgar.

European Commission 2006, *European Steel Technology Platform: From a Strategic Research Agenda to Implementation*, Brussels: European Commission.

Heal, D.W. 1976, *The Steel Industry in Post War Britain*, Newton Abbot: David and Charles.

Holland, S., ed. 1972, *The State as Entrepreneur. New Dimensions for Public Enterprise: The IRI State Shareholding Formula*, London: Weidenfeld and Nicolson.

Houseman, S.N. 1991, *Industrial Restructuring with Job Security*, Cambridge, Mass.: Harvard University Press.

Jones, T.T. and A.J. Cockerill 1984, "The Steel Industry," in *Structure and Performance of Industries*, eds. T.T. Jones and A.J. Cockerill, Oxford: Philip Allan Publishers.

Jörnmark, J. 1993, *Coal and Steel in Western Europe 1945–1993: Innovative Change and Institutional Adaptation*, Göteborg: Publications of the Department of Economic History of the University of Gothenburg 67.

Keeling, B.S. and A.E.G. Wright 1964, *The Development of the Modern British Steel Industry*, London: Longmans.

Martin, S. and D. Parker 1997, *The Impact of Privatisation: Ownership and Corporate Performance in the UK*, London: Routledge.

Meny, Y. and V. Wright, eds. 1987, *The Politics of Steel: Western Europe and the Steel Industry in the Crisis Years (1974–1984)*, Berlin: Walter de Gruyter.

Millward, R. 1997, "The 1940s Nationalizations in Britain: Means to an End or the Means of Production," *Economic History Review* 1(2): 209–234.

Millward, R. 2000, "State Enterprise in Britain in the Twentieth Century," in *The Rise and Fall of State-Owned Enterprises in the Western World*, ed. P.A. Toninelli, Cambridge: Cambridge University Press.

Millward, R. and J. Singleton, eds. 1995, *The Political Economy of Nationalisation in Britain*, Cambridge: Cambridge University Press.

Milward, A.S. 2002, *The United Kingdom and the European Kingdom*, Vol. 1, *The Rise and Fall of a National Strategy, 1945–1963*, London: Frank Cass.

Osti, G.L. 1993, *L'industria di stato dall'ascesa al degrade: Trent'anni nel gruppo Finsider, conversazioni con Ruggero Ranieri*, Bologna: Il Mulino.

Ovenden, K. 1978, *The Politicals of Steel*, London: Macmillan.

Owen, G. 2000, *From Empire to Europe. The Decline and Revival of British Industry since the Second World War*, London: Harper Collins.

Parker, D. 2003, "Privatization in the European Union," in *International Handbook on Privatization*, eds. D. Parker and D. Saal, Cheltenham: Edward Elgar.

Pedrocco, G. 2000, *Bresciani dal rottame al tondino: Mezzo secolo di siderurgia (1945–2000)*, Milano: Jaka Book, Fondazione Micheletti.

Petri, R. 2002, *Storia economica d'Italia /Dalla Grande guerra al miracolo economica (1918–1963)*, Bologna: Il Mulino.

Ranieri, R. 1993, "Inside or Outside the Magic Circle: The Italian and British Steel Industries Face to Face with the Schuman Plan and the European Coal and Steel Community," in *The Frontier of National Sovereignty: History and Theory*, eds. A.S. Milward et al., London: Routledge.

Ranieri, R. 1995, "Partners and Enemies: The Decision to Nationalise Steel, 1945–1948," in *Industrial Organisation and the Road to Nationalization in Britain 1920–1950*, eds. R. Millward and J. Singleton, Cambridge: Cambridge University Press.

Ranieri, R. 1999, "Steel and the State in Italy and the UK: The Public Sector of the Steel Industry in Comparative Perspective (1945–1996)," *European Yearbook of Business History*, Vol. 2, ed. W. Feldenkirchen and T. Gourvish, Aldershot: Ashgate.

Ranieri, R. 2000, "Remodelling the Italian Steel Industry: Americanization, Modernization and Mass Production," in *Americanization and Its Limits: Reworking American Technology and Management in Post-War Europe and Japan*, eds. J. Zeitlin and G. Heriggel, Oxford: Oxford University Press.

Ranieri, R. 2002, "The Productivity Issue in the UK Steel Industry, 1945–1970," in *Americanisation in 20th Century Europe: Business, Culture, Politics*, Vol. 2, eds. M. Kipping and N. Tiratsoo, Lille: Université Charles-de-Gaulle.

Ranieri, R. 2004–2005, "Il Piano Sinigaglia e la ristrutturazione della siderurgia italiana (1945–1958)," *Annali di Storia dell'Impresa* 15–16: 17–45.

Ranieri, R. and L. Tosi, eds. 2004, *La Comunità Europa del carbone e dell'acciaio (1952–2002): Gli esiti del trattato in Europa e in Italia*, Padova: CEDAM.

Ross, G. 1965, *The Nationalization of Steel: One Step Forward, Two Steps Back?* London: Macgibbon and Koe.

Sinigaglia, O. 1948, "The Future of the Italian Iron and Steel Industry," *Banca Nazionale del Lavoro Quarterly Review* 4: 240–245.

Tivey, L.J. 1966, *Nationalization in British Industry*, London: Cape.

Tolliday, S. 1987, *Business, Banking and Politics: The Case of British Steel 1918–1939*, Cambridge, Mass.: Harvard University Press.

Tomlinson, J. 1994, *Government and the Enterprise since 1900: The Changing Problem of Efficiency*, Oxford: Clarendon Press.

Tomlinson, J. 1999, "Learning from Italy? The British Public Sector and IRI," in *European Yearbook of Business History*, Vol. 2, eds. W. Feldenkirchen and T. Gourvish, London: Ashgate.

Vaizey, J. 1974, *A History of British Steel*, London: Weidenfeld and Nicholson.

Wurm, C. 1993, Business, Politics and International Relations: Steel, Cotton and International Cartels in British Politics, 1924–1939, Cambridge: Cambridge University Press.

# 11 From Craftsmanship to Post-Fordism

## Shipbuilding in the United Kingdom and Italy after WWII

*Giulio Mellinato*

## QUANTITY AND QUALITY: FROM WAR TO RECONSTRUCTION

After World War II (WWII), the resumption of international trade involved the Italian and British maritime engineering in two completely different ways. In the United Kingdom, the shipbuilding sector was still a "staple industry" (Elbaum and Lazonick 1984), which had recovered from the contractions of the 1930s, and was fully riding the wave of growing demand. The national fleet was the first in the world, with 22% of the total tonnage in 1948, and a clear global leadership with regard to quality, reliability, and security, guaranteed everywhere by London-based Lloyd's Register of Shipping. In 1953, all major producing districts of the United Kingdom had exceeded the tonnage launched in 1938 (Pope 1990), and British maritime engineering had fully regained its place as world leader. In itself, the great size of the domestic market created the conditions whereby the characteristics of British demand coincided with the main trend for the entire global maritime market. From this point of view, the internal dynamics of continuity with the last prewar period prevented the British producers from changing methods and building practices which, in most cases, dated back to the 1920s and, in some ways, even before (McTavish 2005, 63–98).

In Italy, during the years of reconstruction, the national maritime engineering had to find its place somewhere between two rather uncomfortable positions: on one side, the production overcapacity represented a legacy of fascism difficult to manage, while on the other, the almost complete destruction of the national mercantile fleet during the war required a quick construction of a significant number of new ships, to ensure the country an early resumption of vital supplies from abroad, after a devastating conflict.

For different reasons, for both countries the years after WWII were therefore a particularly positive period, at least until the mid-1960s. In the UK, the production of new vessels remained high and stable for an unusually long period (Parkinson 1960), while in Italy the maritime sector created by the fascist government between 1936 and 1938 was essentially confirmed, albeit with some adjustments over time. After the conclusion of the conflict, in both countries the policies developed were aimed at revitalizing, as soon as possible, a sector that absorbed labor hardly reusable elsewhere, providing the national economy with vessels that would permit a full reintegration into the channels of international trade.

In both countries, the exceptionally favorable conditions (steady demand and high public interest to support the industry, lack of concern for technological innovation or a lowering of costs) prevented politicians and entrepreneurs from perceiving the importance of changes which had occurred during the war. These changes would create a deviation of the productive trajectories followed by the two countries from the development of a world market.

## LESSONS NOT LEARNED

During the early months of WWII, the vulnerability of Britain's maritime links with the traditional areas of supply had become one of the most serious strategic priorities. Between September and December 1939, 215 merchant ships were sunk, totaling close to 750,000 tons of shipping lost. Such a serious weakness in the long-range routes was jeopardizing the British ability to withstand the German assault (Hornby 1958, 33). The situation worsened further in the following months, when the number of ships sunk far surpassed the British productive capacity (Hancock and Gowing, 1949, 80, 241; Skinner Watson, 1950, 368),[1] even after the concentration of production on a single type of ship, highly standardized. Following the fall of France, the British Admiralty shifted more resources toward the construction of naval vessels, and in the summer of 1940 it was decided to transfer abroad the construction of merchant ships (Hornby 1958, 41). Thanks to the convergent efforts of the British and U.S. governments, an Emergency Shipbuilding Program was launched (Lane 1951; Thornton and Thompson 2001),[2] which led to the construction of thousands of ships in very few years.

The most important results were achieved thanks to new building practices: welding, prefabrication, and reorganization of different working stations so as to minimize the processing activity on the building berth. In other words, whereas previously the whole ship, one metal sheet at a time, was built on the slipways, the construction of Liberty ships adopted a system similar to the assembly line, where the individual sections of ship were assembled in workshops, organized in a way that facilitated the linear flow of pieces, and put together on the building berth.

The final product, though far from excellent in maritime terms, was better than expected. Such a result was achieved by combining the British original drawings and the American manufacturing organization. Out of this union emerged a new paradigm for shipbuilding, but in the short term it remained confined inside the exceptional conditions of war production.

In fact, only government action could ensure the success of a construction plan so remote from the operational practices followed by major shipping companies and so different from the markets' habits that the specificity of a ship and its perfect adhesion to the particular type of use (cargo, route, characteristics of the ports called) were considered economically essential. Moreover, welding techniques had been tested only partially, and not always with positive results; this discouraged private owners who remained loyal to the tried and tested (and, at least before the American experience, relatively cheap) riveting system (Hornby 1958, 42–58).

## EMERGENCIES IN WAR AND PEACE

During the development of the Anglo-American program for emergency construction, the huge increase in productivity was mainly due to "learning by doing" processes (Thompson 2001), but also to a clear choice that privileged quantity over quality in every stage of production. After the war, such an option was deliberately rejected by the British side, where operators remained committed to high standard ships, built according to traditional systems (Lorenz and Wilkinson 1987, 124). Initially, the market appeared to reward such a policy, and the British yards built about half the ships launched in the world during the first postwar decade, with rising prices which in 1955 reached a maximum of twice the average value per ton achieved in 1938 (Murray 1960, 42).

In November 1946, the construction and repair shipyards employed 220,000 people (Pope 1990, 53) and operated in a dynamic market that showed excellent growth prospects (United Nations 1948, 13). In the following years, until 1958, British ship production was stable or slightly increasing, rising from 1.2 million tons launched in 1948 to 1.4 million tons 10 years later, with a growing domestic market, which gradually absorbed from 64% of national production in 1948 to over 83% in 1958 (Johnman and Murphy 2002, 102, Table 18). Focusing primarily on Atlantic and "Imperial" routes, the UK merchant fleet was not much affected by international competition, until the opening, in the late 1950s, of new passenger services (fast and luxurious because competition from air travel was beginning to be felt) for Canada or Australia, and cargo services to Africa or the Far East.[3]

But, in the meantime, the world fleet was growing rather quickly (the UK share fell from 24% to 13% between 1948 and 1965) and introduced new services: ships were conceptually different from those in the British traditions, and business strategy was directed primarily to price reduction, a view far different from the quality-based practices followed in the United Kingdom. Inside merchant shipbuilding, the worldwide tendency was to concentrate on simple vessels, very basic but economic both in construction and in maintenance, perfectly suitable for the international mercantile system which emerged out of WWII. The productivity gap between the United Kingdom shipyards and international standards was already visible in the late 1940s,[4] when trade unions began to express some worries, but the strength of the internal market prevented the triggering of social distress. Until the early 1950s, there was no concrete action by the British government,[5] but with the return of a Conservative leadership, serious concerns emerged, both from the merchant side and from the military sector.


## THE ITALIAN MARITIME RECONSTRUCTION

In Italy, the entire maritime sector of the national economy was nationalized in the mid-1930s, after fascism had heavily overexpanded it, with the aim of generating international prestige.[6] The Istituto per la Ricostruzione Industriale (IRI) controlled over 90% of the Italian shipping companies and over 80% of the shipyards' production capacity: this was employed almost entirely in building ships commissioned, financed, and managed directly by the government (in the case of military vessels) or by state-owned shipping companies. During the war, the largest manufacturing plants (located in the North of the country) were devastated by bombing and, after the war, most of the ancillary industries were also in trouble, particularly for lack of power and supplies. On the other hand, the national economy was squeezed by the vital need to restore the traditional trade channels, not only with foreign countries but also between different parts of the national territory, which had been divided into autarkic regions since the beginning of the conflict.

In the early postwar years, all this provoked an apparently schizophrenic maritime transport policy: a lot of resources were invested in the reconstruction and upgrading of the bigger shipyards, but many grants were also given to small and obsolete plants. Some of them were employed in the construction of antiquated wooden boats and sail boats, which were nevertheless essential in those years to reactivate coastal communications, where bombings and fighting had rendered impassable the interior roads, especially in the South. Backwardness was consciously supported until production was resumed inside larger plants, which were given the task of reconstructing the national fleet over a much longer span of time.

In the new Republican Parliament, all major parties agreed the state should remain engaged in the maritime sector. In 1948, in a very proactive speech pronounced during the debate on what would be the first law of the Republic for financial assistance to the maritime sector,[7] the liberal deputy, Epicarmo Corbino, supported the idea of public aid to the shipbuilding industry, outlining its precise targets and limits. The reconstruction of the national fleet had to give priority to cargo ships and passenger liners, mainly because people travelling in luxury liners will always be enough to fill the cabins of ships that already exist and those to come. Then there will be emigrants. Here the numerical proportions cannot be assessed but, in any case, the migration flow will resume. [. . .] According to me, one fleet is of good quality when it does not ask anything to the state, is of low quality when it imposes an effort to taxpayers. This is the only distinguishing factor. (Corbino 1948, 15, 18)

Underlying Corbino's optimistic market forecasts was a throwback to the 1930s and a serious underestimation of the technological advances achieved since then. Tourism and emigrants had been recurring themes in Parliamentary debates since the 1920s. The political debate during the late 1940s and the 1950s gave no consideration to some innovative ideas, which came even from the management of public companies (Jacoboni 1949; Lojacono 1951). State action was instead based on the principle of "rebuilding it in the same place and in the same conditions it was" before the war, recreating the problems experienced in the late 1930s of overcapacity, overlapping of responsibilities, and underground competition between companies formally belonging to the same group. The entire shipbuilding sector was made to operate again on the basis of political (links with foreign countries) and social priorities (large employment of the workforce). Even in the positive environment of postwar reconstruction, nobody seriously considered planning for a selective reduction of capacity, based on the specialization of facilities and their adaptation to new technology. Also, the managers of major companies, which had developed under fascism, remained in their place, marking a strong continuity over time of the entire Italian maritime sector.

In 1952, a new regulatory measure was enacted, which introduced for the first time some strategic elements.[8] The purpose of the bill was to grant funds for the construction of a tanker fleet; the funds were to be allocated to shipyards able to produce at lower costs. The effect of the funding was combined with the overall development of the oil transport market, especially after the closing of the Suez Canal. In 1958, the Italian shipyards launched more than 500,000 tons of ships, almost reaching the saturation of estimated capacity (about 600,000 tons).

In late 1950s, the government established a committee to investigate national mechanical engineering. Moreover, a study was commissioned to be undertaken by American experts from Stanford University while Ernesto Rossi performed detailed research on behalf of Cornell University. All reports agreed: the major problems of the Italian maritime engineering industry was excess production capacity, the rationality of productive activities inside the plants, the poor organization of business, and finally the high cost of raw materials and products bought from domestic suppliers (Rossi 1953, 96–100).

Only by the early 1960s did a more interventionist and planning policy emerge inside the technocratic management of IRI, where it found its processing center and the intellectual resources needed to turn vision into reality, with the founding of the Cetena consortium. But in the short run, the technocracy wasn't able to influence political decision making. Only during the 1980s was the top management of state shipbuilding capable of imposing its vision, that is, well after the political interest in the shipbuilding sector was greatly diminished (Fragiacomo 2003). So, in the short run, in Italy, as in the UK, the significant worldwide growth of demand led to an underestimation of the sector's structural weaknesses, or to an overestimation of the companies' ability to find a market for their ships.

## OLD IDEAS, NEW ENVIRONMENT, MISUNDERSTOOD OBJECTIVES

In 1953, a joint report of the British Admiralty and the Treasury pointed to the structural weaknesses of the shipbuilding sector, which, in the long run, could jeopardize Britain's maritime leadership if the government did not intervene (Johnman and Murphy 2002, 110). In similar vein, a few years later, there arose the issue of the technical upgrading of the Royal Navy. The First Lord of the Admiralty informed the Minister of Defence that, because of backwardness and high British naval engineering costs, "there could be no future cruiser program and even a future aircraft carrier program was doubtful, as he dolefully predicted 'the end of our world-wide naval power'" (Johnman and Murphy 2002, 115). All in all, the excessive optimism of the first postwar decade was questioned, for its superficial confidence in the technical superiority of British production, the overestimation of resources available within the Empire (and their exclusivity for British-based enterprises), and the indifference to what was happening in the rest of the world.

In an official meeting at the end of 1958, the industry's position was clearly exposed.

> The view that the British shipbuilding industry was secure for years to come, because of its order books, was unrealistic. [ . . . ] If this country were to compete successfully, then management and men must find a suitable way of securing stabilised costs and fixed prices, and the Government must facilitate credits comparable with those of Japan and other countries.[9]

From the perspective of employers, the main problem was related to the cost of labor (or freedom for entrepreneurs and managers to organize the workforce at their will) and financial aid from the government. The prevailing "craftsmanship" tradition related not only to the need to maintain over time a higher quality of British ships, but also to a precise pattern of interests shared by the workers and manufacturers.

Given the limited nature of the technology available, their own preference for customer-specific production and their inability to organize a
united front within the industry, British shipbuilding employers were
inevitably committed to labour-intensive, low-supervision methods and
to a workforce with high levels of technical skill and task discretion.
Thus the industry's work-force was not confronted with any significant
pressures towards a major transformation in technology or work organization. (Reid 1991, 40)

Moreover, British maritime engineering remained at the edge of the tanker
market, considering that kind of construction unprofitable and of low quality. After 1956, such a production option proved disadvantageous, with
fatal effects for the entire UK shipbuilding industry. In that year, the closure of the Suez Canal made impracticable the "short way" through the
Mediterranean for energy supplies. This led to an immediate explosion of
the demand for tanker ships, forcing the owners into a huge escalation in
the tonnage of new ships to compensate for the higher costs in circumnavi-
gating Africa to transport oil from the Persian Gulf to Europe.

Besides, by 1958, the number of people who crossed the Atlantic by
airplane exceeded that of maritime passengers (Irons-Georges 2002, 186),
and the first regular shipping service using containers began. Within a
few years, the changes were so widespread and deep that they marked the
beginning of a new era in the history of transport.

The entire European maritime community was unaccustomed to changes
and also was jealously anchored in traditions that have proved able to
survive (and allowed producers to survive) through two world wars and
the most devastating crisis of capitalism. In some cases, British maritime
engineering had developed networks of interconnection between the various companies that had remained virtually unchanged since the late 19th
century. Those networks had been one of the competitive strengths of the
sector (Ingram and Lifschitz 2006), but soon became an element of rigidity
incompatible with the new dynamics.

At the public opinion level, the issue of the declining British maritime
role surfaced during the 1959 election campaign, and created the conditions for a subsequent cycle of studies and technical committees which
brought to light British organizational and technological backwardness
which was exposed also in the House of Commons.[10] But even more
typical was a 1961 Parliamentary debate where the main issue was not
whether to grant subsidies, but rather what the conditions of their payment would be and whether that would favor one or the other among the
shipbuilding districts, even though all were suffering from the poor competitiveness of their product.[11] In the long Conservative era (1951–1964),
state intervention became not only an indispensable substitute for the
market but also a tool for the defense of employment and for the promo-
tion of national excellence.

## THE VAIN SEARCH FOR THE "MASTERPIECE SHIP"

Since air travel had begun to divert passengers from transatlantic shipping, competition for the "best" passenger ship started in Europe. Ever more luxurious, more comfortable, and faster vessels had the mission to maintain the prestige of national merchant fleets. They had also the impossible task of countering the declining maritime passenger market, along with the function of maintaining an oversized workforce. But, apparently, in both countries the early 1960s was the most splendid period for the merchant fleet, heavily financed by their own governments for political and social implications.

In the UK, the competition for the "Ship of the Year" rewarded liners for their increasing sophistication and excellent performance, in order to maintain the high reputation of British maritime quality, especially on "Imperial" routes. This gallery of ships included the liner *Oriana* for Australia, in 1961, followed by *Transvaal Castle* in 1962 and ideally ending with *Queen Elizabeth 2* in 1969. The *Queen Elizabeth 2*, built in Scotland at the prestigious John Brown & Co. shipyard, represented the uncertainties of that transitory phase. The hull was laid down in 1965, the ship made its maiden voyage at the end of 1968, and the vessel revealed all its strangeness to the actual maritime world. The propulsion was still steam (turbine), as in the Scottish tradition, but the speed was reduced to save fuel. Onboard services were simplified to save on personnel, and the whole ship could be easily converted from a transatlantic liner to a cruise ship, to take advantage of every favorable condition of use.[12] The last season of the great ocean liners was opened when the market for transoceanic travel was almost entirely controlled by air transport.

In Italy, the race for the luxury shipping market was costing the state dearly, despite the concerns that came from the shipbuilding management (Fragiacomo 2003). Between 1962 (when the system of public subsidies introduced in 1936 was renewed) and 1966, some excellent ships were built, and public annual grants to navigation climbed from 23 billion to 60 billion lire. Turboships *Michelangelo* and *Raffaello* were launched in 1965, and in the following year *Eugenio C* (the largest passenger ship for private shipping) was launched. These were extremely luxurious and prestigious ships, whose construction had been largely financed by the state, mainly to avoid massive manpower cuts in already depressed areas. The work for the construction and refurbishing of *Michelangelo* and *Raffaello* lasted from 1962 to 1965 and was of a particularly high technical standard (and expensive) because the two ships had been given the task of representing overseas the success of the new Italy, coming out of the economic boom. But their use was made possible only by generous state subsidies, and in both cases their active life lasted only a decade, and virtually ended when it was decided to suspend public disbursement for navigation.[13] The run-up between the worsening industrial crisis and the growing financial commitments led to paradoxical situations. In the Genoa province ("the ghost corner of the Italian industrial Triangle," as the Minister Giorgio Bo called it)[14] between 1955 and 1965, about one fifth of all the investments of state-owned enterprises were in companies engaged primarily in the maritime industry, without reaching any long-standing goal.

In essence, a government five-year plan for the renewal of the national merchant fleet led to the construction of many ships, but the sale prices were so low as to put pressure on the finances of the public enterprises engaged in the maritime sector, which between 1961 and 1964 absorbed (losses plus subsidies) about 90 billion lire (CIPE 1966, 18). The trends in shipbuilding over the whole postwar period are shown in Table 11.1.

*Table 11.1*  UK, Italy, and World Shipbuilding Deliveries, 1947–2004 (x 1,000 gross registered tons.) (All self-propelled commercial vessels over 100 gross tons)

| Year | World Total | United Kingdom | Italy |
|------|-------------|----------------|-------|
| 1947 | | 1,202 | 62 |
| 1948 | | 1,176 | 112 |
| 1949 | | 1,267 | 99 |
| 1950 | | 1,325 | 107 |
| 1951 | | 1,341 | 112 |
| 1952 | | 1,303 | 132 |
| 1953 | | 1,317 | 263 |
| 1954 | | 1,409 | 162 |
| 1955 | | 1,474 | 167 |
| 1956 | | 1,383 | 358 |
| 1957 | | 1,414 | 485 |
| 1958 | | 1,402 | 551 |
| 1959 | | 1,373 | 518 |
| 1960 | | 1,331 | 434 |
| 1961 | | 1,192 | 334 |
| 1962 | | 1,073 | 348 |
| 1963 | | 928 | 492 |
| 1964 | 9,724 | 1,043 | 368 |
| 1965 | 11,763 | 1,073 | 442 |
| 1966 | 14,105 | 1,074 | 530 |
| 1967 | 15,157 | 1,188 | 496 |
| 1968 | 16,845 | 1,047 | 499 |
| 1969 | 18,739 | 828 | 364 |
| 1970 | 20,980 | 1,367 | 546 |
| 1971 | 24,388 | 1,233 | 872 |

*(continued)*

*Table 11.1*   (continued)

| Year | World Total | United Kingdom | Italy |
|------|-------------|----------------|-------|
| 1972 | 26,749 | 1,197 | 902 |
| 1973 | 30,409 | 1,067 | 837 |
| 1974 | 33,541 | 1,198 | 953 |
| 1975 | 34,203 | 117 | 792 |
| 1976 | 33,922 | 1,500 | 715 |
| 1977 | 27,532 | 1,020 | 778 |
| 1978 | 18,194 | 1,133 | 339 |
| 1979 | 14,289 | 691 | 231 |
| 1980 | 13,101 | 427 | 248 |
| 1981 | 16,932 | 212 | 271 |
| 1982 | 16,820 | 434 | 176 |
| 1983 | 15,911 | 496 | 255 |
| 1984 | 18,334 | 444 | 273 |
| 1985 | 18,157 | 171 | 88 |
| 1986 | 16,845 | 98 | 34 |
| 1987 | 12,259 | 194 | 312 |
| 1988 | 11,312 | 52 | 161 |
| 1989 | 14,482 | 117 | 343 |
| 1990 | 16,054 | 127 | 392 |
| 1991 | 16,810 | 108 | 508 |
| 1992 | 18,928 | 229 | 397 |
| 1993 | 20,538 | 230 | 480 |
| 1994 | 19,669 | 227 | 517 |
| 1995 | 22,652 | 150 | 404 |
| 1996 | 25,837 | 188 | 665 |
| 1997 | 25,537 | 74 | 415 |
| 1998 | 25,464 | 139 | 827 |
| 1999 | 27,822 | 24 | 756 |
| 2000 | 31,696 | 105 | 569 |
| 2001 | 31,292 | 12 | 571 |
| 2002 | 33,383 | 28 | 572 |
| 2003 | 36,131 | 33 | 664 |
| 2004 | 40,171 | 2 | 599 |

*Source:* For the years 1947–1965 see Appendix H, in *Shipbuilding Inquiry Committee Report 1965–1966*, HMSO, London, 1966, 180–181; for years 1966–2004, see www.shipbuildinghistory.com.

Original data from Lloyd's Register of Shipping.

## COMMITTEES AND REPORTS

It was said of the maritime economic sphere during the 1960s that "No other sector of the British economy came under such intense scrutiny in these years" (Jamieson 1998, 86). In part, such attention was related to the actual decline in production, but in part it was a response to the need to curb the growth of government subsidies to sectors in crisis, and particularly to shipbuilding industries. In response to this double set of stimulations, in London and Rome, as in other capitals, governments organized teams of politicians and experts to try to resolve a puzzle that seemed impossible: to reduce public funding, revitalize the whole sector and contain, as much as possible, the social and political consequences of the inevitable reduction in the workforce.

In 1965, the Labour government assigned the responsibility for analyzing the status of the national shipbuilding to a committee chaired by Ray Geddes (Strath 1987, 119–121). There is a passage, inside the final report, that showed how clear was the perception of the conclusion of an era, marked by the end of British control of the global maritime market.

> When Britain was the dominant shipbuilding power, the strength of the professions of naval architecture and marine engineering in Britain lay in the traditions and experience of their members, which made possible the continuous progress of ship design and technology, based on the accumulated experience of men with high standards of integrity and ability. The dominant position of the industry gave little incentive to alternative approaches based on any complex systematic analysis into problems suitable for treatment by the methods of fundamental scientific research. (Shipbuilding Inquiry Committee Report 1966, 124)

The weakness of the national shipbuilding system was considered a consequence of incompatibility between Fordist practices and the British way of production, at all levels: business, management, and the workforce. Another link was to the excessive resistance of the labor force to changes in production methods (Lorenz 1991), but it seems more accurate to attribute responsibility to a combination of different factors. First there was the structural rigidity of many plants, which made it impossible to adopt new systems or to build larger vessels. The trajectory of development after WWII should be taken into account, with investments directed to upholding outstanding quality, but also to maintaining a flexible work organization, while the market demanded ships which were economic to operate and relatively easy to build, something possible even in countries with little tradition of naval engineering such as Poland, Brazil, and Yugoslavia. Finally, there was the unwillingness of entrepreneurs to invest heavily in new production lines, given the uncertain viability of their enterprises, expecting in the best cases much lower revenues than usual.

A way remained open, which was actually walked: the exploitation of the available market niches, relying on state aid to support employment, while there were still work opportunities on hand.

The British state intervened when the situation was already severely compromised, and imposed a drastic solution, in the sense that the districts in which it was not possible to interact with market demands, to use new technologies and to change working practices saw the collapse of their shipyards. The final outcome was the nationalization of the remaining shipyards, especially those engaged in military construction. A new state-owned enterprise, British Shipbuilders, was created in July 1977.

In Italy, new problems arose when the ability to cope with changes in the international market was handicapped by the need to respect the Treaty of Rome, signed in 1958, which required the end of public aid to enterprises. Allowing for such a need, but also for practical reasons, Fincantieri was founded in 1959, grouping all state-owned shipbuilding firms under a single holding. At that time, its aim was simply to implement the reforms decided by the government, with a little autonomy in resource allocation.[15] Troubles came when the optimistic forecasts for that year proved unfounded, and the industry soon was in need of new financial assistance. It was estimated that from 1945 to 1965, the Italian state was involved in the shipbuilding industry with policies that led to an overall spending of over 360 billion lire (Flore 1970, 532). In 1966, within the Ministry of Bilancio e Programmazione Economica (therefore not inside IRI), a study commission was created, formally with the aim of drawing up a plan for revitalizing the shipbuilding sector, in reality for reconciling the continuation, at least temporarily, of financial aid to companies with the demands of the European Economic Community, which called for its abolition. The solution proposed was a further reduction of Italian employment and production capacity. After shrinking production level by 25% between 1955 and 1965, more than 22,000 employees remained on the job. Particular emphasis was given to "the creation of a new shipyard for the very large units, which are required by the market and that Italy is not currently able to build" (CIPE 1966, 43).

Compared with the past, the government decided on an abrupt change of direction, accepting that IRI should establish Italcantieri (22 October 1966) to gain direct control of every publicly owned shipyard, dismissing the old regional-based firms. It was also decided to build a sort of laboratory-yard, within which to concentrate the attempts to keep control of the national market, or even get some commission from abroad. The Monfalcone shipyard was chosen, in the northern Adriatic area, causing serious social distress in Liguria, where, in exchange, some investments were concentrated. Nevertheless, the planned shutdown of some sites was postponed indefinitely, for political reasons.

## EMERGING MARITIME FORDISM

In the mid-1960s, the opening in Sweden of the Arendal Shipyard demonstrated how new building practices, derived from Japan, could also be adapted to European social conditions, providing significant productivity gains[16] and profits. The catching up with modernity in the shipbuilding industry followed three main lines: the replacement of the traditional vertical construction method with a horizontal one, the shift from a labor-intensive to a capital-intensive organization, and finally an increase in automation in equipment both on land and on board. These three elements are closely related. As for the first point, it had mostly a conceptual nature, consisting in the reversal of the traditional construction which dated from the days of sailing. The decisive phase for the construction of a merchant ship, the final assembly of the hull, changed from a vertically constructed building (from bottom to top, or from the keel to superstructure) to a horizontal one. Coming from shops, prefabricated blocks were assembled linearly in the basin, starting from the rear (stern), gradually encompassing the ship to the bow, or vice versa. Such an organization made production easier, controllable, and predictable, with obvious advantages in cutting time losses and controlling elements of cost. Also, moving the labor-intensive operations from onboard to land, in factories, allowed the complete reconstruction of working procedures, with the introduction of new machinery and an extensive automation of repetitive operations (cutting, shaping, and welding metal sheets, e.g.). The whole process could be serialized, in a fully Fordist perspective.

For the Italian shipbuilding industry, the question of adopting the new procedures was split into two components: on one hand, the investments should be concentrated on a single plant, enough to build a sort of experimental laboratory-yard. In this case, government subsidies were to have a strategic purpose and the technical management, for the first time in the postwar years, was to have full responsibility for the governance of a project that was very important for the revitalization of the entire sector. On the other hand, the inevitable social consequences associated with the closure of less-efficient plants and reduction of the workforce would be managed through state expenditure of a social care nature, with very little economic content.

In Great Britain, the adoption of the new procedures conflicted with the strong capacity for resistance to change expressed by workers' organizations (Lorenz 1991). Besides, there was a clear incompatibility with the full range of choices (and investment) recently made, and especially with the interests of industrialists, who feared the greater capital lock-in of the new system in the face of uncertain profits and a net reduction of revenues. For example, the Scottish Scott Lithgow shipyard— the new company formed after the recommendations of the Geddes Commission to continue the old systems as well as to meet new market demands—used public funds as financial oxygen for their own budgets, instead of carrying out a reorganization of production. In the case of the Harland and Wolff shipyard in Northern Ireland, political reasons (the maintenance of an economic activity essential for the Protestant part of the population) led to an early nationalization, with a state-subsidized refinancing of the company's assets. The results weren't positive from an economic standpoint, even if the political objective of safeguarding Protestant employment was broadly achieved (Connors 2008). Gradually, also in other cases, state support became more and more directed primarily to safeguard workforce employment, in the sense that most of the funding was not used for the modernization and revitalization of businesses, but rather to support the (low) profitability of enterprises and thus to prevent their closure.

Both in Italy and in Great Britain, during the 1960s, government financial efforts were aimed at maintaining the prestige of national naval engineering and thus the maritime reputation of the entire country. But such a partial politics could not be successful because the passenger market was disappearing, and the freight market was regulated only by cost-related logic, with very little weight given to high-quality transport services in which the two governments had invested large amounts since the end of the war.

## FROM FORDISM TO POST-FORDISM

As late as 1964, the Lloyd's Register of Shipping statistics reported that over 50% of merchant shipping launched in the world was produced in Western Europe. Later, European production fell below the psychological barrier of 50%, and kept declining from there on; it dropped below 40% in 1973 and below 30% since 1980. The decline of the European shipbuilding industry is even more significant if we think that throughout the second half of the 1970s, the production of ships was reducing all over the world: therefore in Europe, the fall was double. In Great Britain, the crisis turned into a real collapse.

A few figures are sufficient to describe the decline of maritime engineering in the United Kingdom: during the 1950s, while world production doubled, the UK share of new constructions dropped from 40% to 15%, and fell again to about 5% of world total during the late 1960s. One of the most important British shipbuilding districts, the River Clyde and Glasgow, passed from over 20 yards active in the early 1960s to less than 5 yards in the 1990s. Among the sacrificed were prestigious firms, such as William Denny & Bros., Dumbarton, one of the first to close (in 1963), John Brown & Co. Clydebank (closed in 1987), and the Lithgow yards of Port Glasgow (closed permanently in 1988). Among the survivors, the majority were integrated into a larger group (as Yarrow & Co. in Scotstoun and Fairfield Shipbuilding & Engineering Co. of Govan). At the beginning of this process, in 1972, the British Department of Trade and Industry commissioned a study by Booz, Allen, and Hamilton on the long-term prospects of the national shipyards. The final report emphasized that the companies were suffering because of underinvestment and mismanagement. The industry had a bad reputation with regard to deliveries and industrial relations, and had experienced a slow modernization. To maintain a sufficient degree of competitiveness, the final report suggested improvements in the organization of the production systems, the flow of information, and strategic planning. Substantial government aid was deemed essential and this still would not have prevented a significant downsizing of the workforce and the closing down of less-efficient plants (Jamieson 2003, 73–74). The basic premise seems to be related mainly to the viability of social and political change, rather than the availability of knowledge and appropriate technologies. Indeed, the origin of the Korean shipbuilding industry dates from those years. It was based on imported British technology and business practices, used heavily by Korea to become a world leader. It started with the construction at Ulsan of the Hyundai shipyard, which opened in 1973; full production began in the early 1980s.

In a comparative perspective, though in Italy the incentives to change in maritime engineering came from within the institutional system of reference (public industry, government, European Community), management was able to lead the state-owned company toward a market logic.[17] In the British case, it was the progressive marginalization from international markets that produced the conditions for a radical change, which was announced by Labour in 1974 and, after a complicated parliamentary passage, ended with the nationalization of the sector in July 1977 and the formation of the state-owned firm, British Shipbuilders. In the Act of Parliament that gave birth simultaneously to British Shipbuilders and British Aerospace, the aims were listed as follows: "To provide for the vesting in British Aerospace of the securities of certain companies engaged in manufacturing aircraft and guided weapons and British Shipbuilders in the vesting of the securities of certain companies engaged in shipbuilding and allied industries."[18] Similar considerations were related to the survival of some companies engaged in naval shipbuilding, with particular reference to the completion of the British nuclear program.

At a time when attention to the Italian example was quite high (Tomlinson 1999; O'Hara 2009, 512–514), the concentration of national maritime engineering inside a single state-owned holding seemed to offer the most appropriate instrument to allow the closure of some yards, while exploring other developments, thereby putting aside the quarrels and divisions that had blocked the possible rationalization after the release of the Geddes Report (Parkinson 1968). From this point of view, "The experience of British Shipbuilders was rather more the management of decline than revitalisation" (Sawyer 1991, 165), because its main activities were the organization of plant closures and massive staff reductions (in the presence of decreasing investment) in an attempt to reduce financial losses, which nevertheless remained very high (Peck and Townsend, 1984, 321–326). Indeed, the image was that of an over-bureaucratic company, too tied to political power and a source of permanent losses to the Exchequer.

In 1985, following the well-known reelection of the Thatcher government in 1983, the merged companies were privatized, and the financial aid converted to specific grants, with a view to achieving particular objectives. But even in this case, the result was a failure: plants continued to close and employment collapsed (Thomas 1983, 213). Out of more than 60 construction sites active in 1948, at the end of 2007 only 4 remained officially operating, all belonging to BAE Systems, which was the first private company in Europe active in the defense sector, and the third in the world.

In Italy, during the 1970s public enterprise maritime activity gradually abandoned the passenger sector and focused on freight transport.[19] In the renovated Monfalcone shipyard, technological renewal led to the adoption of the entire set of Fordist solutions: horizontal methods and prefabrication, full automation and simplification of procedures, and extensive standardization of products. The productivity gains were widely evident. Before the yard's restructuring, a 36,000-ton tanker was built in 22½ months; in the mid-1970s, a 250,000-ton turbotanker was completed in 1 year and 4 days after the first steel plate was laid down.[20] For the first time, the full introduction of a Fordist organization of production led to a general de-skilling of the workforce, especially welders, with consequent reductions in the average wage. Strong social tensions emerged during the 1970s, when the oil crisis seemed to make unnecessary the considerable investments made in the previous decade. But during the 1980s, the need for a revival was shared by management and the workforce, both confronting the specter of complete closure, given the government's will to gradually reduce support to the public sector of the economy.

In 1984, the maritime engineering sector was further reorganized, with the incorporation of Italcantieri in Fincantieri, the specialization of yards by product lines, and the profound changes in productive practices, in years of severe crisis. After the restructuring, the company acted in two directions. On the internal side, two important agreements were reached with the labor unions (in 1986 and 1988) with the adoption of flexible specialization of the workforce. Time losses and bottlenecks in production flow were eliminated, ensuring faster production and an increased ability to control product quality during the course of working. On the external side, the management decided for relocation, with a return, after 25 years, back to the private market for passenger ships and the acquisition of up-to-date production technologies. But the main change happened inside the idea of the ship, considering it not only a means of transport but as an essence of 'made in Italy', from the exterior design to the interior decorations, from the artistic details to Italian cooking in restaurants on board. Low value-added market segments (tankers, general cargo) were completely abandoned.

The introduction of computer-based automation in metal blocks processing allowed for an increase in speed and precision, with considerable savings in terms of labor (Di Filippo, Manzon, and Maschio 1997). At the Monfalcone shipyard, in little more than a decade, a carpentry workshop passed from 80 workers to 3, while increasing the amount of steel processed in every time period. Further gains in flexibility were obtained thanks to outsourcing of all the processes not related to the structure of the ship.

In the mid-1980s, the first passenger ship was built by assembling 300 prefabricated pieces (Cerato 1998), while in more recent years, 65 blocks are enough for even bigger ships. The adoption of fully post-Fordist practices such as lean manufacturing, just-in-time and total quality through self-activation of each individual employee were diffused from Monfalcone to other shipyards in Italy during the 1990s, saving other productive centers from collapse. The massive integration of information technology within the production cycle reduced, by approximately 25%, the workforce employed directly in production, while increasing the duties of a clerical nature, certainly less tiring and more acceptable to employees (Mellinato 2009). Now Fincantieri is still a state-owned enterprise, but political interference is reduced to a minimum. It employs a total of more or less 9,500 people (but approximately 20,000 if the supply chain is included) working at eight shipyards, two design centers, one research center, and two production sites for mechanical components. Direct state financial support was progressively reduced from the late 1990s, and ended officially around 2005, but the company is involved in many research programs, financed both by government subsidies and by European Union grants.

## HISTORY IS NEVER MERCIFUL

During the second half of the 20th century, Italian and British governments were unable to manage the social and political consequences of the transformation of maritime engineering. In the years 1958–1960, a brief contraction of the world shipbuilding market abruptly ended one of the most positive upward cycles in the contemporary age (Storch 1995, 16), focusing the attention of producers on topics such as productivity and work organization, and not just on the quality of the product.

During the 1960s, the detailed reports of the Geddes and Caron Commissions led to the implicit conclusion that the disease maritime engineering was suffering in the two countries was only partly due to production overcapacity. After all, in fact, the causes of the competitiveness crisis were multifactorial and "environmental," at root closely linked to the genetic heritage of the European shipbuilding industry.

In the case of Great Britain, the government was progressively more involved in financing the defense of a system composed primarily of private enterprises, who were aware of not having the right tools to compete with international players, who were free from constraints arising from the past and willing to invest huge capital in equipment and installations. The entrepreneurial landscape was marked by ties to tradition, but also to conservation and inertia: in this way, the UK companies literally lost the international market (Todd 1985, 104–126; Jamieson 2003, 60 et seq.). Assistance from the government was intended to preserve, as long as possible, the benefits deriving from former British maritime leadership, but any help was hindered by at least three factors: lack of strategic vision, which involved uncertainties in choosing the financial tools; misunderstanding about the production options actually valid only for the internal market; and finally the regional policy dimensions, with Northern Ireland treated differently from Scotland and England. In conclusion, government actions were too closely related to private entrepreneurs' short termism to produce a true renewal of the sector.

In Italy, the experience of the shipbuilding industry during the post-war decades can easily be divided into two distinct periods: one initial "political" stage (roughly until the mid-1980s), during which the prevalent dynamics of state intervention were directed to use the sector's production capacity to achieve broader policy objectives, recognizing only partially its specificity. It was the long period during which, even in the field of aid and subsidies, quantity (understood as jobs) prevailed over quality. In the second period, when the sector seemed destined to a slow euthanasia, political pressures (from both government and IRI) were reduced, and Fincantieri was able to find new tools within its organization to design, build, and prepare competitive ships, with the cooperation of labor and trade unions, inside a "managerial" second stage of this development.

In both countries, the key decisions were made during the 1970s, when the need to reduce (or at least increase the efficiency of) state subsidies forced decision makers to make decisive choices. In this phase, British and Italian maritime engineering reacted differently to similar issues, depending on the different structure of the production sector in the two countries. The British system was fragmented into various territorial interest groups, even after the nationalization, so that the operational capability of British Shipbuilders was strongly influenced by the same political priorities and trade union expectations that had already limited the effectiveness of previous choices (Daniel 2003, 234–259). The potential synergies between companies were not implemented, and facing the prospect of continuing losses, the Conservative government decided to close the experiment, leaving privatized companies to slowly collapse, within a general program that had significant political objectives, as well as economic ones (Florio 2004, 27 and et seq.).

Italian naval engineering, even on a different scale, was facing very similar problems, but within a system more open than the British, more sensitive to international pressures, and also more flexible in managing the costs of transformation. Above all, the Italian system was less regionalized, more interconnected, and entirely in public hands. In the late 1970s and early 1980s, Fincantieri absorbed the last private shipyards and also major companies producing auxiliary materials, such as engines (Lanzardo 2000), reaching a nearly complete horizontal integration. In those years, governments inclined to adopt deficit spending policies ensured a temporary financial salvation for Fincantieri, but also assured the background for a reorganization of production methods.

After all, the essential difference between the two countries could not be found inside the greater or lesser governments' willingness to spend on financing the sector, or in matters related to the quality of spending, but rather in the selection of mediators entrusted with the responsibility to manage those expenditures. Broadly speaking, organizational responsibilities were delegated to public technicians and managers in the Italian case, to private entrepreneurs in charge of administrating a state company in the British case. In Italy, the gradual decline of private and political interests in what seemed to be a dying industry opened the way to engineers and technicians who, during the 1990s, managed the survival and revitalization of the entire Fincantieri group.

## NOTES

1. Between the fall of France and Pearl Harbor, Britain lost about a third of its merchant fleet, as available in summer 1940.
2. More than 5,700 ships were launched during wartime.
3. As in the case of the P & O steamship *Iberia*, which was specifically devoted to the service with Australia, launched on 22 January 1954. *Shipbuilder and Marine Engine-Builder* 1954, 61(548), March: 156 et seq.
4. "Mr. E. J. Hill, general secretary of the Boilermakers' Society, is also reported to have estimated that some 75,000 men would be surplus to the 'normal' needs of the industry (*The Times*, December 5th, 1949)" (Ross 1952, 524).
5. A Shipbuilding Advisory Committee was set up in 1946, but its action was very smooth (Jamieson 2003, 60 et seq.)
6. For example, to maintain an active route to New York with the liners *Rex* and *Conte di Savoia,* the company Italia received an extra grant of 192 million lire per year (Ogliari 1984, 1459).
7. Law no. 75, 8 March 1949, which took its name from Minister Saragat (Ogliari 1985).
8. It was the "Legge Cappa," no. 949 of 25 July 1952, followed by another strategic measure, the "Legge Tambroni," no. 522 of 17 July 1954.
9. *Shipbuilder and Marine Engine-Builder* 1958, 65( 610), December: 705.
10. "There is no indication that the United Kingdom shipbuilding industry has on balance any marked technical or economic advantage over its major foreign competitors apart from its large home market." *North Atlantic Shipping Bill*, HC Deb 30 May 1961, 641: c. 177.
11. The minutes of the Parliamentary session can be accessed at http://hansard. millbanksystems.com/commons/1961/may/30/north-atlantic-shipping-bill-2.
12. The ship was later transformed and adapted several times: in 1982 as a troop carrier for the Falklands War, in 1986–1987 with a diesel-electric

propulsion replacing the old steam turbine engine, and later in 1994 for an overall modernization.
13. See http://www.michelangelo-raffaello.com.
14. Newspaper article "Non reggono le lamentele genovesi di fronte alla consistenza dei fatti," in *Il Piccolo*, 14 September 1966.
15. Note "Fincantieri. Notizie storiche sulla società," dated Roma, 27 April 1977, in *Archivio storico elettronico Iri, Gruppo Rossa* 69835: 1–2.
16. "A Milestone in Shipbuilding," in *Shipbuilder and Marine Engine-Builder* 1963, 670, 17 July.
17. Since 1973, also the last Italian private maritime engineering company was absorbed by the state-owned Italcantieri.
18. The text may be found at http://en.wikipedia.org/wiki/Aircraft_and_Shipbuilding_Industries_Act_1977.
19. After a prolonged crisis, the shipping holding Finmare went into liquidation in 1999.
20. The two ships were the *Esso Dublin*, launched in 1960, and *Agip Lazio*, launched in 1976.

## BIBLIOGRAPHY

Cerato, S. 1998, "Tecnologia e sviluppo nella produzione delle navi passeggeri," *Il Territorio* 21(9): 35–42.
Comitato Interministeriale per la Programmazione Economica (CIPE) 1966, *Relazione della Commissione interministeriale di studio per i cantieri navali*, Roma.
Connors, D.P. 2008, *The Role of Government in the Decline of the British Shipbuilding Industry, 1945–1980*, PhD Thesis, University of Glasgow, Department of Economic & Social History.
Corbino, E. 1948, *Le costruzioni navali. Discorso pronunciato alla Camera dei Deputati nella seduta dell'11 dicembre 1948*, Roma: Tipografia della Camera.
Di Filippo, G., L. Manzon, and P. Maschio 1997, *An Integrated Steel Workshop for Shipbuilding: A Real Application of Automation*, New Orleans: Ship Production Symposium, 21–23 April.
Daniel, R.J. 2003, *The End of an Era: The Memoirs of a Naval Constructor*, Penzance: Periscope Publishing.
Elbaum, B. and W. Lazonick 1984, "The Decline of the British Economy: An Institutional Perspective," *Journal of Economic History* 44(2): 567–583.
Flore, V.D. 1970, *L'industria dei trasporti marittimi in Italia, parte II, L'azione dello stato dal 1860 al 1965*, Roma: Bollettino informazioni marittime.
Florio, M. 2004, *The Great Divestiture: Evaluating the Welfare Impact of the British Privatization 1979–1997*, Cambridge, Mass.: MIT Press.
Fragiacomo, P. 2003, "I condizionamenti politici nell'industria pubblica: La cantieristica Iri *(1945–1985)*," *Imprese e storia* 28: 183–223.
Hancock, W.K. and M.M. Gowing 1949, *British War Economy*, London: HMSO.
Hornby, W. 1958, *Factories and Plant*, London: HMSO.
Ingram, P. and A. Lifschitz 2006, "Kinship in the Shadow of the Corporation: The Interbuilder Network in Clyde River Shipbuilding, 1711–1990," *American Sociological Review* 71: 334–352.
Irons-Georges, T., ed. 2002, *Encyclopedia of Flight*, Pasadena, Calif.: Salem Press.
Jacoboni, A. 1949, *L'industria meccanica italiana*, Roma: Centro di studi e piani tecnico-economici.

Jamieson, A.G. 1998, "An Inevitable Decline? Britain's Shipping and Shipbuilding Industries since 1930," in *Exploiting the Sea: Aspects of Britain's Maritime Economy since 1870*, eds. D.J. Starkey and A.G. Jamieson, Exeter: University of Exeter Press.

Jamieson, A.G. 2003, *Ebb Tide in the British Maritime Industries: Change and Adaptation, 1918–1990*, Exeter: Exeter University Press.

Johnman, L. and H. Murphy 2002, *British Shipbuilding and the State since 1918: A Political Economy of Decline*, Exeter: University of Exeter Press.

Lane, F.C. 1951, *Ships for Victory: A History of Shipbuilding under the U.S. Maritime Commission in World War II*, Baltimore: Johns Hopkins University Press.

Lanzardo, L. 2000, *Grandi Motori: Da Torino a Trieste culture industriali a confronto (1966–1999)*, Milano: Franco Angeli.

Lojacono, G. 1951, "L'industria delle costruzioni navali in Italia," excerpt *Atti dell'accademia di marina mercantile*, anno IV, fascicolo unico, (Genova).

Lorenz, E. and F. Wilkinson 1987, "The Shipbuilding Industry 1880–1965," in *The Decline of the British Economy*, eds. B. Elbaum and W. Lazonick, Oxford: Clarendon Press.

Lorenz, E.H. 1991, "An Evolutionary Explanation for Competitive Decline: The British Shipbuilding Industry 1890–1970," *Journal of Economic History* 51(4): 911–935.

Mellinato, G., ed. 2009, *I mestieri e la formazione di una comunità: Monfalcone 1908–2008*, Monfalcone: Comune di Monfalcone.

McTavish, D. 2005, *Business and Public Management in the UK, 1900–2003*, Aldershot: Ashgate.

Murray, J.M. 1960, *Merchant Ships 1860–1960*, London: Lloyd's Register of Shipping.

Ogliari, F. (ed.) 1984, *Dallo Smoking alla divisa: La Marina mercantile italiana dal 1932 al 1945*, Milano: Cavallotti.

Ogliari, F., ed. 1985, *Gli anni della Fenice, il Gruppo Finmare, le compagnie sovenzionate dal 1945 al 1985*, Milano: Cavallotti.

O'Hara, G. 2009, "'What the Electorate Can Be Expected to Swallow': Nationalization, Transnationalism and the Shifting Boundaries of the State In Post-War Britain," *Business History* 51(4): 501–528.

Parkinson, J.R. 1960, *The Economics of Shipbuilding in the United Kingdom*, Cambridge: Cambridge University Press.

Parkinson, J.R. 1968, "The Financial Prospects of Shipbuilding after Geddes," *Journal of Industrial Economics* 17(1): 1–17.

Peck, F. and A. Townsend 1984, "Contrasting Experience of Recession and Spatial Restructuring: British Shipbuilders, Plessey and Metal Box," *Regional Studies* 18(4): 319–338.

Pope, R. 1990, *Atlas of British Social and Economic History since c. 1700*, London: Routledge.

Reid, A. 1991, "Employers' Strategies and Craft Production: The British Shipbuilding Industry 1870–1950," in *The Power to Manage? Employers and Industrial Relations in a Comparative-Historical Perspective*, eds. S. Tolliday and J. Zeitlin, London: Routledge.

Ross, N.S. 1952, "Employment in Shipbuilding and Ship-Repairing in Great Britain," *Journal of the Royal Statistical Society*, Series A (General) 115(4): 524–533.

Rossi, E. 1953, *Lo stato industriale*, Bari: Laterza.

Sawyer, M. 1991, "Industrial Policy," in *Labour's Economic Policies 1974–1979*, eds. M.J. Artis and D.P. Cobham, Manchester: Manchester University Press.

*Shipbuilding Inquiry Committee Report 1965–1966*, Cmd. 2937, 1966, London: HMSO.

Skinner Watson, M. 1950, *Chief of Staff: Prewar Plans and Preparations*, Washington DC: Historical Division, Department of the Army.

Storch, R.L., ed. 1995, *Ship Production*, Jersey City, NJ: Society of Naval Architects and Marine Engineering.

Strath, B. 1987, *The Politics of De-industrialisation: The Contraction of the West European Shipbuilding Industry*, London: Croom Helm.

Thomas, D. 1983, "Shipbuilding: Demand Linkage and Industrial Decline," in *Why Are the British Bad at Manufacturing?* eds. K. Williams, J.L. Williams, and D. Thomas, London: Routledge.

Thompson, P. 2001, "How Much Did the Liberty Shipbuilders Learn? New Evidence for an Old Case Study," *Journal of Political Economy* 109(1): 103–137.

Thornton, R.A. and P. Thompson 2001, "Learning from Experience and Learning from Others: An Exploration of Learning and Spillovers in Wartime Shipbuilding," *American Economic Review*, 91(5): 1350–1368.

Todd, D. 1985, *The World Shipbuilding Industry*, New York: St. Martin's Press.

Tomlinson, J. 1999, "Learning from Italy? The British Public Sector and IRI," *European Yearbook of Business History*, Vol. 2, eds. W. Feldenkirchen and T. Gourvish, London: Ashgate.

United Nations, Department of Economic Affairs 1948, *Salient Features of the World Economic Situation 1945–47*, New York: United Nations.

# 12 State Enterprise in British Electricity Supply*
## An Economic Success?

*Robert Millward*

## INTRODUCTION

Electricity supply was at the center of state enterprise activity in Britain in the 20th century. The national transmission grid was developed and owned from 1926 by the Central Electricity Board which was, ignoring the Post Office, the first nationwide infrastructure industry to be owned by the state. Generating and distributing enterprises were taken over as part of the 1947 nationalization under the umbrella of the British Electricity Authority. Then, at the end of the 1980s, it was the first giant utility where privatization was accompanied by a major restructuring of the industry. Generation, transmission, distribution, and retailing were vertically disintegrated and regulated by independent agencies: the Office of Electricity Regulation and the Office of Gas and Electricity Markets.

That new regulatory regime continued a long tradition of monitoring and control of prices and service levels. When electricity emerged in Britain in the late 19th century, both central and local government had already considerable experience of regulating railways, water, and gas supply, and the 1882 Electricity Supply Act is notorious for its toughness. In those early days, transmission was limited spatially, and the industry was populated by a large number of small enterprises, each vertically integrated from generation to retailing. By 1900, there were 65 private companies as well as 165 municipal enterprises whose role seems to have been to generate profits to supplement local taxes ('rate relief'). The Act set price ceilings and allowed local governments to compulsorily acquire private companies after 21 years. The use of electricity for heat and power in industry emerged, but electricity did not make any serious inroads into the lighting market dominated by gas (see Millward 2000a on all the above). Britain was very well blessed with coal, and its gas output per head of population in 1900 was nearly four times that in U.S. and more than all of the rest of Europe combined; it is not surprising to find that electricity lagged somewhat behind other countries not as well endowed. Nonetheless, comparisons were made with the huge expansion in the U.S., where most tramways had been electrified by 1890. The possibility of long-distance transmission was also emerging, but the structure of the British industry seemed to inhibit the development of regional, let alone national, networks. By 1926, there were 233 private companies and 360 municipal enterprises. These small enterprises did not want to combine or merge, and it was these obstacles that first drew in state intervention after World War I.

The aim of this chapter is first to explain the intervention of the state in the 1920s in Britain and how it led to nationalization in the 1940s. Second, an assessment is made of the effectiveness of state ownership in its two phases of Central Electricity Board 1926–1946 and nationalized industry 1947–1988. An important element in that story is played by the huge British coal industry whose decline and troubled industrial relations had a strong effect on its major customer, the electricity industry. Third, in light of the argument put forward in the 1980s by supporters of privatization that restructuring the industry would raise efficiency, the chapter will evaluate quantitatively the productivity performance of state enterprise electricity in Britain relative to that of the privatized regime which followed in 1989 and to that of the electricity supply industries in some other countries for which comparable data are available.

## THE STATE-OWNED TRANSMISSION GRID AND THE ROAD TO NATIONALIZATION, 1920–1947

A good indicator of the way electricity has developed is the movement of its price relative to those of coal and gas. Figure 12.1 illustrates how the price of electricity in Britain (averaged over different consumers and regions) fell in absolute terms from the 1880s all the way down to World War II. This period of falling price was clearly a period of very high growth rates in electricity consumption as coal and gas prices hardly changed in the 30 years up to World War I across which they showed a very large increase as they did across World War II. These very disparate movements of prices are a sign of an immature energy sector with access for some consumers restricted. In fact the interwar period 1920–1939 saw electric lighting outcompeting gas, and the number of electricity consumers shot up from 1 million to nearly 10 million by which time lighting had fallen to less than 7% of the gas industry's load (Wilson 1993, 4). Sales of electricity to the household sector rose from 8% of total electricity sales to 26% by 1938, reflecting not just the advances in electric lighting but also the fact that consumer durables like cleaners, washing machines, and heaters were starting to spread. The industrial market for heat, energy, and light was also very buoyant, with sales increasing fivefold as manufacturing processing in engineering and chemicals forged ahead.

This huge increase in demand was propelled by the fall in electricity prices which was itself made possible by important technological and structural developments on the supply side. The need to shift from the

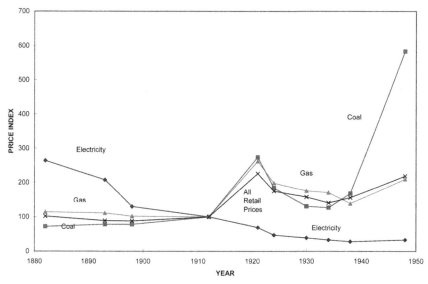

*Figure 12.1* Price indexes for electricity and other goods in the UK, 1882–1948.
*Source*: Millward 2003, Figure 1.

19th-century focus on local undertakings and local markets to a regional or even national market proved difficult, and local government proved a real stumbling block. Practically all electricity in this period was produced from coal-fired thermal generating plants. The development of high-pressure speed turbines meant unit-generating costs were lower in larger stations. In addition, developments in the scientific understanding of electrical current allowed supply to be transformed by stations. Interconnection of areas by grids would therefore allow more use of large generating plants and the elimination of idle capacity. Calls for greater coordination between urban areas were being made in the early 1900s and, immediately after World War I, there was much agitation for the establishment of District Boards. Following the Williamson Committee Report of 1918, the only gain was the establishment of a body, the Electricity Commissioners, to promote technical development. Another government committee was established in 1925 and reported in strong terms on the relatively high cost and low consumption of electricity in Britain, the proliferation of small plants, and the need for interconnection (Weir Committee 1926). The solution, ingenious, said Hannah (1977), in the light of fears of nationalization, was to set up the Central Electricity Board. Its basic functions were to construct a national grid, close down small stations, and standardize electricity frequencies. But it was the institutional arrangement which was truly innovative. Certain stations were to be 'selected'. The Central Electricity Board would buy electricity from them, transmit, and then resell, leaving the job of retailing to the companies and local authority undertakings. It bestowed the honor of being selected rather generously in order to oil the process of transition. The work of Foreman-Peck and Waterson (1985) suggests that the best-practice local authority and private generating plants were equally efficient (though with a longish 'tail' of unselected municipal plants) which also would have facilitated a smooth transition. The managers of the Central Electricity Board were not appointed by the Treasury, and all capital was raised on the stock market without a Treasury guarantee. It was this which allayed the fears, even though the reality was that it was a publicly owned enterprise, as none of the stock was equity.

On the face of it, the Board was a success. The grid networks were set up first on a regional basis with the Board's first chairman, Duncan, experimenting in his home territory in Scotland and the national grid completed in 1933. Capital formation each year averaged £20 million while the number of consumers, as already noted, increased tenfold. With production in nonselected stations dwindling, the thermal efficiency gap with the U.S. eliminated, the system load factor raised from 25% in 1926 to 37% by 1939, and the Battersea 105 megawatt station the largest in Europe, complaints were few.

There were 593 electricity supply undertakings in existence in 1926. This number fell, but only to 581 by 1938 (Ministry of Fuel and Power 1948). They constituted the remnants of the 'local' dimension, mainly involved in retail distribution, many with only a small turnover. In 1934, over 400 undertakings accounted for less that 10% of sales, distribution costs were high, and the multiplicity of boundaries prevented efficient development of networks. The trouble was local authorities accounted for 60% of the undertakings, and they were particularly stubborn. It was not for them to give up empires and profits. Joint electricity authorities had emerged, but the experience was not encouraging, and Herbert Morrison (a leading Labour Party figure who instigated the formation of the London Passenger Transport Board and was later to be a Minister in the 1945–1951 Attlee government) did not see them as the way forward. Civic pride and political rivalries permeated the system. The Member of Parliament for Ashton-under-Lyne observed in 1937 that the local council would rather its electricity undertaking be taken over by a new public board than see it fall into the hands of Oldham borough, the neighboring authority. Later, when nationalization loomed, many municipalities were appalled at the prospect that the loss of their undertakings was to be treated simply as a book-keeping entry within the public sector accounts and hence they would receive as compensation simply the amount of their *net* outstanding debt (Hannah 1979, 331–332). This local parochialism explains, in part, the push to nationalization in the 1940s, but there were wider issues involved.

The problem of the distribution outlets had prompted the government to set up an investigatory body, the McGowan Committee, which in a report of 1936 identified economies which could be realized in marketing and finance from grouping into larger units and from the standardization of voltages.

Insofar as the economies of scale were at a regional (or subnational level), the question was how regional business organizations would emerge. The Committee proposed that they should be developed from existing undertakings but recognized that legislation and compulsory powers would be necessary. Precisely how this would work out was not clear. Herbert Morrison had seen the solution in regional boards publicly owned on the lines of the Central Electricity Board and in both electricity and gas the 'public board' element arose in part from the problems associated with a 'natural' or 'voluntary' emergence of larger units of business organization.

It is important to note that support for public boards did not just come from the Labour Party. In the depressed economic conditions of the interwar period, the Conservative Party could not reject public ownership out of hand, especially given its role in the creation of bodies like the Central Electricity Board and the London Passenger Transport Board. The 'etatist' wing of the Party was barely distinguishable on many issues from the Morrisonian wing of the Labour Party. In 1938, Harold Macmillan described Labour's program for the nationalization of the Bank of England, coal mining, power, land, and transport as mild compared with his own plan (cf. Millward and Singleton 1995, Chap. 2). The public board received support from some civil servants, from the Conservative Minister of Fuel in 1942 and by Liberal Gwillam Lloyd George as Minister in 1943. The Conservatives' Industrial Charter of 1947 opposed nationalization and direct planning in principle but fudged privatization outside one or two small sectors in road and air transport, claiming that privatizing the large public corporations would be too disruptive. Moreover, a large body of professional opinion makers were, by the late 1930s and 1940s, canvassing a more interventionist government stance in industrial matters. Even E.H.E. Woodward, General Engineer and Manager of the North Eastern Electricity Supply Company who wanted larger business units, saw ownership as irrelevant and advocated public boards (Hannah 1979, Chap. 10). In the event the nationalization legislation of 1947 created 12 such regional distribution boards for England and Wales and two for South Scotland to set alongside the North of Scotland Hydro-Electric Board, which had been established in 1943. Finally, the Central Electricity Board was replaced by the Central Electricity Generating Board, which took ownership of all the generating plants and all the national grid and became responsible for all generation and transmission to the Area Boards in England and Wales.

The nationalized electricity industry had many other distinctive features which require some explanation because they affected performance in the 1947–1988 period. There was an overarching supervisory body, the British Electricity Authority which, like the National Coal Board and the Gas Council, was borne in the context of an economy recovering from war and a government committed to planning. Each had to draw up programs for investment in physical capital and training for staff and workers and was answerable to the Minister of the sponsoring government departments.

This was certainly consistent with earlier Labour Party ideas on public boards being subject to the control of a National Investment Board, although the effectiveness of this linkage has been disputed (Ostergaard 1954, 217; Cairncross 1985, 484). There was also the idea that nationalized industries would provide common services (i.e., gas and electricity supply) throughout the country at uniform charges. Fraser (1993) and Chick (1995) have argued that this originated in municipal provision of the 'necessities' of life. By the interwar period, gas, electricity, and water were established items of consumer budgets and probably with low price elasticities of demand. Chick has identified a growing conviction in some quarters that electricity was not a luxury for higher income groups. The musings of the War Cabinet Sub-committee on the future of electricity supply included the argument that "the Public have increasingly come to regard electricity as a necessity and not a mere luxury and it should be regarded from the same point of view as sewerage or water," a position perfectly in line with Morrison's ideas about uniform prices for electricity (Chick 1995, 270). Providing services in this way clearly meant ignoring the costs of supply to different parts of the country and accorded with a one-nation approach to economic issues.

Hence the Nationalisation Acts of 1945–1948 had two central features. First was that the new corporations were to serve the public interest and so a public purpose was written into the Acts and embraced the provision of common services and the development of investment programs. Thus the British Electricity Authority was required "to develop and maintain an efficient, co-ordinated and economical system of electricity supply, . . . the Electricity Boards [to] secure . . . the development, extension to rural areas and cheapening of supplies of electricity" (Electricity Act 1947, Sections 1(1) and 1(6)). Consonant with these aims was the constitution of the Boards, whose members were to be as disinterested as the corporation's objectives. Such had been the philosophy behind the Central Electricity Board. Similarly, the new corporations were not to pursue profit. Finance was to come from fixed interest stock—either the industry's own or government bonds—and any surpluses earned were required by the statutes to be devoted to the public purpose, that is, reinvested in the industry. The investment programs were not simply a commercial matter and had to be approved by the relevant Minister of the sponsoring department. Moreover, the new undertakings were expected to be commercially orientated, innovative, and enterprising. Thus, like the Central Electricity Board and the London Passenger Transport Board, they were to have their own corporate legal status free from Treasury supervision—able to appoint their own employees and be sued in the courts. The injunction to provide "cheap and efficiently supplied services" in the Electricity Act reoccurs in all the statutes and has to be seen in conjunction with another injunction, variously worded, along the lines of "revenues shall not be less than sufficient for meeting all outgoings properly chargeable, on an average of good and bad years." Vague though this wording might be for accountants, it was roundly interpreted to have the straightforward interpretation of breaking even, taking one year with another, and was much more easily monitored than the even vaguer public purposes. This was to prove a source of tension in the years ahead.

## THE NATIONALIZED ELECTRICITY INDUSTRY, 1947–1988

The fortunes of nationalized electricity supply represent something of a paradox. Like all nationalized industries in Britain, they were required to break even financially and yet were given certain public purpose objectives of a noncommercial nature. The Area Boards had to promote rural electrification while the Central Electricity Generating Board did not have free access to imported coal or oil but rather was obliged to enter long-term contracts with the National Coal Board to stave off the long-term decline of that industry. In addition, as a quid pro quo for their monopoly status, the Electricity Boards could not diversify into producing or distributing other fuels or produce any consumer durables or indeed any other commodity or service. Like all the nationalized industries, their prices were closely monitored and controlled (by the Ministry of Fuel and Power for electricity), and this proved very disadvantageous in the 1970s when oil prices were rising steeply and nationalized industry prices were held back. The huge financial losses which resulted provided a useful stick for those writers and politicians marshalling the case for privatization. Indeed in the 1980s, as the agenda for privatization enfolded, it was claimed that much wasteful investment had occurred under nationalization and that privatization would raise economic performance (Johnson, 1988, 61; Secretary of State for Energy 1988).

The paradox is that, by most standards, the industry had performed reasonably well. The years up to the worldwide oil shocks of 1974 witnessed increases in electricity consumption in Britain that were never exceeded, before or since; the productivity record was good, and the financial record was satisfactory and certainly among the best of the public sector industries. The scale of 'electrification' in Britain in this period was among the highest in Europe. Electricity consumption grew in 1959–1973 at 6.4% per annum. This was less than the 7.3% growth rate in the European Economic Community, but British electricity was replacing coal on a big scale so that the saving in primary fuels was much larger (Papadopoulos 1981). The pattern of fuel prices which emerged in the postwar period was very different from that of the prewar period. It was not simply that electricity prices started rising but rather that all fuel prices moved together more closely than ever before. As may be seen in Figure 12.2, up to the early 1960s the average price of electricity rose less than coal and gas, but from the mid-1960s to the end of the 1970s, the price of gas fell relative to electricity.

In the first phase, there was a huge expansion of generating capacity following a large investment program. Capital formation in electricity generating plants and distribution networks in 1950 was £138 million—more than the combined amounts invested in gas, water, and mining. It accounted for 8% of all UK capital formation, a figure that was to rise to 10% by 1965 (Feinstein 1972). Nonetheless, capacity was stretched to the limit and, afterward, industry managers came in for a lot of criticism for poor forecasting of demand. In part this was a failure to predict the fall in the price of electricity relative to gas. In addition, some of the extra demand had bad load characteristics. The construction of the national grid had allowed the system load factor to rise from 25% in 1920 to 37% in 1938. After a further rise across the war, it then flattened off in the 1950s and 1960s at just under 50%. Much of the problem arose in the domestic sector, which was a significantly larger component of consumption than, for example, in France and Canada. It was not the fact that household demand was rising from the diffusion of consumer durables like TVs, electric blankets, and washing machines; rather it was the increase in the use of electric space heating in houses, shops, and offices, demand for which coincided with the daily system peaks and was subject to the same sensitivity to weather conditions. The industrial market on the other hand had good load characteristics, especially when shift work was involved. It also experienced a very high growth rate, which exceeded the growth of manufacturing output (Papadopoulos 1981). Energy costs are only a tiny proportion of industry's total costs (3% in 1979), so that the industrial

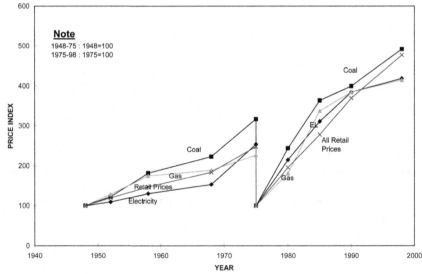

*Figure 12.2*   Price indexes for electricity and other goods in the UK, 1948–1998.
*Source*: Millward 2003, Figure 2.

demand for electricity is largely insensitive to its price. Hence, the paradox was that energy efficiency was rising in this period, even though energy prices were falling relative to the price of labor and capital. Most industrial uses of electricity were in areas like motive power, lighting, electrochemical processes which were electric specific uses, all of which were growing at a rapid rate while solid fuels fell from 71% of industrial energy in 1957 to 23% by 1980 (Thomas and MacKerron 1982). Nonetheless, all of this growth was somewhat overshadowed in terms of system load because the share of industry in total consumption fell in this period, as Table 12.1 shows. Industry accounted for 50% sales in 1938 but only 40% by 1980. The share of the household sector rose across the war, and then held its 40% of the market for the next four decades. Since 1948, the fastest growing sector has been shops, offices, entertainment, and transport (the 'other' sectors in Table 12.1), whose share doubled and heralded the growth of the service sector, which came to be the hallmark of all advanced economies in the second half of the 20th century.

The strains imposed by peak loads and the voracious demands this placed on the electricity investment program stemmed from two sources. The first was that Britain's energy resources were such that supplies

*Table 12.1*  Electricity Generation and Sales in Britain, 1920–1998

| | Electricity Supplied (Net) by Type of Plant (Gigowatt-hours) | | | | Sales by Sector (Percentage shares) | | |
|---|---|---|---|---|---|---|---|
| Year | Hydro | Nuclear | Thermal | Total | Domestic | Industrial | Other |
| 1920 | 12 | 0 | 4263 | 4275 | 8.0 | 68.6 | 23.4 |
| 1938 | 988 | 0 | 23384 | 24572 | 26.3 | 50.6 | 23.1 |
| 1948 | 881 | 0 | 45148 | 46029 | 40.0 | 49.2 | 10.8 |
| 1956 | 1667 | 58 | 85436 | 87161 | 32.3 | 50.6 | 17.1 |
| 1961 | 3196 | 2399 | 121994 | 127589 | 36.3 | 46.9 | 16.8 |
| 1971 | 3754 | 23209 | 204271 | 231234 | 41.5 | 39.5 | 19.0 |
| 1980 | 4497 | 33462 | 222751 | 26710 | 36.1 | 40.0 | 21.1 |
| 1989 | 6457 | 63602 | 220960 | 291019 | 36.1 | 36.1 | 27.8 |
| 1998 | 6677 | 91186 | 240014 | 337877 | 32.9 | 39.2 | 27.8 |

*Notes:* Domestic sales include the farm sector while 'other' includes public lighting, shops, offices, transport, and traction. The supply figures exclude imports and relate to electricity generated minus electricity used in generation and in pumped storage systems. The thermal figure for 1998 includes 95711 gigawatt-hours from combined cycle gas turbines with conventional non-nuclear thermal down to 128513.

*Sources:* For 1920–1980, the source is Mitchell 1988, 264–267. The 1989 and 1998 figures are taken from the Department of Trade and Industry's *Digest of Energy Statistics* 1991 and 1999.

could not be shifted easily to meet variations in demand across seasons of the year and time of day. All countries face this problem to some extent because it is uneconomic to store electricity. Hydroelectric power, however, provides an opportunity for relieving thermal capacity when water supplies are good. Generating equipment like gas turbines can readily be switched from peak to other uses, offering a way of meeting peak demand without lumbering the system with the capital cost of year-round capacity. It can be seen in Table 12.1 that hydroelectricity has played only a minor role in Britain. Much of the thermal capacity initially was coal fired. Even after oil came on the scene and was accounting for 15% of the fuel used in electricity generation, coal still accounted for 81% (all measured in oil equivalents; Department of Trade and Industry 1999). The classic order of merit of generating stations, in terms of operating costs, meant that peak demands were met in the short run by bringing into use the oldest coal plants. Coal was becoming more expensive (cf. Figure 12.2), and the Central Electricity Generating Board was restricted in its ability to import, being bound by governments to long-term contracts with the National Coal Board. In the long run, extra peak demand meant new investment. Nuclear capacity appeared an attractive option in the 1950s and 1960s because of its very low running costs and the immunity it gave from the effects of strikes by British coal miners. Nuclear power ranked highest in the order of merit and was used throughout the year. On the other hand the thermal efficiency of steam plants rose considerably from 21% in 1948 to 27% in 1960 and 32% in 1981 (Ashworth 1991). Moreover, nuclear was very capital intensive, so that the frequent delays in construction led to mounting capital costs. Oil-fired plants were replacing coal and substantial extra oil-fired capacity was ordered in the period 1970–1974, just when oil was to lose its advantage. So oil accounted for 27% of fuel inputs to electricity in 1974, after which came the explosion of oil prices and the long-term disappearance of oil capacity (only 2% in 1998). The main contribution to relief of capacity on the supply side came from gas turbines and the spread of natural gas. By 1998, coal had fallen to 38% of fuel used in electricity generation, with natural gas at 22% and nuclear at 30% (Department of Trade and Industry 1999).

Why was the capacity problem not resolved on the demand side by appropriate time-of-day tariffs and other inducements to shift consumption away from the costly peak hours and seasons? The Central Electricity Generating Board did incorporate incentives in the way it charged for energy transmitted to the 12 Area Boards. The 'bulk supply tariff' included an 'energy charge' per kilowatt-hour to cover operating costs, and this varied with time of day and season. The other part of the tariff was a 'capacity charge', which related to the maximum demands, in kilowatts, of the Area Boards during the peak periods. This tariff, whatever its limitations (Slater and Yarrow 1983), provided incentives for the Area

Boards to shift their consumption away from the system peaks. Moreover, the Area Boards passed on these differentials, in part, to final users in the industrial market, where tariffs included a maximum demand charge. Such industrial users had time-of-day meters, but these never proved economic for the large number of domestic users (Reid, Allen, and Harris 1973). Two-part tariffs (a fixed charge plus a charge per kilowatt-hour) were introduced in the early days of the industry to spread the use of electricity away from simply lighting and with the hope that this would yield such a diversified demand as to raise the system load factor. This never materialized, as domestic space heating came on the scene in the postwar period with very bad load characteristics. The Area Boards promoted the use of special circuits, which allowed reduced charges for demands restricted to off-peak periods. Special 'white meters' extended these off-peak rates, but the prime form of charges to households and shops in Britain remained the two-part or multipart tariff. All of this looks inadequate relative to the marginal cost based 'tarif vert' of Électricité de France. However, as Chick (2006, 2007) has shown, this tariff was restricted to the industrial load, and the French domestic sector was much smaller than the British. In addition, the pressure to economize on coal was strategically much more important for France.

The Electricity Boards were, as noted earlier, criticized for underestimating demand in the 1950s and 1960s. They were criticized also for overestimating demand and, hence, overinvestment from the late 1960s to the end of the 1970s (Johnson 1988, Ashworth 1991). In the latter case, they had not anticipated the rise in the price of electricity relative to gas or the advances in gas central heating, which proved highly popular although they at least had the saving grace of reducing the demands for electric space heating. The system load factor rose in the 1970s and 1980s, reaching 62% in 1989 (Central Statistical Office 1991). How far were these the sort of problems which any business has to face, and how far did they manifest themselves in productivity and profit levels?

Profits are not usually regarded as a good measure of the performance of nationalized industries. On the one hand they have monopolies of the product market, and on the other hand the managers are open to control by Ministers for the furtherance of wider economic and political objectives. Profits do, however, provide some guide as to how far the industries met their stated objective to break even, although blame may have lain outside the control of managers. In the 1950s, the nationalized sector only just covered its operating costs, with no provision for full depreciation or interest charges. This led to two government White Papers (Treasury 1961, 1967) which set financial targets, the effect of which was to improve financial performance by the end of the 1960s. The 1970s saw very high inflation in the Western World, triggered by the way the U.S. financed the Vietnam War and by the 1974 oil price shock. In Britain, price increases for the nationalized industries were held back by both Conservative and Labour governments with the hope that this would set a lead for other businesses and reduce the effects of inflation on working-class household budgets (Hannah 2004). It proved particularly damaging because it led to huge financial losses which were offset only in part by government subsidies from 1975 onward. Whether or not financial performance is really a good guide to managerial performance, there is no doubt these deficits proved useful ammunition for the growing lobby for privatization (Millward 2000b).

Within this context, it seems the Electricity Boards did quite well in achieving their financial targets in the 1960s (Reid et al. 1973) and, throughout the 1947–1980 period, produced higher financial rates of return than most other nationalized industries. One striking indicator is that in the financial year 1968–1969, the Electricity Boards earned £357

*Table 12.2*   Electricity Profits and Rates of Return under Nationalization: Electricity Boards in England and Wales, 1948–1987

| Year | Gross Operating Surplus | | | Profits after Depreciation and Interest | |
|---|---|---|---|---|---|
| | £ million | % Return on Turnover | % Return on Net Assets | £ million | % Return on Net Assets |
| 1948 | 20.9 | | | | |
| 1951 | 28.4 | | | | |
| 1955 | | | 9.7 | | |
| 1958 | | | 11.0 | | |
| 1961 | 138.2 | | 10.6 | | |
| 1963 | | 35.4 | 11.9 | 43 | 6.1 |
| 1966 | | | 12.6 | 85 | 7.6 |
| 1968 | 356.7 | 40.4 | 11.7 | 55 | 6.1 |
| 1969 | | 39.7 | 13.0 | 101 | 7.1 |
| 1971 | | 32.4 | 8.8 | -56 | 4.1 |
| 1974 | | 20.3 | | | |
| 1978 | | 25.0 | | | |
| 1983 | | | | | 2.7 |
| 1985 | | | | | -3.5 |
| 1987 | | | | | 3.2 |

*Note*: Depreciation is at historic cost up to 1978; thereafter depreciation and capital employed are calculated on a current cost accounting basis. The data relate to financial years ending in the year in question. The sources are Reid at al 1993, Johnson 1988, Treasury 1967 White Paper, Pryke 1971, 182; 1981, 31.

*Table 12.3* Productivity Growth in Nationalized Electricity Supply in the UK, 1948–1985 (Annual Average Percentage Growth Rate)

| Year | Output | Labor Productivity | Total Factor Productivity |
|------|--------|--------------------|---------------------------|
| 1948–1958 | 7.94 | 4.46 | 3.58 |
| 1958–1968 | 7.53 | 7.67 | 3.07 |
| 1968–1973 | 3.81 | 8.38 | 0.79 |
| 1973–1978 | 0.20 | 1.91 | 0.57 |
| 1978–1085 | 1.23 | 3.9 | 1.4 |

*Note:* The 1978–1985 figures relate only to England and Wales.
*Sources:* Pryke 1971, 1981; Molyneux and Thompson 1986, 1987.

million profit after depreciation, whereas the nationalized sector as a whole earned only £408 million (Pryke 1971, 182). Consistent long-term data on financial rates of return are not easy to come by, given changing methods of accounting for depreciation. Table 12.2 shows the various estimates which have been made for the period 1948–1987. These estimates suggest that the revenue of the industry as a whole, net of labor, fuel, and other operating costs, yielded a return of about 10% on capital in the late 1950s, rising to about 12% by the end of the 1960s, the latter approximating to a return after depreciation and interest charges of 6%. By this stage, the operating surplus amounted to about 40% of turnover, a figure which collapsed to 26% by 1978, reflecting the price controls mentioned earlier. These rates of return were among the highest in the nationalized industry sector.

What is the evidence on productivity in the use of man-hours and equipment in relation to the growth of output? Comparisons with the U.S. are invariably unfavorable. In 1968, for example, the number of kilowatt-hours supplied per employee in Britain was only 25% of the figure for the U.S. electricity supply industry (Smith, Hitchens and Davies 1982). However, the U.S. has long held an advantage in many industries since the mid-19th century because of its extensive natural resources and inducements to introduce capital-intensive production methods given its relative scarcity of labor (Broadberry 1993). A better guide is the pace at which labor plus capital (total factor) productivity increased in the UK. Table 12.3 shows a very high growth rate in both measures during the golden age of 1948–1973. These growth rates were higher than those in British manufacturing industry and, although the rates declined from the onset of the world recession in the 1970s, the electricity sector thereafter still performed better than manufacturing. The question remains whether this performance was inferior to that of the more privatized electricity supply regime in the U.S. and whether privatization in Britain improved performance.

## PRODUCTIVITY PERFORMANCE UNDER
## PRIVATIZED AND STATE ENTERPRISE REGIMES

When the Conservative government came to privatize the electricity industry at the end of the 1980s, a primary aim was to change the structure of the
industry, not simply its ownership. The government had experimented with
competition, even before privatization, by introducing, in the 1983 Energy
Act, permission for new entrants to produce electricity as a main business
and with rights to use the grid and distribution networks. The power of
the incumbent Central Electricity Generating Board was such that entry
conditions were difficult so that more was expected when transmission and
generation were separated (Hammond, Helm, and Thompson 1986). The
White Paper setting out the government's privatization proposals declared
that the "electricity industry has a record of technical and professional
excellence acknowledged throughout the world. What hampers the industry is its structure" (Secretary of State for Energy 1988, 2). The White
Paper produced no evidence of poor performance although some writers
pointed to the poor record on forecasting (mentioned earlier), overordering
of plant, high plant costs, and long delays in installing it. But even those
sympathetic to privatization acknowledged that energy efficiency, output,
and other physical indicators were good and that the public service and
security of supply obligations had been met (Johnson 1988). As described
in the last section, productivity and profit performance were as good as
could be expected. The government, however, was in no doubt that more
competition at each stage of the production process would improve matters,
and the bad publicity associated with the way British Telecommunications
and British Gas had been privatized as whole entities—almost as private
monopolies, albeit regulated—was further encouragement to innovate in
organizational structure.

Generation was separated from transmission and was initially dominated
by three undertakings, although access was open to anyone. There were two
large private companies: National Power, which accounted for 52% of supplies in 1993, and PowerGen which accounted for 33% of supplies in the
same year. The government was unable to attract buyers for nuclear capacity, which remained in state ownership as Nuclear Electric. Privatization left
transmission across the national grid as a monopoly, carrying on the traditions of the Central Electricity Board and the Central Electricity Generating
Board. It is operated by a privately owned National Grid Company, with tariff increases regulated on the basis of RPI-X (RPI being the annual percentage increase in the national retail price index and X an assumed efficiency
gain). Initially this company ran an auction system of bids for supplies from
the companies in the generating sector. There were few signs in the early
1990s of new entrants to the generating sector, so that the spot prices for supplies to the grid were seen by some as reflecting the market power of a private
duopoly and an output maximizing state enterprise. As a result, in 2001 the

'Pool' was dropped and replaced by a set of bilateral contracts (Helm 1987, 2003; Weyman-Jones 1993; Chick 2007).

Distribution was vertically separated from transmission and from retail supply and was effected through a system of licenses for companies to act as sole distributors in each region. Initially there were 12 Regional Electricity Companies corresponding to the regions of the old Area Boards, and these distributors also held exclusive joint ownership of the National Grid Company. Access to retail supply is now unregulated; any company (including generators and distributors) can offer retail supply services. In some quarters, Britain has been seen as lenient when it comes to profit regulation. Laity (1997) has suggested this explains why only 5 of the original 12 distribution companies remained even by 1997, the rest having been swallowed up by mergers, especially those involving the U.S. multinationals. Retail supply has had unheard-of competition with the generating companies now operating at this end of the market in competition with distributors and other competitors.

How much difference did privatization and restructuring make to productivity performance, and how does the British performance under state enterprise compare with that in other countries? Findings by O'Mahony (1999) and O'Mahony and Vecchi (1999) show that output per man-hour grew very strongly in the 20 years up to 1980 in all of the four countries they investigated: 6% per annum in the UK, France, and Germany and 4.4% in the U.S. Taking capital into account, the UK performance was still good, confirming earlier studies (Millward 1991; Iordanoglou 2001). Total factor productivity growth during 1950–1979, the classic era of state-owned British electricity, exceeded that in Germany and in the more privately owned U.S. industry although probably not as good as the publicly owned French industry (see Table 12.4).

After privatization in Britain, there was much labor shedding, and labor productivity (output per man-hour) grew dramatically—7.3% per annum in the years 1989–1997. This high growth has often been invoked as evidence of the benefits of privatization. However, the decline in employment was offset by large capital investment, which meant that "the aggregate input

*Table 12.4*  Productivity Growth in Electricity Supply in the UK, France, Germany, and the U.S., 1950–1997 (Annual Average Percentage Change in Total Factor Productivity)

| Year | UK | U.S. | France | Germany |
|---|---|---|---|---|
| 1950–1973 | 5.51 | 3.93 | n.a. | n.a. |
| 1960–1979 | 2.54 | 1.85 | 3.08 | 1.52 |
| 1979–1989 | 1.78 | 2.60 | 4.17 | 2.84 |
| 1989–1997 | 1.22 | 2.55 | 3.09 | 1.32 |

*Source:* Derived from O'Mahony 1999 and O'Mahony and Vecchi 2001.

growth was about static in Britain in the period post 1989" (O'Mahony and Vecchi 2001, 92). Although output was rising, it was only at about 0.5% per annum in the 1990s, and the overall growth in total factor productivity in 1989–1997 was 1.22 % per annum, inferior to that in the other three countries. Over the whole period 1960–1997, the publicly owned French electricity industry performed better, on this measure, than did the industry in the other three countries. So, as O' Mahony and Vecchi (2001, 92, 95) have stated, "the bottom line is that privatization and restructuring of the UK [electricity industry] have not, to date, delivered the improvements in productivity which were expected. . . . Relative to its own past experience, or that in other countries, productivity in the UK privatized industry does not appear to have shown any pronounced improvement."

## CONCLUSION

State enterprise in British electricity supply had its origins in three factors. One was the difficulty of constructing an integrated national transmission network, given the structure of the industry by the 1920s. There were over 500 separate undertakings, many of them unwilling to merge with other companies or their fellow municipal corporations to concentrate generation in large units and develop long transmission lines. The state stepped in to form the Central Electricity Board, and by the mid-1930s Britain was alone in Europe in having an integrated network, and its technical efficiency gap with the U.S. had been significantly reduced. Once off the ground, it might have been turned into a regulated private monopoly, as in the U.S. or 1990s Britain. Both generation and distribution might also have been added, but arms' length regulation had lost much of its appeal after the 1930s Depression, and this was a significant factor in the shift to public ownership of all the industry. What emerged in 1947 was a publicly owned industry on a nationally integrated scale, and this was because it was born in an era of national reconstruction after World War II and because of the Labour Party's ideas about the scope and organization of public enterprise.

Like all nationalized industries in Britain, electricity supply suffered from being expected to break even financially and yet, often without explicit subsidies, to meet certain public interest obligations, including security of supply, providing cheap electricity to rural areas, and contracting to buy supplies of coal only from the National Coal Board, for whom it was a priceless customer in the latter's period of decline. The managers of the electricity industry had considerable difficulties in forecasting demand, which was a central concern because of the commitment to ensuring security of supply. It tended to underestimate demand in the 1950s, when its price did not rise as much as that of other fuels, and it fed a rather wasteful expansion of peaky household heating. Then, from the mid-1960s, it overestimated demand as gas prices fell relative to electricity and gas central heating proved popular. Nonetheless, by all reasonable standards of security of supply, profitability, and financing, it performed well. In particular, its productivity record compares favorably with the the U.S.'s mainly privately owned industry and with the privatized British regime which emerged in the 1990s. Perhaps state enterprise in Britain did not do as well as Eléctricité de France but, for the 20th century, that is hardly a critique of public ownership.

## NOTES

\* Sections 2 and 3 were first published in Italian as part of my chapter "L'Organizzazione economica e lo sviluppo della distribuzione dell'energia elettrica nella Gran Bretagna del XX secolo" in A. Giuntini and G. Paoloni (eds.), *La città elettrica: Esperienze di elettrificazione urbana in Italia e in Europa fra ottocento e Novecento*, Rome, 2003, pp. 99–124: This was published by Gius, Laterza & Figli and ENEL, 2003 to both of whom thanks are due for permission to use the material in my chapter here.

## BIBLIOGRAPHY

Ashworth, W. 1991, *The State in Business: 1945 to the Mid 1980s*, London: Macmillan.

Broadberry, S. 1993, "Manufacturing and the Convergence Hypothesis: What the Long Run Data Show," *Journal of Economic History* 53(4): 772–795.

Cairncross, A. 1985, *Years of Recovery: British Economic Policy 1945–51*, London: Methuen.

Central Statistical Office 1991, *Annual Abstract of Statistics 1991*, London: HMSO.

Chick, M. 1995, "The Political Economy of Nationalisation: Electricity Supply," in *The Political Economy of Nationalisation in Britain 1920–50*, eds. R. Millward and J. Singleton, Cambridge: Cambridge University Press.

Chick, M. 2006, "The Marginalist Approach and the Making of Fuel Policy in France and Britain, 1945–72," *Economic History Review* 59(1): 143–167.

Chick, M. 2007, *Electricity and Energy Policy in Britain, France and the United States since 1945*, Cheltenham, UK: Edward Elgar.

Department of Trade and Industry 1991, 1999, *Digest of UK Energy Statistics*, London: HMSO.

Electricity Act 1947, (10 and 11, Geo. 6), *Public General Acts and the Church Assembly Measures of 1947*, Vol 2, London: HMSO.

Feinstein, C.H. 1972, *National Income, Expenditure and Output in the United Kingdom 1865–1965*, Cambridge: Cambridge University Press.

Foreman-Peck, J.M. and M. Waterson 1985, "The Comparative Efficiency of Public And Private Enterprise in Britain: Electricity Generation between the World Wars," *Economic Journal* 95(380a Suppl.): 83–95.

Fraser, H. 1993, "Municipal Socialism and Social Policy," in *The Victorian City: A Reader in British Urban History: 1820–1914*, eds. R.J. Morris and R. Rodger, London: Longman.

Hammond, E.M., D.R. Helm, and D.T Thompson 1986, "Competition in Electricity Supply: Has the Energy Act Failed?" *Fiscal Studies* 7(1): 11–33.

Hannah, L. 1977, "A Pioneer of Public Enterprise: The Central Electricity Generating Board and the National Grid," in *Essays in British Business History*, ed. B.Supple, Oxford: Clarendon Press.

Hannah, L. 1979, *Electricity before Nationalisation*, London: Macmillan.

Hannah, L. 2004, "A Failed Experiment: The State Ownership of Industry 1945–90," in *The Cambridge Economic History of Britain since 1700: Structural Change and Growth 1939–2000*, eds. R. Floud and P. Johnson, Cambridge: Cambridge University Press.

Helm, D.R. 1987, "Nuclear Power and the Privatisation of Electricity Generation," *Fiscal Studies* 8: 65–73.

Helm, D.R. 2003, *Energy, the State and the Market: British Energy Policy since 1979*, Oxford: Oxford University Press.

Iordanoglou, C.F. 2001, *Public Enterprise Revisited: A Closer Look at the 1954–79 U.K. Labour Productivity Record*, Cheltenham, UK: Edward Elgar.

Johnson, C. 1988, "The Economics of British Electricity Privatisation" in *Privatisation and Ownership: Lloyds Bank Annual Review*, Vol. 1, ed. D. Glynn and C. Johnson, London: Lloyds Bank.

Laity, P. 1997, "Big G and Little G," *London Review of Books*, 6 February.

McGowan Report 1936, *Report of the Committee on Electricity Distribution*, London: Ministry of Transport, HMSO.

Millward, R. 1991, "The Nationalised Industries," in *Labour's Economic Policies 1974–79*, eds. M. Artis and D. Cobham, Manchester: Manchester University Press.

Millward, R. 2000a, "The Political Economy of Urban Utilities in Britain 1840-1950," in *Cambridge Urban History of Britain*, Vol. 3, ed. M. Daunton, Cambridge: Cambridge University Press.

Millward, R., 2000b, "State Enterprise in 20th Century Britain," in *The Rise and Fall of State-Owned Enterprise in the Western World*, ed. P.A. Toninelli, Cambridge: Cambridge University Press.

Millward, R. 2003, "L'Organizzazione economica e lo sviluppo della distribuzione dell'energia elettrica nella Gran Bretagna del XX secolo," in *La Citta elettrica: Esperienze di elettrificazione urbana in Italia e in Europa fra ottocento e Novecento*, eds. A. Giuntini and G. Paoloni, Rome: Gius, Laterza and Figli.

Millward, R. and J. Singleton, eds. 1995, *The Political Economy of Nationalisation in Britain 1920–50*, Cambridge: Cambridge University Press.

Ministry of Fuel and Power 1948, Engineering and Financial Statistics of all Authorised Undertakings 1946/7, Electricity Supply Act (41–211–0-47), London.

Mitchell, B.R. 1988, *British Historical Statistics*, Cambridge: Cambridge University Press.

Molyneux, R. and D. Thompson 1986, "The Efficiency of the Nationalised Industries since 1978," *Institute of Fiscal Studies Working Paper* 100.

Molyneux, R. and D. Thompson 1987, "Nationalised Industry Performance: Still Third Rate?" *Fiscal Studies* 8(1): 48–52.

O'Mahony, M. 1999, *Britain's Productivity Performance: An International Perspective*, London: National Institute of Economic and Social Research.

O'Mahony, M. and M. Vecchi 2001, "The Electricity Supply Industry: A Study of an Industry in Transition," *National Institute Economic Review* 177: 85–99.

Ostergaard, G.N. 1954, "Labour and the Development of the Public Corporation," *Manchester School* 22: 192–226.

Papadopoulos, R. 1981, "Growth and Overcapacity in the UK Electricity Industry," *Energy Policy* 9(2): 153–155.

Pryke, R. 1971, *Public Enterprise in Practice*, London: MacGibbon and Kee.

Pryke, R. 1981, *The Nationalised Industries: Policies and Performance since 1968*, Oxford: Martin Robertson.

Reid, G.L., K. Allen, and D.J. Harris 1973, *The Nationalised Fuel Industries*, London: Heinemann.

Secretary of State for Energy 1988, *Privatising Electricity*, Command 322, London: HMSO.

Slater, M.D.E. and G.K. Yarrow 1983, "Distortions in Electricity Prices in the UK," *Oxford Bulletin of Economics and Statistics* 45(4): 317–338.

Smith, A.D., D.M.W.N. Hitchens, and S.W. Davies 1982, *International Industrial Productivity: A Comparison of Britain, America and Germany*, Cambridge: National Institute of Economic and Social Research, Cambridge University Press.

Surrey, J., ed. 1996, *The British Electricity Experiment*, London: Earthscan Books.

Thomas, S. and G. MacKerron 1982, "Industrial Electricity Consumption in the UK: Past Determinants and Possible Futures," *Energy Policy* 10(4): 275–294.

Treasury, H.M. 1961, *The Financial and Economic Obligations of the Nationalised Industries*, Command 1337, London: HMSO.

Treasury, H.M. 1967, *Nationalised Industries: A Review of Financial and Economic Objectives*, Command 3437, London: HMSO.

Weir Committee 1926, *Report of a Committee Appointed by the Board of Trade to Review the National Problem of the Supply of Electricity Energy*, London: Board of Trade, HMSO.

Weyman-Jones, T.G. 1993, "Regulation of the Privatised Electricity Utilities in the UK," in *The Political Economy of Privatisation*, eds. T. Clarke and C. Pitelis, London: Routledge.

Williamson Committee 1918, *Report of a Committee Appointed by the Board of Trade to Consider the Question of Electric Power Supply*, Command 9062, Parliamentary Papers 7, London: HMSO.

Wilson, J.F. 1993, "Competition between Electricity and Gas in Britain, 1880–1980," *International Economic History Association*, Pre-Conference on the Development of Electrical Energy, Paris, May.

# 13 Industrial Policy and the Nationalization of the Italian Electricity Sector in the Post-World War II Period

*Renato Giannetti*

## INTRODUCTION

Historically, state ownership has been invoked for the supply of specific goods: public goods (defense), merit goods (health and education), or in order to achieve social equity goals, such as universal access to certain public services (utilities). Pleas for public ownership of an industrial sector came about as a by-product of the theory of imperfect markets (monopolies and oligopolies), a representation of market and firm behavior developed between economists and politicians in the 1920s and 1930s (Shakle 1967). According to this view, competition among producers is a wasteful process that restrains supply in order to maintain high prices, which leads to a monopolistic or an oligopolistic condition. State ownership is a way of overcoming this condition and of increasing supply. In the field of networking sectors, such as electricity or communications, a specific version of monopoly theory has been advanced (see, e.g., Berg 1988). An industry is said to be a *natural monopoly* if multiple firms providing a good or a service are less efficient (more costly to a nation and its economy) than would be the case if a single firm provided the self-same good or service. In the case of electricity, all companies provide the same product, the infrastructure required is immense, and the cost of adding one more customer is negligible. Adding one more customer may increase the company's revenue and lowers the average cost of providing for the company's customer base. As long as the average cost of serving customers is decreasing, the larger firm will serve the entire customer base more efficiently. This fact represents the *supply* side of public ownership advantage, but economic theory, in the same period, also suggested that public investments had strong *demand* effects in terms of positive externalities. With regard to producers, the heavy investments required in the electricity supply sector would increase the demand for the products of the electromechanical industry and, more generally, contribute to enlarging the industrial matrix of a country and improve its economic growth. With regard to end users, ensuring the availability of the service to everyone would increase the demand for new consumer goods.

State ownership of these industries also reduces the cost of financing long-term investments by exploiting the appropriate financial tools (such as, at that time, bonds were considered to be) at government interest rates, which are almost always lower than the less secure tools issued by the private sector. Finally, public ownership can improve the pursuit of productivity gains by promoting better cooperation from workers. Employees may be more inclined to view their work positively if it is directed by a management appointed by a government that they have a say in electing, rather than a management representing a minority of shareholders.

In this chapter, the following themes are discussed: the ideologies and policies of nationalization in Italy; the ownership and organization of Ente Nazionale per l'Energia Elettrica (ENEL); the expansion of plants and research and development (R & D); the financing of nationalization; the tariff policy; efficiency and productivity; industrial relations and work costs; and the industrial externalities.

## THE IDEOLOGIES AND POLICIES FOR NATIONALIZATION

The nationalization of the electricity supply industry in Italy was decided by the law issued on 6 December 1962, n.1643. From the immediate period following World War II (WWII), the left-wing parties, communist (Partito Comunista Italiano [PCI]) and socialist (Partito Socialista Italiano [PSI]), and a small but very active group of radicals (clustering around the magazine *Il Mondo*) criticized the private companies which owned the electricity supply industry, maintaining that the companies should be a monopoly (Mori 1994). The *amici del Mondo* group (Scalfari 1955) based their battle against the *electricity barons* (Bocca 1960) upon the theory of natural monopoly. In contrast, the Socialist (PSI) and Communist (PCI) parties considered the industry to be a typical example of an oligopoly, that is, the collusive behavior of a few firms which restricted supply in order to maintain high prices. In their view, nationalization was the way both to solve this restrictive practice and to expand production, thereby exploiting economies of scale and reducing prices for consumers (Silari 1989). According to their view, the nationalization of the electricity supply industry also represented the opportunity to show that a planned economy was a better way to achieve both economic growth and social equity, at least, in the strategic sectors, energy included (Mori 1994). Energy, in general, and electricity, in particular, were, in fact, considered a strategic factor for economic growth; an abundant supply of cheap energy was considered a prerequisite to expand and to complete the national matrix of production in iron and steel, chemicals and machinery, and, more generally, to overcome the export-led growth phase of the latecomers, based upon low wages and limited mechanization of production, in comparison with the more advanced countries (Cozzi et al. 1983).

## OWNERSHIP AND CONTROL

The main point of discussion was the ownership and control of the new enterprise; the choice was between the formula of a state holding and that of the state economic body (Caia and Aicardi 1994; Roversi Monaco 1989). From the very beginning, the solution of organizing the electricity supply industry as a state agency was discarded, despite the fact that it was the arrangement adopted for railways in 1905 and for other public services, such as the post office and most of the public water utilities managed by local governments. The state-holding formula had been adopted in 1933 to save the Italian universal banks (Banca Commerciale, Banca di Roma, and Credito Italiano) from bankruptcy, and a financial holding was established to manage their extensive involvement in many industrial firms. Due to this bailout, the Istituto per la Ricostruzione Industriale (IRI) was already present in the electricity supply industry, in Società Idroelettrica Piemontese (SIP) and Società Meridionale di Elettricità (SME) via a financial holding, Finelettrica. The main feature of this way of arranging state ownership and control was the separation between ownership and management: the state was the main shareholder while the directors managed the firm according to private rules and strategies. According to this arrangement for ENEL, the organization and the management had to operate according to a generic public purpose to provide cheap energy, and the government had the power to intervene in the "public interest." However, the Christian Democrats (DC) and the Republican Party (PRI) favored the IRI formula, while the Socialist Party (PSI) was in favor of adopting the "state body solution," which they considered better for controlling the management and implementing the energy policy that they intended to introduce. According to the Italian civil law, a public body is controlled by public administration in two ways: government appoints the board and establishes the aims of the public body activity; a public accounting organ—Corte dei Conti—supervises its bookkeeping according to general public rules (Jaeger and Denozza 2000).

The "state body" formula was finally adopted. As will be discussed later, this solution influenced the way in which the nationalization of the electricity supply industry was accomplished in Italy (Barbato 1963; Mori 1984). The new enterprise (ENEL) had to refund the private companies within 10 years by a direct compensation of around 2,000 billion lira, which had to be paid by a biannual cash compensation at an interest rate of 5.5%. This solution was very different from that adopted in the British and French nationalizations of electricity supply. In the British case, for example, the interest rate was 3% over 20 years and was financed by issuing bonds (Castronovo 1989). Moreover, ENEL did not receive any funding from the state, in the wake of the optimistic hypothesis that the natural monopoly profits could finance everything: the compensation to be paid to the former owners of the newly nationalized companies;

the heavy new investments in production, transmission, and distribution required by a national grid; and a new tariff structure to promote the expansion of the consumption of electricity both by industry and by private consumers. The profits of the private companies were roughly estimated to be 150 billion lira a year for the period 1957–1961, but this was insufficient to achieve all the targets.

## GOVERNANCE AND MANAGEMENT

The strategy of ENEL was strongly oriented toward increasing the number of plants for the production, transmission, and distribution of electric power. This approach was the traditional one, as it had also been pursued in the former private companies, in which the influence of engineers prevailed. It lasted up to the 1970s in ENEL, when a new generation of managers took control, mainly skilled in the management of industrial relations. In the 1960s, the directors were still engineers and this composition of management favored the continuance, and probably even a further development of, a managerial structure strongly oriented to solving the technical problems in the production, transmission, and distribution of electrical power, giving a minor role to financial or consumption strategies. This was due mainly to the fact that ENEL's mission was to supply cheap energy to both industry and consumers and that its tariff policy essentially depended on the government, which managed the company either according to macroeconomic targets, such as inflation control, or to industrial policy, such as establishing a cheap tariff for private consumers in order to promote the diffusion of the new durable consumption goods.

This is why engineers and science graduates prevailed among personnel in ENEL; for example, in 1963, they represented 66% of the total of the personnel with university degrees; in 1970, they represented 68%, and in 1983, 60%. This situation was different from other utilities in Europe in which, even in the 1960s, most graduates came from the faculties of law and economics. This change in the composition of the personnel with university degrees was, for example, accompanied by a change in tariff policy in France, where an attempt to establish a tariff system which corresponded more closely to the cost of supplying energy to different categories of consumers had already been introduced in 1961 (*tarif vert*).

## THE EXPANSION OF PLANTS OF PRODUCTION, TRANSMISSION, AND DISTRIBUTION

One of the main goals of the supporters of nationalization was to increase the supply of electricity. ENEL accomplished this goal (Table 13.1).

*Table 13.1*   The Electricity Plants in Italy, 1951–1973 (Megawatts and Shares)

| | Hydropower | | Thermopower | | Geothermal | | Nuclear | | Total |
|---|---|---|---|---|---|---|---|---|---|
| | | | Oil and Coal | | | | | | |
| 1951 | 6770 | 0,85 | 979 | 0,12 | 239 | 0,03 | | 0 | 7988 |
| 1952 | 7170 | 0,80 | 1559 | 0,17 | 239 | 0,03 | | 0 | 8968 |
| 1953 | 7919 | 0,78 | 2041 | 0,20 | 242 | 0,02 | | 0 | 10202 |
| 1954 | 8300 | 0,79 | 2022 | 0,19 | 242 | 0,02 | | 0 | 10564 |
| 1955 | 8743 | 0,79 | 2118 | 0,19 | 246 | 0,02 | | 0 | 11107 |
| 1956 | 9513 | 0,78 | 2399 | 0,20 | 246 | 0,02 | | 0 | 12158 |
| 1957 | 9939 | 0,78 | 2464 | 0,19 | 265 | 0,02 | | 0 | 12668 |
| 1958 | 10476 | 0,76 | 2981 | 0,22 | 293 | 0,02 | | 0 | 13750 |
| 1959 | 10822 | 0,71 | 4055 | 0,27 | 293 | 0,02 | | 0 | 15170 |
| 1960 | 11468 | 0,70 | 4556 | 0,28 | 287 | 0,02 | | 0 | 16311 |
| 1961 | 11699 | 0,68 | 5098 | 0,30 | 289 | 0,02 | | 0 | 17086 |
| 1962 | 12118 | 0,62 | 5731 | 0,29 | 294 | 0,02 | 0 | 0 | 19437 |
| 1963 | 12517 | 0,57 | 6684 | 0,31 | 305 | 0,00 | 200 | 0,01 | 21813 |
| 1964 | 12728 | 0,54 | 8225 | 0,35 | 313 | 0,01 | 546 | 0,02 | 23552 |
| 1965 | 12788 | 0,51 | 9795 | 0,39 | 336 | 0,01 | 632 | 0,03 | 24941 |
| 1966 | 12943 | 0,48 | 11026 | 0,41 | 339 | 0,01 | 632 | 0,02 | 26949 |
| 1967 | 13061 | 0,46 | 12912 | 0,46 | 358 | 0,01 | 617 | 0,02 | 28125 |
| 1968 | 13106 | 0,46 | 14040 | 0,50 | 361 | 0,01 | 617 | 0,02 | 28256 |
| 1969 | 13226 | 0,42 | 14028 | 0,45 | 384 | 0,01 | 617 | 0,02 | 31332 |
| 1970 | 13408 | 0,39 | 16955 | 0,50 | 391 | 0,01 | 577 | 0,02 | 33965 |
| 1971 | 13561 | 0,39 | 19435 | 0,55 | 391 | 0,01 | 577 | 0,02 | 35020 |
| 1972 | 13838 | 0,37 | 20213 | 0,54 | 391 | 0,01 | 577 | 0,02 | 37686 |
| 1973 | 14612 | 0,37 | 22091 | 0,55 | 405 | 0,01 | 577 | 0,01 | 39875 |

*Source:* Adapted from *ENEL, Produzione e consumi di energia elettrica in Italia*, Roma: ENEL, various years.

In the period from 1963 to 1973, the average rate of growth of capacity thermo plants (oil and coal fueled power stations) was 12% per year. This growth of power stations had already begun in the 1950s in all the European countries, and, even in Italy, private companies had made large investments in these plants (19%+ on average). ENEL shows several original features in comparison with the contemporary French and German experiences. First, the transition to the prevailing oil and coal fueled power stations was much stronger and rapid. In the early 1950s, the hydroelectric plants were still producing 84% of the total electrical power, in contrast to all other national experiences; moreover, hydroelectric power still covered the base load, while oil and coal fueled power stations covered the peak load. Comparing, for example, Italy, France, and Germany in the period 1955–1973, Italy experienced the most important change toward oil and coal fueled power stations, passing from less than 5% in 1955 to almost 100% in 1973 (Cozzi et al. 1983).

This change was, in part, due to the exhaustion of the economic hydroelectric power sources and had already been highlighted by a United Nations report in 1953 (United Nations 1953), but, for the most part, it was due to a strategic decision by ENEL which strongly revised upward the private companies' forecast in the late 1950s of the total consumption (IEFE, 1969). ENEL achieved these results by building very large plants which were able to exploit new technology, and, especially, economies of scale, thereby reducing consumption of coal and oil per kilowatt-hour (kWh) of electricity produced at a rate of 1% per year on average; net consumption decreased from 2585 kilocalories (Kcal) per kWh (1963) to 2345 (1973). Also the 1973 share of large oil and coal fueled power stations changed in comparison with 1963, mainly in the size class over 200 megawatts (MW), which increased its share of total plants from 9% to 61%.

The efficiency of Italian oil and coal power stations built in this period was higher than that of France or Germany (Cozzi et al. 1983). At the same time, the hydroelectric plants were rapidly converted from the base load supply to the peak load supply, reducing the marginal cost of peak supply in comparison with the oil and coal fueled power stations used in other countries (Giannetti 1998).

This expansion of plants was not the only intervention made by ENEL; the main one was, in fact, in the transmission and interconnection system (Ninni 1994). As shown in Table 13.2, the 380 kV voltage quickly expanded: the length of the transmission cables at 380 kV increased from 247 kilometers (km) in 1963 to 2,869 km in 1973; the average distance of electric energy decreased from 201 km in 1963 to 129 km in 1973; the losses of transmission decreased from 11.7% in 1963 to 9.4% in 1973 (Table 13.2).

Thanks to the interconnection, ENEL was able to coordinate the production of electric energy *both* inside the system *and* with external producers, also reducing the breaks in distribution to consumers, thanks to the presence of a centralized dispatching center directly connected with the regional ones (1965).

*Table 13.2*    Composition of the ENEL Grid (by Voltage): Length of Long-Distance Transmission Lines (in Kilometers) and Losses of Transmission and Distribution at 380 Kilovolts (kV)

|  | *380 kV* | *220 kV* | *130-150 kV* | *60 kV* | *Average* | *Low* |
|---|---|---|---|---|---|---|
| 1963 | 247 | 8,840 | 15,446 |  | 120,000 | 215,000 |
| 1964 | 603 | 9,180 | 16,016 |  | 126,075 | 232,770 |
| 1965 | 675 | 9,975 | 16,350 |  | 132,150 | 250,540 |
| 1966 | 675 | 10,296 | 17,156 |  | 138,225 | 268,310 |
| 1967 | 918 | 10,546 | 17,888 |  | 144,300 | 286,080 |
| 1968 | 1110 | 10,715 | 18,111 |  | 150,750 | 299,500 |
| 1969 | 1125 | 11,081 | 18,884 |  | 156,830 | 314,760 |
| 1970 | 1639 | 11,091 | 20,060 |  | 164,830 | 330,900 |
| 1971 | 1951 | 11,568 | 20,848 |  | 171,630 | 354,070 |
| 1972 | 2612 | 11,962 | 21,843 |  | 178,250 | 364,850 |
| 1973 | 2869 | 11,910 | 22,260 |  | 185,360 | 387,610 |

|  | *Length of Transmission Lines (km)* | *Average Distance of Energy (km)* | *Losses of Transmission and Distribution (GWh)/ Demand* |  |  |  |
|---|---|---|---|---|---|---|
| 1963 | 247 | 201 | 11.1 |  |  |  |
| 1964 | 603 | 171 | 11.3 |  |  |  |
| 1965 | 675 | 168 | 10.2 |  |  |  |
| 1966 | 675 | 147 | 10.6 |  |  |  |
| 1967 | 918 | 140 | 10.8 |  |  |  |
| 1968 | 1110 | 142 | 9.7 |  |  |  |
| 1969 | 1125 | 143 | 9.4 |  |  |  |
| 1970 | 1639 | 137 | 9.1 |  |  |  |
| 1971 | 1951 | 134 | 8.8 |  |  |  |
| 1972 | 2612 | 129 | 8.8 |  |  |  |
| 1973 | 2869 | 129 | 8.9 |  |  |  |

*Source:* Adapted from Ninni 1994, 270; Giuntini 1994, 878.

## RESEARCH AND DEVELOPMENT

Electricity is a high-tech sector, and thus the private electrical companies had managed many laboratories since the early 1920s (Hughes 1983). In Italy, these were not proper R & D departments, but technical offices which pointed out empirical problems to researchers working in universities—mainly in Turin and Milan, where two advanced engineering faculties had been established (Polytechnics), supplying even plant and other equipment for eventual experiments by researchers (Galbani, Paris, and Silvestri 1994). In an early phase, the core of research activities concerned the interconnection of different plants, whereas, later on, after the 1920s, they took care of private regional grids and interregional interconnections. For example, CONIEL (CONsorzio Imprese ELettriche) was a consortium (1936), which was among the main companies to manage technical interconnections. According to this formula, private companies maintained an autonomous management of their own network, but they were also able to supply eventual overcapacity to the network of the other companies by bilateral contracts. These initiatives were relatively modest in comparison with building up a national grid: for example, the frequency of transmission was unified at 50 hertz (Hz) only on the eve of nationalization. Centro Elettrotecnico Sperimentale Italiano (CESI) in 1956 was the most important initiative of private companies in this field. This was, in effect, the first large R & D center in Italy, organized as a joint stock company operating both in the electrical and in the electromechanical sectors. It had laboratories for the projecting and testing of different types of electrical equipment and for studying networks, both at high and low voltage (Catenacci 1965). Nationalization did not change this constellation of R & D companies, which were now supervised by the Direzione Studi e Ricerche/Studies and Research Direction (DSR), attracting the leading people from the private centers in order to coordinate them at the central level. In 1966, the relationship between DSR and the other centers and external institutions were better defined, but they remained autonomous even later on. They were organized as specialized laboratories and were mainly engaged in solving the problems created by the unification and standardization of the national network, particularly CESI.

## FINANCING THE NATIONALIZATION

As stated earlier, the project of nationalization of the electricity supply industry was based upon overoptimistic perspectives about profits which quickly turned out to be difficult to achieve (Dami 1963; Zanetti and Fraquelli 1979). For example, even in the first report of the managing director (1963), the problem of financing both the compensations of the former owners and new investments was already being raised. The compensation, a biannual cash indemnity, required a biannual payment of 105 to 111 billion lira for 10 years, plus a 5.5% yearly interest rate, amounting on the whole to between 1,600 and 1,700 billion lira. These compensation payments corresponded on average to 25% of total outflows (Table 13.3).

ENEL also had to finance heavy investment in plants for the production of electrical power and in transmission and distribution equipment, which represented its specific mission of industrial policy (Zanetti and Fraquelli 1979; Sembenelli, 1994). This policy was strongly pursued in the decade

*Table 13.3*   Flows of Funds in ENEL, 1963–1973 (Percentage)

| FUNDS | 1963 | 1964 | 1965 | 1966 | 1967 | 1968 | 1969 | 1970 | 1971 | 1972 | 1973 |
|---|---|---|---|---|---|---|---|---|---|---|---|
| Self-financing | 34.43 | 37.62 | 32.81 | 30 | 26.81 | 19.18 | 26.61 | 22.6 | 15.96 | 5.88 | 4.37 |
| Public funds | 0 | 0 | 0 | 0 | 0 | 0 | 0 | 0 | 0 | 0 | 9.94 |
| Long-term debts | 50.55 | 62.96 | 85.59 | 84.07 | 60.03 | 80.51 | 71.21 | 50.06 | 58.7 | 86.12 | 125.15 |
| Short-term debts | 15.03 | -0.58 | -18.4 | -14.07 | 13.15 | 0.3 | 2.19 | 27.34 | 25.34 | 8 | -39.46 |
| Investments | 71.04 | 58.28 | 53.82 | 60.74 | 65.6 | 64.8 | 63.24 | 71.24 | 56.83 | 72.54 | 67.69 |
| Compensations to for-mer electrical firms | 0 | 25.73 | 24.13 | 27.22 | 26.14 | 24.77 | 22.24 | 21.54 | 16.38 | 20.57 | 21.27 |
| Repayments on long-term debts | 8.74 | 6.63 | 8.85 | 12.04 | 12.31 | 12.39 | 12.47 | 13.49 | 27.99 | 16.92 | 19.98 |
| Others | 20.22 | 9.36 | 13.19 | 0 | -4.05 | -1.96 | 2.06 | -6.27 | -1.19 | -9.93 | -8.95 |

*Source:* Adapted from Sembenelli 1994, 740–741.

under consideration, as seen from the increase in investments and in the capacity which was able to provide the increase in energy consumption. During the decade, ENEL made investments of 5,172 billion lira. The burden of these investments drastically changed the expectations about their financing nurtured at the moment of nationalization. The returns on investment quickly revealed themselves as being unable to furnish adequate resources, as can be seen from the strong decrease in self-financing from 34.3% in 1963 to 4.37% in 1973. In the meantime, long-term indebtedness grew from 50.5% of total debt in 1963 to 125.5%. In the decade, the total debt amounted to 6,118 billion lira, which was mainly covered by bonds, so that the debt–profit ratio doubled from 2 to 4. Despite this extraordinary growth of the debt, the income statement was on balance up to 1973, when, for the first time, it showed a negative result of 269 billion lira.

This satisfactory result essentially depended on the policy of depreciation which reduced from 3.5% of the capital cost per annum in 1963 to 0.7% in 1972 (Sembenelli 1994). There was much discussion on this point: in fact, traditionally, the critics of the former private companies pointed to the depreciation policy as a way of hiding profits (Scalfari 1963), while other experts replied that this criticism might be valid for hydroelectric plants, which require a very long period of depreciation, but it was, at least, inappropriate for oil and coal fueled power stations, which had a more rapid obsolescence. The growing indebtedness was financed mainly by bonds up to the end of this period, when the financial turbulence that followed the dollar crisis in 1971 forced ENEL to finance even long-term investments by use of short-term debts (Sembenelli 1994).

Investments and compensation payments were financed separately. The latter were financed by bonds, sold off-market to Cassa Depositi e Prestiti (a public bank collecting Post Office savings) up to 1964, and afterward to Istituto di Credito delle Casse di Risparmio (ICCRI), collecting funds from the system of savings banks. This way of arranging the cash payments of the compensation was intensively debated: whether it was to be paid by issuing bonds, by cash, or in a wide variety of mixed formulae. The main worry was of reducing the impact of a large emission of bonds on the national financial market. According to the monetary authority, Banca d'Italia, issuing a large number of bonds had to reckon with the behavior of the former shareholders of the electrical companies. In order to prevent them from selling the bonds, their rate was to be higher than market value and indexed to inflation, implying a potential general rise of interest rates. Otherwise, former shareholders might sell the bonds, causing a decrease in the price of the bonds, which would endanger the issuing of new bonds. The central bank mainly feared this effect, as the issuing of bonds was to be the main tool to finance the new industrial policy of the Center-Left government. Moreover, the absorption of these bonds by the monetary authority in order to maintain their value could cause new liquidity problems and eventually lead to an increase in inflation. The arrangement that finally was selected allowed the former companies to survive. The monetary authority thought that the cash flow from the compensation indemnity could force the former shareholders of electricity supply companies to reinvest in real activities, instead of financial ones, or sell their own shares with no significant implication for the bond market. The former companies could also finance their new investments, obtaining a discount on their compensation funds at Istituti Speciali di Credito, but, in this case, the monetary authority could authorize discount operations in order to invest in a specific sector, as happened in the chemical industry with the merger of Edison and Montecatini in 1965.

Investments were financed mainly by bonds guaranteed by the state. These were purchased by Mediobanca (the only Italian merchant bank at that time) for a consortium of national banks (mainly public banks) which, in turn, sold them to savers. Foreign investors were not involved in this system up to the end of the period here analyzed, because the institutional organization of the banking system strongly depended on the monetary authorities, who, as we have seen, feared destabilizing effects on the money market from a heavy issue of bonds. In July 1965, Mediobanca did issue a loan in foreign currencies of 137.5 billion lira (100 billion in Italy and only 37.5 billion on foreign markets) with the formula of "parallel loan"—that is, bonds were issued in the currency of the countries involved, and they were characterized by common conditions, but by different yields, obtained by fixing different prices for any issue. Foreign markets began to be used in 1970, when, to overcome troubles on the financial markets, bonds were issued on the Eurodollar market, at first at fixed rate, and subsequently at a variable rate. The first loan was repaid in 1971—following the declaration of U.S. dollar inconvertibility—with an intervention by Banca d'Italia, which bought bonds issued by ENEL off market. Banca d'Italia also intervened in the following two years buying bonds issued in dollars by ENEL.

## TARIFF POLICY

Tariff policy was conceived as a tool for implementing the aims of nationalization. Economic policy considerations could lead to tariffs with goals different from the goal of realizing profits according to standard allocation decisions: for example, controlling inflation, subsidizing poor consumers, establishing standard national charges for consumers with different costs of supply, and so on. The latter were the main objectives pursued by ENEL in the decade after nationalization (Abate 1994). In Italy, the regulation of electricity tariffs for containing inflation or subsidizing different types of consumers had been a long-established practice since the very beginnings of the electricity supply industry. Tariffs had been established by the government since the post–World War I period in order to control inflation, and this practice lasted until WWII and afterward. Usually, the intervention limited itself to periodically reevaluating tariffs according to an inflation index, without intervening on their structure. For example, in the post-WWII years, tariffs were reevaluated several times according to a multiplier of 5.54 in 1945, and of 41.24 in 1953; then they remained unchanged until 1961 and were decreased (39.40) in that year with no intervention on the tariff structure (Rey 1991; Giannetti 1998). By 1953, an equity goal (universal service) was added among the conditions for establishing tariffs: unifying tariffs throughout the entire national territory. This intervention was completed in the year before the nationalization, in 1961. This intervention established only a two-part tariff, composed of a fixed charge for capacity and a variable one according to energy consumption for the five classes of consumers: domestic, industrial, commercial, agricultural, and public illumination. In fact, the changes in the structure of the various plants, more diffused over the national territory, and the improved coordination of the grid partly justified this intervention, which favored mainly the southern regions, the consumers in small towns, and isolated consumers in the countryside. No trace can be found in Italy of charging consumers according to their own peak load, as, for example, in France, where, in 1961, a marginal cost approach was adopted for industrial consumers only with the so-called *tarif vert* (Sanna 1967).

The aim of a marginal cost tariff—the approach that was implemented in this phase of the electricity supply industry in France—is that consumers pay for their consumption according to the different costs of providing them with energy produced in different seasons of the year and in different times of the day. For example, during the night, there is a low load, and therefore lower tariffs can be offered to consumers. The Italian tariff system remained a system based essentially upon the average cost of supply, implying cross subsidization among different classes of consumers (CIRIEC 1983). In this phase, small domestic consumers and small industrial consumers up to 30 kW benefited most, according to an economic policy oriented toward improving the consumption of the new domestic appliances and supporting small firms, rather than large firms, as had happened, for example, in the 1930s. Several explanations were advanced for this long-lasting structure of ENEL's tariff. The first one concerned the costs of managing a marginal cost system; it required all of the installed meters to be changed, and the management of ENEL estimated this cost to be too high to compensate for a flatter load on the system. The main argument was that Italian firms were, for the most part, small and characterized by low consumption of energy, and therefore they had no real interest in changing the organization of their work in order to profit from lower off-peak tariffs. On the other hand, the large, energy-intensive firms in electrochemical and electric steel industry or in aluminum production were mainly self-producers of electricity and, in other cases, had *historically* special tariffs that contributed to flatten the load in the seasons and in the hours of low load of the electrical system.

*Table 13.4*   Costs and Revenues in ENEL, 1963–1973 (1963 = 100)

|      | Costs | Revenues |       |
|------|-------|----------|-------|
| 1963 | 100   | 100      |       |
| 1964 | 95.9  | 94.4     | -1.5  |
| 1965 | 92.8  | 91.7     | -1.1  |
| 1966 | 91.2  | 89.9     | -1.3  |
| 1967 | 87.6  | 86.7     | -0.9  |
| 1968 | 88.1  | 85.4     | -2.7  |
| 1969 | 83.4  | 80.1     | -3.3  |
| 1970 | 80    | 75.2     | -4.8  |
| 1971 | 79.9  | 73       | -6.9  |
| 1972 | 88.8  | 68.8     | -20   |
| 1973 | 73    | 62.8     | -10.2 |

*Source:* Adapted from Giuntini 1994, 870.

To summarize, ENEL's strategy of supplying more energy at homogenous prices according to the few, large classes of consumers, was mainly driven by the ideology of economic planning of the Socialist Party (PSI) which, at that time, entered the ruling coalition. But this strategy had strong roots in the history of the electricity supply industry in Italy, which allowed the government to establish tariffs according to a roughly average cost approach (Giannetti 1998). Generally, the results of this tariff policy were negative for ENEL's profits, as shown in Table 13.4.

## PRODUCTIVITY GROWTH

This section considers the evolution of the productivity of the factors of production: labor, capital, and total factor productivity (TFP) (Fraquelli 1994). An increasing productivity reduces costs and allows an enlargement of the resources for new investments in a virtuous circle which reduces tariffs and therefore increases consumption. Here, it is evaluated whether this virtuous circle was at work in the nationalized electricity supply industry by considering the evolution of the productivity of labor and capital, and of their combination, TFP (see Table 13.5).

First we examine labor productivity by the ratio between the gross gigawatt-hour (GWh) sold and the average number of employees. In the decade 1963–1973, productivity grew by 57%, mainly due to the expansion of production. If we consider that a large number of employees work in the distribution phase of electricity supply (around 60% on average), a better measure for labor productivity is represented by the users per employee

*Table 13.5* Labor, Capital, and Total Factor Productivity (TFP) in ENEL 1963–1973 (1963 = 100)

| Years | Labor Productivity | | | TFP | | |
|---|---|---|---|---|---|---|
| | Gross GWh per employee | Total sales per employee | Users per employees | Total sales (a) | Total costs (b) | TFP (a/b) |
| 1963 | 100 | 100 | 100 | 100 | 100 | 100 |
| 1964 | 108.1 | 108.5 | 98.1 | 113.8 | 110.5 | 103 |
| 1965 | 105.3 | 106.5 | 95 | 121.8 | 119 | 102.3 |
| 1966 | 102.9 | 105.2 | 90.6 | 133.3 | 132 | 101 |
| 1967 | 104.5 | 105.8 | 88 | 145.2 | 146.2 | 99.3 |
| 1968 | 104.8 | 106.8 | 84.4 | 158.8 | 160.7 | 98.8 |
| 1969 | 108.8 | 111.4 | 83.4 | 173.3 | 173.2 | 100.1 |
| 1970 | 118.7 | 120.8 | 84.7 | 190.7 | 183.2 | 104.1 |
| 1971 | 126.3 | 128.4 | 86.7 | 204.4 | 192.9 | 106 |
| 1972 | 142.5 | 144 | 92.1 | 222 | 196.1 | 113.2 |
| 1973 | 157 | 158.9 | 96.7 | 239.7 | 205.1 | 116.9 |

| | Capital Productivity | | |
|---|---|---|---|
| | Gross GWh/ total equipment | Sales/total equipment (1990 price) | Sales/depreciation funds (1990 price) |
| 1963 | 100 | 100 | 100 |
| 1964 | 99 | 99.4 | 97.1 |
| 1965 | 96.4 | 97.4 | 92.8 |
| 1966 | 93 | 95.1 | 88 |
| 1967 | 94.8 | 95.9 | 87.2 |
| 1968 | 95.2 | 97.1 | 86.5 |
| 1969 | 95.5 | 97.9 | 85.8 |
| 1970 | 98 | 99.7 | 85.7 |
| 1971 | 96.4 | 98 | 83.1 |
| 1972 | 99.6 | 1007.7 | 84.7 |
| 1973 | 101.5 | 102.7 | 86.2 |

ratio. According to this index, the period considered shows unsatisfactory results; in fact, the index decreased from 100 in 1963 to 96.7 in 1973. In this phase, the evolution of labor productivity was strongly influenced by political intervention. At the moment of nationalization, ENEL was obliged by law to hire employees directly from the subcontracting firms of private companies, greatly increasing the total number of employees. Also, the rapid improvement in labor productivity observed between 1971 and 1973 depends on the issue of a law which accorded anticipated retirement to all dependent employees who had fought in WWII.

The electricity supply sector is capital intensive, and therefore the productivity of capital is a crucial factor to be considered. The usual way to measure the productivity of capital is the ratio between gross GWh sold and gross equipment. ENEL shows a decline of the productivity of capital in the period considered, from 100 in 1963 to 93 in 1966, and a small increase afterward, to 101.5 in 1973. If we consider the ratio between total sales and depreciation—a more adequate measure of capital productivity—the evolution is much less satisfactory, going from 100 in 1963 to 86.2 in 1973. This result can be explained by three main factors: the difficulties of integrating different equipment in a national system; the changing composition of plants in favor of the thermal plants, which have a shorter economic life than hydro ones and therefore need higher depreciation rates; and the changing composition of total equipment in favor of investments in the transmission and distribution phase of the system (Fraquelli 1994).

The partial productivity of the factors of production is not sufficient to evaluate the performance of ENEL; in fact the results of any economic activity depends mainly on combining the factors of production. This effect is represented by TFP, here represented by the ratio between total sales (lire) and total costs (lire). In the period 1963–1973, there was a small increase in the index of sales/cost, from 100 in 1963 to 116.9 in 1973. These results reflect mainly the expansion of the workforce, noted earlier, especially in the period from 1963 to 1968, and the new public mission of universal service that ENEL had to satisfy, in contrast to the former private firms.

## LABOR COSTS AND INDUSTRIAL RELATIONS

As mentioned earlier, the supporters of nationalization thought that the workers would be more cooperative in a work organization managed by the state, expecting to receive higher wages and better working conditions. Table 13.6 shows that the wage percentage increase in public utilities 1963–1973 was very close to that of manufacturing in the same period (55% versus 52%) and lower, for example, than in chemicals (83%), while it was more rapid than in transport equipment (45%).

This evidence is explained, in part, by the fact that the total labor-costs of electricity employees were higher than those in other sectors even before nationalization (Coriasso 1993) and, in part, by the fact that their increase depended mainly on the general increase of wages that started in 1969 throughout the economy. This fact is confirmed in the decade of the 1970s when the percentage increase of labor-costs of utilities was lower than in total manufacturing and in chemicals, while it also converged with labor-costs in transport equipment.

*Table 13.6*   Sectoral Wages in Italy 1963–1973 (1963 = 100)

|  | Manufacturing | Chemicals | Transport Equipment | Public Utilities |
|---|---|---|---|---|
| 1963 | 100 | 100 | 100 | 100 |
| 1964 | 101 | 106 | 98 | 107 |
| 1965 | 103 | 109 | 100 | 102 |
| 1966 | 107 | 114 | 103 | 103 |
| 1967 | 102 | 119 | 109 | 104 |
| 1968 | 106 | 124 | 111 | 108 |
| 1969 | 111 | 133 | 112 | 110 |
| 1970 | 128 | 153 | 133 | 119 |
| 1971 | 136 | 160 | 136 | 129 |
| 1972 | 138 | 173 | 134 | 152 |
| 1973 | 152 | 183 | 145 | 155 |

*Source:* Giannetti 1989, 67.

The main change of nationalization, therefore, was in the field of industrial relations (Zoppoli 1989; Coriasso 1993). In the private companies before nationalization, industrial negotiations were conducted mainly at the central level in order to reduce the role of trade unions in negotiating working condition and skills formation; after nationalization, new guarantees were introduced in terms of trade union presence at different levels of firm, of basic collective rights, of the regulation of extra contractual wages, and, in particular, of the regulation of individual functions and of career progress in 1966, which became the critical point later, after the 1970s. In addition, in ENEL, cooperation between management and trade unions in setting wages and, moreover, in the organization of work, was a strategy that anticipated an orientation which a few years later was generalized (Negrelli 1989). This strategy could explain the slow rate of growth of labor productivity, in line with a contemporary political slogan: "by working less, work for all."

## INDUSTRIAL EXTERNALITIES

Private companies maintained, from the very early years of electricity supply, a close relationship with electromechanical firms. It was usually arranged by a network of jointly owned laboratories, as was mentioned earlier with reference to the R & D of private companies, by a direct shareholding in electromechanical firms and by informal or cartel agreement with regard to the management of equipment. One of the expected effects of nationalization was an increase in the demand for new equipment for the national electromechanical industry due to the heavy investments required. Moreover, the contemporary industrial economic policy gave great importance to the expansion of the national industrial matrix by the tools of industrial policy to support economic growth. In the Italian case, this demand effect on the national electromechanical industry represented only a temporary boost for the Italian electromechanical industry in the second half of the 1960s. National suppliers benefited from the increase in demand, but it seems that this was managed according to the former practices of price agreements, which hindered the growth of company size and efficiency as well as the diversification in production plants. In fact, the Italian producers were not able to enlarge their size or to strengthen their R & D capabilities in order to compete in the oligopolistic market of heavy electrical equipment. In fact, later in the 1980s, the Italian firms were absorbed by big multinational firms such as Siemens, Brown Boveri, or General Electric (Giannetti 2001).

## CONCLUSION

The first decade after the nationalization of private electricity supply companies corresponds mainly to what the supporters of nationalization expected, in terms of their economic representation of a natural monopoly and of the role of electric energy for growth. ENEL was, in fact, able to improve the technical efficiency of the national network, continuing the transition from hydroelectric generation to oil and coal fueled generation, which private companies had already begun in the early 1950s. But ENEL adopted bigger oil and coal fueled plants for generation—reducing energy consumption per Kwh—and heavily invested in long lines of transmission equipment and new distribution, which improved the efficiency of the network and reduced the losses in transmission and distribution. R & D was, however, less successful.

The pattern of financing of the nationalization of the former private companies, and the heavy investments which it implied, was also consistent with the expectations of the supporters of nationalization, up to the end of the 1960s, especially for financing new investments. The institutional configuration of the Italian credit system—mainly public and controlled by the administrative tools of the national central bank—allowed ENEL to place a growing volume of bonds until the exogenous shock in the financial market, following the 1971 dollar crisis, which also stopped the attempt to issue bonds on foreign markets. The formula of biannual cash compensation indemnity to private companies also mattered: it was implemented with heavy conditions, but it revealed itself to be compatible with the strategy of preserving the national financial market from shocks due to a heavy issuing of bonds, and of allowing the former electrical companies to make *real* investments in new sectors such as the chemical industry. Later these initiatives turned out a failure, but this did not depend on the financial formula adopted to pursue this industrial policy.

Tariff policy results were much more controversial, but they seem to be the effect of a path-dependent way of conceiving tariffs in Italy, at a crossroad between macro-policy to control inflation and a public service vision of electricity supply, strongly rooted in the private sector.

The results, in terms of productivity of labor and capital, and of their combined effect, TFP, are very disappointing. In the case of labor, the low productivity growth reflected partly on the way the hiring of personnel was arranged by law—both at the beginning and at the end of the period—and partly on the growing role of trade unions in controlling work conditions and careers. These features of industrial relations also contribute to explain why wages did not grow more than in other industrial sectors in the decade, as expected; in fact, trade unions concentrated their strategy on the control of work conditions and organization, instead of trying to obtain better wages and salaries as a result of an eventual increase in productivity.

More generally, it can be concluded that how contemporary actors represent the economic process—in terms of economic theories—and how they conceive society, institutions, and the role of policy are very important factors in explaining such a complex phenomenon as nationalization.

## BIBLIOGRAPHY

AA. VV. 1990, *La nazionalizzazione dell'energia elettrica*, Bari: Laterza.

Abate, A. 1994, "Problemi tariffari dalla nazionalizzazione a oggi," in *Storia dell'industria elettrica in Italia*, Vol. 5, *Gli sviluppi dell'ENEL, 1963–1990*, ed. G. Zanetti, Bari: Laterza.

Barbato, M. 1963, *La nazionalizzazione dell'industria elettrica*, Roma: Presidenza del consiglio dei Ministri.

Berg, S. 1988, *Natural Monopoly Regulation: Principles and Practices*, Cambridge: Cambridge University Press.

Bocca, G., ed. 1969, *Le baronie elettriche*, Bari: Laterza, 1960.

Caia, G. and N. Aicardi 1994, "La struttura organizzativa dell'ENEL e il regime giuridico della sua attività," in *Storia dell'industria elettrica in Italia*, Vol. 5, *Gli sviluppi dell'ENEL, 1963–1990*, ed. G. Zanetti, Bari: Laterza.

Castronovo, V. 1989, "Le nazionalizzazioni nelle politiche economiche del secondo dopoguerra in Europa," in *La nazionalizzazione dell'energia elettrica*, ed. AA. VV., Bari: Laterza.

Catenacci, G. 1965, "Il CESI: Le sue risorse e le sue attività," in *L'Elettrotecnica* 62: 313–318.

CIRIEC, ed. 1983, *Rapporto sulle tariffe*, Milano: Franco Angeli.

Coriasso, R. 1993, *Tra partecipazione e conflitto. Le relazioni sindacali all'ENEL*, Milano: Franco Angeli.

Cozzi, G., et al. 1983, *Sistema elettrico e sviluppo economico. Il caso italiano*, Milano: Franco Angeli.

Dami, C. 1963, "Indennizzi alle imprese elettriche e problemi finanziari dell'ENEL," *Moneta e Credito* 17(62): 240–266.

ENEL 1965, *La ricerca scientifica e tecnologica nelle aziende di Stato e la partecipazione statale*, Milano.

ENEL 1978, *I primi quindici anni di attività*, Roma.

Fraquelli, G. 1994, "La produttività dell'ENEL durante i trent'anni di monopolio pubblico," in *Storia dell'industria elettrica in Italia*, Vol. 5, *Gli sviluppi dell'ENEL, 1963–1990*, ed. G. Zanetti, Bari: Laterza.

Galbani, A.M., L. Paris, and A. Silvestri 1994, "La ricerca nel settore elettrico," in *Storia dell'industria elettrica in Italia*, Vol. 5, *Gli sviluppi dell'ENEL, 1963–1990*, ed. G. Zanetti, Bari: Laterza.

Giannetti, R., 1989, "Le relazioni industriali all'ENEL (1963–1986): Strategia e struttura," in *Le relazioni industriali all'ENEL*, eds. A. Accornero and T. Treu, Milano: Aisri/Franco Angeli.

Giannetti, R., 1998, "Tecnologie di rete e intervento pubblico nel sistema elettrico italiano (1883–1996)," in *Rivista di Storia economica* 14(2): 127–160.

Giannetti, R. 2001, "Il meccanico e l'elettrotecnico," in *Storia dell'Ansaldo, 8, Una grande industria elettromeccanica (1963–1980)*, ed. V. Castronovo, Bari: Laterza.

Giuntini, A. 1994, "Fonti statistiche," in *Storia dell'industria elettrica in Italia*, Vol. 5, *Gli sviluppi dell'ENEL, 1963–1990*, ed. G. Zanetti, Bari: Laterza.

Hughes, T.P. 1983, *Networks of Power. Electrification in Western Societies, 1880–1930*, Baltimore: Johns Hopkins University Press.

IEFE 1969, *Le previsioni a lungo termine dei consumi di energia in Italia*, Milano: Giuffrè.

*La nazionalizzazione dell'industria elettrica in Italia. Leggi e decreti di attuazione* 1963, Roma: Studium.

Jaeger, P.G. and F. Denozza 2000, *Appunti di diritto commerciale: Impresa e società*. Milano: Giuffrè.

Mori, G. 1994, "La nazionalizzazione in Italia: Il dibattito politico-economico," in *Storia dell'industria elettrica in Italia*, Vol. 5, *Gli sviluppi dell'ENEL, 1963–1990*, ed. G. Zanetti, Bari: Laterza.

Negrelli, S. 1989, "Modelli di contrattazione collettiva nella storia dell'ENEL," in *Le relazioni industriali all'ENEL*, eds. A. Accornero and T. Treu, Milano: Aisri/Franco Angeli.

Ninni, A. 1994, "Interconnessione e standardizzazione," in *Storia dell'industria elettrica in Italia*, Vol. 5, *Gli sviluppi dell'ENEL, 1963–1990*, ed. G. Zanetti, Bari: Laterza.

Rey, G. M., ed. 1991, *I conti economici dell'Italia*, Bari: Laterza.

Roversi Monaco, F. 1989, " Scenario istituzionale e legislazione in materia elettrica con riguardo alla nazionalizzazione," in *La nazionalizzazione dell'energia elettrica*, in ed. AA. VV., Bari: Laterza.

Sanna, F.M. 1967, *Produzione, costi e tariffe dell'energia elettrica in Italia, Francia e Gran Bretagna (1967–1974)*, Roma: Editrice Elia.

Scalfari, E. 1955, *La lotta contro i monopoli*, Bari: Laterza.

Scalfari, E. 1963, *Storia segreta dell'industria elettrica*, Bari: Laterza.

Sembenelli, A. 1994, "Investimenti strategie e vincoli finanziari," in *Storia dell'industria elettrica in Italia*, Vol. 5, *Gli sviluppi dell'ENEL, 1963–1990*, ed. G. Zanetti, Bari: Laterza.

Shakle, G.L.S. 1967, *The Years of High Theory: Invention and Tradition in Economic Thought 1926–1939*, Cambridge: Cambridge University Press.

Silari, F. 1989, "La nazionalizzazione elettrica in Italia. Conflitti di interessi e progetti legislativi (1945–1962)," in *Italia contemporanea* 177: 49–68.

United Nations 1953, *Hydro-electric Potential in Europe and Its Gross, Technical and Economic Limits*, Geneva.

Zanetti, G., ed. 1994, *Storia dell'industria elettrica in Italia*, Vol. 5, *Gli sviluppi dell'ENEL, 1963–1990*, Bari: Laterza.

Zanetti, G. and G. Fraquelli 1979, *Una nazionalizzazione al buio. L'ENEL dal 1963 al 1978*, Bologna, Il Mulino.

Zoppoli, L. 1989, "Profili giuridico istituzionali, contrattazione collettiva e gestione del personale," in *Le relazioni industriali all'ENEL*, eds. A. Accornero and T. Treu, Milano: Aisri/Franco Angeli.

# Acronyms

| | |
|---|---|
| AGIP | Azienda Generale Italiana Petroli |
| AIOC | Anglo-Iranian Oil Company |
| ALITALIA | Linee aeree italiane |
| ANIC | Azienda Nazionale Idrogenazione Combustibili |
| APOC | Anglo-Persian Oil Company |
| ASIRI | Archivio Storico IRI |
| AUTOSTRADE | Concessioni e Costruzioni Autostrade |
| BISF | British Iron and Steel Federation |
| BISPSA | British Independent Steel Producers' Association |
| BL | British Leyland |
| BMH | British Motor Holdings |
| BNOC | British National Oil Corporation |
| BP | British Petroleum |
| BRP | Bureau de Recherches de Pétrole |
| BSC | British Steel Corporation |
| BTDB | British Transport Docks Board |
| CAMPSA | Compañía Arrendataria del Monopolio de Petróleos Sociedad Anónima |
| CESI | Centro Elettrotecnico Sperimentale Italiano |
| CFP | Compagnie Français des Pétroles |
| CIPE | Comitato Interministeriale per la Programmazione Economica |

| | |
|---|---|
| COMIT | Banca Commerciale Italiana |
| CONIEL | Consorzio Imprese Elettriche |
| CREDIOP | Consorzio di credito per opere pubbliche |
| DC | Italian Christian Democrat Party |
| DETR | Department of the Environment, Transport and the Regions |
| DfT | Department for Transport |
| DSR | Direzione Studi e Ricerche |
| EAGC | Ente Autonomo Gestione Cinema |
| EAGAT | Ente Autonomo Gestione Aziende Termali |
| EC | European Community |
| ECMT | European Conference of Ministers of Transport |
| ECSC | European Coal and Steel Community |
| EDF | Électicité de France |
| EEC | European Economic Community |
| EFIM | Ente Finanziamento Industria Manifatturiera |
| EGAM | Ente Gestione Attività Minerarie |
| ENEL | Ente Nazionale per l'Energia Elettrica |
| ENI | Ente Nazionale Idrocarburi |
| ENM | Ente Nazionale Metano |
| ERAP | Entreprise de recherches et d'activités pétrolières |
| FFSS | Azienda Autonoma delle Ferrovie dello Stato |
| FINCANTIERI | Finanziaria cantieri navali |
| FINELECTTRICA | Finanziaria elettrica nazionale |
| FINMARE | Società finanziaria marittima |
| FINMECCANICA | Società finanziaria meccanica |
| FINSIDER | Società finanziaria siderurgica |
| FINSIEL | Finanziaria per i sistemi informativi elettronici |
| GDF | Gaz du France |

| | |
|---|---|
| GDP | Gross domestic product |
| GWh | Gigowatt-hours |
| HABCP | Harvester Archives of the British Conservative Party |
| HGV | Heavy Goods Vehicles |
| IBM | International Business Machines |
| ICIPU | Istituto di credito per le imprese di pubblica utilità |
| ICL | International Computers Limited |
| IDAC | Imports Duties Advisory Committee |
| IEA | Institute of Economic Affairs |
| IMI | Istituto Mobiliare Italiano |
| INA | Istituto Nazionale Assicurazioni |
| INDENI | Società per la promozione di nuove iniziative industriali |
| INI | Instituto Nacional de Industria |
| IRC | Industrial Reorganisation Corporation |
| IRI | Istituto per la Ricostruzione Industriale |
| ISSRI | Istituto di Credito delle Casse di Risparmio |
| ITALSTAT | Società italiana per le infrastrutture e l'assetto del territorio |
| MINPASTA | Ministero delle Partecipazioni Statali |
| MW | Megawatt |
| NAUK | National Archives of the United Kingdom |
| NCB | National Coal Board |
| NEB | National Enterprise Board |
| NHC | National Hydrocarbons Corporation |
| NPV | Net present value |
| ONS | Office of National Statistics |
| OPEC | Organization of Petroleum Exporting Countries |
| PCI | Partito Comunista Italiano |

| | |
|---|---|
| PFI | Private Finance Initiative |
| PPP | Public–Private Partnership |
| PRI | Italian Republican Party |
| PRT | Petroleum Revenue Tax |
| PSI | Partito Socialista Italiano |
| R & D | Research and development |
| RAI | Radiotelevisione italiana |
| ROMSA | Raffineria Oli Minerali Società Anonima |
| RPI | Retail price index |
| SAMIM | Azionaria minero-metallurgica |
| SGW | S.G. Warburg Archives |
| SIAP | Società Italo-Americana pel Petrolio |
| SIFA | Società immobiliare e finanziaria per azioni |
| SIP | Società Idroelettrica Piemontese |
| SISMA | Società industrie siderurgiche meccaniche e affini |
| SME | Società Meridionale di Elettricità |
| SMF | Società meridionale finanziaria |
| SNAM | Società Nazionale Metanodotti |
| SNOM | Società Nazionale Olii Combustibili |
| SNP | Scottish National Party |
| SOE | State-owned enterprise |
| SOFID | Società finanziamenti idrocarburi |
| SOFIN | Società finanziaria di partecipazioni azionarie |
| SOPAL | Società partecipazioni alimentari |
| SPA | Società finanziaria di partecipazioni azionarie |
| STET | Società torinese esercizi telefonici |
| TFP | Total factor productivity |
| TML | Transmanche-Link |
| TNA | The National Archives (UK) |

| TPC | Turkish Petroleum Company |
| UCS | Upper Clyde Shipbuilders |
| USSR | Union of Soviet Socialist Republics |
| VEBA | Vereiningten Elektriziitats u. Bergwerk AG |
| VIAG | Vereiningten Industrie Unternehmungen AG |

# Contributors

**Franco Amatori** is Professor of Economic History as well as Director of the Institute of Economic History at Bocconi University. His research interest in business history covers both Italian and international cases. He has published extensively, including *Big Business and the Wealth of Nations* (co-editor with A.D. Chandler and Takashi Hikino, Cambridge University Press, 1997) and *Business History around the World* (co-edited with G. Jones, Cambridge University Press, 2003).

**Martin Chick** is Reader in Economic and Social History at the University of Edinburgh. He is currently writing the final volume of the Economic and Social History of Britain book series published by Oxford University Press. His previous books are *Electricity and Energy Policy in Britain, France and the United States since 1945* (Edward Elgar, 2007) and *Industrial Policy in Britain, 1945–1951* (Cambridge University Press, 1998).

**Leandro Conte** is Professor of Economic History at the University of Siena. He has published extensively on the history of bank and financial systems in modern time.

**Renato Giannetti** is Professor of Economic History at the University of Florence. He has written widely on the history of technology and business, especially on the post-1861 Italian experience. Among his publications are "Leaping Frogs" and "Big Business, 1913–2001" (co-written with M. Vasta), both chapters in *Forms of Enterprise in 20th Century Italy*, edited by A. Colli and M. Vasta (Edward Elgar, 2010).

**Terry Gourvish** is Director, Business History Unit, London School of Economics and Political Science. He is the author of *The Official History of Britain and the Channel Tunnel* (2006). Other recent publications include *British Rail 1974–97: From Integration to Privatisation* (Oxford University Press, 2002) and *Britain's Railways 1997–2005: Labour's Strategic Experiment* (Oxford University Press, 2008). As an adviser to the Department for Transport, he contributed a report *The High Speed Rail Revolution: History and Prospects* (2010).

**Giulio Mellinato** is Senior Lecturer in Economic History at the Faculty of Economics, University of Milan-Bicocca. His main interests are maritime transport and business history in Italy and abroad. He has recently published books on the maritime and shipbuilding history of Northern Adriatic region and on the Cosulich shipping family.

**Robert Millward** has been Professor of Economic History at the University of Manchester, UK, since 1989 and Professor Emeritus since 2005. Recent research has focused on Europe's infrastructure industries and its demography, as in his contribution to the new *Cambridge Economic History of Modern Europe* (edited by S. Broadberry and K.H. O'Rourke, 2010) and his own book, *Private and Public Enterprise in Europe: Energy, Telecommunications and Transport: 1830–1990* (Cambridge University Press, 2005).

**Glen O'Hara** is Senior Lecturer in Modern History at Oxford Brookes University. His main research interests lie in the field of modern British government and policy, and he is the author or editor of four books on this subject. His most recent publications are *Britain and the Sea since 1600* (Palgrave Macmillan, 2010) and *Statistics and the Public Sphere in Britain since 1750* (Routledge, forthcoming).

**Giandomenico Piluso** is Assistant Professor in the Department of Economics at the University of Siena and the editor of *Imprese e storia*, the Italian business history journal. He has published extensively on banking and business history. Recent publications include "From the Universal Banking to the Universal Banking: A Reappraisal" in *Journal of Modern Italian Studies* (2010) and "Financing the Largest Italian Manufacturing Firms: Ownership, Equity, and Debt (1936–2001)" (with L. Conte), in *Forms of Enterprise in 20th Century Italy,* edited by A. Colli and M. Vasta (Edward Elgar, 2010).

**Daniele Pozzi** is Research Fellow at the Department of Institutional Analysis and Public Management at Bocconi University (Milan, Italy) and lecturer at LIUC University (Castellanza, Italy). Among his recent publications are "Entrepreneurship and Capabilities in a Beginner Oil Multinational: The Case of ENI" in *Business History Review* (2010) and *Dai gatti selvaggi al cane a sei zampe. Tecnologia, conoscenza e organizzazione nell'AGIP e nell'ENI di Enrico Mattei* (Marsilio, 2009).

**Ruggero Ranieri** is currently Visiting Professor at the Universities of Padua and Perugia. He was Jean Monnet Professor and Senior Lecturer in

Economic History at the University of Manchester from 1999 to 2004. He has written widely on the history of the steel industry in postwar Europe and the economic history of European integration.

**Pier Angelo Toninelli** is Professor of Contemporary and Business History at the Department of Economics of the University of Milano-Bicocca. He has published extensively on the history of state-owned enterprise, of accounting, of comparative economic growth, and entrepreneurship. He has just edited the volume *The Determinants of Entrepreneurship: Leadership, Culture, Institutions* (with J.L. Garcia-Ruiz, Pickering and Chatto, 2010).

**Michelangelo Vasta** is Professor of Economic History at the University of Siena. His main interests are the economic development and business history of Italy. Among his recent publications are "Was Industrialization an Escape for the Commodity Lottery? Evidence from Italy 1861–1939" (with G. Federico) in *Explorations in Economic History* (2010); "Companies' Insolvency and 'the Nature of the Firm' in Italy, 1920s-1970s" (with P. Di Martino) in *The Economic History Review* (2010); and *Forms of Enterprise in 20th Century Italy* (co-edited with A. Colli, Edward Elgar, 2010).

# Index

## A

Abate, A. 252, 259
Aberdeen 156
Abromeit, H. 188, 198
Abruzzo Molise 90, 91
Acciaierie di Cornigliano 132
Acemoglu, D. 119, 139
Accornero, A. 260, 261
Adlam, D. 55, 63
Affuso, L. 101, 116
Africa 203
Aganin, A. 57, 63, 76, 98
Aghion, P. 119, 139
AGIP (Azienda Generale Italiana
      Petroli) 5, 9, 10, 34, 35, 36,
      44, 69, 76, 95, 96, 164–173,
      176–179, 181
AGIP Carbone 96
AGIP Mineraria 95
AGIP Nucleare 96
AGIP Petroli 48, 49
Agnelli, G. 40, 166
Aicardi, N. 244, 259
Alberta 148, 162
Alfa Romeo 35, 38, 41, 44, 48
Alitalia Linee Aeree Italiane 95
Allen, K. 233, 241
Amato, G. 47
Amatori, F. XIII, 3, 8, 31, 37, 47, 48,
      56, 63, 68, 69, 121, 124, 125,
      127, 139, 140, 166, 173, 180,
      183, 184, 191, 197, 198
Amersham International 26, 28
Amyot, G. 56, 63
Anglo-Iranian Oil 31
Anglo-Iranian Oil Company (AIOC) 5,
      6, 165, 172, 179
Anglo-Persian Oil Company (APOC)
      14, 167, 168, 178, 179

Anguera, R. 103, 107, 108, 112, 116
ANIC (Azienda Nazionale Idrogenazi-
      one Combustibili) 36, 95, 96,
      172, 173
Ansaldo 47, 125
Anson, M. 116
Antonelli, C. 48
Arcelor 197
Arendal Shipyard 213
Arguden, R.Y. 105, 117
Argyll 151, 158
Armanni, V. 166, 180
ARMCO 190
Armstrong, R. 157, 162
Arrighetti, A. 68, 76, 97, 98
Artis, M. 240
Aston-under-Lyne 226
Ashford 106
Ashworth, W. 232, 233, 239
Asia 164, 180
Assider 182
Assonime 138
Atomic Energy Authority 28
Attlee, C. R. 50, 54, 61, 63, 65, 226
Auk 151, 158
Auroux, J. 114
Austen 58
Australia 147, 203, 219
Austria 31
Autostrade (Concessioni e Costruzioni
      Autostrade) 95
AVIOFER Breda 96
Aylen, J. 188, 189, 194, 198
Azienda autonoma delle Ferrovie dello
      Stato (FFSS) 33

## B

BAE System 216
Bagnoli 132

274 *Index*

Balconi, M.a 36, 37, 43, 48, 132, 137, 139, 191, 192, 195, 197, 198
Balkans 167
Ball, S. 66
Ballestro, A. 167, 181
Balogh, T. 55, 63, 152, 158
Bamberg, J.H. 172, 180
Banca Commerciale Italiana (COMIT) 49, 95, 132, 166, 167, 182, 183, 244
Banca d'Italia (Bank of Italy) 34, 39, 133, 176, 251, 252
Banca Italiana di Sconto 4, 39, 47
Banco di Roma 4, 39, 47, 95, 244
Banco di Santo Spirito 95
Bank of England 12, 19, 20, 51, 53, 115
Barbato, M. 244, 259
Barber, J. 114
Barbero, M.I. 47, 48
Barca, F. 45, 47, 48, 57, 63, 120, 124, 125, 127, 139, 140, 180, 183, 198
Bargigli, I. 47, 48, 96
Barnett, C. 18, 28
Barrett, S.D. 14, 28
Basilicata 90, 91
Bastogi 41
Beauman, C. 182, 189, 197, 198
Belgium 147
Beltran, A. 178, 180
Bénard, A. 115
Beneduce, A. 34, 41, 47, 127, 140, 183
Benn, T. 57, 58, 60, 63
Beresford, A.K.C. 101, 118
Berg, S. 242, 259
Berle, A.A. 97, 98
Berlin 3
Berliner Elektrizitäts-Werke 17
Bertrand, M. 71, 98
Bianchi, M. 139
Bianchi, P. 57, 63, 124
Bianco, M. 124, 139
Bigazzi, D. 39, 180
Binks, M. 112, 113, 116
BISF (British Iron and Steel Federation) 182, 185, 186, 187, 188, 189, 196
Blackaby, F. 65
Bo, G. 209
Bocca, G. 243, 259
Bodsworth, C. 189, 199
Bognetti, G. 68, 76, 97, 98
Boldrini, M. 171, 179

BNOC (British National Oil Corporation) 6, 8, 11, 12, 26, 28, 145, 146, 152, 153, 154, 155, 160, 161
Bo, G. 174
Bonelli, F. 39, 48, 127, 132, 140
Booz, Allen and Hamilton 215
Bottiglieri, B. 33, 48, 132, 140
Bourg-St. Maurice 106
Bowens, M. 199
Braibant, G. 114
Brazil 211
Brech, M.J. 62, 63
Breda Ferroviaria 96
Brescia 168
Bretton Woods 7
Briatico, F. 176, 180
Bricco, P. 138, 140
Brioschi, F. 47, 48, 124, 125, 139, 140
Britain 4, 5, 11, 12, 13, 14, 16, 17, 26, 27, 50, 51, 52, 56, 60, 61, 62, 63, 64, 65, 66, 67, 100, 105, 106, 117, 147, 151, 160, 182, 196, 211, 213, 214, 217, 221, 223, 229, 232, 233, 235, 237, 238, 239, 241
Britain's Department for Transport 106
British Aerospace 9, 11, 12, 26, 215
British Airways 14, 20, 28, 50, 62
British Broadcasting Corporation 51
British Electricity Authority 17, 19, 28, 223, 227, 228
British Electricity Authority and Area Boards 7, 12, 227, 228
British European Airways Corporation 28
British Gas 13, 20, 26, 28, 62
British Independent Steel Producers' Association 189
British Iron and Steel Federation. *See* BISF
British Leyland (BL) 11, 17, 58, 59, 61
British Motor Holdings 58
British National Oil Corporation. *See* BNOC
British Overseas Air 28
British Overseas Aircraft Corporation 14
British Overseas Airways Corporation (BOAC) 12, 26, 50, 51
British Petroleum (BP) 11, 12, 14, 17, 26, 52, 150, 159 179, 180
British Rail 11, 13, 21, 25, 100, 102, 106, 109
British Railways Board 117

British Shipbuilders 12, 17, 212, 215, 218
British Steel Corporation (BSC) 6, 12, 19, 28, 51, 189, 192, 193, 194, 196, 197, 198
British Steel PLC 194
British Telecom 7, 13, 20, 28, 62
British Transport Commission 12, 17, 19, 100
British Transport Docks Board (BTDB) 13, 26
British Waterways 12, 28, 50
Britoil 28, 160
Broadberry, S.N. 24, 28, 59, 63, 235, 239
Brown Boveri 258
BRP (Bureau de Recherches de Pétrole) 172
Brussels 106, 112
Bruzelius, N. 105, 116
Buckley, M.S. 163
Burk, K. 63, 187, 199
Burmah Oil Company 146
Burn, D.L. 185, 188, 198
Butler, Rab 52
Buxton, T. 65
Buzzacchi, L. 140
Byé, M. 55, 64

**C**

Cable and Wireless 11, 12, 17, 26
Cable and Wireless Co. 13
Caia, G. 244, 259
Cairncross, A. 51, 63, 228, 239
Calabria 90
Calais 111
Callaghan, J. 155
Cameron, P.D. 146, 147, 162
Campania 88, 90, 91
CAMPSA (Compañìa Arrendataria del Monopolio de Petróleos Sociedad Anónima) 165, 167, 172
Canada 148, 203, 230
Carnevali, F. 62, 63
Caron Commission 217
Carparelli, A. 140
Casavola, P. 124, 139
Cassa Depositi e Prestiti 251
Cassa Nazionale per le Assicurazioni Sociali 34, 165
Cassese, S. 34, 46, 48
Castle, B. 114
Castronovo, V. 41, 43, 48, 244, 259, 260

Catenacci, G. 249, 259
Cavazza, F. 47, 48
Caviaga 170
Cefis, E. 175, 176, 177, 178, 179
Central Electricity Board 6, 11, 12, 15, 21, 223, 224, 225, 226, 227, 236, 238
Central Electricity Generating Board 17, 28, 50, 227, 229, 232, 236, 240
Central Statistical Office 21, 23, 28, 233, 239
Cerato, S. 217, 220
CESI (Centro Elettrotecnico Sperimentale Italiano) 249, 259
Cetena 206
Chambers, P. 62
Chandler, A. D. 48, 138, 140, 180
Chapman, P. 65
Chatillon 41
Chester, N. 13, 20, 28, 51
Chick, M. 7, 8, 12, 15, 28, 61, 64, 186, 199, 228, 233, 237, 239
Chrysler 61
Church, R. 58, 59, 64
Cianci, E. 35, 38, 39, 41, 47, 48
Ciocca, P. 124, 140
CIPE (Comitato Interministeriale per la Programmazione Economica) 177, 178, 209, 212, 220
Civil Aviation Board 19
Clark, J.G. 165, 180
Clarke, T. 241
Clifton, J. 49, 99, 101, 116
Clyde 214
Coase, R.H. 48, 151, 162
Coates, D. 60, 64
Coates, K. 60
Cobham, D. 240
Cockerill, A.J. 193, 199
Cohen, J.S. 56, 64
Colajanni, N. 125, 140
Colitti, M. 47, 48, 174, 178, 180
Colli, A. 99, 138, 140
Colombo, M.G. 140
Coltorti, F. 125, 140
Comìn, F. 49, 99, 101, 116
Commonwealth 187
Compañìa Arrendataria del Monopolio de Petróleos Sociedad Anónima. *See* CAMPSA
Compagnie Français des Pétroles (CFP) 165, 167
Confalonieri, A. 39, 48

Confindustria 40, 65
CONIEL (Consorzio Imprese
  Elettriche) 249
Connors, D.P. 214, 220
Consorzio di Credito per Opere Pub-
  bliche (CREDIOP) 34
Consorzio Sovvenzioni Valori Indus-
  triali (CSVI) 34, 39, 47
Conte, L. 7, 8, 47, 119, 123, 124, 127,
  138, 140
Conti, E. 165, 167, 168, 180
Cooke, P. 57, 64
Coopey, R. 66, 116
Corbett, G. 113, 116
Corbino, E. 204, 205, 220
Coriasso, R. 256, 257, 259
Cornigliano 132, 184, 190
Cornwall 156
Cortemaggiore 170
Corus 197
Costa, A. 40
Costain and Dumez 144
Cottino, G. 181
Cozzi, G. 243, 259
Coventry Gauge 59
Crafts, N.F.R. 64, 141
Credito Italiano 95, 182, 244
Croatia 166
Crompton, G.W. 15, 29, 100, 116
Cronin, J. 51, 64
Cuccia, E. 56

**D**

Daimler 58
Dalmine 132, 170, 184, 190, 192
Dalton, H. 50, 186
Dam, K. W. 151, 162
Dami, C. 249
Danish Gas Company 17
Dankbaar, B. 59, 64
*Daily Telegraph* 116
D'Arcy, W. 165
Daniel, R.J. 218, 220
Darmstadter, J. 165, 179, 180
Daunton, M. 240
Davies, S.W. 235, 241
Davidson, A. 116
Davidson, F. 116
De Cecco, M. 39, 48, 121, 140
De Gasperi, A. 171
Dell, E. 152, 153
Denmark 147
Denozza, F. 244, 260
Denison, E.F. 56, 64

Díaz Fernández, J.L. 167, 181
Diaz Fuentes, D. 49, 99, 101, 116
Dienel, H.-L. 29
Di Filippo, G. 217, 220
Disneyland Paris 106
Doria, M. 125, 140
Dover 108
Dudley, G.F. 193, 194, 196, 199
Dumbarton 214
Duncan, A. 186, 226
Dunkerley, J. 24, 29, 51, 64

**E**

EAGAT (Ente Autonomo Gestione
  Aziende Termali) 36
EAGC (Ente Autonomo Gestione
  Cinema) 36
Easyjet 109
ECSC (European Coal and Steel Com-
  munity) 121, 187, 190, 196,
  198, 200
Edinburgh 116
Edison 35, 41, 170, 252
EDF 17
EFIM (Ente Finanziamento Industria
  Manifatturiera) 6, 36, 41, 45,
  46, 69, 73–87, 96, 97, 127
EGAM (Ente Gestione Attività Minerarie)
  36, 38, 41, 45
Einaudi, L. 46
Einaudi, M. 16, 29, 55, 64
Ekofisk 151
Elbaum, B. 201, 220, 221
Électricité de France (EDF) 28, 239
Electricity Boards 22, 26, 233, 234
Elektriciteist-Værk 13
Electricity Council 28, 53
Elliott Automation 57
Emilia Romagna 90
Encaoua, D. 47, 48
ENEL (Ente Nazionale per l'Energia
  Elettrica) 9, 17, 36, 77, 243–
  250, 252–261
ENI (Ente Nazionale Idrocarburi) 6–8,
  17, 31, 36–38, 41, 42, 44, 46,
  57, 63, 69, 73–81, 83–88, 95–97,
  150, 152, 160, 164, 172–180
Enichimica 96
ENM (Ente Nazionale Metano) 172
England 158, 159, 218, 227, 234, 235
English Electric 57, 58
E.ON 28
ERAP (Entreprise de Recherches et
  d'Activités Pétrolières) 152, 160

Europe 6, 11, 13, 16, 17, 20, 26, 49, 103, 104, 106, 149, 162, 166, 196, 197, 200, 207, 208, 214, 216, 223, 229, 238, 239, 245, 260
European Conference of Ministers of Transport (ECMT) 113, 116
European Economic Community 191, 212, 215, 229
European Passenger Services 109
European Union 217
Eurostar 109, 111
Eurotunnel 103, 104, 106, 109, 111–113, 115, 117
Groupe Eurotunnel (GET) 111, 117

**F**

Fairfield Shipbuilding & Engineering Co. 214
Falck 139, 183, 184, 191
Falklands 219
Favretto, I. 62, 64
Federico, G. 56, 64, 137, 140
Feinstein, C.H. 230, 239
Feldenkirchen, W. 200
Felisini, D. XIII, 10
Ferguson, N. 54, 64
Ferrier, R.W. 165, 180
FIAT (Fabbrica Italiana Automobili Torino) 38, 41, 44, 125, 139, 166, 170, 183, 184, 190
Financial Times 105, 111, 116
Finanziaria Ernesto Breda 96
FINCANTIERI (Finanziaria Cantieri Navali) 35, 95, 131, 132, 218–220
FINELETTRICA (Finanziaria Elettrica Nazionale) 35, 94
FINMARE (Società Finanziaria marittima) 47, 94, 95, 220, 221
FINMECCANICA (Società Finanziaria Meccanica) 94, 95, 123, 127, 131–134, 136–138, 141
Finniston, M. 189
FINSIDER (Società Finanziaria Siderurgica) 38, 44, 47, 94, 95, 123, 127, 131–138, 182, 183, 184, 189, 190–192, 195
FINSIEL (Finanziaria per i Sistemi Informativi Elettronici) 95
Firth, W. 185
Fisman, R. 124, 140
Fiume. *See* Rijeka
Flore, V.D. 220

Florio, M. 101, 102, 116, 218, 220
Floud, R. 240
Flyvbjerg, B. 105, 108, 116
Fogarty, S. 114
Foote, G. 60, 64
Ford 59
Foreman-Peck, J.M. 15, 29, 62, 64, 226, 239
Fragiacomo, P. 206, 208, 220
Fraquelli, G. 249, 254, 260, 261
France 11, 13, 16, 31, 64, 105, 109, 147, 165, 179, 180, 202, 219, 230, 233, 237, 239, 245, 253
Frankel, P.H. 175, 180
Frasca, F.M. 125, 140
Fraser, H. 228, 239
Fratianni, M. 55, 64
Freud, D. 108, 116
Friuli-Venezia Giulia 88, 90, 91

**G**

Gaitskell, H. 50, 188
Galbani, A.M. 249, 260
Galli, G. 179, 180
Gallup 53
Gamble, A. 51, 62, 64
Gas Boards 51
Gas Council 17, 19, 152
Gas Council and Area Boards 12, 28
Gazpom 28
GDF 17
Geddes Commission 211, 217
Geddes Report, 213
General Electric 258
Genova (Genoa) 208
Germany 11, 13, 17, 26, 31, 64, 109, 165, 237
Gerschenkron, A. 39, 48
Ghosal, S. 24, 28
Giarratana, A. 9, 168, 171, 177, 178, 181
Giannetti, R. 7, 46, 48, 96, 98, 99, 126, 137, 140, 242, 247, 253, 254, 257, 258, 260
Gibellieri, E. 198
Gioia Tauro 133, 139
Gingell, O. 114
Girotti, R. 178
Giuntini, A. 239, 240, 248, 254, 260
Glasgow 214
Glasgow's Shipyards 60
Glynn, D. 240
Goldstein, A. 178, 180
Goto, A. 47, 48

Gounon, J. 111
Gourvish, T. R. 6, 7, 61, 64, 100, 101,
    103, 107, 109, 116, 117, 200
Govan 214
Gowing, M.M. 202, 220
Graham, A. 58, 64
Granovetter, M. 47, 48
Grant, W. 55, 64, 159
Graubard, S.R. 47, 48
Grayson, L.E. 169, 172, 178, 179, 180
Green, E.H.H. 52, 65
Greenland 155
Grierson, R. 54, 55, 63
Grimond, J. 159
Grimsey, D, 103, 105, 117
Groupe Eurotunnel (GET) 111
Gunter, R.152

**H**
Hackett, A. 16, 29
Hackett, J. 16, 29
Hague, D. 58, 65
Hall, G. 66, 117
Hammond, E.M. 236, 239
Hancock, W.K. 202, 220
Hannah, L. 16, 22, 29, 53, 64, 225–
    227, 234, 240
Hare, P.G. 24, 29, 51, 64
Harland and Wolff 214
Harriman, G. 58
Harris, D.J. 233, 241
Harris, N. 65
Hart, P.T. 199
Hay, A. 105, 108, 109, 112, 117
Heal, D.W. 189, 199
Healey, D. W. 155, 163
Heath, E. 22, 59, 60, 66, 114, 157, 193
Helm, D.R. 236, 239, 240
Hendry, J. 58, 65
Herbert Group 59
Herrigel, G. 200
Hennessy, P. 50, 65
Heslop, A. 109, 117
Hikino, T. 48, 180
Hine, D. 65
Hirschfield, A. 17, 29
Hitchens, D.M.W.N. 235, 241
H.M. Telegraph 12
H.M. Telephone 12
Hydrocarbons International Holdings
    S.A. 96
Hogwood, B.W. 50, 65
Holland 13
Holland, S. 55, 60, 65, 195, 199

Hollingsworth, J.R. 64
Hoogovens 197
Hornby, W. 202, 203, 220
Houseman, S.N. 193, 199
Howell. D. 63
Hughes, T.P. 248, 260
Hurd, D. 117
Hyundai 215

**I**
IBM 57
ICCRI (Istituto di Credito delle Casse di
    Risparmio) 251
ICIPU (Istituto di Credito per le
    Imprese di Pubblica Utilità) 34
ICL (International Computers Limited)
    57
ICT (International Computers and
    Tabulators) 57, 58
IFI 41
Ilva 125, 132, 140, 184, 191
Ilva Laminati Piani 192
IMI (Istituto Mobiliare Italiano) 34, 38,
    47, 131
Imperial Airways Company 14
INA (Istituto Nazionale Assicurazioni)
    33, 34, 165
INI (Instituto Nacional de Industria)
    172
INDENI (Società per la Promozione di
    Nuove Iniziative Industriali) 96
INI 17
Ingham, B. 163
Ingram, P. 207, 220
INPS (Istituto Nazionale della Previ-
    denza Sociale) 34
Institute for Worker's Control 60
Institute of Economic Affairs (UK) 103
Insud 96
International Monetary Found 3
Iordanoglou, C.F. 29, 237, 240
Iran 175
Iraq Petroleum Co. 10
IRC (Industrial Reorganisation Cor-
    poration) 7, 17, 54, 57, 58, 59,
    60, 65
IRI (Istituto per la Ricostruzione Indus-
    triale) 5–8, 17, 31, 34–36, 38,
    40–42, 45–47, 54–57, 69–79,
    81, 83–88, 94, 96–98, 119–123,
    126–141, 170, 173, 181–184,
    191, 192, 195, 204, 205, 212,
    218, 222, 244
Irish Free State 14

Iron and Steel Board 51, 53, 185, 187, 188
Iron and Steel Corporation 12, 28, 51, 186
Irons-Georges, T. 207, 220
Istituto di Liquidazioni 47
Italcantieri 220
Italgas 35, 40
ITALSTAT (Società Italiana per le Infrastrutture e l'Assetto del Territorio) 95
Italcementi 170
Italia (Italy) 4–11, 13, 17, 19, 26, 35, 36, 38, 41–43, 45, 54–56, 61, 64, 65, 88, 89, 139–141, 150, 165, 167–170, 174, 175, 179, 182, 188–190, 195–197, 200, 201, 204, 206, 208–210, 214, 216, 218, 219, 222, 239, 246, 259
ITALSIDER 184

**J**

Jackson, P.M. 102, 117
Jacobini, O. 10
Jacoboni, A. 205, 220
Jacquemin, A. 47, 48
Jaeger, P.G. 244, 260
Jaguar 58
Jamieson, A.G. 211, 215, 220
Jannaccone, P. 46
Japan 188
Jay, D. 50
John Brown & Co. 208
Johnman, L. 203, 206, 221
Johnson, C. 229, 233, 234, 240
Johnson, P. 240
Jones, T. 56, 65
Jones, T.T. 193, 199
Jörnmark, J. 198, 199
Joseph, K.h 7

**K**

Kamel, K. 105, 117
Kay, J. 108, 117
Kavanagh, D. 51, 65
Kearton, Lord 26, 154
Keeling, B.S. 196, 199
Kemp, P. 114
Kent 105, 117
Kipping, M. 200
Koike, K. 47, 48
Korea 215
Kramer, D.C. 61, 65

Kuisel, R.F. 16, 29

**L**

Laity, P. 237, 240
Lane, F.C. 202, 221
Lanerossi 96
Lanzardo, L. 219, 221
La Porta, R. 71, 98
Lavista, F. 121, 135, 140
Law, J. 151
Lazio 87, 88, 90, 91
Lazonik, W. 201, 220, 221
Leali 192
Leff, N. 47, 48
Lemass, S. 14
Lever, H.d 152, 153
Lewis, M.K: 103, 105, 117
Leyland Motor Corporation 58
Li, C. 109, 117
Liberty Shipbuilders 222
Libya 175
Licini, S. 184, 198
Lifschitz, A. 207, 220
Liguria 88, 90, 91
Lipartito, K. 13, 29
Liquichimica 45
Lloyd George, Gwilam 227
Lloyd's Register of Shipping 201
Locke, R.M. 57, 65
Lojacono, G. 221
Lombardia (Lombardy) 88, 90, 94
London 19, 106, 109, 112, 157, 201, 211
London Passenger Transport Board 18, 226, 227, 228
London Stock Exchange 8
Lopez-de-Silanes, F. 71, 98
Lorenz, E. 203, 211, 213, 221
Lucchini 192, 197
Love, I. 124, 140
Lowe, A.V. 58, 67
Luraghi, G. 44, 48
Lyall, A. 114
Lyth, P.J. 29, 116

**M**

MacDonald, Margo 158
MacDonald, Mott 105
MacGregor, I. 194
Mackay, G.A. 148–151, 162
MacKay, D.I. 148–151, 162
MacKerron, G. 231, 241
Mackie, P. 113, 117
Macmillan, H. 66, 227

Maddison, A. 55, 65
Magatti, M. 48
Maillot, J. 111
Malgarini, M. 68, 98
Mallaby, C 115, 117
Manning, A. 108, 117
Manzon, L. 217, 220
Maraffi, M. 40, 41, 48, 65
Marcel, V. 180
Marche 90
Marchi, A. 140
Marchionatti, R. 140
Marotta, G. 125, 140
Marquand, D. 50, 65
Rapporto Marsan, 68
Marsh, R. 152
Martin, B. 117
Martin, S. 102, 117, 194, 199
Martinelli, A. 55, 56, 64, 65
Maschio, P. 217, 220
Masson, J. 101, 116
Mattei, E. 6, 8, 35, 36, 42, 44, 164, 169, 170, 171, 173–177, 179–181
Mattesini, F. 54, 65
Matthewman, R. 106, 117
Mattioli, R.49
Mauroy, P. 114
McDonnel L.M. 105, 117
McGowan Commitee 226, 240
MCS 96
McTavish, D. 201, 221
Meade, J. 50
Means, G.C. 97, 98
Mediobanca 56, 57, 66, 123, 124, 126, 136, 138, 140, 141, 252
Mediterranean 207
Meeks, G. 59, 65
Melchett, P. 189
Melis, G.do 8, 10
Mellinato, G. 7, 88, 201, 217, 221
Meny, Y. 198, 199
Meredith, K. 105, 117
Merrill Lynch Capital Markets 112
Merseyside Docks and Harbour Boards 18
Middle East 149, 150, 180
Middleton, D.d 103, 105
Midlands (UK) 157
Milano (Milan) 63, 88, 169, 248
Miguet, N. 111
Millward, R. XIII, 3, 7, 8, 9, 11, 13, 15, 16, 20, 29, 51, 62, 64, 65, 67, 103, 117, 138, 145, 160, 162, 185, 186, 195, 199, 200,

223, 225, 227, 230, 234, 237, 239, 240
Milward, A.S. 187
Ministero delle Partecipazioni Statali 121, 174, 177, 178, 191
Mitchell, B.R. 231, 240
Mittal 197
Mitterand, F. 115
Moch, J. 16, 29
Molyneux, R. 24, 30, 235, 240
Monfalcone 212, 216, 217, 221
Monger, G.W. 162
Monopolies and Mergers Commission (MMC) 109, 117
Montecatini 42, 46, 252
Montedison 8, 125, 140, 176
Montrose 158
Morgan, K. 57, 63
Morck, R. 71, 98
Mori, G. 243, 244, 260
Morris Co. 58
Morris, D. 59, 65
Morris, P. 51, 65
Morris, R.J. 239
Morrison, H. 18, 30, 50, 186, 226, 227, 228
Morrow, E.W. 105, 117
Mortara, A. 76, 98
Morton, A. 115
Mossul 6
Mossul Oil Field Co. 10
Mottershead, P. 58, 65
Mucchetti, M. XIII
Mullainathan, S. 71, 98
Murphy, H. 203, 206, 221
Murray, J.M. 203, 221
Mussolini, B. 34, 38, 40, 41, 167
Myddelton, D.R. 117

**N**

NAFTA 166
Napoli (Naples) 44
Nardozzi, G. 124, 140
National Coal Board 11, 12, 17–21, 51, 152, 227, 229, 232, 238
National Coal Board (Exploration) Ltd. 146
National Enterprise Board (NEB) 60, 65, 195
National Freight Company 26
National Grid Company 236, 237, 240
National Health Service 5
National Hydrocarbons Corporation. *See* NHC

National Investment Board 228
National Power 236
National Research and Development
  Corporation 54
National Water Council 12, 28
Negrelli, S. 257, 260
Netherlands 31, 147
New York 113, 219
Newbery, D. 101, 116
NHC (National Hydrocarbons Corpo-
  ration) 152, 153, 154, 160, 162
Ninni, A. 247, 248, 260
Nordvestsjællands 13
Nord-Pas de Calais 117
North America 49
North Eastern Electricity Supply Com-
  pany 227
North Sea 6, 25, 145–153, 156–163,
  179
Northern Rock Bank 3
Northern Ireland 214, 218
North of Scotland Hydro-Electric
  Board 227
Norway 13, 145, 147, 148, 150, 155
Nouschi, A. 167, 180
Nuclear Electric 236
Nuovo Pignone 96

**O**
Office for Electricity Regulation 223
Office of Gas and Electricity Markets
  223
Office for National Statistics (ONS)
  109, 117
Officine Savio 96
Ogliari, F. 219, 221
O'Grada, C. 14, 30
O'Hara, G. 5, 6, 7, 8, 12, 17, 50, 215,
  221
Oil and Pipeline Agency 160
Oldham 226
Olivetti, A. 138
O'Mahony, M. 24, 25, 30, 237, 238,
  240
OPEC 148, 152
Organisation for European Co-Opera-
  tion and Development (OECD)
  55
Orkneys 159
Orsenigo, L. 36, 37, 43, 48, 192, 198
Ostergaard, G.N. 17, 30, 228, 240
Osti, G.L. 42, 44, 48, 131, 137, 141,
  184, 197, 199
Ovenden, K. 188, 200

Owen, G. 187, 194, 196, 200

**P**
Padoa Schioppa, F. 57, 66
Pagano, M. 124, 141
Paoloni, G. 239, 240
Panama 105
Panetta, F. 124, 141
Pantaleoni, M. 46
Papadopoulos, R. 229, 240
Paria, Gulf of 147
Paris 106, 109, 112
Paris, L. 249, 260
Paris Gas Company 17
Parker, D. 20, 25, 30, 118
Parker, D. 117, 118, 191, 194, 199,
  200
Parker, Peter 100, 102
Parkinson, J.R. 210, 215, 221
Pastorelli, S. 46, 48, 126, 140
Paterson, W. 55, 64
Pavitt, K. 198
Pearl Harbor 219
Peck, F. 216, 221
Pedone, A. XIII, 39, 48
Pedrocco, G. 192, 200
Penrose, E.T. 181
Pepy, G. 108
Persian Gulf 207
Pesenti 57
Peters, G.B. 199
Petri, R. 183, 200
Peugeut Citroën 61
Peyton, John 114
Phoenix 193
Piemonte (Piedmont) 46, 88, 90
Piluso, G. 7, 8, 47, 119, 123, 124, 125,
  127, 138, 141
Piombino 132
Pirelli 57, 125, 139, 166
Pirelli, G.B. 40
Pirelli, P. 166
Pisani, E. 114
Pitelis, C. 241
Pizzigallo, M. 165, 166, 168, 181
Plessey Co. 57
Po Valley 36, 170–173, 175, 177
Poland 16, 211
Ponsolle, P. 115
Pope, R. 201, 221
Port London Authority 18
Port Talbot 189
Portugal 13
Posner, A.R. 66

Posner, M.V. 34, 37, 49, 55, 57, 65, 66, 68, 98, 119, 120, 121, 139, 141
Post Office 12, 13, 28, 223
PowerGen 236
Pozzi, D. 6, 9, 164, 167, 178, 179, 181
Prahova AG 167, 181
Pressenda, A. 172, 173, 180
Preston, J. 106, 109, 112, 113, 117, 118
Prosser, R. 162
Prussia 13
Price, C.M. 102, 117
Pryke, R. 24, 30, 55, 62, 66, 235, 240
Puglia 90, 91

**Q**

Quintieri, B. 54, 65

**R**

Radio Chemical Centre 12, 28
RAI (Radiotelevisione Italiana) 95
Rail Freight Distribution 106
Rail Freight Group 106, 118
Rail Link 115, 116
Rajan, R. 124, 141
Ramsden, J. 51, 52, 66
Rand Corporation 105
Ranieri, R. 6, 9, 19, 30, 62, 66, 121, 132, 141, 182, 184, 186, 187, 190, 197–200
Ratcliffe, R. 47, 49
Ravenna 170
Raymond, JL. 111
Recoaro 46
Reed Paper Group 58
Regional Water Authorities 28
Reid, A. 207, 221
Reid, G.L. 233, 234, 241
Rey, G. 253, 260
Renault 16, 31
Richard Summers, 189
Richard Thomas & Co. 185
Richard Thomas & Baldwins Ltd, 187, 189
Richardson, J.J. 193, 194, 196, 199
Ricketts, M. 145, 163
Ridley, N.s 59, 60, 114
Rijeka 166
Rinaldi, A. 56, 66, 96, 98
Rio Tinto 102
Ripalta 170
Riva 192, 197
Robson, W.A. 18, 30

Rocca, A. 132, 183
Rodano, G. 34, 49
Rodger, R. 239
Roll, E. 63
Rolls Royce 11, 12, 17
Roma (Rome) 42, 63, 87, 88, 170, 211
Romanelli, R. 48
Romania 181
Romeo, R. 35, 49
ROMSA (Raffineria di Oli Minerali Società Anonima) 95, 166
Rooke, D. 26
Ross, G. 186, 200
Ross, N.S. 221
Rossi, E. 55, 64, 205, 221
Rossi, N. 120, 141
Rothengatter, W. 105, 116
Rotherham 193
Rover 11, 58
Rover Group (British Leyland) 12
Roversi Monaco, F. 244, 260
Royal Dutch-Shell 166
Royal Bank of Scotland 3
Russolillo, F. XIII
Ryanair 109

**S**

Saipem 96
Sanna, F.M. 253, 260
Salsomaggiore 46
SAMIM (Società Azionaria Minero-Metallurgica) 96
Sapelli, G. 34, 36, 44, 48, 49, 76, 98
Saraceno, P. 36, 40, 41, 44, 47, 49, 68, 77, 98
Sardegna 90
Sartori, R. 68, 98
Saskatchewan 148, 162
Saville, R. 51, 66
Sawyer, M. 215, 221
Scalfari, E. 47, 49, 243, 251, 260
Scandinavia 11
Scapa Flow 156
Scholes, H. 151, 162
Scholey, R.194
Scotland 146, 156, 157, 158, 159, 163, 188, 208, 218, 226, 227
Scott Lithgow Shipyard 213, 214
Seiscom 151
Sembenelli, A. 249, 250, 251, 260
Seldon, A. 65, 66
Segreto, L. XIII 56, 66
Shakle, G.L.S. 242, 260
Sheffield 193

Shell 150
Shetland Islands 159
Shiba, T. 47, 49
Shimotani, M. 47, 49
Shleifer, A. 71, 98
Schmitter, P.C. 63
Shonfield, A. 40, 41, 47, 49, 56, 66,
    146, 162
Sicilia ((Sicily) 90, 91
Siciliano, G. 124, 141
Siemens 258
SIFA (Società Immobiliare e Finanziaria
    per Azioni) 95
Silari, F. 243, 260
Silvestri, A. 249, 260
Singleton, J. 16, 30, 51, 61, 65–67,
    195, 199, 200, 227, 239, 240
Sinigaglia, O. 44, 132, 182, 183, 189,
    190, 191, 200
SIAP (Società Italo-Americana pel
    Petrolio) 166
SIP (Società Idroelettrica Piemontese)
    41, 244
Sip-Stipel Group 132
Sir 45
SISMA (Società Industrie Siderurgiche
    Meccaniche e Affini) 95
Skinner Watson, M. 202, 222
Slater, M.D.E. 232, 241
SME (Società Meridionale Finanziaria)
    95
SME (Società Meridionale di Elettricità)
    244
Smith, A.D. 235, 241
SNAM (Società Nazionale Metan-
    odotti) 95, 96, 172
SNAM Progetti 96
SNOM (Società Nazionale Olii Com-
    bustibili) 166, 178
Snia 41
Società del Canale Cavour 46
Società Finanziaria per il Traforo del
    Monte Bianco 95
Società Italiana per le Strade Ferrate
    Meridionali 39
Società Nazionale Metanodotti 36
Società Veneta 39
SOFID (Società Finanziamenti Idrocar-
    buri) 96
SOFIN (Società Finanziaria di Parteci-
    pazioni Azionarie) 95
Sofindit 183
SOPAL (Società Partecipazioni Alimen-
    tari) 96

Soviet Union 35
SPA (Società Finanziaria di Partecipazi-
    oni Azionarie) 95
Spagnolo, C. 68, 76, 97, 98
Spain 11, 17, 26
Spinelli, F. 55, 64
Standard Oil New Jersey 166, 180
Standard Triumph 58
Stansfield, G. 68, 98
Starkey, D.J. 221
Statoil 145, 155
Steel Company of Wales 189
STET (Società Torinese per l'Esercizio
    Telefonico) 47
STET (Società Finanziaria Telefonica)
    94, 95, 123, 131–134, 136
Stokes, D. 58
Storch, R.L. 217, 222
Strath, B. 211, 222
Streek, W. 64
Suez Canal 105, 205, 207
Supple, B. 16, 30
Surrey, J. 241
Sweden 13, 213
Szymanski, S. 108, 117, 118

T
Taranto 44, 132, 133, 139, 184,
    190–192
Tata 197
Taylor, R. 60, 66
Techint 197
Teesside 156, 189
Teksid 8
Telve 132
Temple, P. 65
Terni 4, 39, 132, 190
Terninoss 190
Texas 156
Thatcher, M. 7, 15, 38, 65, 100, 114,
    115, 194
Thomas, D. 216, 222
Thomas, S. 231, 241
Thompson, D. 24, 30, 235,236, 239,
    240
Thompson, P. 202, 203, 222
Thornton, R.A. 202, 222
Timo 132
Tiratsoo, N. 200
Tivey , L. 18, 30, 187, 195, 200
Todd, D. 218, 222
Tolliday, S. 62, 66, 185, 200
Tomlinson, J. 53, 54, 55, 61, 66, 141,
    186, 194, 195, 200, 215, 222

Toninelli, P.A. XIII, 3, 7, 8, 31, 33, 36,
    37, 43, 45, 46, 48, 49, 63, 68,
    69, 77, 97–99, 141, 180, 192,
    198, 240
Toniolo, G. 35, 49, 120, 141
Torino (Turin) 221, 248
Tortella, G. 167, 172, 181
Toscana 90
Tosi, L. 190, 200
Townsend, A. 216, 221
Toye, R. 66
Transmanche-Link (TML) 105, 113
Transport Commission 50
Transport Statistics Great Britain
    (TSGB) 101, 118
Trentino Alto Adige 90
Trento, S. 45, 48, 57, 63, 125, 127,
    139
Treu, T. 260, 261
Trieste 221
Troilo, C. 181
Tube Investments 59
Turani, G. 47, 49
Turati, A. 168
Turkish Petroleum Co (TPC) 14, 165
Tyssen Krupp 197

**U**
Ulsan 215
Umbria 90
United Kingdom (UK) 3–8, 14, 17,
    22, 25, 31, 38, 55–57, 59,
    61, 105, 109, 118, 141, 145–
    149, 150–152, 155, 156, 158,
    159, 161, 162, 165, 179, 182,
    184, 187, 188, 192–197, 199,
    200, 201, 203, 204, 206–210,
    218, 219, 225, 230, 235, 237,
    240
United Nations 55, 203, 222, 247,
    260
United States (US) 9, 13, 24, 25, 27,
    59, 64, 137, 147, 149, 150,
    165, 169, 170, 178, 185, 190,
    196, 197, 202, 223, 226, 233,
    237, 238, 239
United Steel Company 189
Upper Clyde Shipbuilders (UCS) 60–1
U.S. Steel 190
USSR 175
Utton, M. 59, 66

**V**
Vaizey, J. 182, 200

Valle d'Aosta 90
Vanoni, E. 171
Vasta, M. 7, 45, 47, 48, 49, 56, 66,
    68, 69, 77, 96, 97, 98, 99, 126,
    138, 140
Vattenfall 13
Vauxhall 59
Veba 17
Vecchi, M. 25, 237, 238, 240
Veneto 90
Venezuela 147
Vetritto, G. 33, 49
Viag 17
Vickerman, R. 106, 117
Vickers, J. 146, 160, 163
Vietnam 233
Virno, C. 68, 98
Volpi, G. 166, 167, 168
Volpin, P.F. 57, 63, 76, 98
Votaw, D. 181

**W**
Wales 156, 187, 189, 227, 234, 235
Walkland, S. 51, 64
Wall, G. 106, 109, 112, 118
Warburg, S. 54, 55, 58, 63, 64
Warne, E.J.D. 162
Waterson, M. 226, 239
Wearing, R. 103, 109, 113, 118
Webb, M. 145, 163
Wentworth, M.A. 101, 118
West Germany 64, 147, 179, 188,
    196
Weyman-Jones, T.G. 237, 241
Wickham-Jones, M. 60, 61, 66
Wilkinson, F. 203, 221
Wilkinson, G. 58, 65
William Denny & Bros. 214
Williams, J.L. 222
Williams, K. 222
Williamson Committee 241
Wilson, H. 22, 54, 56, 63, 188
Wilson, J.F. 61, 67, 224, 241
Winch, G.M. 105, 113, 118
Wisconsin Central 106
Woodward, E.H.E. 227
Woodward, N. 64, 66
Woolf, S.J. 34, 37, 49, 55, 66, 68, 98,
    119, 120, 121, 139, 141
Wolfenzon, D. 71, 98
Wright, A.E.G. 196, 199
Wright, E. 162
Wright, V. 198, 199
WTO (World Trade Organization) 3

Wurm, C. 200

**Y**
Yarrax, G. 163
Yarrow, G.K. 146, 160, 232, 241
Yarrow & Co. 214
Yergin, D. 165, 167, 181
Yeung, B. 71, 98
Young, S. 58, 67
Yugoslavia 211

**Z**
Zamagni, V., 35, 49, 133, 141
Zane, M. 168, 181
Zanetti, G. 249, 259, 260, 261
Zanmatti, C. 169, 170
Zeitlin, J. 47, 49, 200
Zilibotti, F. 119, 139
Zingales, L. 124, 141
Zoppoli, L. 257, 261
Zweininger-Bargielowka, I. 53, 67

Printed in the United States
by Baker & Taylor Publisher Services